CITIZENS OF PHOTOGRAPHY

CITIZENS OF PHOTOGRAPHY

The Camera & the Political Imagination

EDITED BY CHRISTOPHER PINNEY WITH THE PHOTODEMOS COLLECTIVE

(Naluwembe Binaisa, Vindhya Buthpitiya, Konstantinos Kalantzis, Christopher Pinney, Ileana L. Selejan, and Sokphea Young)

DUKE UNIVERSITY PRESS DURHAM AND LONDON 2023

Printed in the United States of America on acid-free paper ∞
Project Editor: Ihsan Taylor
Designed by Aimee C. Harrison
Typeset in Portrait Text and Helvetica Neue Std by Copperline
Book Services

Library of Congress Cataloging-in-Publication Data
Names: Pinney, Christopher, editor, contributor. | Binaisa, Naluwembe, editor, contributor. | Buthpitiya, Vindhya, editor, contributor. | Kalantzis, Konstantinos, editor, contributor. | Selejan, Ileana, editor, contributor. | Young, Sokphea, editor, contributor.
Title: Citizens of photography : the camera and the political imagination / edited by Christopher Pinney ; with the PhotoDemos Collective (Naluwembe Binaisa, Vindhya Buthpitiya, Konstantinos Kalantzis, Christopher Pinney, Ileana L. Selejan, and Sokphea Young).
Description: Durham : Duke University Press, 2023. | Includes bibliographical references and index.
Identifiers: LCCN 2022045929 (print)
LCCN 2022045930 (ebook)
ISBN 9781478020769 (paperback)
ISBN 9781478020004 (hardcover)
ISBN 9781478024590 (ebook)
ISBN 9781478093619 (ebook other)
Subjects: LCSH: Photography—Political aspects. | Photography—Social aspects. | Documentary photography. | Photography in ethnology. | BISAC: PHOTOGRAPHY / History | SOCIAL SCIENCE / Anthropology / Cultural & Social
Classification: LCC TR184 .C58 2023 (print) | LCC TR184 (ebook) | DDC 770—dc23/eng/20230223
LC record available at https://lccn.loc.gov/2022045929
LC ebook record available at https://lccn.loc.gov/2022045930

Cover art: Photographers gathered around a mourning family, Mullaitivu, Sri Lanka, 2018. Photograph by Vindhya Buthpitiya.

This book is part of a project that has received funding from the European Research Council (ERC) under the European Union's Horizon 2020 research and innovation program (grant agreement No. 695283).

European Research Council
Established by the European Commission

CONTENTS

Acknowledgments

Generous funding from the European Research Council (ERC) made it possible for me to spend several years working alongside a remarkable and inspiring group of young scholars in the PhotoDemos Collective. To Naluwembe Binaisa, Konstantinos Kalantzis, Ileana L. Selejan, Sokphea Young, and Vindhya Buthpitiya, profound thanks. Our collaborative investigations were enhanced immeasurably by the friendly support of Rahaab Allana, Ariella Aïsha Azoulay, Elizabeth Edwards, NayanTara Gurung Kakshapati, Susan Meiselas, Mark Sealy, and Karen Strassler. Along the way we have benefited from the editorial and design assistance of Dominik Hoehn and Helene Leuzinger.

Others who have helped in various important ways include Shahidul Alam, Taslima Akhter, Nadvi Abdullah, Ahsan Habib, Pratyoush Onta, Kunda Dixit, Usha Titikshu, Nayanika Mookherjee, Lotte Hoek, Nestan Nijaradze (and Tbilisi Photo Festival!), Rosemary Grennan, George Agbo, Pascale Searle, Wendy Chandler, and Myriam Verri.

To explore other results from the PhotoDemos project, readers are encouraged to visit https://www.citizensofphotography.org.

Working again with Duke after two decades has been a pleasure. Ken Wissoker's enthusiasm and alacrity have been much appreciated, as also the work of Ryan Kendall and Ihsan Taylor and the invaluable comments of two generous, anonymous readers. We are grateful to Aimee Harrison, whose cover design, using Vindhya Buthpitiya's powerful photograph, captures so much of the dynamics of the phenomena we have been investigating.

—Christopher Pinney

Introduction

Photographing

OR, THE FUTURE OF THE IMAGE

CHRISTOPHER PINNEY

Anyone who stands in any relation whatsoever to photography has membership of the citizenry of photography—by virtue of the fact she is a photographer; that she views photographs; comments on or interprets them; displays them to others or is herself photographed.—**ARIELLA AZOULAY, *CIVIL IMAGINATION***

This collection of essays presents a series of reports on photography as actually existing practice. Its concern is with pragmatic, demotic, everyday routines, interventions, and predicaments, which only ethnography can capture. However, whereas the standard anthropological reflex anticipates an endless diversity of appropriation driven by the creativity of human subjects, this collection highlights a set of recurring tropes and architectures that point to photography's ambivalently determining presence. This volume hopes to contribute to photographic theory through the study of grounded practice and to advance anthropological thinking on the relationship between media and culture by taking the nature of technics seriously. One of its tasks is to reach a conclusion about the complexity of photography rather than dissolving photography in observations about the complexity of culture.

It also seeks to contribute to the recognition of what might be termed "world system photography." It is still the case that if you study European photography, you are likely to be considered a photographic theorist or a historian of photography sui generis. Europe "remains the sovereign, theoretical subject of all [photographic] histories."[1] By contrast, if you study Nigerian photography, for instance, you are likely to be considered a commentator on Nigerian photography. In the first instance, the European placement fades away while, conversely, Nigeria is underlined as a location, a "belated" case study, stuck in the "waiting room of history," of what has already happened elsewhere in a purer form.[2]

Work in the "periphery" has to confront a deeply embedded structure of knowledge that distinguishes between normative and variant practices. India (or equally Peru or Japan) becomes the site for footnoted descriptions that are intended to counterpoint a core photographic history, European in its sources and nature, but that declines to name itself as such. *Ex-nomination* is the term Roland Barthes uses in *Mythologies* to describe the process through which an ideological fact disappears. The category he is concerned with is the bourgeoisie, "*the social class which does not want to be named.*"[3] For Barthes, the bourgeoisie was the source of an ideology that "can spread over everything and in so doing lose its name without risk."[4] By naming, by studying other locations that we consider to be equally important for the study of photography, and by assuming that the study of diverse practices can contribute to an understanding of photography's coherence, this collection hopes to contribute to the erosion of this still-powerful ex-nomination.

The case studies (covering Bangladesh, Cambodia, Greece, India, Nepal, Nicaragua, Nigeria, and Sri Lanka) are empirical anthropological investigations of a central hypothesis about the relationship between photographic self-representation and different societies' understanding of what is politically possible. The collection explores, through field research, recent ideas about the metaphorically "prophetic" nature of photographic visibility, and the possibility that the camera can offer a form of political recognition in advance of ordinary citizenship. "Citizenship" is loosely understood as describing the rights and duties that come from recognition within a political community, and, like Robert Hariman and John Lucaites, we acknowledge that "one sign of its importance is its complexity."[5] It will be seen that the concept is invoked in diverse ways that testify to this complexity.

If a hypothesis is sound, it should be capable of falsification, and so this collection does not in any sense merely seek confirmation of initial ideas. Its method is, we hope, seriously empirical, embracing the likelihood of refutation, and seeks advances in description and understanding through the meticulous accumulation of data acquired through in-depth anthropological participant observation. All the contributions to this volume embrace the view that ethnographic theory can only be produced through good ethnography.

The Civil Contract Provocation

This volume builds upon earlier work by Georges Didi-Huberman, Deborah Poole, Christopher Pinney, Elizabeth Edwards, and Corinne Kratz that has stressed the irreducibility of photography to the ideological contexts in which it appears. Didi-Huberman, in his searing study of photographs from Auschwitz, argues that "we ask too little of images" if "we sever these from their phenomenology, from their specificity." Honoring their phenomenology, he continues, gives access to "everything that made them an *event*." Images, he concludes, endure "in spite of all."[6]

Poole's study of early photography in the Andes underlines the medium specificity of photography, noting the role that cartes-de-visite "aesthetics of the same" played in configuring motions of race as visible difference.[7] Pinney's ethnography of the camera in central India puts particular emphasis on the unruly performative dimensions of small-town studio practices and highlights the creatively destabilizing effects of this on "identity."[8] A further anthropological perspective, this time emerging primarily from archival engagement, is offered by Edwards. Her fine-grained work stresses the need to engage "*specific* photographic *experiences*: how photographs and their making actually operated."[9] Rather than a capture by discursive regimes, Edwards underlines the "rawness" of photography and the manner in which even the seemingly "most dense of colonial documents can spring leaks."[10] Furthermore, photographs were acknowledged to be capable themselves of making history and of generating a "beyond."[11] Kratz echoes this, suggesting that diverse Kenyan responses to the excessive "mnemonic" qualities of photographs entail a "going beyond what was shown."[12] These insights suggest that the Foucauldian model, although dominant within photography studies, was often contested.

The various inquiries collected here also engage recent work by photographic theorists, including Ariella Azoulay, on the "political ontology" of photography that explicitly addresses the political "beyond" intrinsic to photography. She has argued, in her early work at least, that photography makes possible a new form of "civil imagination" because of its inclusiveness and contingency.[13] Azoulay develops her argument in the context of historical images and also in relation to contemporary photojournalism and the manner in which photographic images appear to provoke actions with political consequences. At the heart of this hypothesis is a refusal to reduce "representation" to mere power (as in the Foucauldian approach) and to instead see it, following Walter Benjamin's insights, as an active, unpredictable, and potentially transformative process.[14] Azoulay argues that photography "has created a space of political relations that are not mediated exclusively by the ruling power," inculcating "civil skills" that create "civil knowledge" and facilitate a "citizenship of photography."[15] These are aspects of the "civil contract," which Azoulay notes she has encountered "at any and every site where there has been photography—and that is almost everywhere."[16]

Azoulay offers an alternative to the use of Michel Foucault in theorizing photography. That approach, propounded initially by Victor Burgin, John Tagg, and others, undoubtedly cast a useful skepticism on the claims of documentary photography and delivered a necessary critique of naive celebrations of the camera's "realism." However, it also conceived of photography as a mere epiphenomenon of the state, photography's power being in actuality, it was claimed, the power of the state to document, surveil, and archive. Far from being characterized by an indexical exorbitance, photographs were best viewed as "paltry pieces of paper," underdetermined scraps that required inscription by powerful discursive formations in order to be able to advance their (fraudulent) claims that they were capable of describing the world through direct reference. Photography as a technical practice characterized by contingency and uncontrollability was overscripted by state-dominated narratives that inserted a totalizing and normalizing power into the social. Photography, even (or, in fact, *especially*) when it thought it was acting in the interests of freedom, was merely acting as an insidious agent of state power. As Tagg famously wrote, photography "as such" has no identity, being simply the reflection of the power that informs it.[17] It is in this context that Tagg asks whether "power" should ever be afraid of photography.[18] Tagg's answer was "no." The importance of stressing photography's "rawness" and its making visible of the "beyond" is that it allows us to imagine the conditions under which it might be possible once again to say "yes."

For Foucauldian photographic theorists, there is an anxiety about the photograph as a window, a kind of trick that asks us to see through it and discover reference and figuration as though these were somehow capable of existing independently. We "dream in the ideological space of the photograph," Tagg wrote, and he sought to shatter this dream, directing attention instead to the societal expectations and conventions that swirled around the occluded surface of the picture plane.[19]

Skepticism in the face of naturalizing claims is entirely justified, but Tagg's strategy allows "ideology" to occupy the complex and paradoxical space of the photographic event and index that Benjamin and several of the other theorists mentioned here have opened up. Perhaps the most damaging impact of the Foucauldian consensus in photographic theory was this foregrounding of the ideological work of the image at the expense of the contingencies and logistics of its making. It is these unruly contingencies that the contributions to this volume explore in detail.

Azoulay's early provocations open up possibilities and political potentials that an earlier orthodoxy foreclosed. However, Azoulay's foundationalist and utopian paradigm inevitably encounters problems when we start to pit her hypothesis against the empirical evidence of actual practices.

The research presented here takes some of Azoulay's insights and seeks to explore them at a local level, through the examination of actual practices, in relation to popular, vernacular, or "demotic" photography. This involves taking a set of claims formulated exclusively in relation to documentary and journalistic photography and scrutinizing them in the context of different genres such as studio portraiture and the "messianic" potential of digital media.

The locations for the ethnographic investigations were chosen because they are sites of current crisis or former political conflict, sites where differences in religious practices are evident, or sites that have significance in the history of visual anthropology. Some of the locations, most notably Nicaragua and Sri Lanka, would be seared by new conflicts during the research period.

In summary, this volume presents a series of social science investigations, through intensive ethnography, of a hypothesis that has been much discussed by photographic historians and political theorists as a foundational and philosophical issue that could be settled by a priori evidence. We, by contrast, focus on how different groups of people actually use photography and what they have to say (and what they do) about politics. At its core is the question of the relationship between visual representation and political representation in social practice.

The Photographic Event and the Event of Photography

Benjamin, and his legacy in thinkers as diverse as Didi-Huberman and Azoulay, offers escape from reductive positions into the ambivalence and complexity of the photographic event. This richness can be grasped through the concepts of "contingency" and "exorbitance." When Barthes wrote about the "sovereign Contingency" of the corps, he was perhaps deliberately recalling Benjamin, who had linked contingency and the event much earlier.[20] Benjamin's much-cited observation in the "Little History of Photography" essay marks a key breakthrough and demands careful attention. "No matter how artful the photographer, no matter how carefully posed his subject," he writes, "the beholder feels an irresistible compulsion to search such a picture for the tiny spark of contingency, the here and now, with which reality has, so to speak, seared through the image-character of the photograph, to find the inconspicuous place where, within the suchness [*Sosein*] of that long-past minute the future nests still today—and so eloquently that we, looking back, may rediscover it."[21] Barthes's punctum is in many ways an echo of Benjamin's "tiny spark of contingency," although one that could be seen as neutralizing its political charge by converting it into a matter of idiosyncratic subjective interpretation that is removed from social and historical interrogation.

Here Benjamin provides a description of the fragility of what E. H. Gombrich would later have described as a visual filter. Benjamin starts with an account of that filter through which the photographer attempts to screen the real through "artfulness" and "careful" posing. Benjamin, of course, does not deny that the photographer is likely, perhaps certain, to attempt to massage or finesse the profilmic. We might also add here that much of the work of the many photo studios that appear in this volume is devoted to attempting to manage and minimize contingency through overpainting or photoshopping images (figure I.1).

But the crucial point is that attempts to eliminate contingency will never be wholly successful. The screen or filter will never be complete because the complexity of the mise-en-scène in its minute and infinite details will always evade the anxious control of the photographer. The image is "seared" with the event, which deposits more information than the photographer can ever control. It is this searing that deposits those "tiny spark[s] of contingency," which make the photograph such a rich resource for future viewers.[22] Konstantinos Kalantzis offers many examples of this, tracing the ways in which commercial images (for instance, postcards) of Sfakians that are narrowly encoded by their producers as images of anonymous consumer-friendly shepherds are sufficiently "unruly" for his Sfakian interlocutors to narratively and materially reanimate the images so that they escape their earlier framing (figure I.2).[23] Note here that "reappropriation" marks not so much the triumph of a later interpretation as the discovery of a possibility intrinsic to the original ontology of the image.

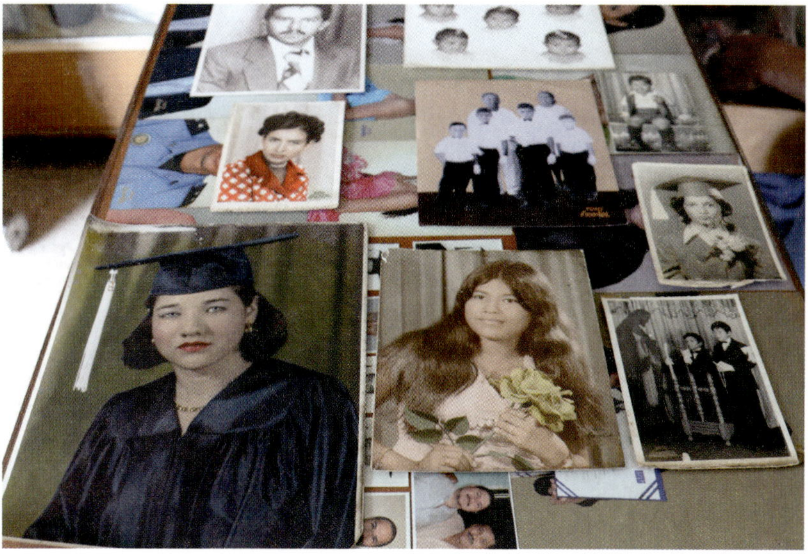

I.1 Selection of images, several overpainted, from Foto Luminton, Managua, Nicaragua. Photograph by Ileana L. Selejan.

Vindhya Buthpitiya and Sokphea Young provide further examples of image "transcoding" or repurposing. In Sri Lanka (Buthpitiya, this volume), National Identity Card (NIC) photographs have been widely photoshopped into memorial images that are mobilized in spaces and acts of resistance demanding accountability from the state for enforced disappearances (figure I.3). These photographs, in many cases the only images of the disappeared that remain, possess extraordinary afterlives, conjugated into new forms and uses. Through a process of copying, retouching, and overpainting, initially with brush and ink and now with Photoshop on desktop computers, each photographic incarnation is recast and remade. State-mandated images form the basis for widespread antistate visual practices. In a parallel manner in Cambodia (Young, this volume), the pre-execution identity photographs made in the Khmer Rouge S-21 Tuol Sleng security prison have become national icons of postgenocide conciliation.

This contingency is central to Azoulay's understanding of the productive nature of the photographic event. Both Benjamin and Barthes might be seen as first and foremost interested in how the event leaves its trace in image content, whereas Azoulay emphasizes the event as plural and paradigmatic

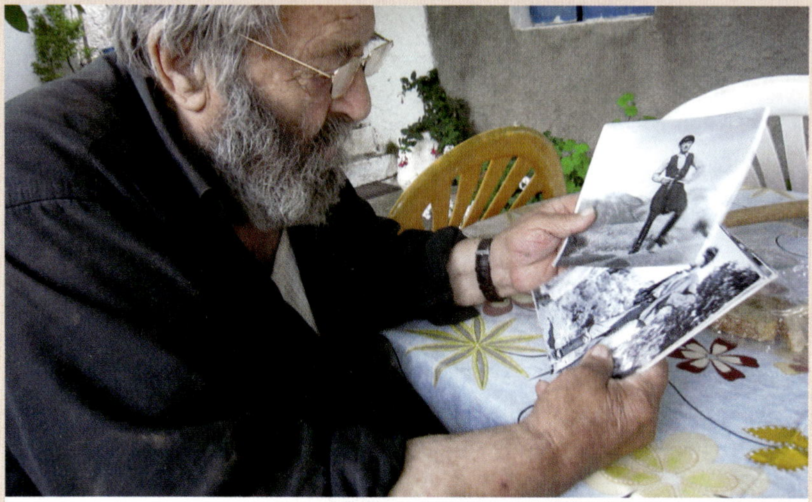

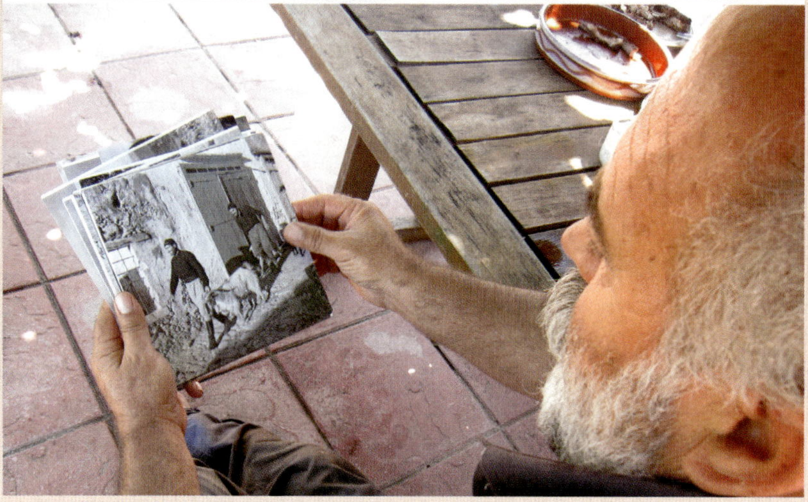

I.2 Sfakian men looking at images taken by professional photographer Nelly, working under commission from the Metaxas regime's Under-Ministry for Press and Tourism in the 1930s and by Voula Papaioannou in the 1950s. Both photographers, and especially Nelly's portraits, emblematizing Sfakia through an emphasis on traditional highland men are highly prized by Sfakians—particularly the sitters' descendants. These images triggered enthusiastic responses, and local viewers who examined them were primarily concerned with identifying and naming the subjects. Interlocutors also commented on sitters' life histories and local reputations, and some photos even uncovered stories of feuding and discord that were otherwise left uncommented on in public. Such commentaries, emphasizing the distinctive properties and materialities of the subjects, break with these images' original typological aesthetic (the Sfakian as an anonymous shepherd type). Historical photos by Nelly, ca. 1939, and by Voula Papaioannou, ca. 1955, copyright Benaki Museum Photographic Archive. Photographs of viewing by Konstantinos Kalantzis, 2007–12.

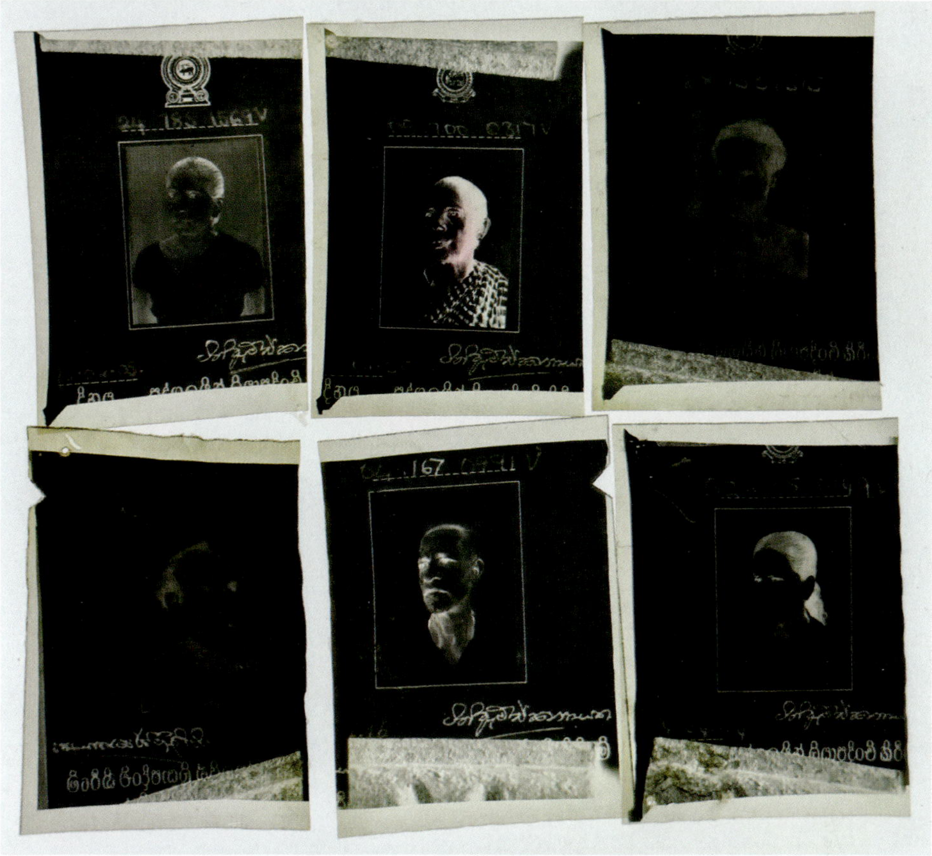

I.3 Copying negatives, Kugan Studio, Jaffna, 2018. These demonstrate the repurposing of National Identity Card (NIC) photographs to create memorial portraits. Rephotographed by Vindhya Buthpitiya.

of possibilities that are subversive of established politics. Azoulay starts by declaring that "the photograph bears the seal of the photographic event" before developing, through a discussion of Mayer and Pierson's 1859 studio image of Napoleon III's son (figure I.4), a deeply Benjaminian understanding of the structuring nature of contingency.[24] This leads her to the conclusion that the encounter between subjects in photography is "never entirely in the sole control of any one of them: no one is the sole signatory to the event of photography."[25]

The photograph depicts the son seated on a horse in front of a screen. Additionally, reflecting the "dynamic field of power relationships that the pho-

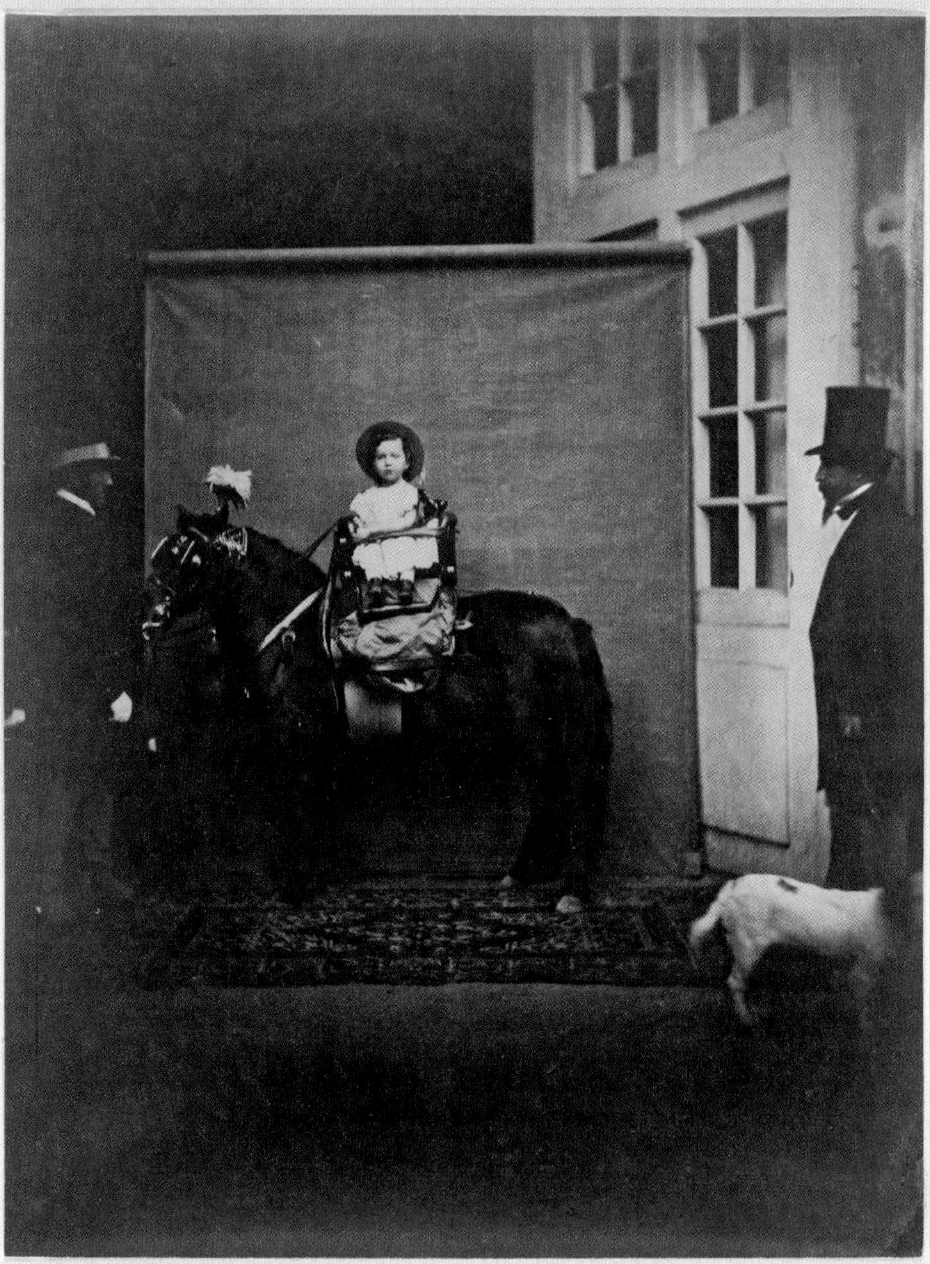

I.4 Pierre Louis Pierson, *Napoleon III and the Prince Imperial*, ca. 1859. Getty Research Institute.

tographic situation portrays," we also see Napoleon III standing on the right side of the image and on the other side a figure that may be that of a servant or equerry.[26]

The visible presence of the sovereign, whose image Azoulay suggests has been "pilfer[ed]," testifies to the explicitly Benjaminian conclusion that "the photograph . . . does not exclusively represent the photographer's will or intention. . . . In fact the photograph escapes the authority of anyone who might claim to be its author, refuting anyone's claim to sovereignty."[27] Azoulay also goes on to make a distinction between "the event of photography and the photographed event" as a way of understanding images that "never come into being."[28] The event of photography, photography's ubiquity and permeation into almost every aspect of human existence, establishes a "photographability" even where no photographs exist. Consequently, some of the most heightened discussions about photography concern photographs that do not exist but that "ought" to, their hypothetical existence becoming an expectation of "modernity," "transparency," "equity," or, most fundamentally, of "history" itself. This was already the underlying idea in the poet Paul Valéry's striking philosophy of history and photography, which transformed an assumption about the concrete conditions of photography into a general model of the event that would allow history to escape from "mere story telling." Lecturing in 1939 on the centenary of Louis Daguerre and Henry Fox Talbot's announcements, and as Europe descended into atrocity, Valéry's text offers many insights. He argues, for instance, that not only did photography teach the eye "not to see non-existent things which, hitherto, it had seen so clearly," but the eye also "grew accustomed to anticipate what it should see."[29]

There are prefigurations here of what Edwards terms the "beyond" and of the distinction that Azoulay makes between the event of the photograph and the event of photography: photograph*ability*, or what Valéry calls "the mere notion of photography," creates expectation and reorients our demands of what will be. "The mere notion of photography, when we introduce it into our meditation on the genesis of historical knowledge and its true value," Valéry explains, "suggests this simple question: *Could such and such a fact, as it is narrated, have been photographed?*" Note the hypothetical and speculative nature of this anticipation: History is not so much what *was* photographed but was rather what was "caught in 'quick takes' *or could have been caught had a cameraman, some star news photographer, been on hand.*"[30]

It is in the light of this that a 1961 article in the Indian newspaper *The Current* could proclaim that the "World's Greatest News Picture" was one that didn't exist (figure I.5).[31] When asked what was the "greatest photo [she] had missed taking," the photographer Homai Vyarawalla responded that it was of Mahatma Gandhi's assassination. As on many previous occasions, she had special permission to attend the prayer meeting at Birla House on January 30, 1948. She took her camera and left her office, but after she went out of the gate, "something cropped up" and she decided that she would go the next day instead. After all, as she recalled, she had photographed the Mahatma many, many times. Her decision would prove fateful: within half an hour, news came of the assassination, at the very spot where she habitually photographed Gandhi, and she realized that she had missed the "one big chance for taking the biggest picture ever." In retrospect, she concluded it was destiny, a force that does "strange things to people" that prevented her attendance that day and resulted, as a later news story proclaimed, in her missing "the world's greatest news picture."

I.5 Article by Ratan Karaka published in *The Current*, 1961. Courtesy of Sabeena Gadihoke and the Alkazi Collection of Photography.

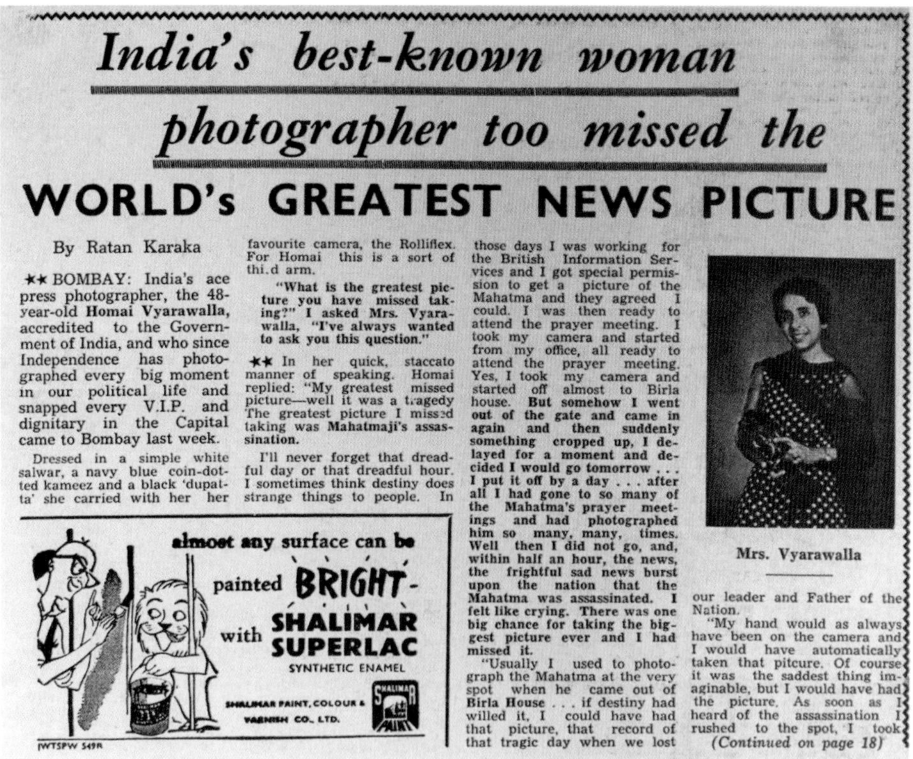

India's best-known woman photographer too missed the

WORLD's GREATEST NEWS PICTURE

By Ratan Karaka

★★ BOMBAY: India's ace press photographer, the 48-year-old **Homai Vyarawalla**, accredited to the Government of India, and who since Independence has photographed every big moment in our political life and snapped every V.I.P. and dignitary in the Capital came to Bombay last week.

Dressed in a simple white salwar, a navy blue coin-dotted kameez and a black 'dupatta' she carried with her her favourite camera, the Rolliflex. For Homai this is a sort of thi.d arm.

"What is the greatest picture you have missed taking?" I asked Mrs. Vyarawalla, "I've always wanted to ask you this question."

★★ In her quick, staccato manner of speaking. Homai replied: "My greatest missed picture—well it was a t.agedy The greatest picture I miss:d taking was **Mahatmaji's assassination.**

I'll never forget that dreadful day or that dreadful hour. I sometimes think destiny does strange things to people. In those days I was working for the British Information Services and I got special permission to get a picture of the Mahatma and they agreed I could. I was then ready to attend the prayer meeting. I took my camera and started from my office, all ready to attend the prayer meeting. Yes, I took my camera and started off almost to Birla house. **But somehow I went out of the gate and came in again and then suddenly something cropped up, I delayed for a moment and decided I would go tomorrow . . . I put it off by a day . . . after all I had gone to so many of the Mahatma's prayer meetings and had photographed him so many, many, times. Well then I did not go, and, within half an hour, the news, the frightful sad news burst upon the nation that the Mahatma was assassinated. I felt like crying. There was one big chance for taking the biggest picture ever and I had missed it.**

"Usually I used to photograph the Mahatma at the very spot when he came out of **Birla House** . . . if destiny had willed it, I could have had that picture, that record of that tragic day when we lost our leader and Father of the Nation.

"My hand would as always have been on the camera and I would have automatically taken that pitcure. Of course it was the saddest thing imaginable, but I would have had the picture. As soon as I heard of the assassination I rushed to the spot, I took

(Continued on page 18)

Mrs. Vyarawalla

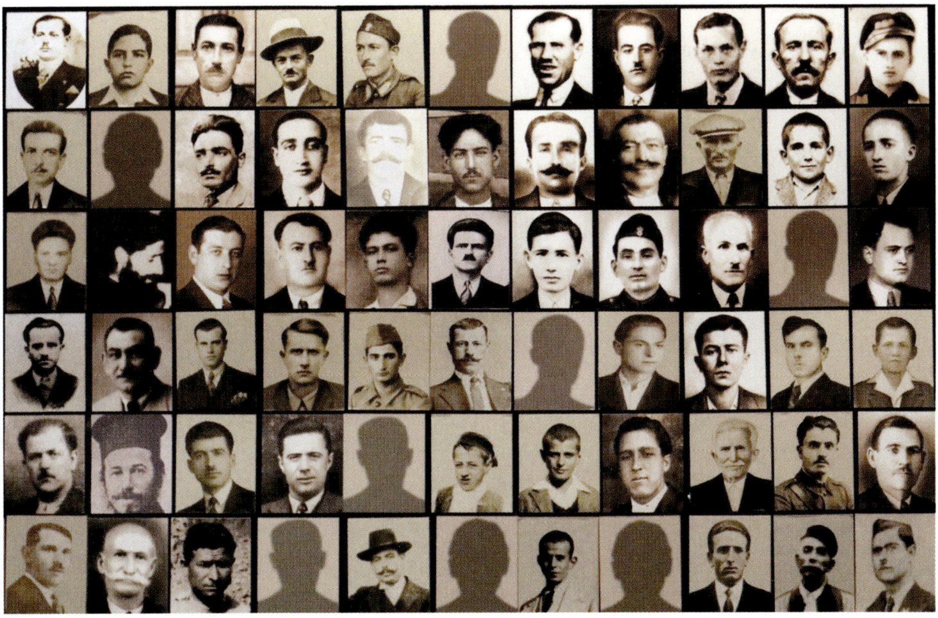

I.6 Detail of photo collage in the final hall at the Municipal Museum of the Kalavritan Holocaust, Greece. Collecting images of the murdered town residents was one of the museum's key missions since its inception. Note the silhouettes used for those cases where photos of the deceased were impossible to retrieve. Photograph by Konstantinos Kalantzis, 2018.

An even more poignant triumph of the event of photography over the event of a specific photograph can be found in Kalantzis's account (this volume) of mainland Greek's valorization of primordial originary footage that could/might/ought to have been taken to document the slaughter of civilians by Nazi troops. He reports that a space in a commemorative museum had been left vacant to accommodate this yet-to-materialize footage (figure I.6).

There are echoes of this, too, in the response of the Bangladeshi Ready Made Garment Workers activists to the group photograph of Rana Plaza victims reported in Pinney's essay in this volume. The absence of an individuated portrait of one of the victims (her face was recoverable only through an image of her together with seven fellow workers) provoked the demand that there *should have been* such an (individuated) image. To recall Valéry, the eye became "accustomed to what it *should* see."[32]

The core Benjaminian idea of the "event" that lies at the heart of the "civil contract" hypothesis ultimately depends on the medium specificity of photography and on photography's emergence as a kind of historical rupture. At its heart, the hypothesis assumes that photography is a self-authenticating form of autopticism (eye-witnessing). The revolution that photography brought can be established through the consideration of a rather haunting lithograph depicting "the apparition at Knock" in County Mayo, Ireland, in 1879 that shows the Virgin Mary and other figures appearing in an ethereal burst in front of a number of astonished foregrounded figures (figure I.7). Much more significant for our current purposes is the elaborate caption, which reveals what it is that photography renders redundant. It describes how "this view was taken on the spot by W. Collins and submitted to and approved by the several persons who saw the above." The image, in other words, required further authentication beyond its simple creation: its "seeing" demanded affirmation from those who had seen the original event. Photography abruptly shortens this sequence, for it allows the viewer of the photograph to see the event itself. To this we might add that the photograph—in its "pure" form—is not only self-authenticating (i.e., not requiring the kind of social consensus after the fact that the Knock image clearly did). Its indexicality is radically "unfiltered" when compared to the socially managed consensus of the Knock image's iconic and symbolic properties. Recall that for C. S. Peirce, who first formulated the trichotomy of symbol, icon, and index, the icon's association with its referent (through likeness) was not dependent on the existence of that referent ("an *Icon* is a sign which refers to the Object that it denotes merely by virtue of characters of its own . . . whether any such Object actually exists or not"[33]). The icon, in Webb Keane's words, refers to a "possible object."[34] To this we might add that inasmuch as the "likeness" was arrived at through social agreement, then like the "symbol," the relationship between sign and interpretant (signifier) depends on "an association of general ideas."[35]

In contradistinction to what is sometimes referred to as the "ontological turn," the essays in this volume adhere to a universal semiotics for the purposes of our analysis while recognizing that local semiotic ideologies (semiotic evaluations as "social facts") frequently diverge. Thus we do not see the fact that in much of India, chromolithographs of deities are widely described as *photos*, as requiring us to accept that lithography can acquire the power of the index. They *are* indexes of the stone or offset roller with which they are impressed but *not*, analytically speaking, indexes of gods.

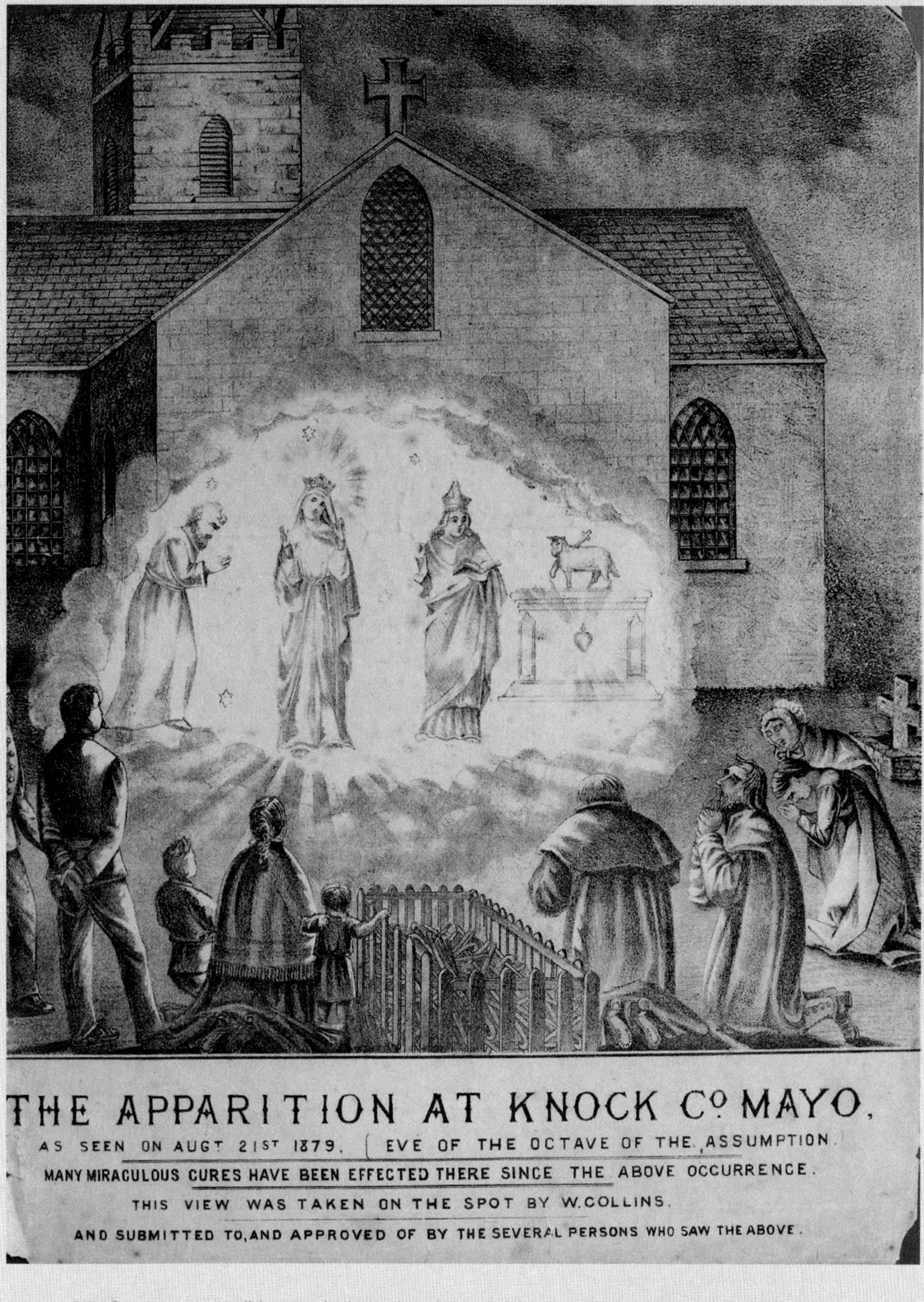

I.7 Contemporary lithograph depicting the apparition at Knock, Ireland, in 1879. Private collection.

The requirement, therefore, is not to affirm local sign systems (this would be impossible since they contradict each other and cannot all be affirmed simultaneously[36]) but rather to describe them adequately. Part of this description must communicate the strange "not-quite-secular" power that photography has to capture performative enactments (what Barthes termed the "corps" or "body") and the widely distributed idea that the photograph serves as a space of heightened revelation.[37] The "not-quite-secular" is a marvelous phrase devised by Kajri Jain to describe the power and modality of Indian calendar art, a genre of mass-produced popular art that, while frequently celebrating the modern (e.g., bicycle-riding women), also simultaneously invoked mythic and divine archetypes.[38] Photography, too, exemplifies this paradoxical duality, being at the cutting edge of technical innovation and also, at the same time, saturated with an archaic magic. This is an observation made by Nadar (Gaspard-Félix Tournachon), who noted how "awesome night—dear to all sorcerers and wizards—reigned supreme in the dark recesses of the camera."[39] This sentiment was echoed by Benjamin in his suggestion that the photographer might be considered the descendant of the "augurs and haruspices"—the diviners of the classical world—and that photography makes the "difference between technology and magic visible *as a thoroughly historical variable*."[40]

How does this concern with normative semiology and the possibility of "pure" photography play in the context of actually existing photographic practice? Consider, for instance, a framed print of a *sati* (the self-immolation of a widow on her husband's funeral pyre) that was photographed in the home of a central Indian factory worker, a former native of Jhunjhunu, a town in the arid north of Rajasthan famous for its martial Rajput culture (figure I.8).

The print is titled *Sri 1008 Kotadivali Sri Sati Savitri Mata* (Sri 1008 female from Kotadi village Sri Sati Savitri mother), below which is given information on the date of the sati (2025 in the Vikram Samvat calendar = 1969 or 1970 CE). At the center of the images is a color reproduction of a painting that possibly incorporates photographic faces. This image is surrounded by eight black-and-white halftone photographic images that show Savitri with her brother (*bhai milan*) as well as the preparation of the pyre (*chita ki taiyari*) and the priestly ritual (*brahman puja*). The image presents two central questions for the Azoulayean hypothesis. First, it problematizes the differential evaluation of "atrocity photography," for the black-and-white photographs serve for most of the image's viewers as celebrations of the renunciatory act of the widow (sati as "blessing").[41] It is only for a smaller audience of metropolitan activists that the photographs serve as evidence of atrocity (sati as "curse") of

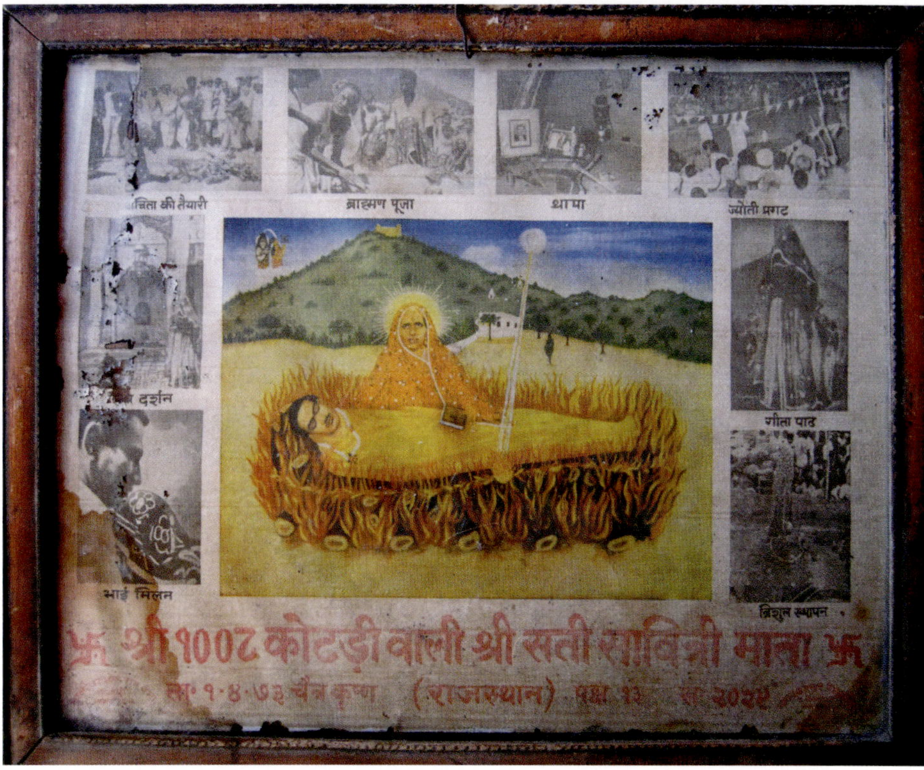

I.8 *Sri 1008 Kotadivali Sri Sati Savitri Mata*. Framed offset lithograph with halftone photographic elements. Photograph by Christopher Pinney, 2015.

the sort on which Azoulay focuses.[42] This duality underwrites the dangers of assuming that there is a single public, one equally committed to agreed civic virtues. We are faced by contrast with "counterpublics" constituted by fundamental disagreements. *Counterpublics* was the term that Michael Warner adopted from Nancy Fraser's optimistic claim for a late twentieth-century US feminist subaltern alternative sphere.[43] However, Warner's reworking of the concept, in line with his general proposition that "political confidence is committed to a strange and uncertain destination," is not confined to politically approved "subalterns."[44] He asks why counterpublics should not include "US Christian fundamentalists" or other entities that do not privilege "the hierarchy of faculties that elevates rational-critical reflection as the self-image of humanity."[45] Those who eulogize sati "as blessing" (and in western India, they are many) would certainly qualify as a counterpublic not enamored of Habermasian critical rationality.

Second, the print offers a fine example of "mixed media." The black-and-white photographs play a secondary role to the central image, which is largely painted and duplicated through offset chromolithography. The "failure" of photography at the center of this image reflects the difficulty or impossibility of capturing the event that authenticates sati: the transmission of a beam of fire from the god Shiva that certifies the divinely approved status of the act and initiates the immolation. In the central image, we can see Shiva and his consort Parvati in the sky on the left; the beam of fire emerges from the right-hand side of the image. The other subsidiary point to make concerns the image's intervisuality. The arrangement of a central devotional image surrounded by contextualizing and historicizing images is a peculiarity of visual culture in this part of Rajasthan. The most illuminating parallel is that of images of Baba Ramdev Pir, whose *samadhi* (tomb) is near Pokharan, also in northern Rajasthan. In one widely circulated print (versions of which were produced by Harnarayan and Sons in the 1930s and Sharma Picture Publications in the 1950s), known as *Ramdevji ki chaubis parche* (The twenty-four proofs of Ramdevji), Ramdev is show on horseback in the center and is surrounded by twenty-four medallions or *tondi* that record the "proofs" (*parche*) of the deity's divinity.[46] The sati image reproduces this basic visual structure and reveals photography's work in this context not to be the self-authenticating historical reflex about which Valéry commented but to demonstrate conformity to a local visual-cultural convention (i.e., the authority of parche rather than, or not simply, the Peircean index).

At this point, cultural relativists, or radical adherents of the "ontological turn," might argue that anthropology faces a choice between embracing a universal or a locally sensitive semiotics. Keane stresses that for Peirce, signs gave way to more signs opening up semiotics to "sociability, struggle, historicity, and contingency," thus opening up the conditions for what Keane calls "semiotic ideology," in which "different ontologies . . . underwrite different sets of possible signs," or as he later puts it, the manner in which signs, agentive subjects and acted-upon objects, "are found in the world."[47] Keane advocates the relocation of semiotic research from the closed confines of philosophy into the "messier, open-air landscapes of ethnography," an aim with which this collection is in total agreement.[48]

Keane cites Peirce to the effect that indexes in themselves "assert nothing" and require "instructions," this being the work of semiotic ideology.[49] In light of this, we would have to acknowledge for Hindu viewers of the sati image that the central painted/chromolithographed element may well be more indexically powerful than the black-and-white photographic elements. This conundrum recalls an intriguing discussion by Jain of a photomontage not dissimilar to the central element of the *Kotadivale* image reproduced here, depicting the eighteen-year-old 1987 sati Roop Kanwar.

The Roop Kanwar image, which concerns Jain, shows her being "consumed by flames as her hands are joined in prayer over her husband's body; in the air in front of a tree hovers the mother goddess (*devi/mata*), who is sending a beam of light toward Roop Kanwar's haloed head."[50] This image plays a significant role in Anand Patwardhan's 1994 film *Trial by Fire*, in which we hear Patwardhan interrogating a Rajput women named Godavari about the semiotic status of the photograph. Has it been "faked," he asks, to which she replies, "No . . . that's the way it is in the photo." Patwardhan then asks how it is possible to photograph god, at which point she insists that "he'll definitely come in the photo. . . . He hides and then appears in the photograph." It must be god in the photo, she concludes, because otherwise how would you know that it was god's beam of fire that ignited the pyre? This stages what Jain refers to as "a radical incommensurability" grounded in different evaluations of what constitutes a "photo" (the term *photo* being used in Hindi to denote any kind of two-dimensional image) and an equally significant divergence about what the capabilities of the gods are.[51]

"Secular" demands can of course also be made of photographs. In Cambodia, according to the sub-decree on Khmer identification and identity cards, a Buddhist monk is not entitled to a Khmer citizen ID. Consequently, monks occasionally ask photographers to photoshop "Buddhist images" (images that they already have that show them attired as monks) into something that looks like a civil photo ID by adding a shirt, moustache, hair, and eyebrows (figure I.9).

Elsewhere in South Asia, family portraiture dips in and out of the transcendent. In Indian Hindu practice (Pinney, this volume), framed photographs of ancestors are routinely worshipped (in theory for seven generations after their death). Pinney often experienced villagers in central India complaining (if upon returning to his field site without a portrait photo he had pledged to a sitter), "So what will they do when I'm dead?" (meaning, what would their relations do in the absence of a suitable image for memorial purposes?). Buthpitiya (this volume) documents a kind of "remixing" that underlines the "not-quite-secular" status of photographic images—a material embedding of images of the departed in Sri Lanka within small temple-like wooden structures. Studio practitioners transform staid NIC photographs into extrava-

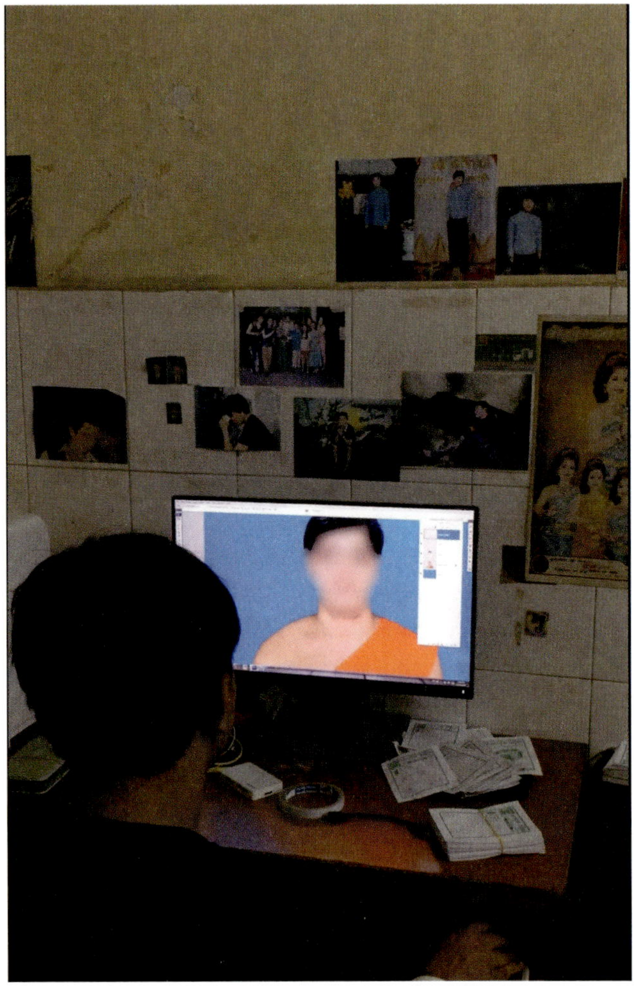

I.9 A Phnom Penh studio photoshopping a monk's portrait so that it can be used for a national ID card. Photograph by Sokphea Young, 2019.

gant memorial portraits made even grander by frame makers with twinkling electric lights and neon plastic flowers, to be placed and worshipped among Hindu or Catholic household pantheons (figure I.10).

Ileana L. Selejan documents similar crossovers between photographic ensembles and devotional assemblages of ex-votos in Nicaragua. She notes that photographs are frequently displayed alongside religious images. This spillover between auratic registers also encompasses revolutionary displays of martyrs' portraits and portraits of the victims of the 2018 repression, which are incorporated into portable saints' altars. The latter are displayed during subsequent Semana Santa (Catholic Holy Week) precessions and placed alongside the figure of the Virgin Mary within altars erected in homes and neighborhoods during the celebrations of La Purísima (the immaculate conception).

The "not-quite-secular" characteristic of photography suggests, however, not that we need a relativistic semiology but that we need to not lose sight of the commonalities that underlie the diversity in semiotic ideologies and that most of all we need to understand the centrality of the photographic event to the semiotics of photography. Although local "Hindu" semiotic ideology would insist that the colored centerpiece and the black-and-white "proofs" in the Indian sati image are equally indexical, we should not experience any embarrassment in making the contrary claim that this is not the case: the black-and-white images are signs of events, whereas the "event claim" of the central colored element can only be equivalent to that made by the Knock lithograph: it meets with social "approval" after the fact.

Consider in this context a photoshopped image of a Cambodian graduate with Prime Minister Hun Sen, as discussed in Sokphea Young's contribution

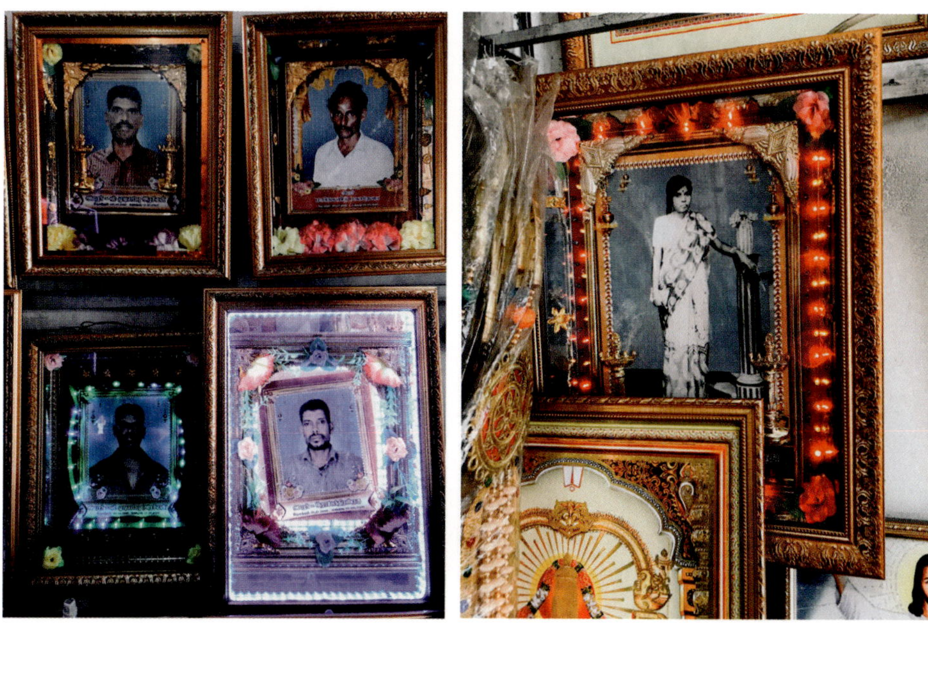

I.10 Memorial portraits awaiting collection at framing shops. Jaffna, 2018. Memorial portraiture, inextricable from wartime public remembrance practices and aesthetics, has a significant social presence. These were placed among Tamil Hindu and Catholic pantheons in households and commercial establishments and incorporated into rituals of daily worship. Photograph by Vindhya Buthpitiya, July 2018.

(this volume). Believing that being photographed in the presence of a powerful figure will bring fortune and facilitate a flow of power, many Cambodians desire such images. However, only a few students are fortunate enough to be photographed with the premier. The poor graduate shown in figure I.11 paid a photographer to photoshop himself with Hun Sen with the intention of displaying the image at home or in the office to show relatives and friends his indexical connection to power. The "semiotic ideology" is clear: the graduate hopes that beholders of the image will believe that he was in physical proximity to the fountainhead of power. However, analytically we can safely dispute this indexical claim, concluding that it is merely "iconic" trickery.

The Political and Optical Unconscious

Intrinsic to the Benjaminian event is also his idea of the "optical unconscious" and the sense that photography, rather than simply confirming our vision and view of the world, *extends* and *subverts* it.[52] This intuition was most perfectly expressed in his response to Karl Blossfeldt's close-ups of the structure of plants. Originally conceived as a contribution to scientific botany, they were received upon their belated publication in 1928 as *Urformen der Kunst*, as somewhere "between New Objectivity and Surrealism."[53] Blossfeldt's work ("the forms of ancient columns in horse willow, a bishop's crosier in the ostrich fern, totem poles in tenfold enlargements of chestnut and maple shoots") had provoked Benjamin to a memorably poetic vision of "the image worlds, which dwell in the smallest things—meaningful yet covert enough to find a hiding place in waking dreams."[54] This "perceptive inventory" opened up the possibility of an optical unconscious.[55]

To Benjamin's idea of the optical unconscious we might add the idea of a "political unconscious." Although this is a phrase associated with Fredric Jameson, its usage here directs our attention not so much to fundamental questions of *form*, as in Jameson, as to the manner in which "subjunctive" performances in front of the camera find a place in "waking dreams."[56] Photographs, as Vilém Flusser puts it, are "projections . . . images of the future" that encourage covert explorations of what, once made conscious, we would readily recognize as conventionally "political." Photographers, Flusser continues, "are pursuing new possibilities."[57] There is already ample ethnographic evidence for this, perhaps most notably through Karen Strassler's work on photography in Indonesia, which has advanced important propositions con-

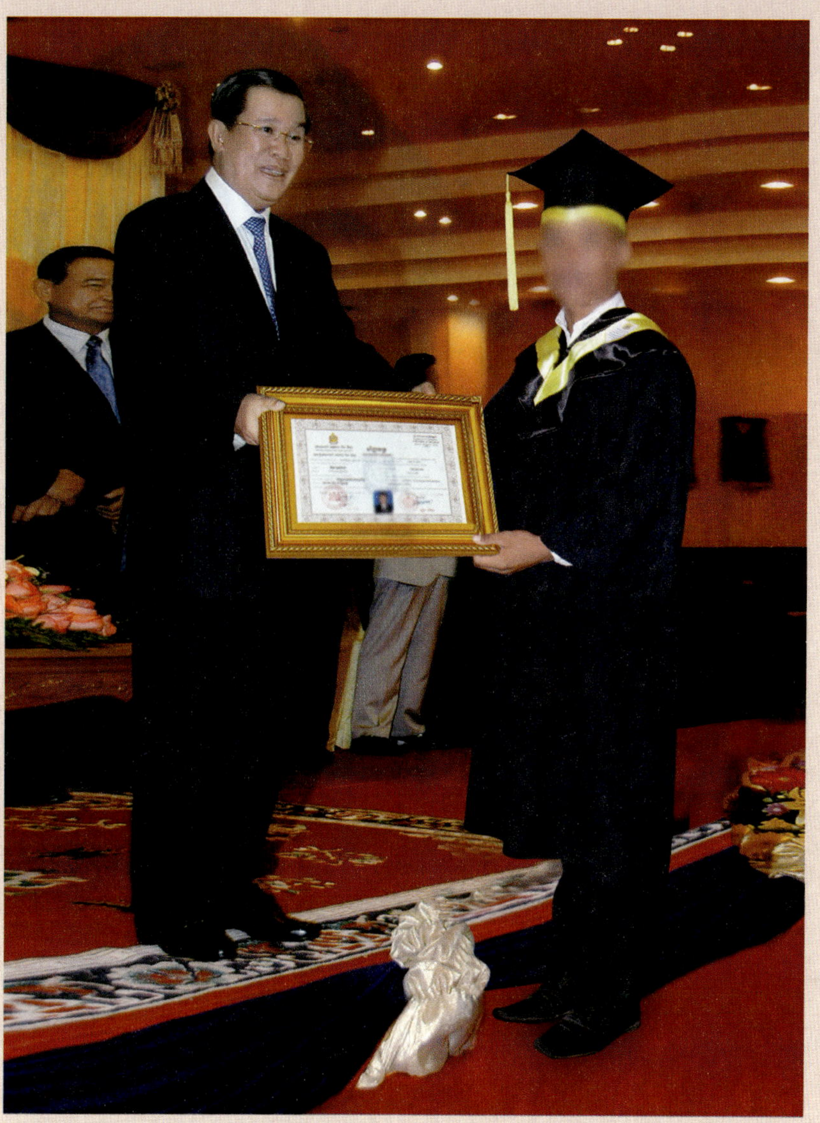

I.11 A photoshopped image of a graduate with Hun Sen, the prime minister of Cambodia. Rephotographed by Sokphea Young, 2018.

cerning the nature of "visual history," the role of affect and visuality in nationalism, the relationship between intimate and public spheres, and the "messianic" potential of photography.

Strassler emphasizes the subjunctive nature of photography, what she terms the "as if" quality of the image. This involves photography's *inability* to do other than capture the proleptic future-made-present of the performative self-presentation so commonly found in popular images. Strassler's *Refracted Visions* is replete with insights about the political identifications, projections, fluidities, and erasures that photography facilitates. In the process, it delivers a subtle analysis of the role of visual practices in political imaginaries. She writes, for instance: "In posing for—and with—the camera, people place themselves (and are placed) within the visual landscapes, temporal logics, and affective and ideological structures of Indonesia's national modernity. Popular photographic practices thus register how people pose as 'Indonesians' and the ways that 'Indonesian' itself has been posed: as a problem, a proposition, a possibility, and a position from which to occupy the world."[58]

The covert dimension of the political unconscious partly speaks to the problem identified by Judith Butler concerning how different behaviors and issues come to be framed as "perceptible reality" or how, conversely, they may never enter the field of visibility: "how we articulate political analyses, depends upon a certain field of perceptible reality having already been established."[59] Strassler provides tangible evidence that the study of photographs can give us access to the political unconscious and in the process make visible what would otherwise be occluded: "Popular photographs . . . reveal the larger currents of Indonesian history as they are refracted through the prism of the intimate and the everyday. At the same time, they show the visual to be a domain crucial to the very making of history itself. History, after all, encompasses not only the main events and central plots but also people's barely registered efforts to orient themselves to new narratives and possibilities, to assimilate alien ideas and practices, to see and be seen in new ways."[60]

Photography's political unconscious realizes what would otherwise remain latent, hidden, as Benjamin put it, "in waking dreams." It is through photography that images of "'imagined' social entities like nations become visible and graspable."[61] Photography is central to becoming, to emerging identities and identifications, to selves in the process of being forged. This subjunctive and unconscious modality suggests that the gerund *photographing* may better capture this processual and emergent quality than the noun *photograph* or the abstract noun *photography*.

It is for this reason that the study of photography can provide access to "affective dimensions of national belonging that have remained elusive to scholarship—not (or not only) the strident emotions of nationalist fervor and patriotism but the more subtle and often ambivalent sentiments that attach to the nation."[62] Kalantzis (this volume) provides equally powerful documentation of the way in which photography allows access to a level of the social imagination, a political unconscious of sorts, in which Sfakians mobilize affects that are in tension with the formal political rhetoric that would otherwise attach to concepts like "Germany." He further shows in other work how Sfakian men use photography to both perform and deform nineteenth-century warrior archetypes, reanimating motifs and identifications that have the potential to reorient the terms of conventional political debate.[63]

The Sfakian case study speaks to a long history of asymmetry in the area's representation: Sfakians are always the subject of others' photographs and texts—never, until very recently, the producers. However, out of this asymmetry is forged a dialogical mediation in which outsiders drawn to local idioms encounter locals posing in ways that fit their own sense of self and outsiders further inflate that local sense through their presence and through their images that locals reimport.[64] This echoes the negotiations through which Sfakians ameliorate an unequal image economy by partly erasing the role of photographers through their emphasis on the aura of ancestors as in some sense the authors of photographs. This is less the egalitarian space of the civil contract and more a patrilineal and hieratic valorization of sacred ancestors.

The *overt* uses of photography for political purposes are documented by Buthpitiya in Sri Lanka (where atrocity images feverishly circulate as part of ongoing Tamil political claims [figure I.12]) and by Naluwembe Binaisa in Nigeria (where elaborate photographic billboards promote political candidates in state elections). Selejan documents how in the 2018 uprising in Nicaragua, portraits of victims of the regime were repeatedly brought into view during months of protests, marches, and assemblies (figure I.13). One might say they were embodied by the mass, and *performed* and revivified in public space through the prominent display of images of the martyrs. These strategies resemble practices from the earliest revolutionary period (late 1970s and 1980s), signaling certain continuities that nevertheless many protesters sought to contradict.

Bangladeshi photo studios are also unusually vocal about their competition for the patronage of local politicians, each studio claiming they can deliver "cleaner" and "shinier" portraits for campaign images. But these practices

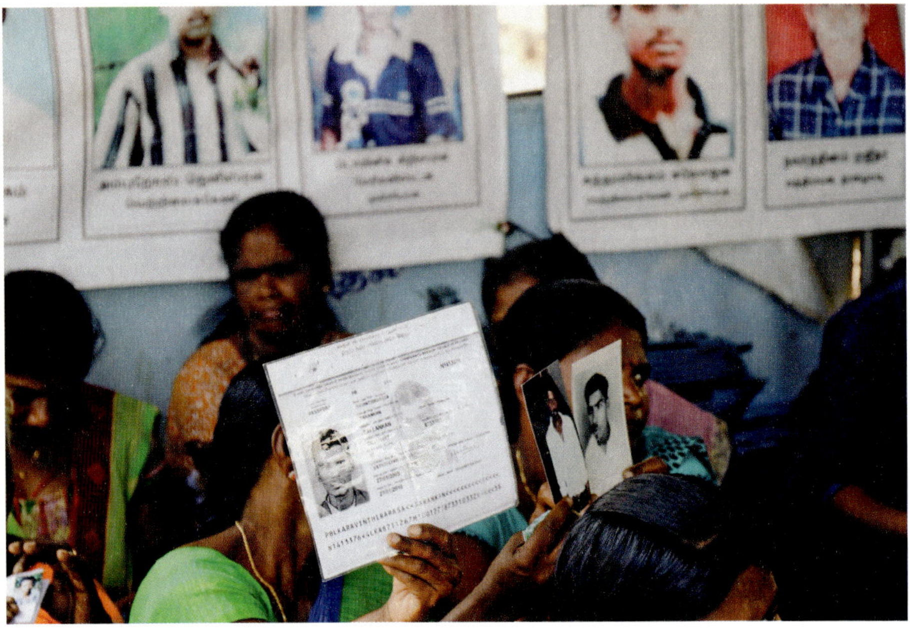

I.12 Family members hold up photographs of their loved ones at a protest of the Families of the Disappeared in Maruthankerny, Jaffna, March 2018. Continuing for more than 2,000 days since February 2017, the Families of the Disappeared in the north and east of Sri Lanka have gathered in various locations to demand answers from the state about the whereabouts of their loved ones, a number of whom surrendered to the state security forces at the end of the civil war. Photographs of the protesters, wielding photographs of missing family members, have become a visual metonym for the injustices and grievances that characterize the postwar period. Photograph by Vindhya Buthpitiya.

usually have a covert underside: in Osun, Nigeria, Binaisa reports a liking among politicians and dignitaries for "mirror portraits" offering an amplitude through doubling. In Cambodia, as we have seen, the image of Premier Hun Sen is photoshopped into images where individuals crave the benefits of supposed physical contiguity. In small-town central India (studied by Pinney), mobile phone covers with photographic prints of the local Member of the Legislative Assembly (MLA), or their political competitors, are popular, the image of the politician here acting as talisman, compressed through daily use, into the intimate bodily space of the loyal devotee.

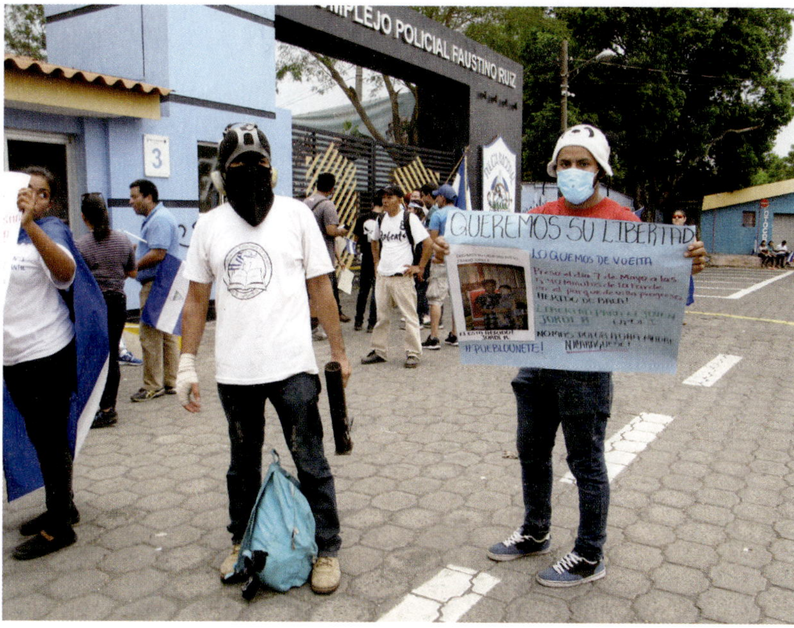

I.13 Students demand the release of political prisoners in Nicaragua as part of an antigovernment solidarity protest in front of the police headquarters in Managua. The poster includes a family photograph of one of the protesters, with details surrounding his arrest provided in the text. Photograph by Ileana L. Selejan, May 9, 2018.

Performance and Imagination

Karen Strassler also persuasively affirms James Siegel's observation that in the late colonial Indies, photography "emblematized the pervasive fantasy" of a lingua franca of modernity, establishing a zone of translatability and transmission, a space of performative invention and consumption, a laboratory for the development of new selves and identities.[65]

The current collection presents many examples that echo this insight as well as photographic practices that consolidate powerful narratives of "tradition." To focus only on South Asia, we can find strikingly explicit visualizations that place photography itself in the vanguard of progress. Early twentieth-century South Indian studios picture photographic packaging virtually laminated against clocks as though they could be harnessed to the onward march of time or perhaps propel that time ever forward. Images from

1960s Kathmandu similarly foreground photographic packaging's high symbolic yield. A parallel genre deploys photography to record or imagine mobility: bicycles were frequently brought into the studio, and the studio in turn became a staging space for travels in airplanes and automobiles. Frequently, this was tied to the desire and/or necessity of transnational migration (figure I.14).

Motorbikes, for long a means of surveying urban glamour within profilmic space, still feature as a prop in the photographic studios that accompany traveling fairs in central India. Pinney's research in South Asia revealed numerous images where the motorbike featured as a prop, including a poignant late 1970s one made in a traveling studio at a fair in Birgunj, Nepal, in which two brothers straddle a Royal Enfield Bullet bike, one wearing a policeman's cap in reference to the then popular Yash Chopra 1975 film *Deewaar* (figure I.15).

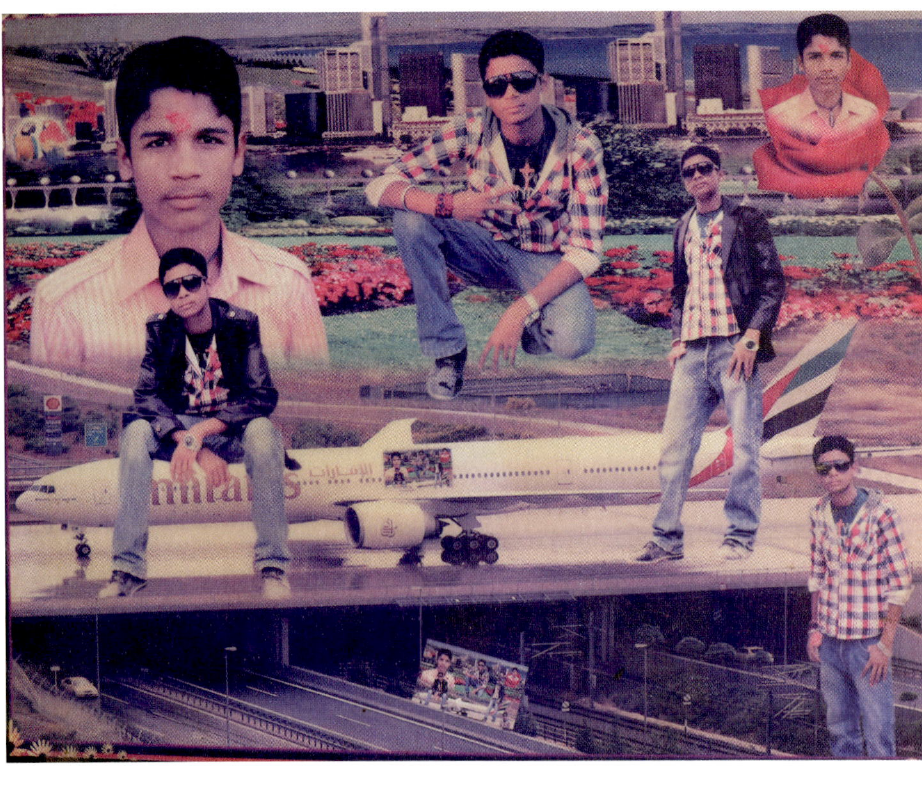

I.14 Elaborate photomontage of a prospective migrant, visualizing a future in the Gulf. Birgunj, Nepal. Rephotographed by Christopher Pinney, June 18, 2019.

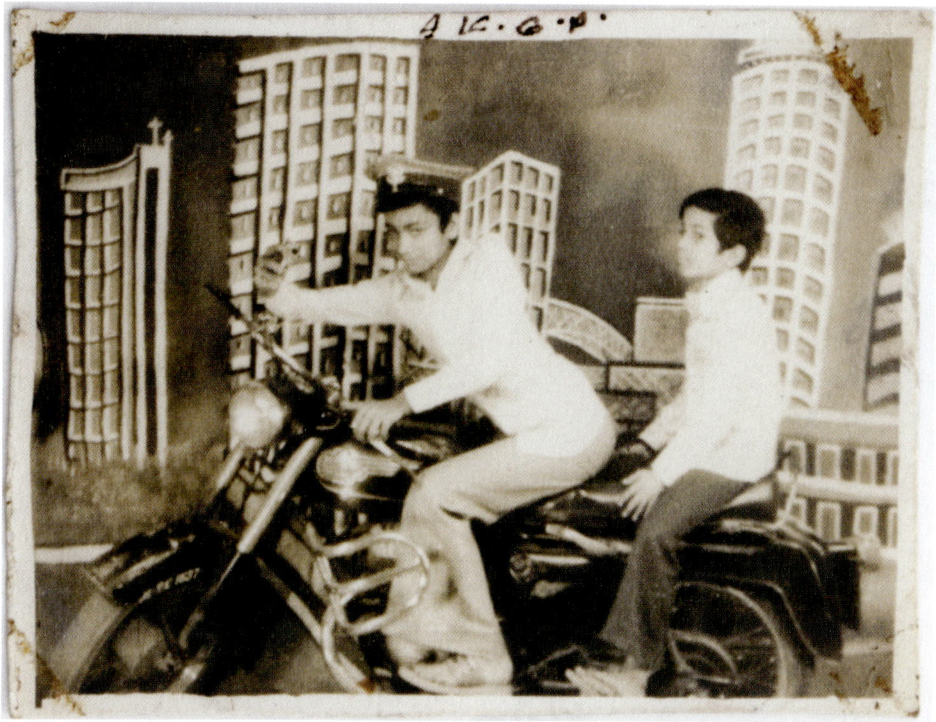

I.15 Ganesh Lath and his brother photographed in a traveling studio in a *mela* at Birgunj, Nepal, late 1970s. Courtesy of G. P. Lath. Rephotographed by Christopher Pinney, June 19, 2019.

The expressionistic Dr. Caligari–like painted backdrop beautifully conjures the access to modernity opened up by the space of the photographic studio.

In Nicaragua (Selejan, this volume), Photoshop has of course replaced artisanal practices of overpainting and adornment with new aspirational backdrops indicative of the desire for economic prosperity, usually through some iteration of the American Dream (villas, cars, luxurious interiors). Some image types have remained consistent (figures I.16–I.18): standard graduation photographs in Sri Lanka will have the hand-painted library backdrop replaced with an almost identical digital one; family portraits posed against painterly gardens will be juxtaposed with an equivalent chosen by the sitters from a multitude of floral backdrops "harvested" online. In Nigeria (Binaisa, this volume), aspiration is embodied in ornate golden chairs found in many studios. There are resonances here with Krista Thompson's work on Bahamian photography and Tobias Wendl's documentation of Ghanaian studio images.[66]

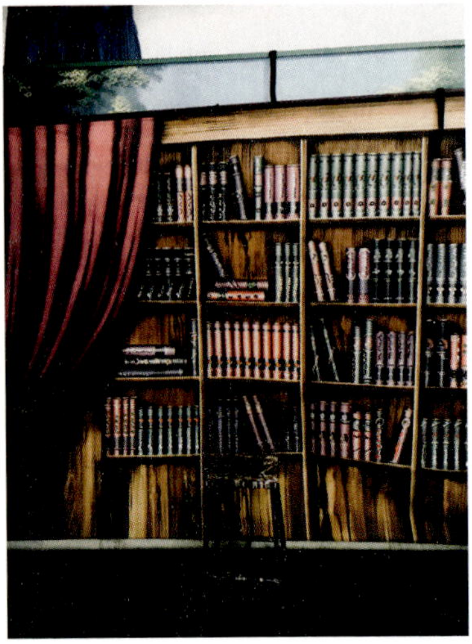 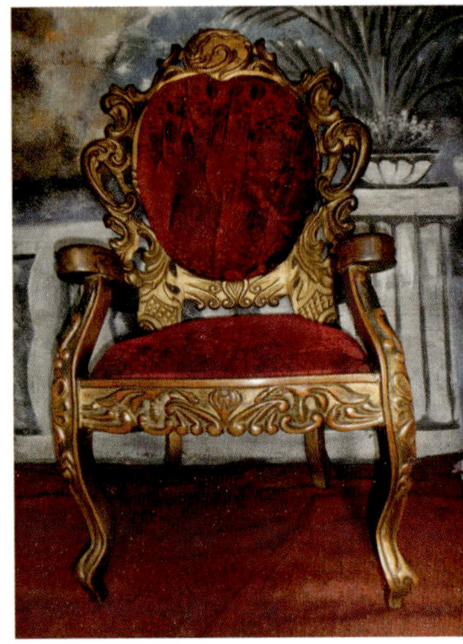

In Crete, the circuit is rather more complex. Kalantzis (this volume) dissects the process through which Germans, envisioned by Cretan shepherds as arch agents of modernity (exemplified by their presence as early photographers of local life but also through other vectors such as the engineering prowess embodied in cars, and Germany itself as a high-value migration destination), were the chief propagators and image preservers of the antimodern traditional Sfakian archetype (figure I.19). Thus a German modernity invested itself (through a Romantic Orientalism) in the image of what it had itself lost.[67]

Demotic versus Vernacular

The connections between the different practices documented here suggest the need for a new theory of "demotic" photography as opposed to "vernacular" practice. This, following J. F. Champollion (who elaborated this concept in his engagement with the Rosetta Stone), denotes a "ground-up" practice "of the people" rather than the reactive "top-down" trajectory of theories of vernacularity.[68] "Vernacularity" has certainly done useful work in the past, and we do not propose its complete abolition.[69] However, "demotic" assumes a widespread subaltern practice that is "more than local and less than global." "Vernacular," based on linguistic models, assumes popular practices that are reactive to dominant hierarchies, as for instance in Pierre Bourdieu's influen-

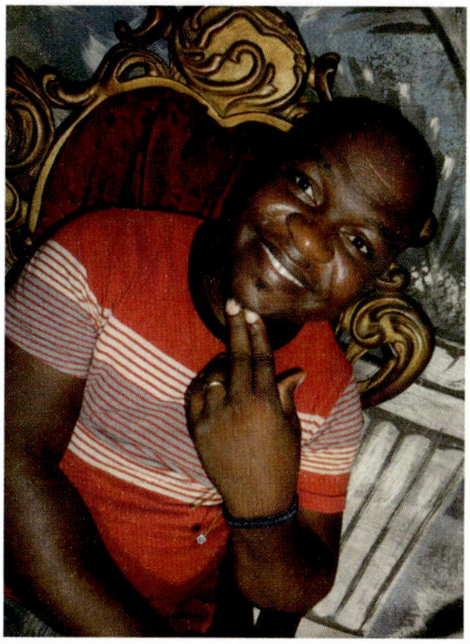

I.16 (left) Studio backdrop, Kumaran Photo Studio, Jaffna, Sri Lanka. Library backdrop as used for university graduation portraits either on-site at the studio or as part of official photography services offered at graduation ceremonies. On both occasions, sitters typically pose standing with a cap, gown, and rolled-up diploma in hand. Photograph by Vindhya Buthpitiya, April 2018.
I.17 (center) Throne chair, the central studio backdrop in Dr. Lukson Star Photo Studio, Ilé-Ifè, Osun, Nigeria. In a highly segmented society, a photograph posed in the throne chair invokes and visually cements aspirations for future social mobility. Photograph by Naluwembe Binaisa, 2018.
I.18 (right) A client, Oladimeji Ogunoye, a PhD student at Obafemi Awolowo University. Image taken in 2017 by Dr. Lukson Star Photo Studio, Ilé-Ifè, Osun, Nigeria. Rephotographed by Naluwembe Binaisa. 2018.

tial work on French popular photography.[70] "Vernacular" may accurately describe certain practices (such as Bourdieu's), but it is inappropriate in many instances, including several documented in this book.

The linguistic paradigm of vernacularization involves a distilling out of local idioms from much larger cosmopolitan structures; as the Sanskritist Sheldon Pollock puts it: "in conscious opposition to some larger world, in relationship to which they chose to speak more locally."[71] Pollock contrasts vernacular "place" with cosmopolitan "space," describing vernacularization as choosing "to write in a language that did not travel . . . as easily and as far as the well-traveled language of the older cosmopolitan order."[72]

It is apparent how models of vernacularization, applied to media, suit a rather conventional mode of anthropology invested in emphasizing localization as active cultural practice. It affirms the heroic estimation of the human subject who always proves capable of overcoming the potential tyranny of technology and unwittingly feeds ex-nominating narratives through its celebration of divergent local appropriations.

The desire to move away from the concept of the "vernacular" lies in the recognition of its hierarchical origins in the "language of the *verna*, or houseborn slave of Republican Rome."[73] It was this sense of a local, subordinate practice developed in opposition to dominant class practices that Bourdieu advances in his work on photography and visual culture. While this may well be an appropriate characterization of the hierarchical dynamic of 1960s French photographic practice, it is this volume's contention that it fails to accurately describe the dynamics and contours of all "popular" photographic activity.

"Demotic" seems a better descriptor than "vernacular" for much of the popular practice documented in this volume for two central reasons. First, a good deal of popular photography reveals a desire to engage with (rather than withdraw from) the cosmopolitan: telephones, cityscapes, motorbikes, and airplanes are all symptoms of a modernity and mobility that connects, rather than disconnects, localities. This mélange of speed, glamour, consumption, and aspiration forms the core repertoire of much global popular photography.

Second, much global popular photography looks very similar. This is the "more than local, less than global" space of the *demotic*, a distributed horizontal space of popular practice whose dynamic space is quite different from

I.19 A woman holds up a portrait of her father-in-law, Charitos Protopapas, taken originally by a tourist, most likely a German, in the 1970s at a highland village in the Sfakia region of Crete. This particular sitter had been photographed on various occasions in his lifetime by passing travelers and professionals and had been featured in various media, including the German travel magazine *Merian*. Such images of "traditional" rugged men acquire complex social lives and often become cherished photos of ancestors for Sfakians in the absence of other locally produced images. Original photographer unknown. Photograph by Konstantinos Kalantzis, 2018.

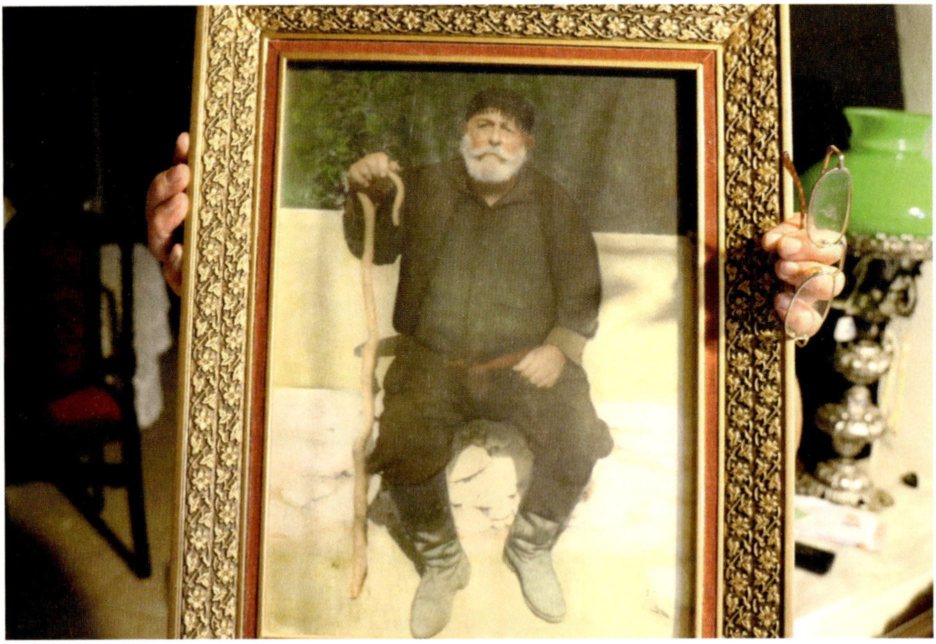

the vertical place of the *vernacular*. It is worth adding here that Bourdieu's nation-state space of aesthetic hierarchy seems especially ill-suited to (for instance) the diasporic space of Tamil nationalism in which image flows configure a landscape that massively exceeds the northern part of Sri Lanka (see Buthpitiya, this volume).

The Photograph as a Scarce Resource

Photographic theory in its ex-nominated form frequently bemoans the anaesthetizing properties of simulation. From Ludwig Feuerbach in 1843 onward, this has combined a Platonic disparagement of the image with complaints about the sheer numbers of images and the velocity of their circulation. Guy Debord's profoundly Platonic 1960s regret about the triumph of "spectacle" opens with Feuerbach ("the present age . . . prefers the sign to the thing signified, the copy to the original").[74] This gets rebooted in Susan Sontag's popular account and Baudrillard's account of modernity's "simulation" in which the precession of simulacra drives out the "original."[75] In the 1990s, Paul Virilio would emphasize the importance of speed in "dromospheric circulation."[76] In the digital age, what Sontag referred to as photography's "usurpation" of reality appears complete, for the digital image is (ostensibly) divorced from its referent by the lack of any indexical contiguity.[77] We have too many images, and they are not even indexes!

But before we assent too readily to this position, we should consider how some of the most powerful accounts of photography are predicated upon its scarcity and the extreme difficulty of its making. The photographers Adam Broomberg and Oliver Chanarin provide a memorable introduction to *Mr. Mkhize's Portrait*, noting that their eponymous South African subject had only been photographed twice before (for a Pass Book and then an Identity Book) and that their picture, taken in 2004, was the first portrait of him made "for no official reason."[78]

In Cambodia, Greece, India, and Nigeria, the fluctuating "demographics" of the image (its literal presence and absence, abundance and scarcity) provide a vital way of understanding history (figure I.20).

Sokphea Young's and Konstantinos Kalantzis's contributions are fundamentally about scarcity. In Greece, in wartime slaughter towns, people are desperate to acquire images of relatives. Martyrdom is predicated on scarcity, the gallery of Nazi victims being peppered, as we have seen, with shadow figures where photos don't exist. Scarcity is also a feature of Sfakian image ecol-

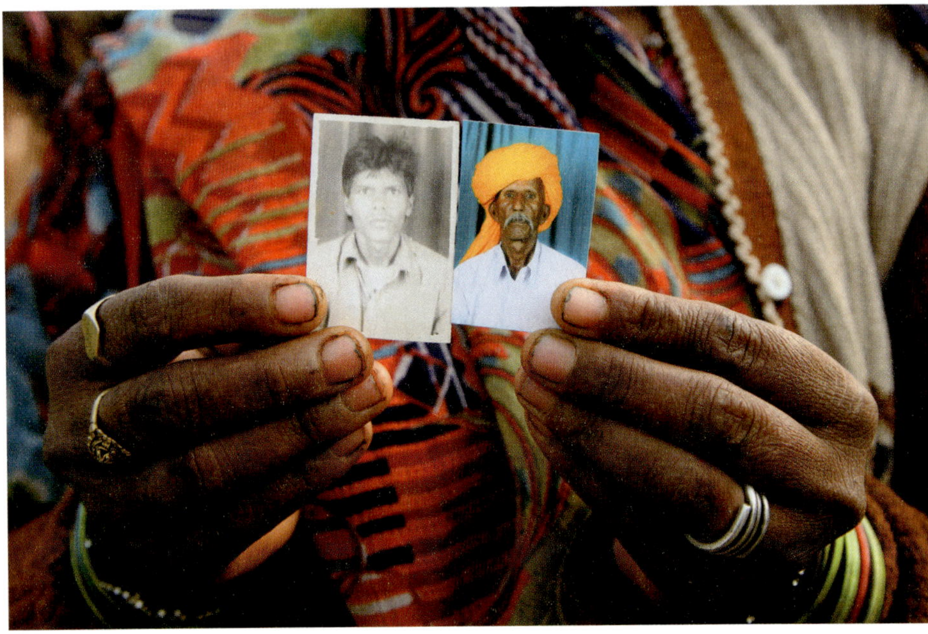

I.20 A villager in central India holds out the only images she possesses of her deceased husband and son for rephotography. Photograph by Christopher Pinney, 2017.

ogies and is the condition for the compromises and intimacies precipitated by the dependence on German tourists for photographs. There is a deep yearning for photographs of co-villagers, and in practical terms this involves appropriating images produced by powerful outsiders such that the external authorship of those images is partially erased.

Young discusses an image of his own grandparents, a photograph taken in a studio in Phnom Penh around the 1930s during the French colonial period (figure I.21). The photograph survived apocalyptic and political calamities, from peace to war, from war to genocidal regime, and to peace again. Recently it was colorized in Photoshop and shared among a wider group of relatives. The photograph's complex career reveals that photography in Cambodia for much of the twentieth century was a scarce resource, not part of an anesthetizing deluge of images.

Indeed, modern Cambodia's history can be seen as involving an image deficiency with projects such as Charles Fox's *Found Cambodia* serving to recuperate image worlds that Khmer Rouge tyranny attempted to destroy. The photographer Kim Hak's powerful (2014–ongoing) series *Alive* rephotographs objects (including family photographs) that were hidden as repositories of family memory during the dark days of Khmer Rouge rule (figure I.22). Photographs were frequently hidden, stitched inside clothing or buried for fear that they would incriminate through their intrinsically "bourgeois" existence, the mere fact of being able to afford to have a photograph made serving as an index of culpability. Hak's series, as also Young's contribution here, highlights the significance of not only the epidemiology of representation but also the political stakes of the "distribution of the visible."[79]

Pinney's research notes the huge difficulty in obtaining apparatus and film in Nepal. One leading photographer recalls swapping a transistor radio with a farmer who had found a Leica camera left by Japanese tourists in a temple. The same photographer had many tales of waiting months for color film sent by post to be processed in Pakistan and India. Pinney's chapter reports the difficulty the Nepali photographer Gopal Chitrakar experienced prior to the 1990s in getting photographic images reproduced in local newspapers. Mass

I.21 The only image of the grandparents of Sokphea Young, ca. 1930s. Unknown Phnom Penh studio, recently colorized.

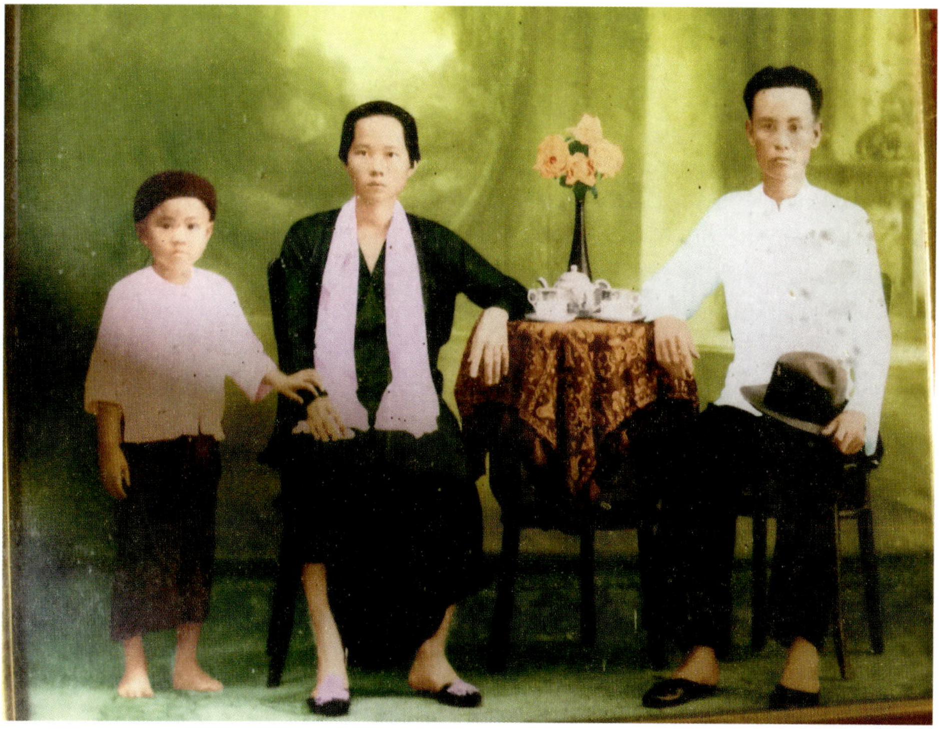

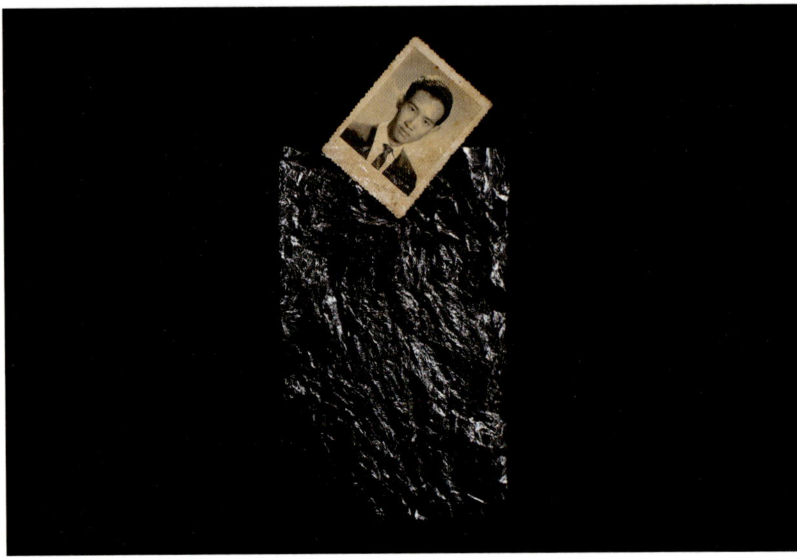

I.22 Kim Hak, "Photo and Plastic Bag" from the *Alive* series, 2014. The subject of the photograph was Chhoa Thiem, a friend of Hak's father who buried his photo along with other treasured mementos during the Khmer Rouge period.

media was no guarantee of a superfluity of images: halftones were badly made and frequently, literally, could not be "seen." Selejan reports a similar experience during the revolutionary period in 1980s Nicaragua due to general scarcity as well as a US-imposed embargo. Local photographers were thus at a great disadvantage when compared with foreign correspondents who had access to plentiful supplies.

The fragility and silencing of the archive run in tangent through Nigeria's visual history and underscore the scarcity of atrocity photographs. A black-and-white photographic history is hard to access in the public domain, hence the growth and popularity of online platforms like the Nigeria Nostalgia Project, whose popular (but private) Facebook profile displays photographs from the mid-nineteenth century to 1980. The silencing of the archive is loudest when it comes to conflict photographs depicting the atrocities in Biafra. Despite the overflow of images depicting the Biafra war within the international domain (a reflection of the large numbers of international photojournalists who covered the war), almost none of these images circulate in Nigeria's public sphere. This asymmetry of demand and visibility across the transnational media space continues and is reflected in the coverage of contemporary conflicts in Nigeria, where images are commissioned by the international press and press agencies, shot by photographers within Nigeria, but seldom appear in the country's mainstream press.

Selejan argues that although photography in Nicaragua was quantitatively scarce, especially if measured by the incidence of professional photographers and studios (it was not unusual to encounter interlocutors whose entire life span had resulted in only one or two photographs), this was belied by the recognition of its importance as a social practice. Many interlocutors observed a surfeit of images of the revolution and deficit of images recording the history of their community as though a nationally authorized visual narrative had squeezed out the intimate and covert identities discussed by Strassler.

Within the context of war in Sri Lanka, photographs became exceedingly vulnerable to loss and destruction, not simply on account of the frequent and pervasive displacement that the northern Tamil community was subject to but also on account of the political allegiances they might betray. For example, in the postwar, personal photographs of those pictured in Liberation Tigers of Tamil Eelam (LTTE) uniforms had to be concealed or destroyed for fear of repercussions from state security forces as the groups' iconography was immediately perceived as a threat to national security and Sri Lanka's territorial integrity. This was especially challenging within spaces of commemoration and personal remembrance where such portraits were the only images available to family members. By contrast, an excess of digital atrocity photographs captured on cell phones and compact digital cameras by "victims" and "perpetrators" began circulating locally and internationally, underpinning political claims for self-determination.

Mnemosyne versus Iteration, or "Never Again" (Again)

Ariella Azoulay observes that "political imagination does not always provide us with the wings we need to soar. Political imagination runs the risk of remaining cramped, limited and circumscribed. It often re-inscribes existing forms, but remains a form of imagination all the same."[80] Although the photographic event is endlessly capable of generating contingency and newness, established images frequently persist. Aby Warburg gave the name of Mnemosyne, the Greek goddess of memory, to his 1920s atlas of visual archetypes. Concerned at one level with the "afterlife of antiquity," it was also immersed in tracing the tension between historical change and recurrence.[81]

If we can be allowed to detach the idea of Mnemosyne from Warburg's very specific understanding of it and use it as a metaphor for the complex intersection of visual continuity and transformation (a certain tenacity of iconicity mixed with mutability), we can also put it in conversation with the Derridean notion of "iteration," that is, the suggestion that there can be no repetition without difference. As Derrida puts it, "iteration alters, something new takes place" because of the "logical force of the *iter* which 'ties repetition to alterity.'"[82] In the matrix produced by this conjunction of Mnemosyne and iteration, we can start to think about what stays the same and what changes. This theme is further expanded by Silvia Rivera Cusicanqui's understanding of collective memory as "a series of montages that are updated according to the ebb and flow of struggle and are deployed as auspicious gestures of justice."[83]

A Jamesonian approach might investigate the "shape of seeing" as a route to grasping the fundamental *forms* that change or don't change (for instance, aspect ratios, which were so variable until the introduction of 35 mm [4:3] and which in the digital era have once again endlessly morphed between square Instagram and smartphone panoramas). Future work might still find this to be a productive and strangely underexplored area.

In terms of image content and the politics that attaches to it, the Nepali editor and curator Kunda Dixit's wry observation about his book *A People War* and his photographic exhibition on the Nepalese Civil War points to a paradox from which it is difficult to escape. He noted that he and his collaborators had come up with the slogan "Never Again" as a way of condensing their political and ethical demands.[84] It was only subsequently that "we realized . . . that everyone demands 'Never again!'" In other words, it was "never again (again)," a resigned repetition when what is demanded is cessation.

This may be one way of framing the observation that while some photographic genres privilege contingency and "newness," others—such as pilgrimage photography in Dakshinkali in Nepal, or north Indian *manorathas* (Pinney, this volume)—can be considered machines for the suppression of contingency by strictly imposing repetitive templates that attempt to mobilize an "eternal time" of photography that suppresses iteration. But of course, contingency seeps through, and repetition always reveals itself to be a form of iteration. Repetition as iteration is clear in the afterlife of Susan Meiselas's famous "Molotov Man" from the Sandinista Revolution. This is endlessly quoted in other images circulating in Nicaragua and exemplifies a wider practice of citationality and deformation of images, a circulating constellation of images that establish the parameters of what Selejan calls "hauntology." During the April 2018 events, Nicaraguan activists urgently scoured the internet for material

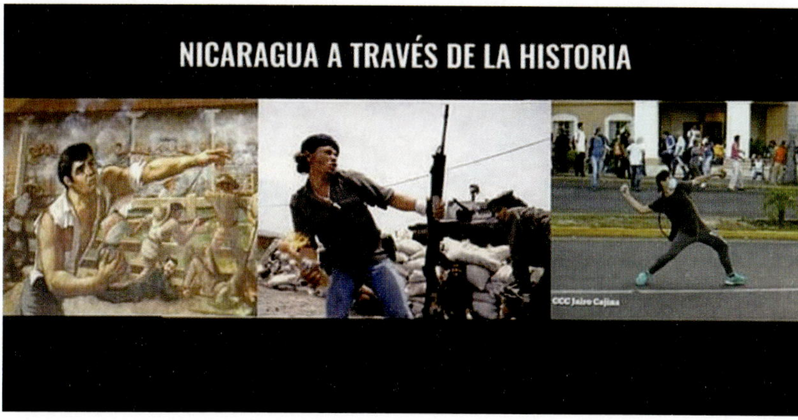

I.23 Digital collage showing a timeline of protest in Nicaragua (*from left*): an image of national hero Andrés Castro, who in 1856 fought against the invasion of US filibuster William Walker (sourced from a 1964 painting by Luis Vergara Ahumada); Susan Meiselas's "Molotov Man" photograph from the historic Sandinista insurrection taken in 1979 in the town of Esteli; and a contemporary image taken by Jairo Cajina during an April 2018 protest in the capital city, Managua.

for memes that could be redeployed as part of a digital campaign (figure I.23). In part *detournement* ("rerouting") of the kind beloved of the Situationist International, this strategy also contributed to the construction of genealogies through the repetition of highly recognizable images: Meiselas's *guerrillero* was materialized within the bodies of recognizably contemporary student protesters, again and again.

Kalantzis provides a compelling study of gendered photographic transformation. Digital media, and especially social media, enable possibilities of self-display that extend preexisting modes of envisioning, specifically through the placing of women in a highly gendered landscape previously occupied by older "warrior" men. Sfakian women use social media to humorously comment on the novelty of this scenography (figure I.24). While echoing a global-media normativity, this nevertheless opens up distinctly new possibilities of existing and imagining oneself in a place that social media is transforming into a cosmopolitan space.

Binaisa points to the tenacity of certain poses coded as "traditional" in Nigeria. During election season, whole streets in towns and cities are inundated, seemingly overnight, with posters of prospective political candidates. Rival gangs overlay opposing candidates' campaign posters thick and fast in a

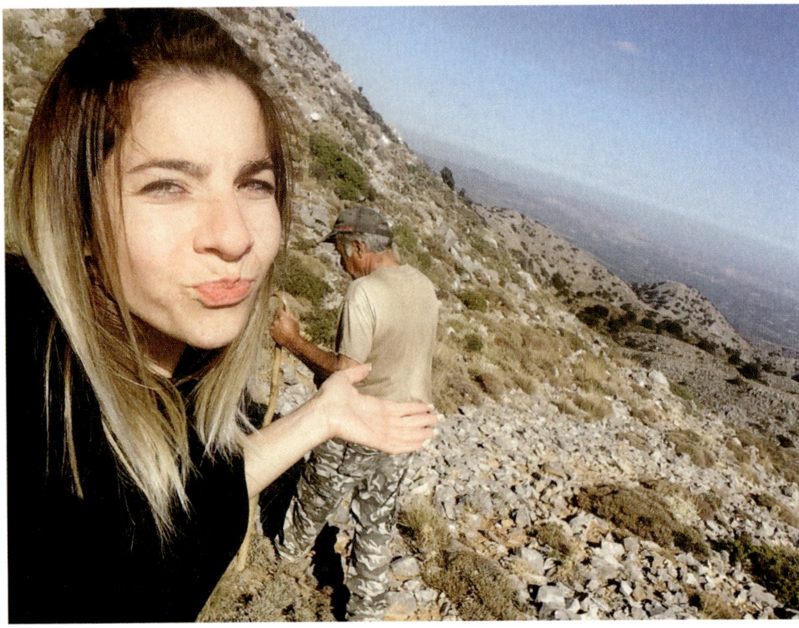

I.24 "Since Dad doesn't have a son." Photograph by Iosifina Lefaki, 2017. This photograph was taken by a young Sfakian woman and originally posted on her Instagram page. Konstantinos Kalantzis later asked her to submit it to the exhibition of local digital photography *The Sfakian Screen*, which he curated in 2018; the photographer opted for the caption "Since Dad doesn't have a son." The photograph represents an emerging genre of imagery in Sfakians' social media pages in which young women visually highlight the perceived contradiction of a female subject posing on the mountain (her father is a shepherd who would in the formalist Sfakian scenario have sons to assist him at work). Image collected by Konstantinos Kalantzis.

race for maximum visibility. There is a striking similarity of pose despite differences of gender and political persuasion, with most candidates adopting a similar facial demeanor. The poster shown here features just the upper half of the body instead of the full body of the "traditional" pose (figure I.25). By making the head prominent, the portrait alludes to the Yoruba philosophical linkage of *Orí-inú* (inner spiritual head) to *íwa* (the essential nature of the person) visualized through the symmetrical body pose and the characteristic "cool" set of facial features.[85]

Buthpitiya, by contrast, documents practices that explicitly strive for greater fixity: Sri Lankan Tamil activists compile photographic memorializa-

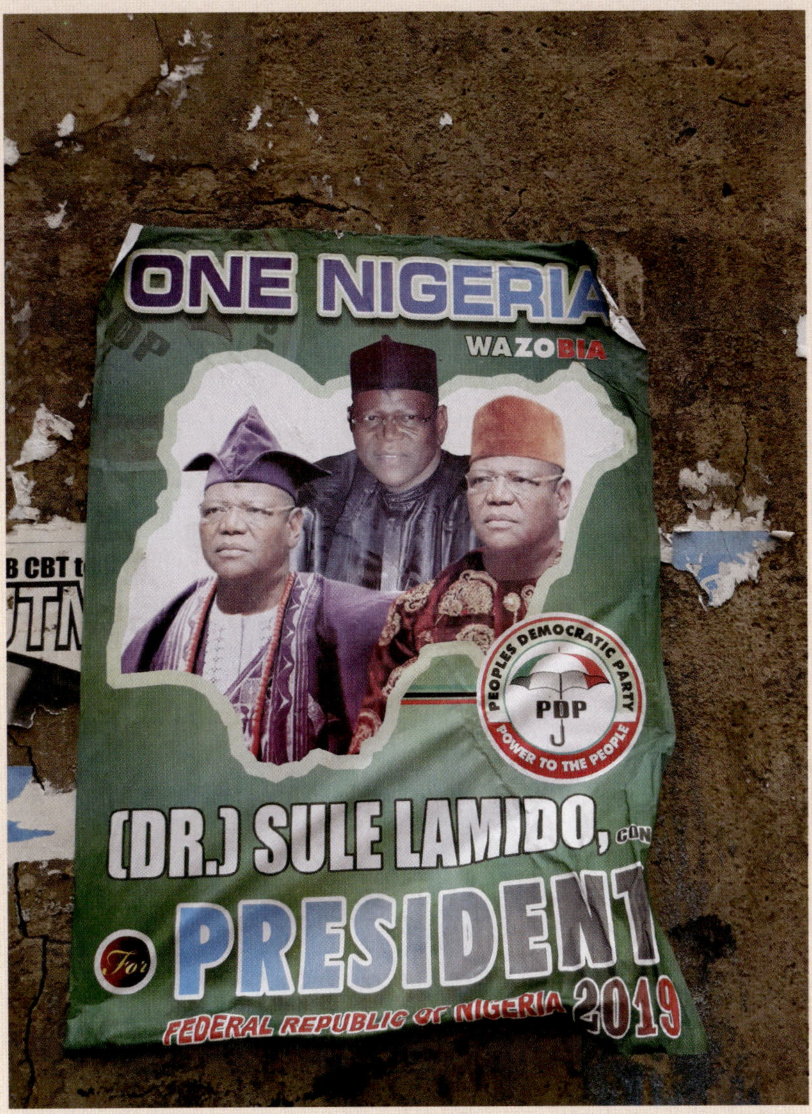

I.25 Poster of Dr. Sule Lamido competing for the nomination as People's Democratic Party (PDP) presidential candidate for the 2019 federal presidential elections. In this triple portrait under the banner Wazobia, he is depicted wearing the three hats that indicate the dominant ethnic groups in the country (*left to right*): Yoruba, Fulani, and Igbo. Wazobia is the common phrase for One Nigeria. Here, iteration is performed in the cause of suturing identity back into a master narrative of a singular Nigeria. Photograph by Naluwembe Binaisa, 2018.

tion books that amass individual images of the dead into fixed assemblages of suffering that are then duplicated across international borders throughout the diaspora. Scanning and printing open up a new space of standardized dissemination.

Augurs and Haruspices

The contingency of the event also returns us to photography's divinatory potential. Benjamin's vision of the photographer as a modern-day "augur" or "haruspex" can find much support from recent anthropological commentaries on demotic imaging practices that stress the dangerous liminality of the moment of exposure of the negative. Tobias Wendl notes the use of photography in Ghana as a mode of exorcism, a kind of "photo-therapy," and also that negatives were referred to as *saman* or "ghosts of the dead." Pregnant women commonly avoided the camera for fear of exposing their unborn child to various dangers.[86]

The essays in this volume provide numerous affirmations of Benjamin's insights into photography's double identity as simultaneously modern and archaic. Its "optical unconscious" provides access to an underneath that is not straightforwardly clarifying but endlessly refracted. Binaisa (this volume) recounts meeting Simple Photo and Sir Special, elder photographers in the ancient city of Ìlá Òràngún, Nigeria, whose work appeared in Stephen Sprague's seminal article "Yoruba Photography: How the Yoruba See Themselves." Fifty years since this article was published, Sir Special (who is now known as Uncle Special to reflect his elder status) explained to Binaisa how he perfected the art of merging photographs within mirrors, a technique that first came to him in a dream.

Photography's relationship to the "otherworld" is also clearly evident in Pinney's account of how a photograph revealed the presence of King Cobra (Nag Maharaj) at an Indian village festival. It can also be opaque but no less interesting. Kalantzis reports a Sfakian who spent much of his time in the mountains and declined to take a smartphone with him because he deemed it "too bulky." Kalantzis then heard a story narrated by a friend of this intrepid trekker and hunter recounting that after an encounter at high altitude with some demonic force, he had taken to traveling with a bulky icon of Panagia, over which he would loudly say the Lord's Prayer to exorcise the demonic threat. Subsequently, this mountaineer did acquire a phone and became an avid Instagram uploader of images from his treks. The narratives that circle around him are offered humorously, and though they do not assert the direct equivalence of the icon and smartphone, they nevertheless bring them into a zone of proximity where their similarities can be evaluated.

In Cambodia, the "not-quite-secular" nature of photography is apparent in its connection to death and the afterlife. The country is in part defined by the chilling portraits from S-21—images, like Alexander Gardner's 1865 photograph of Lewis Payne before his execution, that allowed Barthes to caption the portrait "he is dead and he is going to die" and establish an uncanny doubled temporality.[87] As is also the case in much of South Asia, demotic photographs of ancestors are photoshopped with modernized backdrops, such as mansions, flower gardens, and utopian landscapes often featuring a car. The Sino-Cambodian diaspora also makes use of ghost passports to enable their ancestors to travel to industrially developed countries in the West and in North America. The passports include a space on the main page intended for an ID photo of the deceased (figure I.26). Visas for desirable destinations (the one shown here features the United States) also require completion through the addition of photographs. Once the photograph is attached, the passports (together with boarding passes, cardboard cars, and cell phones) are burned during Qingming, the annual ceremony honoring the dead, and the ancestral ghost can then use the passport. Through these practices, which propel the aspirational props of the photo studio in a reverse direction, the deceased ancestors can acquire the benefits of a modernity they were denied in their earthly life.

Liquid Photography

Georges Didi-Huberman, in his discussion of photographs of the Holocaust, provides an unforgettably powerful account of a kind of pure analog materiality and phenomenology.[88] The question is what, if anything, of this endures after the "end of photography"? One account might emphasize the dissolution of the photographic "event" as the empirical world of the analog image gives way to the simulacrum of the digital.

In fieldwork in central India, I formerly used a cassette tape recorder with a graphic equalizer. The dizzying rows of red lights, like an undulating cityscape, always attracted eager villagers to participate in conversations for my microphone. They were being captured by the glamour of a foreign city, happy that their voices would be transported halfway across the world. Now they

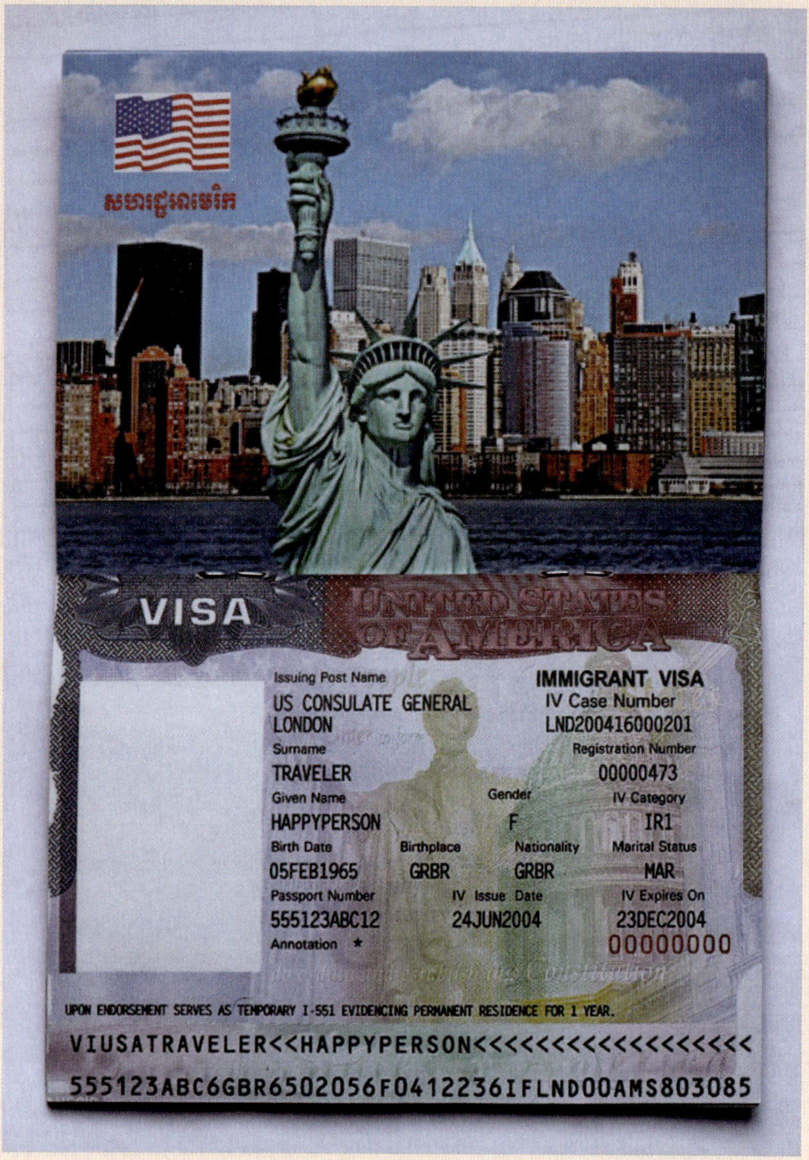

I.26 The US visa page of a Cambodian "ghost passport." Collection of Sokphea Young, purchased in Phnom Penh, 2018.

do the same for my camera lens. What enchants them so? In India, before the spread of mobile phones, strangers would often ask to have their picture taken, but they rarely asked for the print, or they gave an address to which it might be sent. Standing in front of the lens was sufficient. Or to put it another way, which resonates with recent arguments about the circulation of photographs on digital platforms, we glimpse a practice that is outside of, or beyond, representation and materialization. What matters is participation and flow, not the stasis of the frame of the photograph as it was formerly known. Kalantzis's observations echo this, for he reports elderly Sfakians who had never traveled widely expressing their pleasure that their images would (through the agency of commercial photographers and tourists) become globally disseminated. José van Dijck suggests that photography for "digital natives" has more the quality of conversation, a communicative to-and-fro, rather than the monumental ethos of the analog era.[89] The materiality of photography is here compressed in the zone in front of the lens through performativity and enactment, and in the digital mobility of its trace.

Against this narrative of transformation, consider a dialectical triptych composed of three images glimpsed in quick succession in Suhag Studio in central India in early 2020 (figures 1.27a–1.27c). Viewed together, they suggest a technomaterial thesis, antithesis, and synthesis in which each image anticipates the next. The first reveals a dashing young Suresh Punjabi, the studio proprietor, photographed by his brother in the early days of the studio (almost certainly in the late 1970s). Obviously *filmi* inspired (one thinks of the eager Sashi Kapoor in *Deewaar*), Suresh talks on the phone while reading a copy of the newspaper *Dainik Bhaskar*.[90] Perhaps he is a journalist following one of his colleagues' stories, or a politician or businessman following pressing current events. At any rate, he is a connected man of action, connected both to the national space of the newspaper and to his unseen (and, in actuality, nonexistent) interlocutor at the other end of the phone. The image wonderfully conjures the imagined community that Benedict Anderson famously theorized. Anderson pivots his idea of the imagined network of like-minded national citizens with whom one can identify in the absence of any face-to-face experience through an account in an Indonesian serially published novel of a "young man . . . seated on a long rattan lounge reading a newspaper" in which there is a story about the death of a vagrant.[91] The "imagined community" is "confirmed by [this] doubleness of our reading about our young man reading," Anderson concludes.[92] We might imagine Suresh in a similarly doubled location asking his interlocutor whether they have read the same story that he is

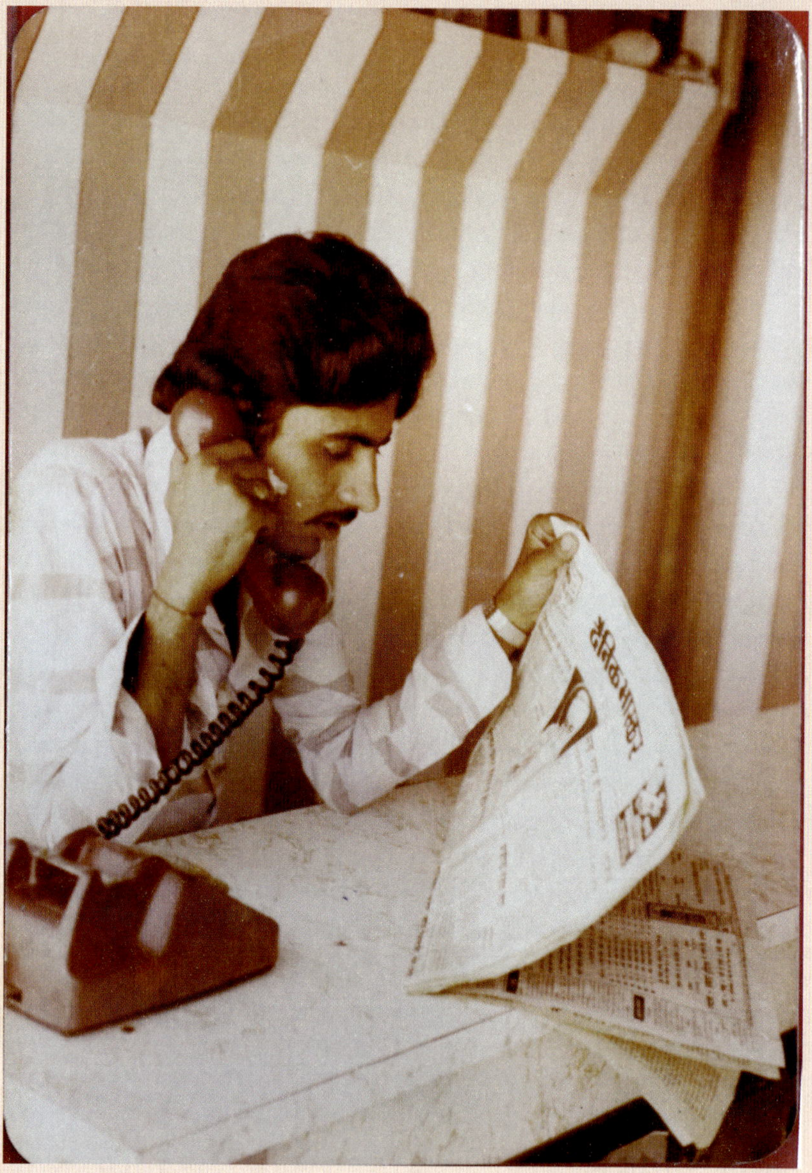

I.27a (above), I.27b (right), & I.27c (overleaf) Three images from Studio Suhag, in central India, photographed by Suresh Punjabi. Figure I.27a dates from the late 1970s. The other two date from 2019 (I.27b) and 2020 (I.27c).

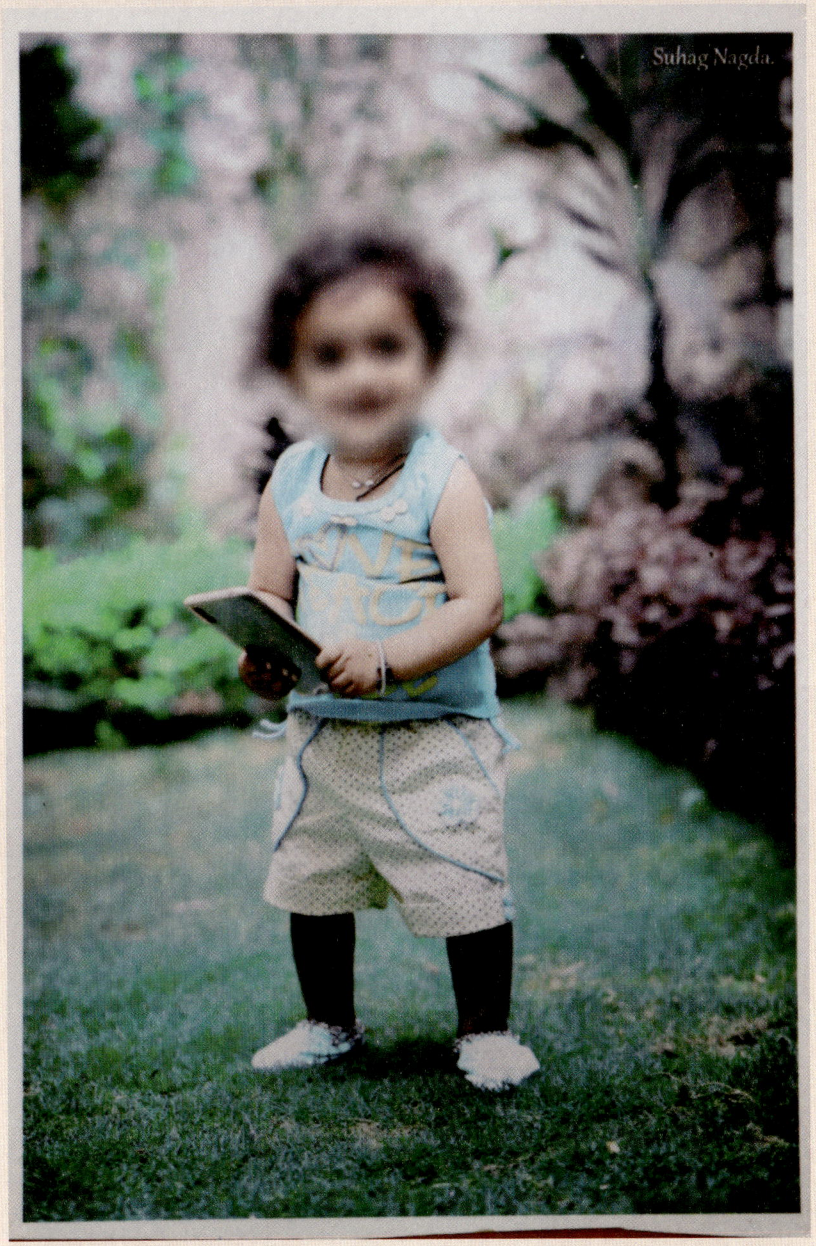
Suhag Nagda.

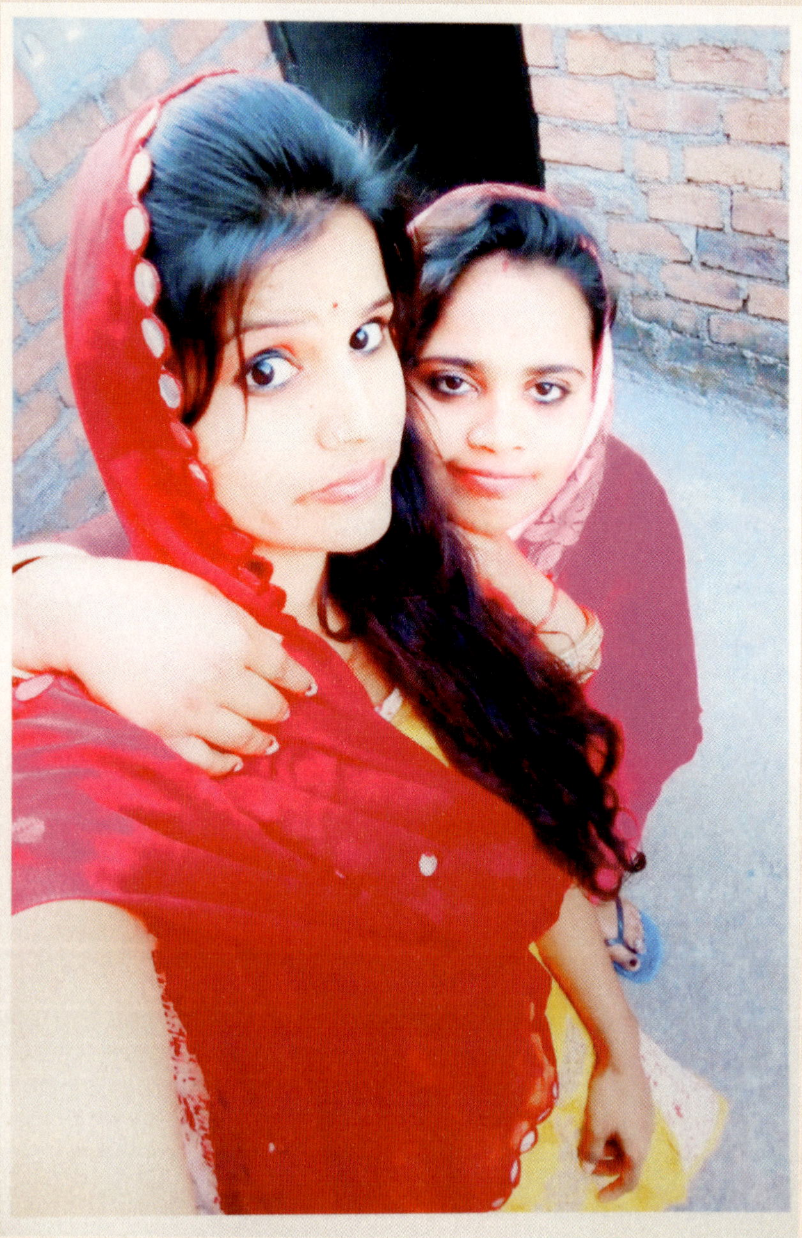

looking at, as they both, at a distance, in the same "meanwhile," consume and internalize the same narrative.[93]

The phone and the camera, which are allied as separate entities in the first image, are fused in the second image, which depicts a small boy gleefully clutching a mobile phone, shot in 2019 in the garden that is a unique feature of Suhag Studio's new premises. The mobile here is incarnated as a kind of poison, for it heralds the assault on the aesthetics and economics of studio practice. The third image is a 2020 example of the selfie images captured on a mobile that are brought to the studio for transformation into a physical paper print. One sees in the invisible apparatus into which the two women gaze a harbinger of the likely ultimate destruction of the studio system.

In the analog era, every photograph was a wager. Every exposure was made in the world. But after days (or sometimes months) had passed and you received the prints, that world had changed. In the digital era, the photograph becomes coeval with its world. There are other changes too. Edgar Gómez Cruz and Eric Meyer note that "giving away a photograph is no longer a subtractive process but an additive one."[94] "Sharing" as "flow" hence entails amplification: WhatsApp and YouTube serve as broadcast channels whose "width" contrasts with that of the "strange, confined space" of the analog photograph.

The additive (rather than subtractive) dimension of social networking has been theorized by Daniel Rubinstein and Katrina Sluis as a sensual plenitude: "Proliferation and abundance create a pornographic effect whether in the context of the App Store, Facebook timeline or Twitter stream. For that reason it becomes misleading to talk about the photographic 'frame' or the singular image for the image is everywhere at once, accessible from any point in the network, establishing a regime of intoxication and plenitude through its rapid multiplication and profusion."[95] It's not a "frame," or a "confined space," but a rolling frontier of superabundance.

In all regions, and especially India, Sri Lanka, and Cambodia, image-saturated social media plays a central role in socially and culturally polarizing politics. As such, these digital practices seem to undermine several of the foundations on which the "civil contract" thesis is built. Frequently, in the digital realm, cohesion around a shared image-world forms the basis for political division. Limitless and instantaneous sharing (at least until WhatsApp's recent constraint on the number of forwardees in India) facilitated the rapid circulation of idiosyncratic narratives, news, and opinions and has been directly implicated in political crimes and ethnic cleansing in Sri Lanka, Myanmar, and India.[96] In Sri Lanka, the circulation of image- and text-based memes propagating hate speech on social media, notably Facebook and WhatsApp, has stoked ethnic violence directed at several different communities. Photographs, which were often of indeterminate origin (identical images have been found circulating in both Sri Lanka and Myanmar), fostered racist and xenophobic fears against the Muslim community, offering commentary on the group's increasing numbers and espousal of Wahhabi practices that were condemned as a threat to the Sinhalese majority's future. During various pogroms, trophy photographs documenting damage inflicted by Sinhalese mobs were also shared widely on social media.

Classical photography's first chronotope entailed the physical coincidence of apparatus, operator, and subject. These were necessary for the creation of an image, underwritten by an "event" with claims to persuasive power. In photography's second chronotope ("after the end of photography"), such conjunctions are no longer required, and it is more appropriate to talk about photography's image act as "perlocution" (its ability to persuade) rather than its "indexicality."[97] Photoshop would now allow Homai Vyarawalla to "photograph" Gandhi's assassination after the fact, just as various technologies facilitate Indian prime minister Narendra Modi's digital distribution into spaces and times that his corporeal body has yet to encounter.

In spaces of low literacy, social media, especially Facebook, becomes a vital source of visual readability and new forms of politics. The impact of the new fusion between the camera and the phone cannot be overstated. While social media can affirm preexisting practices, there is clear evidence from Greece and Nigeria that it encourages new forms of images that break with conventional hierarchies of gender and politics.

The attraction of a notion like "liquid photography" lies in its suggestion of a radically new material form and ecology of imaging. The examples given here notwithstanding, it is not the case in the new liquid ocean that all the antique artifacts of photographic practice float away. The ethnographic investigation of actual practices reveals how much in the photographic landscape remains nonliquid (from photo studios to framed prints) and how much within liquid formats is filled by recognizably archaic structures and content (from Facebook "albums" to the ritualized modalities of Nepali pilgrimage prints). In a symmetrical fashion, we should note that analog techniques such as montage prefigured some of the transformations that we associate with the digital. The ethnographic reports in this collection do not support the view that the "real" has disappeared under a deluge of circulating representations detached from any "event."

If the event is no longer as relevant in this new perlocutionary chronotope, what are the conventions and limits of this new regime?[98] Are they burning the mimetic capital accumulated by the first chronotope (an entrenched memory of photographic "objectivity")? One of the most striking symptoms of the new chronotope in South Asia was a photograph of the face of convicted Bangladeshi war criminal Delwar Hossain Sayadee in the moon. Propagated via the Jamaat-Shibir Facebook page, this "divine" image was widely received as an omen, an interpretation reinforced by announcements from mosque loudspeakers. Many Bangladeshis then reported seeing the face directly in the moon (see Pinney's chapter in this volume).[99] A wonderful example of pareidolia (the discovery of a familiar pattern where none exists), this may conjure memories of Georges Méliès, and it raises the question of the extent to which digital perlocution remains indebted to codes established during the first chronotope of photographic "objectivity."[100]

The perceived nature of technical change may underwrite the longing for archaic modes: Kalantzis reports that Cretans have a tenacious attachment to the real valorized as analog. Although younger women have started to appropriate patriarchal mountain landscapes by means of social media, older males often reject what they see as the ephemeral color photography of the present, which is seen as secondary and less "historical." Black-and-white analog photographs are eulogized as repositories of value and affirmed as repositories of the aura of the ancestors.

Conclusion: Lifting the Veil That Hides the Future

Azoulay's comment that "the image is always the point of departure for a voyage whose route . . . is never known in advance" marks her difference from Foucauldian photographic theorists for whom the destination was sadly all too familiar.[101] But it also points to the prophetic dimension of photography to which Strassler also directs us and which Siegfried Kracauer long ago identified as a peculiar property of the visual. Pinney (this volume) cites Kracauer's memorable account of the response to Eugène Delacroix's *Liberty Leading the People* in the Paris Salon of 1831. Kracauer describes the crowds gathered around the image each day and speculates that the attraction of the picture may have reflected the suspicion in "the minds of some of those who came to gaze at it that this picture was not just a graphic representation of the three glorious days of July [i.e., the July Revolution of 1830], but that it also lifted a corner of the veil that hid the future."[102] Kracauer here suggests a popular understanding and desire for pictures to point to what is yet to be rather than merely objectify what has already happened.

Photography's subjunctive invitation positively encourages experimentation. As Strassler notes, "Far from signs of an interior essence, studio portraits exploit the illusionistic potential of photography to bring into material, tangible proximity a fantasy portrayed 'as if' it were real."[103] This subjunctive dimension has also been identified by Thy Phu and Elspeth Brown as "enacting a future, right now, in the present" and by Tina Campt as an element of "black futurity," the future real conditional, or "*that which will have* **had to** *happen*."[104] Mohamed Shafeeq Karinkurayil has recently applied these prompts to an insightful analysis of Keralan migrants to the Arabian Gulf's "aspirational" photographs of mobility and travel as proleptic "image acts." Richard Vokes and Darren Newbury, in an important intervention, note how photography "has always been as much about fantasy, imagination and projection as about recording the visible social world."[105]

Consider also the case of simple ID photographs, for so long the exemplar within Foucauldian photographic theory of objectified state power and the end-point materializations of visibility and identity. In the high-migration ecologies described in this volume (such as Sri Lanka, Cambodia, Nepal, Bangladesh, and Nigeria), the passport and visa photograph is future-oriented, embodying the aspiration to leave and prosper (figure I.28). Both Buthpitiya and Pinney (in Sri Lanka and Bangladesh) encountered narratives of "lucky studios" where the descendants of customers who had success with visas attributed an auspiciousness to the work of the photographers.

The "subjunctive invitation" is facilitated by the fact that the *corps* of the photographic event has nothing to do with the *corpus*. This is a key differentiation made by Barthes in *Camera Lucida*; his observations about these two concepts are compressed in the following single paragraph: "In the Photograph, the event is never transcended for the sake of something else: the Photograph always leads the corpus I need back to the body I see; it is the absolute Particular, the sovereign Contingency, matte and somehow stupid, the *This* (this photograph, and not Photography)."[106] Corpus appears fleetingly here, as that thing "I need," which the photograph in its indestructible particularity refuses. The corpus is that "something else" that the particularity of the photograph can never be transcended to provide. The corpus signifies all those normalizing generalities that we expect the real to generate but that in its photographic specificity it is unable to produce. Indeed, this is the central point made by Barthes: the particularity of the corps cannot generate the

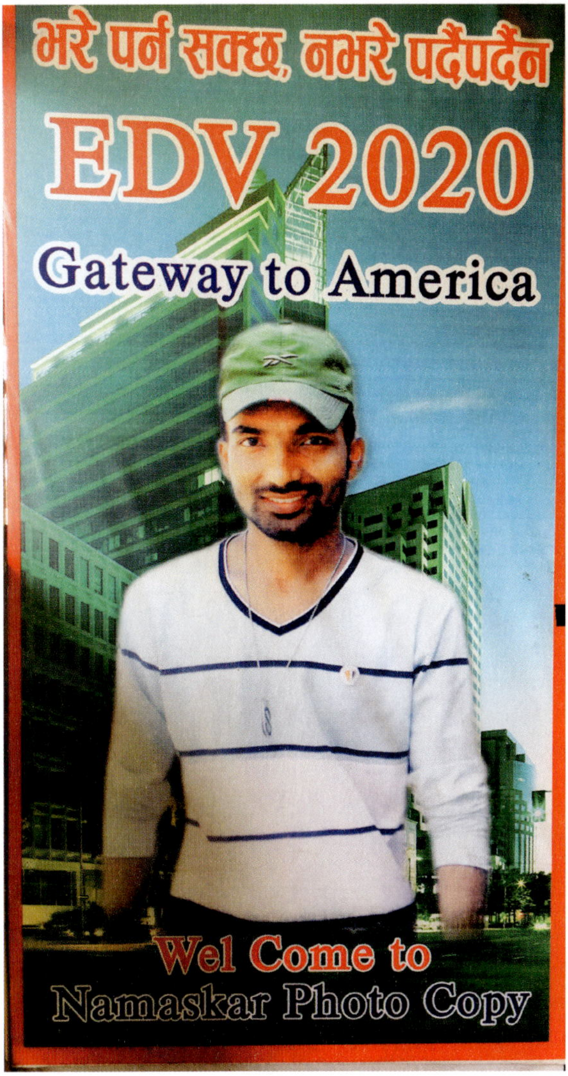

I.28 Advertisement for the US Electronic Diversity Visa 2020 program outside a photo studio in Birgunj, Nepal. Nepal has a particularly high application and success rate in the lottery for green cards. Most photo studios become data-processing centers during the lottery period, filing applications for their clients as well as preparing the correct biometrically formatted ID photos. Rephotographed by Christopher Pinney, June 18, 2019.

corpus. The camera delivers the *event* ("this photograph"), and this cannot legitimately be fused with the broader narrative of the corpus. The camera records what is placed in front of it and on its own is incapable of making distinctions about the relationship of its visual trace to psychic, social, or historical normativity. This is why it is for many consumers so liberating, and why rather than simply monumentalizing or ossifying already existing identities, it plays a prophetic role, adopting a vanguard posture, precipitating future possibilities.

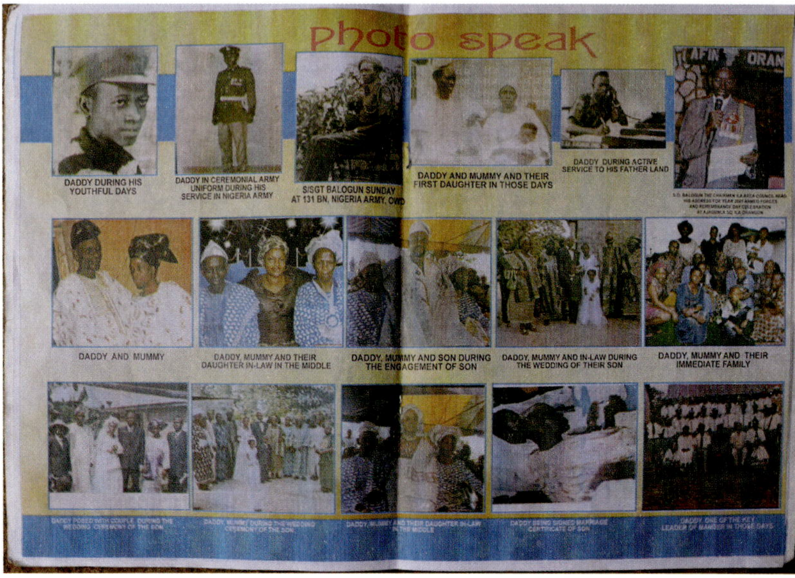

I.29 Funeral brochure for S.O. Balogun, former chairman, Ila Area Council. Photo Speak in the center pages depicts the key stages of his life biography. The studio photographer who compiled the brochure, Hajj Hammed, and other local interlocutors remarked that his future success was already visible in the first photograph of his "youthful days." Rephotographed by Naluwembe Binaisa, 2018.

In Nigeria, the booking calendar of studio photographers revolves around clients' major life events such as naming ceremonies for newborns, birthdays, marriages, funerals, and other important occasions. These image-events invoke the life-yet-to-come with a liveliness that one hears in the oft-repeated phrase "the photographs are always speaking." Attendees are captured as witnesses, searing the future within the reciprocity of communal life. The deceased person's life is depicted as "Photo Speak," a pictorial biographical layout printed in the compulsory funeral brochure and in which images of the past are granted a predictive role in subsequent events (figure I.29).

Many of the photographic practices documented in this volume demonstrate a deeper concern with future potential than past events. Photography's peculiar power is to turn the "as if" (the hypothetical and conjectural) into the proleptic or the already achieved, a consequence of the "sovereign contingency" of photography's "body" rather than the "corpus." A significant part of the appeal of the studio system has derived from its opening of the

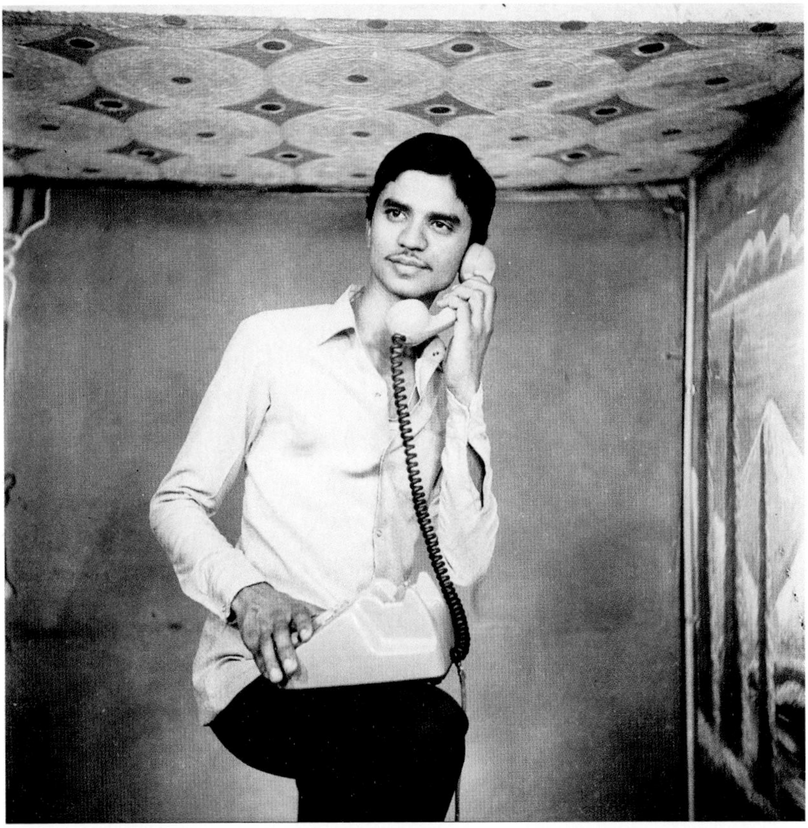

I.30a (above) & I.30b (overleaf) Suresh Punjabi, scans made in 2012 by Thomas Pinney from negatives made in the late 1970s by Studio Suhag in Nagda, Madhya Pradesh, India.

future into the present. Bourdieu's endless tautologies about the solemnization of the past (see Pinney, this volume) bear very little relation to the futuristic obsessions documented in this volume. Images such as those made in Suhag Studio in the late 1970s may seem now to invite a backward glance at a past that seems irretrievably lost (figures I.30a and I.30b).[107] But in fact most of the images speak in prophetic mode to a future that is yet to be. There are young men with phones, because phones could only be easily found in photographic studios. Suhag's customers posed wistfully, listening carefully to an interlocutor who is not yet there. They were lifting a corner of the veil that hides the future, using photography, as Azoulay suggests, to chart uncertain destinations.

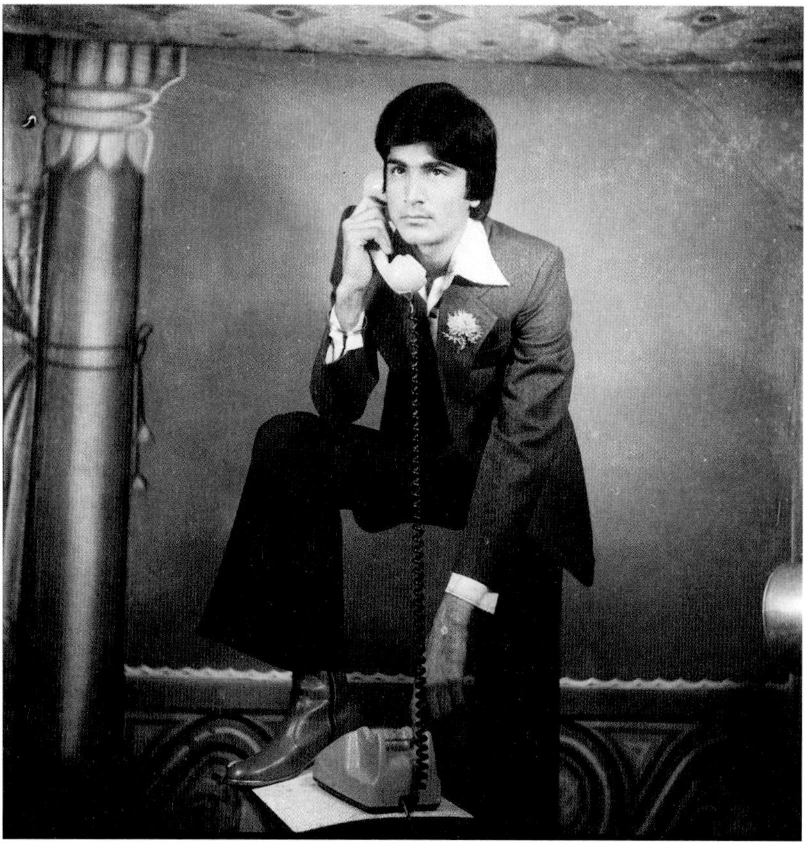

More dramatically, but in a similar key, memorial photographs in South Asia are often possession "trigger objects"; that is, their presence and worship, especially if the subject died a violent and sudden death, can provoke the appearance of the photographic subject in the body of a medium (usually a consanguine) (figure I.31). Commonly the unsettled spirit of the deceased will offer advice about future predicaments and make predictions and prognostications (*bhavisvani*).

Photography is allied to the future in other ways: in Nepal, many photo studios offer a "cultural dress" service, usually through the provision of ethnicized costumes for clients to inhabit emergent new "indigenous" identities (such as Newar, Pahari, Tharu, etc.) of the kind encouraged by the Maoist government. They are not all yet widely embraced in society at large but can be commonly found inside studios.

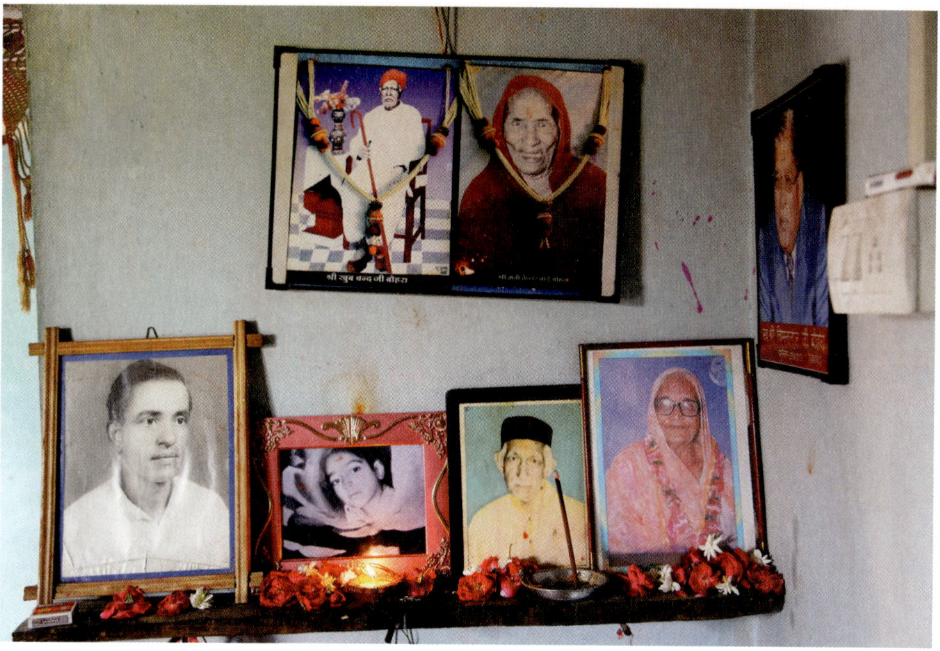

I.31 Memorial portraits of ancestors in a rural Jain home in central India. The images of the boy (*second from left*) and the male (*far right*), both of whom died untimely deaths, regularly trigger possession events entailing future predictions. Photograph by Christopher Pinney, 2014.

If under the influence of Foucault the idea of a singular photography was smashed into the discursively nuanced multiplicity of photograph*ies*, in our present moment we might think of photography as being better conceptualized through the gerund *photographing*, which stresses the becoming of the image, the coming into being, and also the future life of the image. If earlier debates focused on what kind of noun *photography* was (singular or plural), the present debate, in part through the effect of Azoulay's generative thinking, focuses more on photography as a verb. As Patricia Spyer and Mary Steedly observe, images "move": they are mobile, unpredictable, and "world-making."[108] Karen Strassler underlines this, noting that images "are themselves eventful in that they are always *taking place* and *open-ended*."[109]

Photographing, conceived of as a gerund, enables us to ask new kinds of questions about how the visual reveals a cultural practice that is covert, latent, and, most importantly, *yet to be*. It allows us to think of the metaphor of the developing image in a new manner. The latent image not simply *develops* to the point where it is "fixed" but continues to "become."[110] The evidence it provides is not the tautology of Bourdieu's "empty gravestone" but that of an inscriptional surface that endlessly multiplies and begins to form an image subject to as-yet-unknown gazes.

Notes

1 Chakrabarty, *Provincializing Europe*, 27.

2 Chakrabarty, *Provincializing Europe*, 8.

3 Barthes, *Mythologies*, 132.

4 Barthes, *Mythologies*, 139.

5 Hariman and Lucaites, *No Caption Needed*, 16.

6 Didi-Huberman, *Images in Spite of All*, 32, 36, 3.

7 Poole, *Vision, Race, and Modernity*, 119–32.

8 Pinney, *Camera Indica*, 178–86.

9 Edwards, *Raw Histories*, 3.

10 Edwards, *Raw Histories*, 5, 12

11 Edwards, *Raw Histories*, 17, 19.

12 Kratz, *The Ones That Are Wanted*, 148.

13 Azoulay's Benjaminian embrace of the positivity of contingency is a feature of her early writing. Her more recent intervention, *Potential History*, is much more ambivalent, as when she declares her intention as a writer to "refuse to become the photographer" (xvi).

14 Benjamin, "Little History of Photography" (1999), 510; Azoulay, *Civil Contract*, 23, 29; Azoulay, *Civil Imagination*, 13.

15 Azoulay, *Civil Contract*, 12, 18; Azoulay, *Civil Imagination*, 10, 17.

16 Azoulay, *Civil Contract*, 26.

17 Tagg, *Burden of Representation*, 63. The evidence presented by this collection does not affirm any strong version of the Foucauldian claim that photography has "no identity." Neither does it affirm Friedrich Kittler's equally reductive claim that "media determines our situation" and his dismissal of media ethnography as "cultural-history gossip" (*Optical Media*, 9).

18 Tagg, *Burden of Representation*, 64.

19 Tagg, "Currency of the Photograph," 141.

20 Barthes, *Camera Lucida*, 4.

21 Benjamin, "Little History of Photography" (2008), 276–77.

22 My earlier formulation of this, via Carlo Ginzburg rather than Benjamin, argues that "however hard the photographer tries to *exclude*, the camera lens always *includes*" (Pinney, "Introduction," 7).

23 Kalantzis, *Tradition in the Frame*, 101–9.

24 Azoulay, *Civil Contract*, 14.

25 Azoulay, *Civil Imagination*, 17.

26 Azoulay, *Civil Contract*, 112.

27 Azoulay, *Civil Contr*act, 120. Benjamin had much to say about the radical egalitarianism of photography, which "pried aura from its shell." See Pinney, *Coming of Photography*, 38–49, for a discussion of the consequences of this in nineteenth-century India. James Siegel notes a similar effect through the reproduction of photographs in Indonesian newspapers: "Without their consent the rulers of Java sit next to sellers of soup. . . . It is as though royal presences are actually mingling with the popular classes" (*Fetish, Recognition, Revolution*, 85).

28 Azoulay, *Civil Imagination*, 10, 227–31.

29 Valéry, "Centenary of Photography," 193.

30 Valéry, "Centenary of Photography," 195, emphasis added.

31 Reproduced in Gadihoke, *India in Focus*, 83.

32 Valéry, "Centenary of Photography," 192, emphasis added.

33 Peirce, *Philosophical Writings*, 102.

34 Keane, "Semiotics and the Social Analysis," 417.

35 Peirce, *Philosophical Writings*, 102.

36 This is a key point made by David Graeber in "Radical Alterity."

37 On performative enactments, see Edwards, "Performing Science"; and Pinney, *Photography and Anthropology*, 69–78.

38 "The newness of modernity itself—can be understood within this not-quite-secular frame of the auspicious" (Jain, *Gods in the Bazaar*, 236).

39 Nadar, "My Life as a Photographer," 9.

40 Benjamin, "Little History of Photography" (2008), 294, 279, emphasis added.

41 Batchen et al., eds., *Picturing Atrocity*.

42 Sati is familiar as a trope of atrocity against women, albeit one whose increased intensity is frequently seen as a paradox of colonial proscription (see Mani, *Contentious Traditions*; Hawley, *Sati, the Blessing and the Curse*; Nandy, "Sati"; and Courtright, "Iconographies of Sati"). The print reproduced here should, by contrast, be understood as a celebration of what is seen as a divine intervention. On sati as curse, see Hawley, *Sati, the Blessing and the Curse*; and Courtright's description in that volume of two competing—colonial and Hindu—iconographies of sati (Hawley, "Iconographies").

43 Warner, "Publics and Counterpublics," 85.

44 Warner, "Publics and Counterpublics," 52.

45 Warner, "Publics and Counterpublics," 86, 89.

46 See Pinney, "Accidental Ramdevji," 40.

47 Keane, "Semiotics and the Social Analysis," 413, 419.

48 Keane, "On Semiotic Ideology," 65.

49 Keane, "On Semiotic Ideology," 68.

50 Jain, *Gods in the Bazaar*, 7.

51 "The male voice, appealing to secular reason seeks to establish the falsity of the image on the basis that its human fabrication invalidates its putatively divine authority. . . . For the woman . . . the very existence of the image invalidates the terms of truth and falsity" (Jain, *Gods in the Bazaar*, 9).

52 See Sliwinski and Smith, *Photography and the Optical Unconscious*.

53 Mattenklott, *Karl Blossfeldt*, 6.

54 Benjamin. "Little History of Photography" (2008), 279.

55 Mattenklott, *Karl Blossfeldt*, 5; Benjamin, "Little History of Photography" (2008), 277.

56 Jameson, *Political Unconscious*.

57 Flusser, *Towards a Philosophy of Photography*, 26.

58 Strassler, *Refracted Visions*, 5.

59 Butler, *Frames of War*, 64.

60 Strassler, *Refracted Visions*, 28.

61 Strassler, *Refracted Visions*, 4.

62 Strassler, *Refracted Visions*, 4–5.

63 Kalantzis, *Tradition in the Frame*, 163–68.

64 Kalantzis, *Tradition in the Frame*, 191–97.

65 Strassler, *Refracted Visions*, 13, 27.

66 K. Thompson, *Shine*; Wendl, "Ghana."

67 Inden, "Orientalist Constructions of India."

68 Thomas Young had originally used the term *enchorial* ("of the country") to denote the middle inscription on the Rosetta Stone. Champollion, in his later rival claim, used the term *demotic* ("of the people"), following Herodotus (Wood, *Thomas Young*, 208).

69 See Batchen, "Vernacular Photographies"; and Campt et al., *Imagining Everyday Life*.

70 Bourdieu, *Photography*.

71 Pollock, *Language of the Gods*, 20.

72 Pollock, *Language of the Gods*, 21.

73 Pollock, *Language of the Gods*, 22.

74 Debord, *Society of the Spectacle*.

75 Sontag, *On Photography*, 179; Baudrillard, "Simulacra and Simulations," 166–84.

76 Virilio, *Open Sky*, 40.

77 Sontag, *On Photography*, 154.

78 Broomberg and Chanarin, *Mr. Mkhize's Portrait*, n.p.

79 "Politics revolves around what is seen and what can be said about it, around who has the ability to see and the talent to speak" (Rancière, *Politics of Aesthetics*, 13).

80 Azoulay, *Civil Imagination*, 3.

81 Michaud, *Aby Warburg*.

82 Derrida, *Limited Inc.*, 40, 44. Derrida quotes from his earlier essay "Signature, Event, Context."

83 Gago, "The Silvia Rivera Cusicanqui Principle," xvii.

84 Kunda Dixit, interview with Pinney, December 3, 2017.

85 Abiodun, *Yoruba Art and Language*; R. Thompson, *African Art in Motion.*

86 Wendl, "Ghana," 150–51.

87 Barthes, *Camera Lucida*, 95; see also Zelizer, *About to Die.*

88 Didi-Huberman, *Images in Spite of All.*

89 Dijck, *Mediated Memories*, 113.

90 *Deewaar* is the same 1970s Bombay movie that might have inspired figure I.15.

91 Anderson, *Imagined Communities*, 31.

92 Anderson, *Imagined Communities*, 32.

93 Anderson, *Imagined Communities*, 24.

94 Gómez Cruz and Meyer, "Creation and Control," 213.

95 Rubinstein and Sluis, "The Digital Image in Photographic Culture," 30.

96 See Pinney, "Digital Cows."

97 Austin, *How to Do Things with Words*, 102, 110.

98 A wonderful recent space for the exploration of this question has been provided by the photographer Jonas Bendiksen in *The Book of Veles*, with its AI-generated textual commentary and almost entirely confected photographic "documentation" of the North Macedonian town infamous as the origin of much "fake news."

99 See Zuberi, "The Man on the Moon," 262, 264, for analysis of "contested" and "polyscopic" Bangladeshi visual regimes.

100 Méliès directed *Le voyage dans la lune*, a 1902 Jules Verne–influenced film that might be best described as satirical science fiction.

101 Azoulay, *Civil Imagination*, 56.

102 Kracauer, *Orpheus in Paris*, 3–4.

103 Strassler, *Refracted Visions*, 27.

104 Phu and Brown, "The Cultural Politics of Aspiration," 157, cited by Karinkurayil, "Reading Aspiration"; Campt, *Listening to Images*, 17, italics and bold in original.

105 Vokes and Newbury, "Photography and African Futures," 2.

106 Barthes, *Camera Lucida*, 4.

107 Punjabi and Pinney, *Artisan Camera.*

108 Spyer and Steedly, "Introduction," 8.

109 Strassler, *Demanding Images*, 14.

110 Bajorek, *Unfixed*, 241.

1

"The Truth Is in the Soil"

THE POLITICAL WORK OF PHOTOGRAPHY IN NORTHERN SRI LANKA

VINDHYA BUTHPITIYA

The Road to Mullivaikkal

On the 18th of May 2018, the road from Jaffna to Mullivaikkal was punctuated by small towns in mourning.

It was the ninth anniversary of the last day of war between the Sri Lankan state forces and the Liberation Tigers of Tamil Eelam (LTTE).[1] The intensification of hostilities between 2006 and 2009 fatally impacted the Vanni Tamil community, which was caught between the military's indiscriminate offensives and the Tigers' frantic last stand.[2] By January 2009, more than 300,000 displaced civilians were forced into government-declared "No Fire Zones" (NFZs) and trapped between the advancing army and the retreating combatants.[3] Many thousands succumbed to relentless state-directed artillery shelling and aerial bombardment. Essential humanitarian aid, including food and medical supplies, was curtailed, deepening the crisis. Not even hospitals and medical facilities were safe from the armed forces' systematic attacks.[4] Neither warring party showed regard for international humanitarian law or civilian life. As the rebels' command structure collapsed, the able-bodied were drafted in desperation to fight for an independent homeland, Tamil Eelam, that they, like many thousands before them, did not survive to see. The final days of the three-decade-long insurgency led by the Tamil militancy unfolded in Mullivaikkal, where it was brutally extinguished. Between September 2008 and May 2009, an estimated forty thousand to seventy thousand civilians died in the Vanni.[5] Government statistics maintained that the number was no greater than nine thousand.[6] Credible allegations of war crimes and crimes against humanity have been leveled against both the Sri Lankan state and the LTTE.

On Mullivaikkal Remembrance Day, upon which this chapter focuses, war losses were reanimated in makeshift monuments that mobilized photography in relation to a dissenting citizenry that the state had attempted to obliterate. Little roadside shrines were centered around assemblages of photographs. Small pandals showed the carnage of the final months of the war. Others housed portraits of the known dead and missing garlanded with peach hibiscus, white pinwheel flowers, and red Ixora—unscented, commonplace funeral blooms for lives lost. Clay oil lamps of mourning were lit. Shuttered shops draped with black flags announced a region-wide *hartal*.[7] The towns marked their protest with a day of Tamil grief. In the predominantly Sinhalese south, remembering the end of the war took on an entirely different tone indicative of the lack of consensus about the nature of atrocity. Preparations for the annual commemoration of "Victory Day" on May 19 were underway. As former president Mahinda Rajapaksa declared in his May 2009 address to the parliament, the celebration signified "the liberation of the whole country from terrorism."[8]

The photographic debris of war making up the transient memorials in the north challenged this proclamation of hard-won "peace." The government's projection of reconciliation took the form of new highways, ports, and stadiums in southern Sri Lanka and grand monuments in the north as a tribute to the bravery of the armed forces. For those gathered at Mullivaikkal, such concrete accolades amounted to exalting the perpetrators who were responsible for the deaths and disappearances of their family and friends. Until 2015, public gatherings to remember the Tamil war dead were prohibited, taking place in secrecy or hidden away in homes.[9]

Even where the visual and material remains of the *iyakkam* (movement) and the LTTE's efforts at state building have been razed, Tamil imaginaries of the nation and the imperatives of the Sri Lankan state persisted at troubled odds.[10]

In these divergences, the causes and consequences of the war and the contours and histories of the nation and state were quietly but resolutely opposed.

Photography and Nation Making in the Sri Lankan Post/War

Scholarly considerations of Sri Lanka's intractable politics and conflicts have significantly overlooked the possibilities for analysis afforded by the visual. In fourteen months of fieldwork carried out among members of the northern Tamil community, it became evident that photography offered a window into contested questions of war, nation-state, and citizenship. Everyday "photographing" and the endless recontextualization and rematerialization of photographic images presented a compelling means to illuminate both the effects of war and the lingering political frictions and grievances of the postwar.[11] Following Ariella Azoulay's provocations, the ensuing vignettes form an attempt to "watch" the types of photographs that made up the postwar image world of my interlocutors.[12] My analysis extends beyond what is shown in the image to reconstruct the photographic event and its subsequent circulations and reframings to account for the reinscriptions of time and increasingly borderless movement.

Photography was central to the nation-state and citizen-making practices of the island's competing state actors, the Sri Lankan government and the LTTE. The medium was mobilized within personal and collective spheres to mediate both individual and shared political futures. Where sustained conflict resulted in mass displacement and international migration, these imaginings would become transnational in aspiration and character, escaping into a space of global circulation. These serve as an unlikely expansion to Azoulay's proposition of photography's capacity to "deterritorialize."[13] In post/war Sri Lanka, citizenship, as a practical pursuit to remedy inequalities of political status, was made possible by everyday photography.[14] Alongside the contingencies embedded within images, personal and political improvisations facilitated by photography played a crucial role in helping transcend the limits of the sovereign.[15] These enabled, in turn, greater amplification of a *located* claim for a Tamil nation-state and homeland by way of a "nation" deterritorialized through transnational dispersal.

Since gaining its independence from Britain in 1948, Sri Lanka has been troubled by a *longue durée* of emergency rule and increasing securitization and militarization. Two armed insurrections in the Sinhalese-majority south (1971 and 1987–89) and ethno-nationalist conflict fermenting into civil war (1983–2009) in the Tamil-majority north and east exacerbated by a hostile "peacekeeping" intervention by India (1987–90) drastically transformed the island's socioeconomic and political climate. A governing logic of counter-insurgency was espoused by successive administrations to secure and expand state power. In this setting, promoting Sinhala Buddhist nationalism and the demonization of political minorities served as an expedient tool to summon electoral support from the island's majority voter base.[16]

The photographs generated through the Tamil national liberation struggle and its aftermath make up the core of this chapter. In northern Sri Lanka, popular photographic practices have been defined by war in terms of what was photographed, why the photographs were taken, and how these photographs were displayed, shared, concealed, or destroyed. Conflict continues to determine the afterlives of these images, emphasizing how war-affected communities are actively engaged in the re/production, embellishment, and circulation of photographic images that pertain and respond to their civic and political status. Where "conflict photography" has been typically theorized through the lens of documentary images, this compels a necessary and important shift to our understanding of what "frontline" photography can constitute and demonstrates the medium's perceived power to confront harm and erasure and help materialize political aspirations and futures. This chapter speaks principally to the diversity and vibrancy of those photographies and their interminable conjugations. Within a landscape of loss, displacement, war death, and terror, the boundaries between the public and the intimate were blurred, and the social became inherently political.[17] Conflict necessitated the generation of new social, political, and institutionalized image making and expanded their transnational circulations as thousands of Tamils fled the island. As the war escalated, the internationalized social and political arcs and permutations of these images would become increasingly unruly. Following the 2009 victory, the oppression of Tamils under the guise of national security continued. The diverse photographies of the post/war began to reinforce new and competing political claims and demands, transitional justice grievances, and individual aspirations for parity of citizenship.

Karen Strassler uses the metaphor of "refraction" to examine how popular photography mediates between "widely shared representational forms and visual logics and more intimate concerns."[18] As they change contexts, photographs accrue new social meanings and functions. Sri Lanka's territorial boundary also served as a threshold between political suppression and possibility, defining the refractions of the images discussed in this chapter. Photographs that engendered silence or peril on the island conversely allowed for vocalizations of national liberation or pursuits for truth and accountability outside its borders. While acknowledging the extensive visibility and impact of wartime images outside Sri Lanka, I focus on the uses of photography in Jaffna and the Vanni, where freedoms were limited and the risks remained constant. By centering the space of remembrance at Mullivaikkal as a point of departure, I explore the political work of photography in the shadow of ethno-nationalist conflict.

The Political Work of Photography

Writing on photography, Walter Benjamin highlights the "spark of contingency" linked to the "here and now" of a specific time and place that lingers in the photographic image where "the future nestles still today, so eloquently that we, looking back are able to discover it."[19] As elaborated in the introduction to this volume, photography's capacity for "contingency" is vital to its political possibilities. In the context of post/war Sri Lanka, the events of war and their truths were numerous and disputed. We should note also a powerful paradox: the scarcity of personal photographs compounded by loss, displacement, sparse access to cameras, and the costs of studio services coexisted with an excess of images documenting war and suffering. In acts of civilian resistance and remembrance in the postwar, my interlocutors' interests did not necessarily lie in the "punctum" found in a single meaningful image but in multiplicity and the potential for "remixing."[20] Single images were transformed into vibrant and renewed reincarnations and composites that blurred boundaries between genres as well as the public and the private.

The final phase of the Sri Lankan civil war was marked by a significant transition in the technics of photography. In the mid-2000s, analog practice became rapidly supplanted by compact digital cameras and mobile phone cameras. Unrestrained by the finite exposures and the temperamental qualities of film cameras, hundreds of images could be immediately generated, viewed, modified, and transmitted. A surplus of digital images recording the horrors and atrocities of the warzone captured by both victims and perpetrators were a direct result of this shift. Where these "events" were framed and atomized by multiple perspectives, lenses, devices, and image regimes, "contingency," understood as a future uncertainty demanding both personal and political invention, lends itself to grapple with photography's social and political "refractions."[21] Further, as has been highlighted by Konstantinos Kalantzis, who stresses the ambivalence of the photographic image, the "continuous (social) repossession and use" of the image "destabilizes the initial inscriptions."[22]

First, within the social conditions and transformations of the Sri Lankan post/war, new and responsive photographies were continually created in both intimate and official spheres.[23] A large number were intended to manage personal and political contingencies. A surfeit of photographic imponderabilia, as if to visually enumerate the pervasive terrors of the state, reinforced the collective imagining of a Tamil nation-state and its political necessity as well as possibility.[24] The medium's capacity to disturb and trouble was enabled by both volume and ubiquity, magnified by the digital re/production, enhancement, and circulation of photographs rather than a singular punctum or spark of chance.[25] Acts and spaces of Tamil civilian resistance as well as those declaring renewed claims of nation became saturated with images showing the devastations of war. Such photographs drew attention to the countless injuries inflicted on Tamil bodies and the Tamil landscape. These amounted to a visual inventory illustrating claims of genocide boldly papered onto the contested homeland, or pinned digitally onto user-generated maps on social media platforms. It served as a communal act of "evidencing."

The Sri Lankan state has continually expunged community histories and embedded the island's landscape with its violence against Tamil citizens. Within such a setting, an assembly of photographs formed in their fleeting mobilizations was a defiant act of making visible, *in numbers*, the resilience of the nation. Second, even within more intimate realms, seemingly "mundane" portraits, such as identity photography or the contents of wedding albums, performed an important function in aiding individual mobility that was ultimately bound to citizenship aspirations.

The Visual Debris of War

The small dirt road to the grounds of Mullivaikkal was brimming with hundreds of grievers (figure I.1). The path was marked by flamboyant paper and vinyl pandals printed with photographs: maimed children, the injured elderly, the dismembered dead, hundreds fleeing for their lives with their worldly belongings borne on backs and bicycles, others, wounded and emaciated, queuing for *kanji* (porridge).[26] Photographers, both civilian and militant, trapped in Mullivaikkal turned their cameras onto their own suffering.[27] In Sri Lanka, the makers of these public images remained mostly anonymous. Photographers in exile occasionally stepped forward to claim ownership as they began to build lives in asylum elsewhere. Thousands of images circulated online and as part of displays built for commemoration events, echoing a civic demand for recognition. These congregations of images often suggested that the Tamil community's "impaired civic status" can only be remedied by national self-determination.[28] A vinyl banner printed with images of suffering announced, "We will rise again!" (figure 1.2).

Necropolitics of Solidarity

Where death was insistently politicized and ritualized within the context of war, its influence on the visual-material world of the island has been extensive.[29] Effects included the building of cemeteries, the commissioning of cenotaphs, and the circulation of atrocity images and memorial portraiture.[30]

The photographs displayed in Mullivaikkal and in and around the north and east during the time of the commemoration were those captured by both "victims" and "perpetrators." As in the example of American military personnel torturing prisoners in Abu Ghraib, vicious, celebratory records of annihilation were snapped on cell phones and digital cameras by their executioners in the early years of portable digital image making.[31] The soldiers' exultant poses affirmed their heroism in "eradicating terrorism."[32] These men documented their own experiences and making of war on the front lines: compatriots killed by "terrorist" adversaries, rows of brutalized Tamil bodies, the stripped and desecrated "enemy" subjects of deliberate injury, the callous executions of prisoners, and army men posing triumphantly over piles of corpses and recovered weapons hauls. Such photographs, especially those of dead Tiger cadres, bolstered the state's own account of "liberation" and its assertions of a benevolent "humanitarian rescue operation."

Embedded media personnel staged scenes of combat and rescue with cinematic verve. Tamils were simultaneously framed as both victims in need of saving and culprits requiring total destruction. The line between civilian and combatant had been blurred by many decades of state violence coupled with voluntary and forced recruitment.[33] As a result of the state's rhetoric of othering and antagonism, the distinction was one that many southern Sinhalese were willing to overlook. Yet what was made apparent in the images produced during the final months of the war was the perpetrator state's willful and catastrophic failure to protect its Tamil citizens. This continued to permeate the postwar, where Tamilness and the expression of interlinked political grievances were regularly condemned and reprimanded as efforts to resuscitate the LTTE. State violence against those who were cast as threats or suspects persisted.

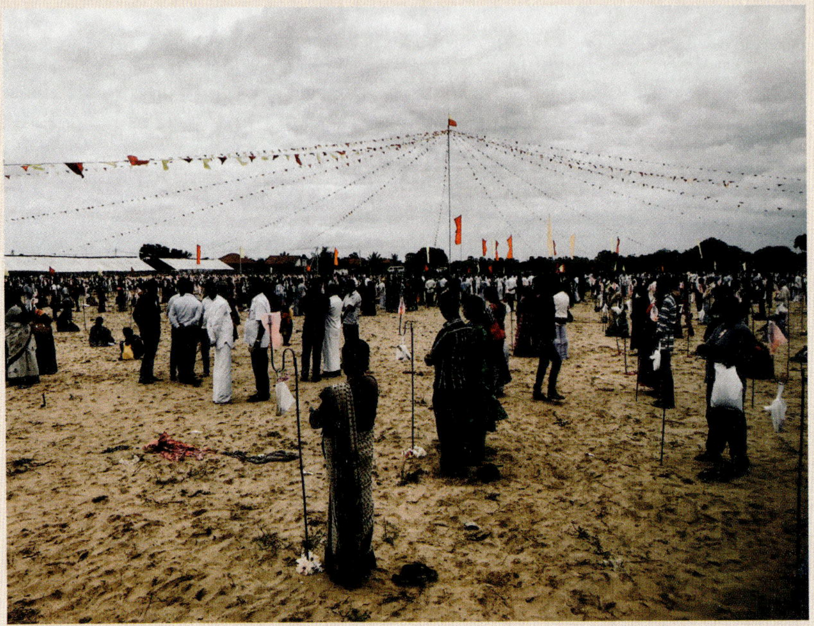

1.1 Mourners gather at Mullivaikkal Remembrance Day. Mullaitivu, May 18, 2018. Photograph by Vindhya Buthpitiya.

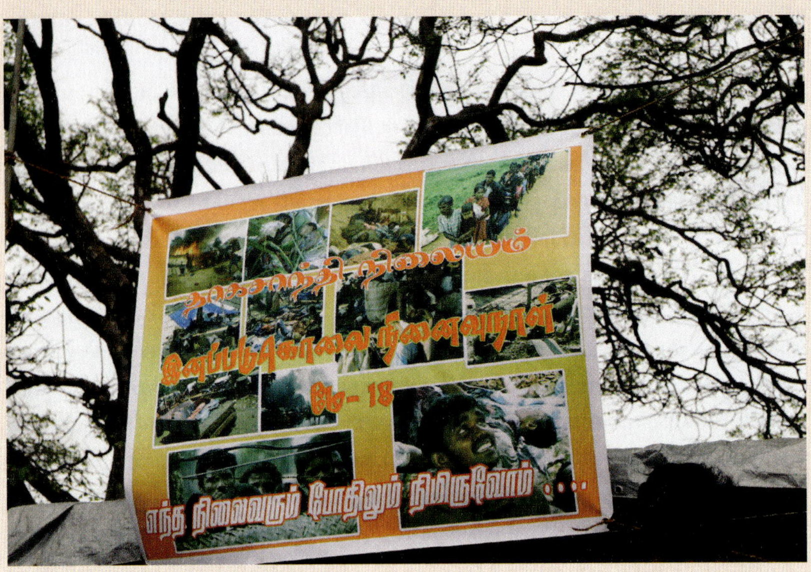

1.2 Sign displayed at Mullivaikkal Remembrance Day. The vinyl banner is made up of various photographs showing the atrocities, suffering, and displacement that the Tamil community trapped in the warzone was subjected to in 2009. Mullaitivu, May 18, 2018. Photograph by Vindhya Buthpitiya.

Tamil photographers trapped in the warzone collectively drew attention to the plight of civilians in the NFZs. While the Sri Lankan state rendered Tamil victims invisible through claims of "zero civilian casualties," thus denying the vast losses that took place, soldiers photographed the brutalities that were deemed *necessary* to win the war. The Tigers, in turn, enhanced civilian visibility through photography to protect their interests. Photographs captured by emergency aid workers verified the government bombings of hospitals and designated humanitarian centers.[34] Journalists and photographers working for the Tigers documented the carnage for transmission to the outside world by way of newswire websites such as TamilNet.[35] These photographs showing the catastrophe of the warzone supplemented the LTTE's repeated requests for a ceasefire, confronted by an "unprecedented humanitarian crisis" weeks before the war finally ended.[36] The witness and testimony of the Tamil survivors of Mullivaikkal have been all-too-often silenced, denied, or rejected on account of their ethnicity and perceived allegiance to the LTTE. In the postwar, these photographs and footage, made with diverse intentions, endured in online and offline circulation. Such images simultaneously motivated contrasting readings and mobilizations: Sinhalese nationalist celebration, Tamil nationalist demands for a separate state, evidence of war crimes, and international calls for accountability, thus emphasizing the unruliness and "remixability" implicit in Benjamin's suggestion of photographic contingency.[37]

On occasions such as Mullivaikkal Remembrance Day, atrocity photographs were momentarily stitched into the landscape in acts of commemoration and resistance. Following the end of the war, the many visual-material markers of the aspiring Tamil nation-state were aggressively demolished by the Sri Lankan government. Resident Tamils described the recasting of the northern landscape under the direction of a military-heritage-development apparatus as a process of "Sinhalization." Such violations were documented by Tamil youth under hashtags on photography-centered social media platforms such as Instagram, registering complaints against the state's "colonial occupation." This is the essential context against which one must grasp the political power of claims upon this landscape.

In a black banner displayed at Jaffna University in May 2018, four photographs showed the suffering of the final months (figure 1.3).[38] A mother tended to a bawling, wounded child whose broken arm was in a sling. Stripped Tamil prisoners of war were rounded up near a mud pit. One appeared to be alive but collapsed into the water, holding his head. A few soldiers watched on, while another group led a naked man to the pit. Their execution was imminent. Among them was also a young boy. It might be readily inferred that this

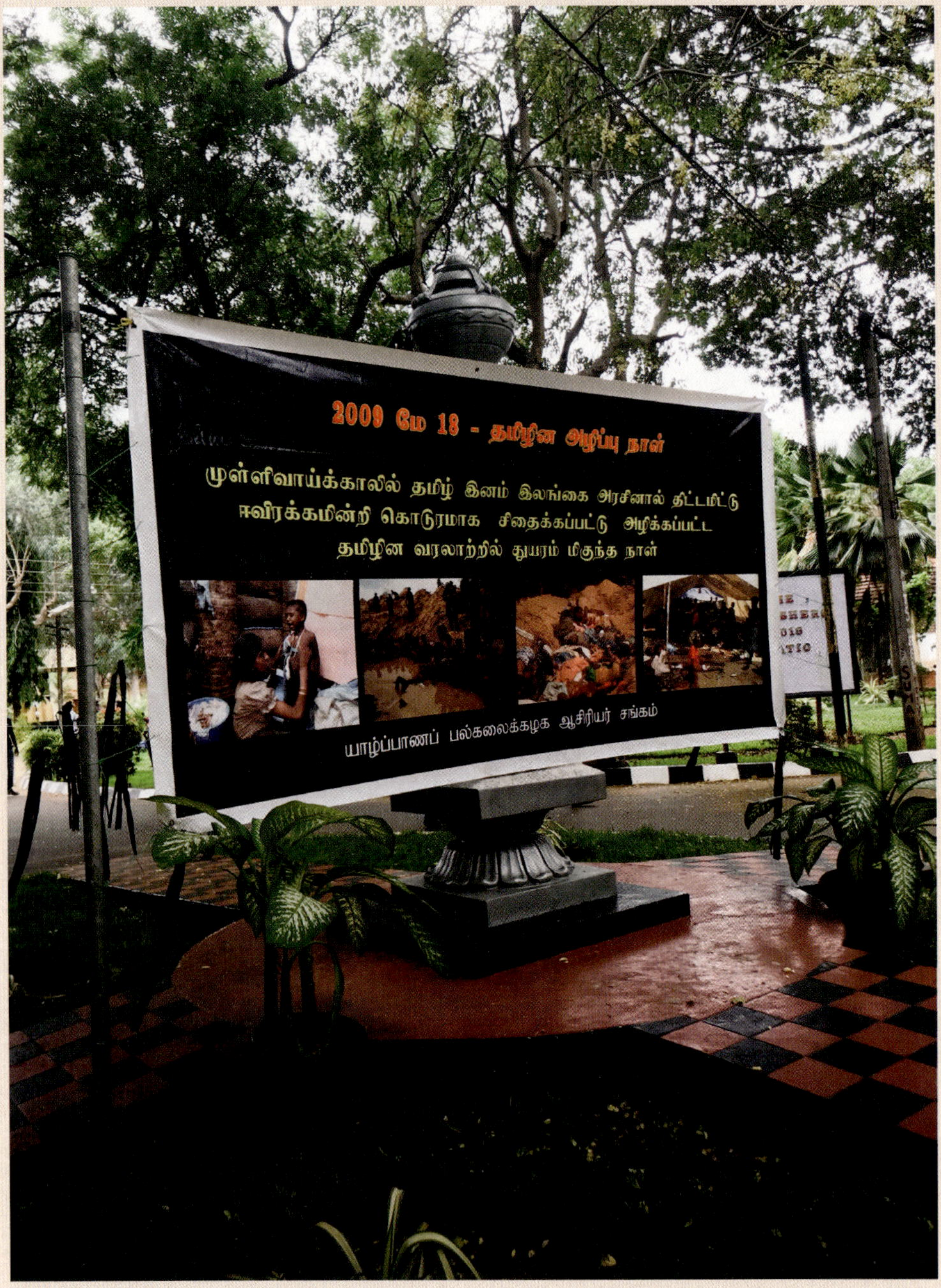

1.3 Banner placed at Jaffna University marking "Tamil Genocide Day." Jaffna, May 2018. Photograph by Vindhya Buthpitiya.

was one of many trophy photographs captured by army personnel. The third photograph showed a pile of corpses half-folded into the soil, perhaps prior to a hasty burial or cremation. The fourth exposed a camp with injured Tamils sprawled on the ground. Where the building of new roads also seeded Buddhist shrines, and civilian land remained occupied by ever-expanding military camps housing the perpetrators of these violences, these images of atrocity directed attention away from the hegemonic script of a victorious peace.

Additionally, postmortem images taken by warzone photographers aided the subsequent identification of the dead.[39] In 2018 a downloadable archive of 577 photographs and 19 video clips taken from the digital camera of an anonymized Tamil humanitarian worker was published online by an exiled journalist, Suren Karthikesu. TamilNet, quoting Karthikesu, notes, "Apart from serving the purpose of documenting the genocide, the material would also be useful to the kith and kin of the victims who perished in the onslaught and to those who are searching for their loved ones."[40] Sightings of the abandoned dead were often conscientiously conveyed to family members outside the warzone. This was one aspect of an enduring preoccupation with the war dead, which was central to the Tamil struggle. The numbers remain the subject of considerable dispute: conservatively estimated by international organizations, deliberately minimized by the Sri Lankan government, and decried as too few by proponents of the Tamil nationalist cause. The losses experienced and remembered by survivors were suspended somewhere in between.

A Visual Economy of Death

Photographic funeral notices remain a highly visible aspect of the Sri Lankan image world. Even during the height of the war, local newspapers, constrained by the state embargo on printing materials, repurposed cardboard, brown paper, and exercise books for printing. At times, a mere two pages listing casualties were published so that relatives might know if a family member had been killed or wounded.[41] Memorial images, in the form of handbills, posters, flex banners, *ninaivu malar* (memorial booklets), and ornate portraits, were ubiquitous in northern Sri Lanka. Prior to the advent of the digital, photographs produced out of "copying negatives" were used to make photo-realistic impressions on zinc blocks that allowed the image to be printed as notices or flyers overnight. These announced the death and details of the funeral to the neighborhood. Copying negatives were typically stored by studios for future use. These photographs of photographs were often sourced from identity cards when family members did not possess usable portraits of the deceased. Fragments of the National Identity Card (NIC) as official document and minutiae from this process endured in the negative: the logo of the state, the individual's unique NIC number indicating their year of birth, and the signature of the registrar of persons who hand-signed each card (figure 1.4a). The printed photographs were retouched and enlarged to erase any marks of the state (figure 1.4b). The resulting portraits were further embellished by overpainting or framing to be displayed and worshipped in households. This "remixing" involved the appropriation of state-mandated documentation for a very different political project. Portraits that had made subjects visible to the state now confronted the state with new demands.

Postwar memorial photography grew more extravagant with the possibilities afforded by the digital to remix, reformat, and reframe. Photographs were scanned, edited, and ornamented. Sedate black-and-white posters were printed in color or morphed into digitally printed decorative flex banners. The material form of the image was also frequently transformed; two-dimensional images transmuted into ostentatious new presences. Studios and framing shops produced lavish memorial frames embellished with electric lights, plastic flowers, and lamps and other elements of the iconography of funerals (figure 1.5). These material alterations also minimized the contingency of the photographic images through the application of bright colors, motifs, and templates.[42]

This economy of embellishment and remixing was also transnational, with overseas Tamils enlisting the cost-effective services of local practitioners. Ganesananthan, an elderly retouching artist in Jaffna, had customers send him photographs from France and Switzerland via WhatsApp. Sitting at a desktop computer that occupied the shrine room of his home, he patiently transfigured these photographs using a Photoshop equivalent. He wielded the mouse with the finesse of a sable brush to turn out digital memorial portraits and posters. The overlaying of saturated colors enhanced the visibility of these images, foregrounding and highlighting desired elements and minimizing the contingent "noise" of the original image.

Pathivu

The events at Mullivaikkal, by contrast, necessitated different sorts of remembrance imagery as a mnemonic of the nation, taking the form of those "martyred" on its behalf.[43] In the midst of shelling and gunfire, Arulraj, an exiled Tamil photographer from Jaffna, photographed the destruction of his community. His family was among the thousands trapped in Mullivaikkal in the brutal final months of the war. Camera in hand, Arulraj climbed onto his motorbike and painstakingly snapped the devastations of war. He narrated his losses and his survival with filmic vigor, repeatedly making clear that his photography was intended to serve not the parties and politics of the conflict but the evidential *pathivu* (record).

"The world needs to know about our suffering," he said simply. Although Arulraj was unwilling to confirm how many images he had in his possession owing to fears for his safety, he hoped that their contents would serve as evidence of "what was done" to his people. Through his photographs, shot in color and sometimes edited into black and white, Arulraj sought to capture moments of stillness amid chaos. In a vivid Tamil image world that draws on Hindu and Catholic iconography and the flamboyance of South Indian Tamil cinema, it was the contrasting solemnity of black and white, a color scheme typically associated with mourning, that demanded the viewer's attention.

In Arulraj's photographs, now circulated and exhibited globally, the war was captured in intense detail. Huddles of young and old fled in chaotic processions, their belongings heaped onto the backs of bicycles and bullock carts. Black clouds of smoke billowed on the horizon, evidence of the shelling that the Sri Lankan state denied. A woman embracing a memorial portrait of a relative led a small convoy of exhausted escapees. Dogs and emaciated cattle followed at their heels. Reedy old men and women knee-deep in saltwater stacked cooking pots, plastic chairs, tin kettles, and old rice sacks full of uprooted possessions into small fishing boats on the lagoon. Young "birds of freedom," recognizable by their braided hair and checkered men's shirts belted around their waists, tenderly wrapped up a dead woman's body in polythene sheets.[44] This image evoked the ambivalence of even those whose who did not support the LTTE's authoritarian methods. The group's contributions to the nation were always recognized, especially in their struggle against the hostilities of the Sri Lankan state. Kovalan, a Tamil activist, who had been critical of the Tigers and had even been briefly forced into exile as a consequence, said, "In 2009, I felt very sad. Like we had lost something."

Other photographs emphasized the seemingly endless tragedy of the Vanni. Sarong-clad old men dug graves to bury the dead laid out on stretchers fashioned out of rush mats and whittled branches. Families sheltered and slept under the abandoned husks of buses or queued for water dispensed from a bowser with plastic buckets. A woman carried a rattan mat in the crook of her arm and a tiny pet monkey in a makeshift chicken-wire cage on her back. A stunned boy in a bright-orange shirt sat on the back of a tractor and cradled

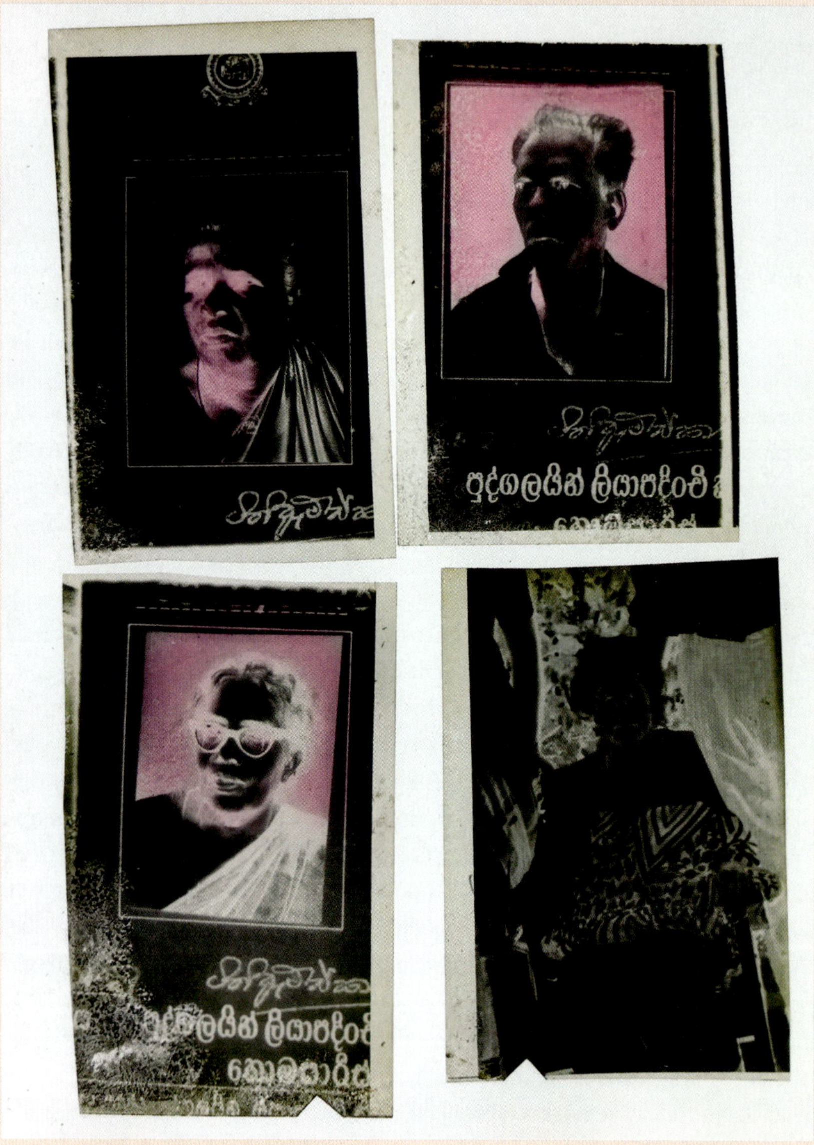

1.4a (above) Copying negatives from the Kugan Studio archive. Jaffna, August 2018. Details of the individual NICs they were copied from, including the iconography of the state, are visible. **1.4b (opposite)** Hand-retouched memorial portrait from a Jaffna framing shop. The pose suggests that it was repurposed from a NIC photo. Photographs by Vindhya Buthpitiya.

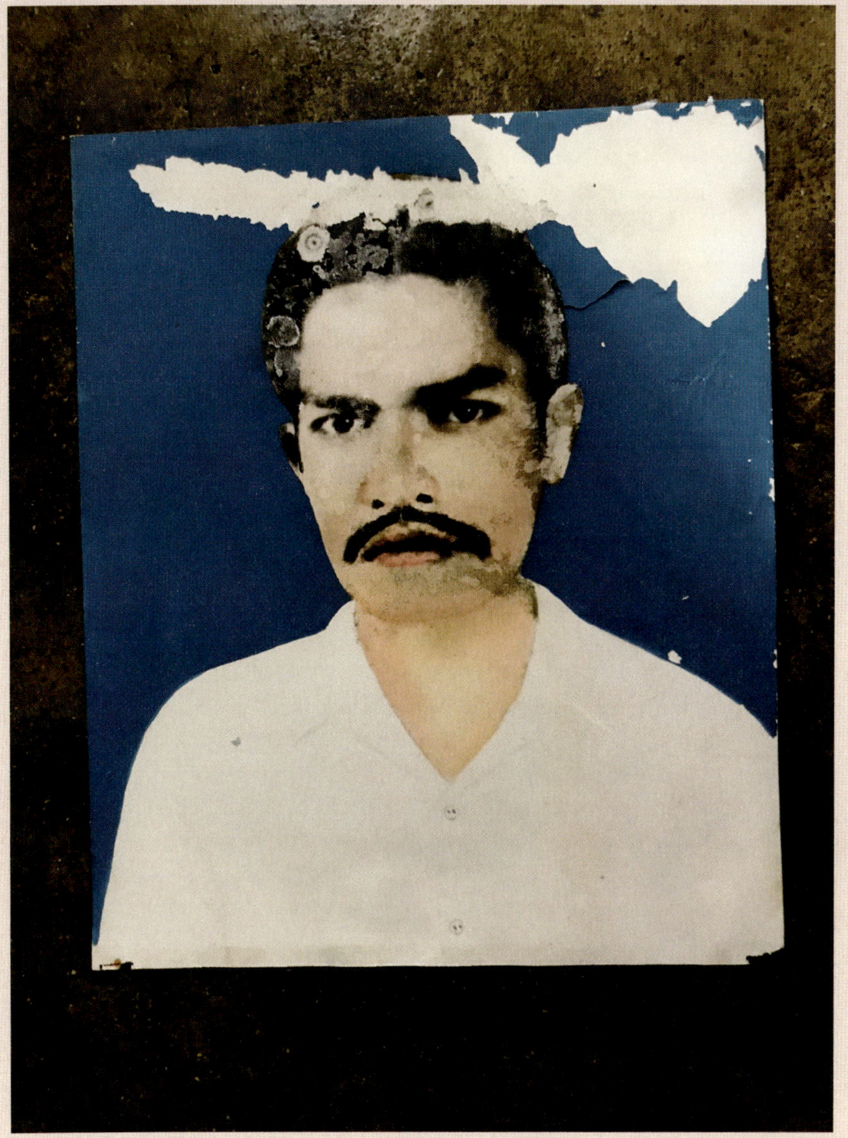

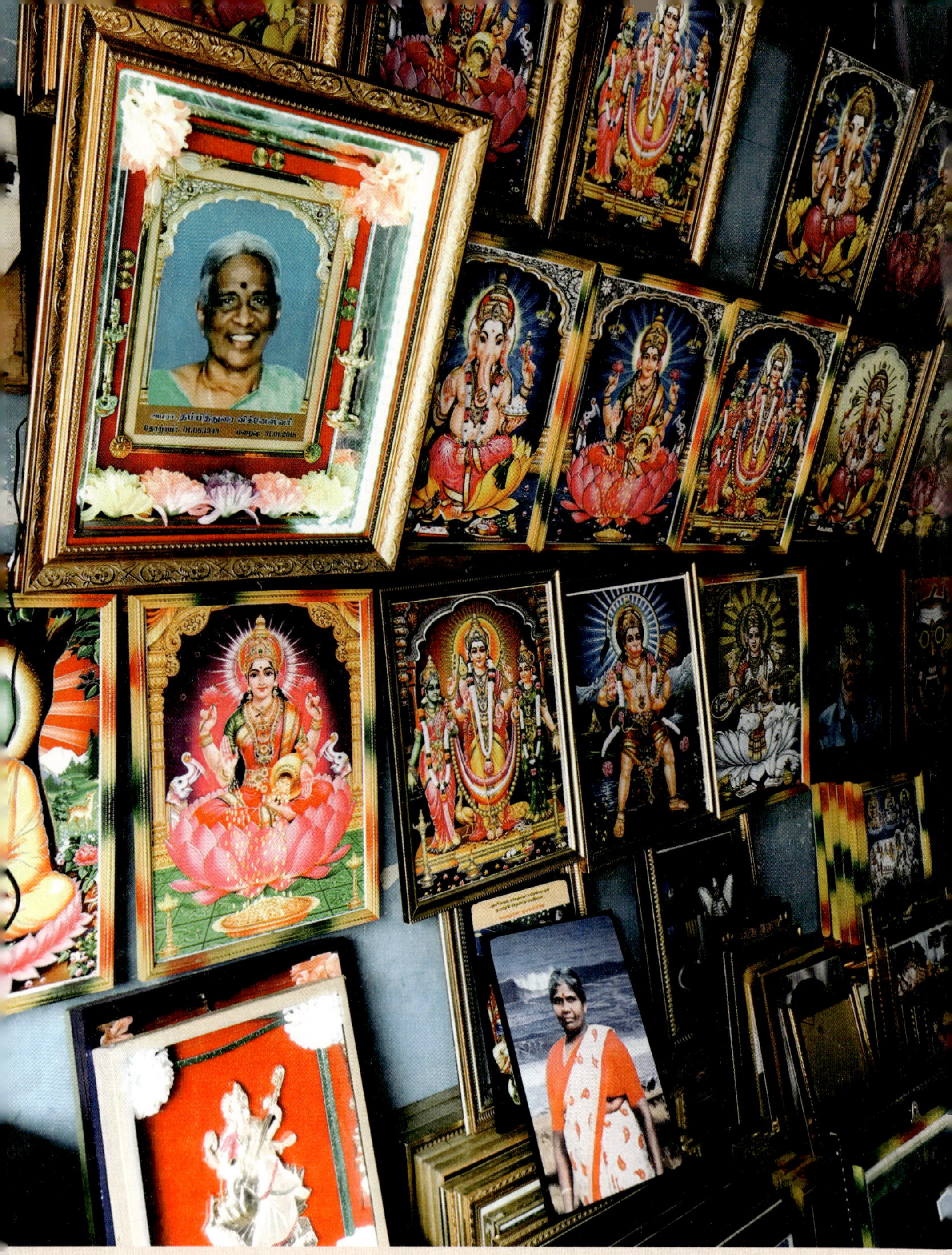

1.5 Framed memorial portraits awaiting collection at framing shops. Jaffna, March 2018. Photograph by Vindhya Buthpitiya.

a baby in his arms: sleeping or dead, it was impossible to say. Two men on a Hero Honda bike gasped in horror at an event unfolding beyond the frame. Sandwiched between them was the half-concealed body of a girl in a blue teddy bear print dress. The jagged bones that jutted out made it difficult to gauge whether there was more of her than a pair of legs spilling over the side. A woman carrying a boy in a red bunny cap looked on at the two-and-a-half passengers in resignation. Amid this turmoil, there were also shy smiling toddlers sitting on sari swings draped on tree branches and tired grandmothers rocking happy babies. Life, too, persevered amid death.

"I wanted to capture the feelings of people through their faces, and so I photographed them directly looking at the camera. No words are required then," Arulraj mused nearly a decade after the war had ended.

> I don't support any side, but I see this as my responsibility to make sure that the injustices, the war crimes committed against the Tamil people, are brought to light. I see these photographs as evidence of genocide. I do not know whether we will get justice, but it is my *nokkam* [purpose]. These photographs must be seen and these injustices need to be inquired into internationally, but no one is speaking on behalf of us Tamils. This is *neradi sakshi* [direct witness]. There needs to be *neethi* [justice] and no one can deny that it happened. *Varalaruka pathivu senji vaikkaṇom* [We must record this for history].

Arulraj's photographs were among many thousands, claimed and unclaimed, mobilized and concealed, appropriated, exhibited, and disputed, that persevered in the aftermath of the armed conflict, speaking to a history and loss that had been silenced in Sri Lanka. As the material remains of war were covered up, the photographic debris continued to challenge the absences contrived by the state.

Arulraj was not alone in his pursuit of photography for the pathivu. Yet in its mimicry of "state" practice echoing that of an archive, the photographic record becomes a screen for ideology, legitimating the necessity of a sovereign Tamil Eelam.[45] The significance of the pathivu was not merely in its role as a source of historical truth. In its photographic incarnation, it was also politically expedient, to be read for its intentions, contingencies, and disturbances. The photographic pathivu was a repository of the past that not only pointed to the future in its present mobilizations but demanded a future alternative tethered to a political claim of the (Tamil) nation.

In the Vanni, Sivapragasam, a studio photographer who had occasionally moonlighted as a photographer for the LTTE, recalled the mass confiscation of cameras by the latter during the final months. Cornered, the Tigers were using photographs from the war zone to both document atrocities by the state and strengthen the expanding appeal for an internationally moderated cease-fire. Photographs uploaded onto news websites such as TamilNet spurred the Tamil diaspora in Europe, North America, and Australia to undertake global protests, drawing attention to the plight of civilians trapped in the NFZs. Sivapragasam buried his cameras in the soil at Mullivaikkal, hoping that he might recover them one day. He had not returned to look for them but was certain that he would not be able to locate them. He reestablished his studio under a new name, looking to secure the future of his children. "We are a people who went to Mullivaikkal and came back," he pondered, implying something of his resilience in the face of adversity, as much as his community's.

Images produced by "victims" or those living in sites of active political violence and unrest in recent years such as Syria and Myanmar are yet to be afforded significant attention within the anthropological literature on photography or conflict.[46] Those like Arulraj, who were caught amid war, saw themselves as exercising something like Azoulay's call for responsibility. This was also central to their ethno-political identity. For the Tamil community confronted by the Sri Lankan state, the atrocity image demanded to be amplified. As perhaps inadvertently implied by Arthur Kleinman and Joan Kleinman, the "local population" is often tacitly categorized and homogenized as the passive, victimized subjects of such photographs.[47] They are seen and theorized as somehow separate from a "global audience" to which they do not appear to belong as producers, audiences, consumers, or intermediaries in their dissemination and circulation. Within this framing, they are also rendered apolitical and lacking in agency, often relegated within tropes of the "suffering other" as opposed to the makers, movers, and manipulators of images. This premise is rendered progressively unwarranted by rapidly expanding access to image-making devices. Their potentials and appropriations were enhanced with internet-based platforms available for the direct dissemination of images.

Un/Civil Spectators

Within the context of the Sri Lankan conflict, atrocity images have a complex history of political use by the state as well as aspirant state actors, notably the LTTE. Visuals of war and violence were actively incorporated into the Tamil image world through photography, film, and other forms of public art and used as a tool for recruitment and political socialization.[48] The "Truth

Tigers" or cadres trained in film and photography for the LTTE's Nitharsanam (Reality) Television Media Unit filmed its land and sea battles against the Sri Lankan armed forces. Central to this distribution were images foregrounding the Sri Lankan state's atrocities against and victimization of the Tamil community. These were featured in exhibitions and pamphlets, circulated online, and broadcast on television to enlist popular support and encourage recruitment locally. In an English-language interview with an Australian documentary crew, an LTTE videography coach noted, "We're looking for two aspects. One, the person has the potential and the courage to undertake this training. The second, film the fighting beautifully with artistic talent."[49] These visuals were also circulated internationally to secure support and financial contributions from the Tamil community abroad. The footage was used by the group's military strategists to assess performance and as instructional material. Moreover, the Tigers' victories over the Sri Lankan forces in various battles were documented often in the form of "kills" showing the bodies of dead soldiers to rouse nationalist sentiment and public motivation for the Tamil political cause.

The Sri Lankan state initially claimed to avoid using atrocity images in its official media campaigns. However, the intensification of the war between 2006 and 2009 saw its adoption of similar visual strategies. This coincided with the switch from analog to digital image making as well as growing access to personal cameras. Consequently, the war effort was enthusiastically documented by Sri Lankan soldiers. The performative "martial virtues" of young troops forced into military service from the rural Sinhalese south by poverty and unemployment animated the war for the screens of Sinhalese audiences.[50] This imagery was regularly revived in election campaign visuals, ranging from posters and billboards to music videos, to remind voters of the Sri Lankan armed forces' triumph over terrorism. Images of violation and violence underpinned ethno-nationalist political claims in which atrocities were not denounced but demanded and celebrated. Photographs became generative of further, future violence. Claims of nation served as a means of consolidating the martial imperatives and powers of the state, which also made visible the consequences to those who did not conform.

A short-lived informal economy of authentic and counterfeit visuals from the final years of war emerged, to satiate morbid public curiosity as well as political assertions, both in Sri Lanka and overseas. In the island's capital, Colombo, video CDs of bloodshed and conquest with Sinhalese titles such as *Ape Viruvange Veera Kriya: Prabhage Avasanaya* (The gallant deeds of our heroes: Prabha's end) sold for a couple of hundred rupees (US$1). The content rejoiced in the grisly death of the Tiger leader Velupillai Prabhakaran and his acolytes at Mullivaikkal. A Sinhalese journalist recalled that the CDs hawked in Colombo included news footage captured from TV broadcasts and "hand-out footage" from the Ministry of Defense. Film and stills were captured on low-grade phones and compact cameras as well as professional equipment and "leaked" for profit. A few months after the end of the war, the Sri Lankan army also hosted a grand exhibition that sought to "bring the heroism witnessed in the Vanni on the television screen" to the capital. The event, described as a *sonduru, sajeevi athdakeema* (beautiful, live experience), drew thousands of Sinhalese citizens to "experience" the war and the *vismitha vijayagrahanaya* (marvelous triumph) for themselves through a display of captured weapons, armored fighting vehicles, soldiers demonstrating their combat skills, and, most significantly, photographs. The images on display showed the visceral, bodily destruction of the LTTE, confirmed by the lined-up corpses of dead cadres over which the triumphant military leadership stood.

In Europe, however, visual evidence of war crimes was purportedly stashed away for future financial gain or secretly proffered for thousands of euros by enterprising soldiers—even though purchase would render them legally inadmissible. Alongside Tamil victims' and international aid workers' images and testimony, soldiers' trophy footage and photographs became the subject of investigative documentaries such as *Sri Lanka's Killing Fields* (dir. Macrae, 2011), *Sri Lanka's Killing Fields: War Crimes Unpunished* (dir. Macrae, 2012), and *No Fire Zone: In the Killing Fields of Sri Lanka* (dir. Macrae, 2013). Similarly, Tamil photographers' images of suffering were transformed into international exhibitions and publications.[51] While the films moved audiences abroad to outrage and advocacy, in Sri Lanka they became the focus of state-sponsored protests against the international community. Widely publicized efforts were made by the government to discredit claims of authenticity through the production of its own documentaries and publications, including *Lies Agreed Upon* (2011), *Ruthless* (2012), and *Corrupted Journalism: Channel 4 and Sri Lanka* (2013). These visuals remained colored by the politicized tensions between ethnic groups. Wartime atrocities, committed based on ethnic difference and a fundamental rejection of the notion of shared humanity and citizenship, continue to be dismissed by the government and the majority of the island's population.

The political work of these atrocity images of varied origin and intent far exceeded the island. Azoulay considers "citizenship through the study of photographic practices," suggesting that the medium affords new means for the photographed, the photographer, and the spectator to untether themselves from the bounds of sovereign power or contracts of the nation-state and economy.[52] Drawing on the context of Israel/Palestine, where the Israeli state governs both citizens and "noncitizens" together even though the former are governed "differently," Azoulay emphasizes that "the nation-state (re)territorializes citizenship."[53] This provides "a protective shield to those declared as citizens within a certain territory, and discriminates between them and others, noncitizens, who are governed with them in the same territory, by the same power."[54] By contrast, Azoulay argues, photography "deterritorializes citizenship, reaching beyond its conventional boundaries and plotting out a political space in which the plurality of speech and action . . . is actualized permanently by the eventual participation of all the governed."[55] This premise, Azoulay suggests, allows for "civil skills that are not subject to nationality, but rather to borderless citizenship" that demands an ethical responsibility toward one another.[56] The deterritorialized circuits and proliferation of these images respond to Azoulay's appeal for civic spectatorship.

Images from the final phase of the war reinforced witness accounts, testimony, and international advocacy efforts that underscored state violations of international humanitarian law. Shared on Instagram and Facebook, compiled into YouTube clips or Flickr albums, printed onto vinyl banners at commemoration events and protests, they endured within political claims in the postwar. Tamils, both located in and dispersed from the island, continue to reimagine their shared political future/s for an independent nation through these images.

At the Mullivaikkal commemoration, photographic montages adorned banners and archways (figure 1.6). Embellished with digital graphics of blood, these installations dramatized Sinhalese state violence inflicted on Tamil bodies, asserting that these crimes would not be forgotten (figure 1.7). Here, the representational format was situated within a register comparable to those made in Jaffna's photography studios, intended to "enhance" eyewitness claims, thus heightening their visibility and effect rather than their "truthfulness." In other instances, the iconography of the Sri Lankan state was caricatured. On one banner, an illustration of the Sri Lankan flag's lion with a bloodied sword standing over an anonymous pile of bodies was superimposed over images of Tamil suffering drowned in flaming red and a photograph of a memorial shrine. The accompanying map of Tamil Eelam too was bleeding. Photographs of the dead and injured served as an index of past violence, signifying the community's grievances tethered to a desired, alternative political future. The caption read, "The martyrs died along with our dreams of a motherland. May 18th, the day we carried the pain."

Uyirayutam

The reference to *thyagi* alludes to the LTTE's vocabulary of martyrdom. An ethos of self-sacrifice was cultivated among fighters as part of the Tigers' single-minded commitment to securing Tamil Eelam.[57] A Tamil citizen's *kadamai* (duty) was total devotion and sacrifice of the self, drawing on ancient Tamil martial concepts. To this end, the LTTE created "new" terms, such as *uyirayutam* (life [as a] weapon) and thyagi (martyr, or one who gifts themselves, implying also an act of killing others while sacrificing oneself).[58] This was embodied in the creation of the Karumpuli or Black Tiger suicide squad. In the de facto Tamil state, photographs of atrocity and displays of ornate martyrs' portraits served as powerful tools for political/ideological inspiration. These were made and wielded to underpin demands for Tamil political

1.6 A temporary paper archway strung with banners showing the horrors of Mullivaikkal. Mullaitivu, May 18, 2018. Photograph by Vindhya Buthpitiya.

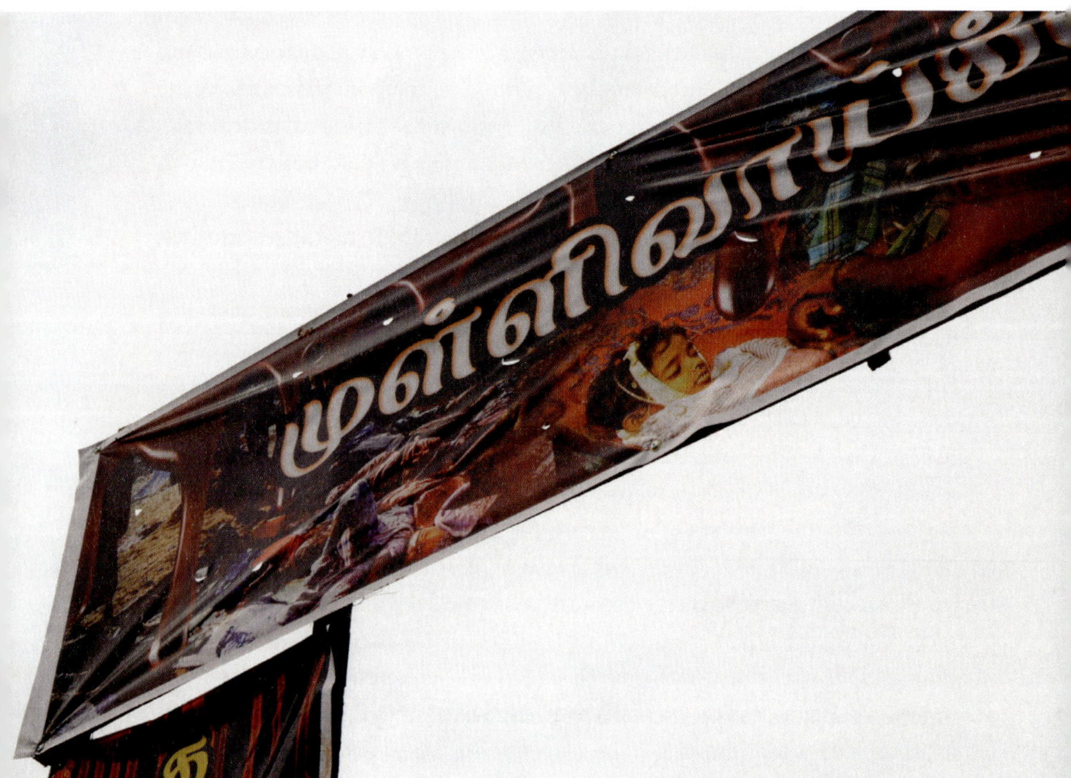

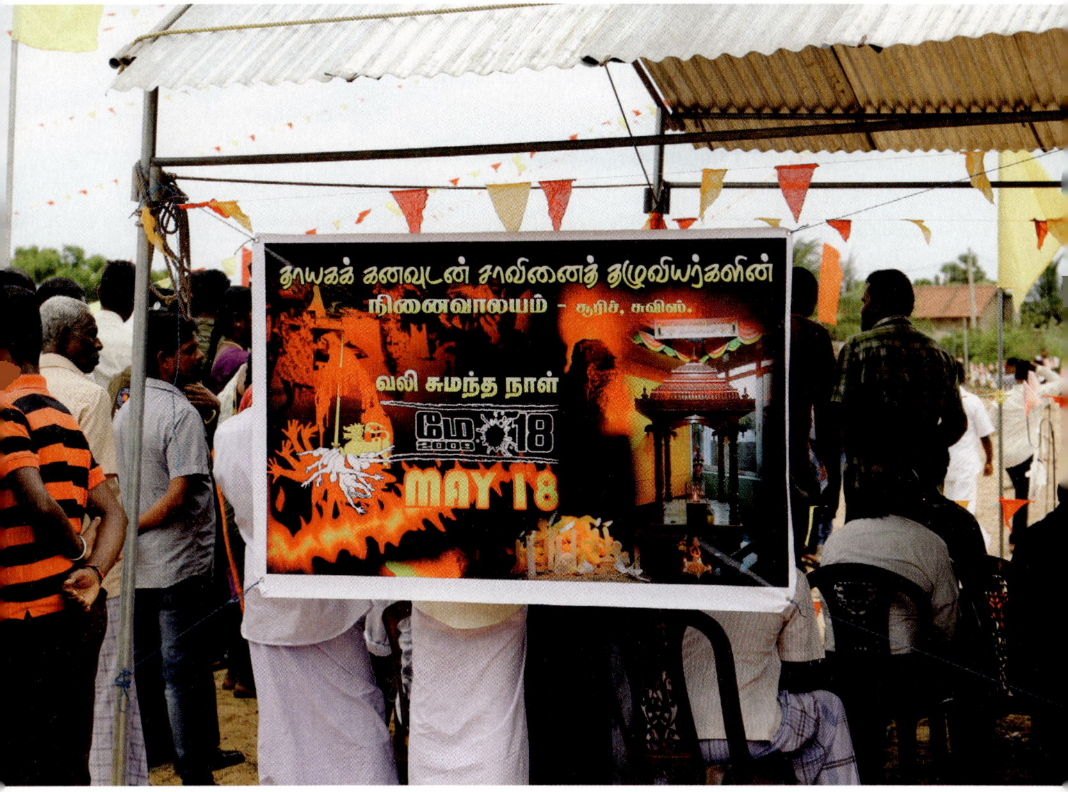

1.7 Mullivaikkal genocide "martyrs" banner. Mullaitivu, May 18, 2018. Photograph by Vindhya Buthpitiya.

self-determination. Such images also served as catalysts in motivating and necessitating politically generative violence: as essential to the liberation of the Tamil nation from the "oppressive" Sinhalese/Sri Lankan state, and the future formation and pictorial idealization of an independent Tamil ethno-state. Photography further underpinned validation for and celebration of the sacrifices expected of its dutiful (future) citizens as fighters and martyrs. Elaborate public rituals focused on death, funerals, and memorialization were established, transforming practices and iconographies in lasting ways. In the south, Tamilness and terror became intertwined in the state's visual narrative of war, mobilizing the menace and fear of death at the hands of the Tigers.

The commemoration of dead cadres reinforced a sense of solidarity among Tamils.[59] The vast LTTE *thuyilum illam* (heroes' cemeteries) were among the first to be destroyed by the state in an act that qualifies as a war crime. These were hastily built over with no respect for those whose kin were interred there. As has been explored by Michael Roberts and Christiana Natali, the thuyilum illam were an important component of Tamil political socialization during the war years.[60] These served as communal spaces for mourning complemented by calendrical rituals such as Maaveerar Naal (Great Heroes Day), which encouraged the participation of bereaved families.[61]

The LTTE's iconography, steeped in the yellow and red of the national flower of Tamil Eelam, *karthigai*, drew heavily on stylized portraiture.[62] Photographic and sometimes painted portraits of men and women who epitomized this virtue of selflessness and loyalty were widely venerated in public. Martyrs' shrines adorned with honor rolls, godlike depictions, and cinematic cut-outs were integrated into local neighborhoods, encouraging memorialization, civic devotion, and voluntary enlistment. Such image making was undertaken by studio photographers and those involved in painting cinema hoardings for the South Indian Tamil films screened in Jaffna before the beginning of the war. Following the destruction of the cemeteries and the prohibition on mourning as well as any visible hints of the LTTE, commemorations took place in secret. In contrast, grand memorial events, centered around these martyrs' pictures, were organized overseas, where migrant Tamils could openly pay their respects to those who had sacrificed themselves for the nation (figure I.8). These events also functioned as fundraisers for the war effort.

In the postwar, proscription by the state coupled with sustained practices of surveillance and intimidation of Tamil civilians and ex-cadres resulted in personal photographs, especially those indicating prior affiliation to the Tigers, becoming contraband, risking keepers' arrest or worse. For many, such photographs, especially those featuring LTTE uniforms, were all too often the only images available to them. Kanthan, an interlocutor formerly allied with the iyakkam, admitted to burying his albums, only to find much of his collection in a state of deterioration. Digital archiving also proved challenging due to the policing of online spaces such as Instagram. "Community guidelines" periodically restricted the use of content tagged under terms such as #TamilEelam due to associations with the LTTE. Effective bypasses were improvised by diasporic Tamils through the use of Sri Lanka–specific hashtags.

In these divergent, even contradictory, postwar registers, wartime images accrued new political meanings and mediated new political potentials for different audiences. For the Tamil community, they signaled the hostility of the state in both the past and the present, underpinning the necessity of a future Tamil nation-state. Within global frameworks of human rights and

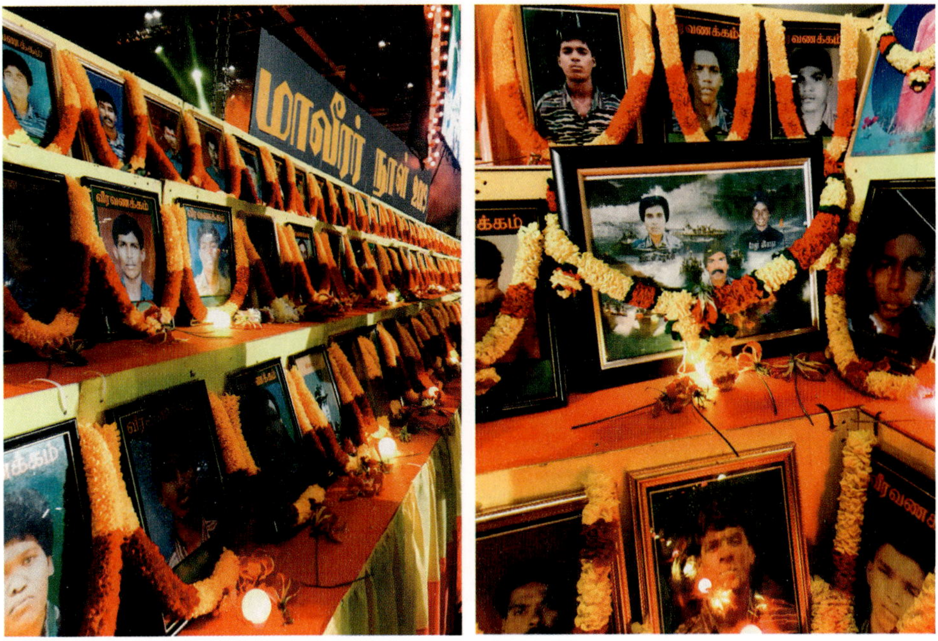

1.8 Maaveerar Naal (Great Heroes Day). London, November 2019. Photographs by Vindhya Buthpitiya.

world peace, where Azoulay's notion of solidarity and responsibility emboldens advocacy and accountability networks, these photographs supplemented demands for international governance commitments and action.[63] The inclusion of these visuals within "Western" documentaries elicited outrage among predominantly Sinhalese Sri Lankans, where it was deemed an "international conspiracy" bolstered by LTTE supporters to undermine Sri Lanka's sovereignty. These visuals confirmed the defeat of the "other" who were a threat to the survival of the Sinhalese body and nation. Such photographs also served as a reminder of individual politicians' and military commanders' roles in vanquishing the enemy, becoming integral to their electoral influence. Elsewhere, these mementos of atrocity were transformed into visual accompaniments to songs of patriotism and lamentation by Tamils, echoing the LTTE's potent legacy of political-cultural production centered on atrocity and the violence of the Sri Lankan state (figure 1.9). The contending image regimes of war endured as Tamils sought to reimagine their personal and political futures in a postwar burdened by the grounds and effects of the extraordinary violence that begot "peace."

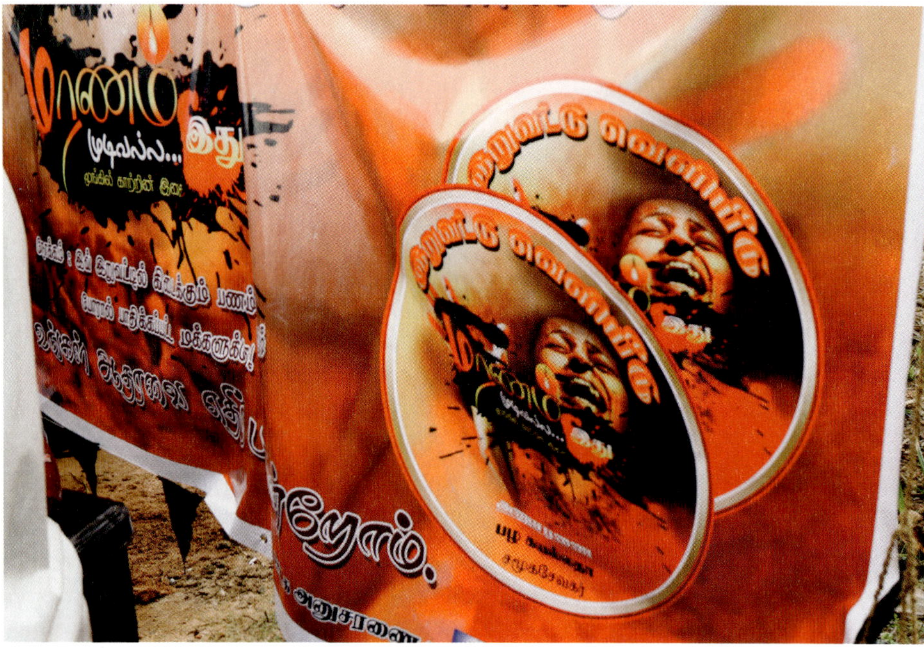

1.9 The cover artwork of music CDs being sold at Mullivaikkal. Mullaitivu, May 18, 2018. Photograph by Vindhya Buthpitiya.

Materialities of Mourning

The complex iconographies of war were evident upon our entrance into the Mullivaikkal commemoration grounds strung with red and yellow flags, illustrations of the karthigai flower, and banners adorned with technicolor atrocities. "This is just like Maaveerar Naal!" Maanavi, one of my companions, exclaimed as we entered the grounds. The young woman employed in a community psychosocial support organization had survived the final phases of the war in Kilinochchi.

In another life, the sandy turf near the ocean may have played host to a game of cricket or football, but it remained irrevocably steeped in the detritus of war (figure 1.10). I was told that the military clean-up took two years and that there was not a human bone to be found. "They brought in an incinerator," someone whispered, "to burn all the bodies." The soil, however, was still tangled and scattered with the remnants of the NFZ. Children's shoes, women's saris, the plastic shells of battery-powered radios, men's rubber slippers, woven mats,

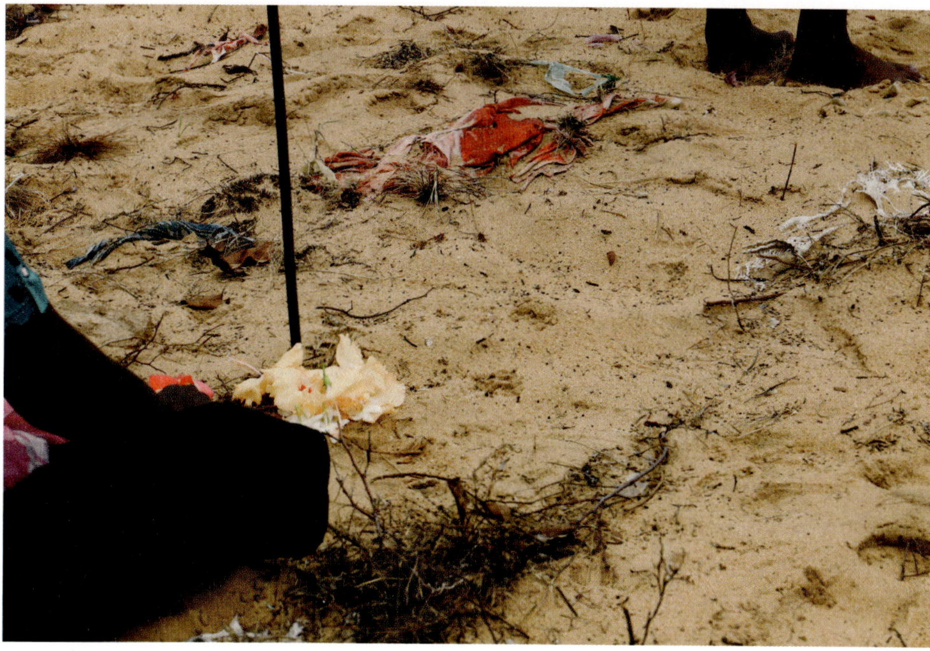

1.10 Material remains of Mullivaikkal. Mullaitivu, May 18, 2018. Photograph by Vindhya Buthpitiya.

and blue tarpaulin all served as indexes of atrocity. Hundreds of mourners had gathered before a crop of metal rods that would be repurposed as torches. Here, they took off their shoes, toes digging into soil consecrated darkly by these relics of nation and violence as if to form an elemental tether to all that was lost.

Examining the everyday materialities of violence in Sierra Leone, Marianne Ferme considers how local histories are bound up in matter whereby, through objects, language, and social relations, "violent historical memory is sedimented and critically appropriated."[64] The visible world, Ferme argues, is "activated by forces concealed beneath the surface of discourse objects and social relations."[65] In Mullivaikkal what was buried, though only barely concealed, served as a material reliquary of the nation upon which political continuities and claims are built. Photographs of the soil, tangled with wartime residue, were posted on Instagram with captions demanding recognition of genocide against the community and justice for the victims.

Where ragged shirts, broken suitcases, and small school bags were half-buried in the dirt, mourners assembled makeshift memorials for their departed loved ones (figure 1.11). Among these were those whose family members had disappeared in the hundreds following their surrender to the state. Flowers and incense encircled photographs. Elegant studio portraits, an occasional family snap, and staid headshots still laminated into identity cards were placed on mounds of soil resembling little graves (figure 1.12). Many were elderly women, often alone, weeping with visceral grief that hung heavy in the air. A stone's throw away, on the strip of beach where the final days of the war had unfolded, scraps of sun- and-salt-bleached family albums carried by victims had survived for many years, before they slowly deteriorated and washed away. Flex banners printed with brightly tinted atrocities were strung on tree branches and tents that offered sweet cordial to the participants.

Community organizers, some of whom wore T-shirts emblazoned with karthigai flowers, helped marshal a lamp affixed onto a truck that had been roving the Northern Province as a mobile temple. Activists quietly discussed the guaranteed presence of state intelligence men weaving in and out of the crowd incognito, photographing and documenting much like the sup-

1.11 A family mourns around a studio portrait at Mullivaikkal. Mullaitivu, May 18, 2018. Photograph by Vindhya Buthpitiya.

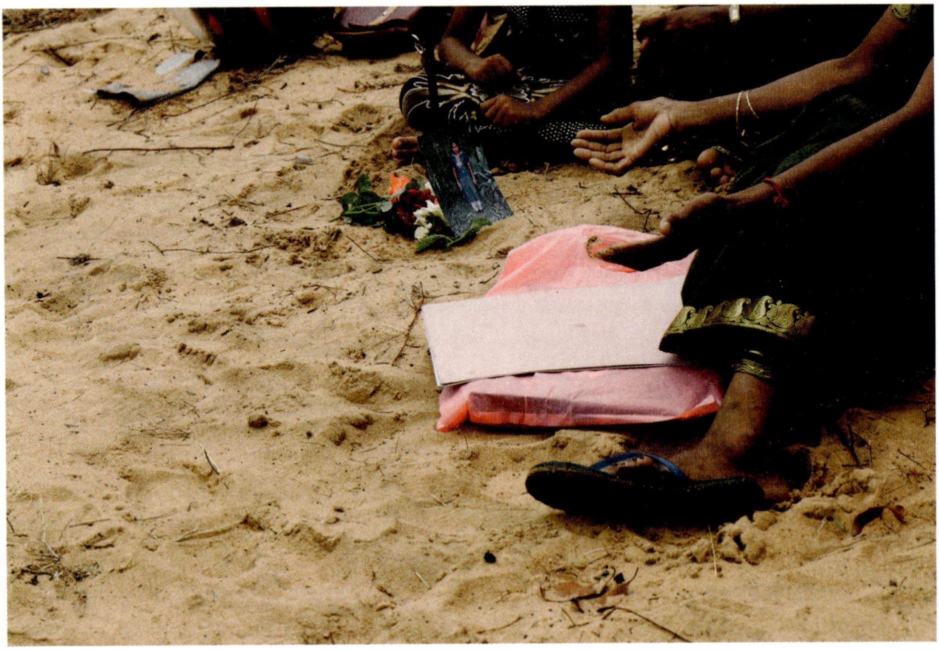

porters themselves. The recruitment of "rehabilitated" LTTE cadres into informal state surveillance networks was common knowledge. Where social stigma and marginalization stemming out of fear were prevalent and opportunities available to them were minimal, many were absorbed into the Civil Security Force to carry out menial labor and information gathering. The line between citizen journalists, activists, state intelligence operatives, and even researchers like myself was blurred, generating a visible tension between the use of the camera as an instrument of the state and a weapon of emancipation.[66]

Visitors took mobile selfies destined for social media against the brightly colored banners printed with dead children and maimed adults to mark their participation in this new ritual of nation and survival. Tamil Eelam, a dispersed nation and desired "state," was thus sustained in hashtags and geotags that stake denied political claims: #mullivaikkal, #tamileelam, #eelam, #tamil, #freetamileelam, #tamilgenocideday, #may18tamilgenocide, #remembranceisresistance, #remember2009, #weremember, and #weresist tether these to a

1.12 A makeshift memorial shrine centered on a Workplace Identity Card (*left*) and a National Identity Card (*right*). Mullaitivu, May 18, 2018. Photograph by Vindhya Buthpitiya.

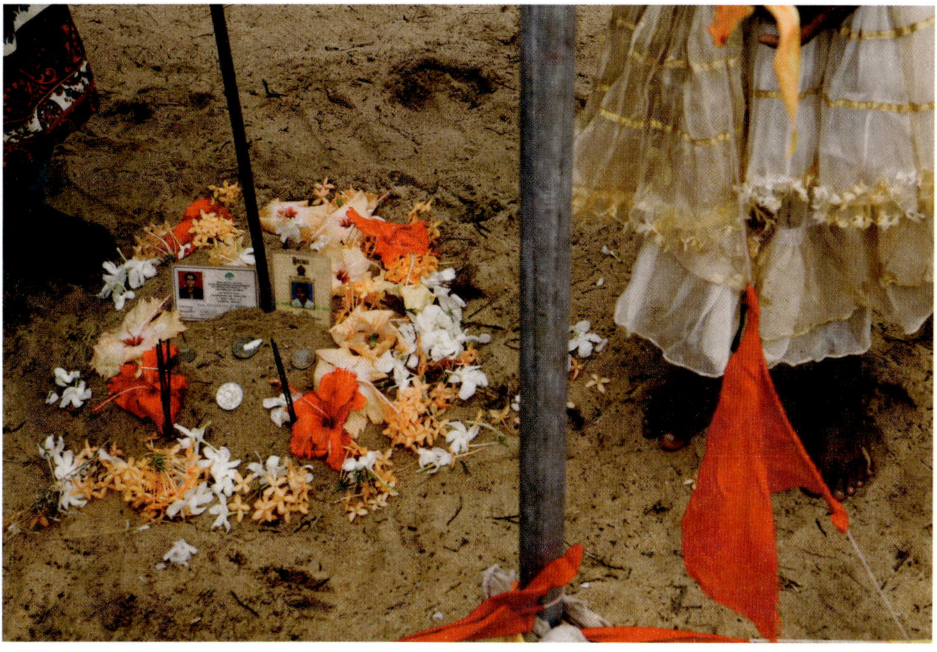

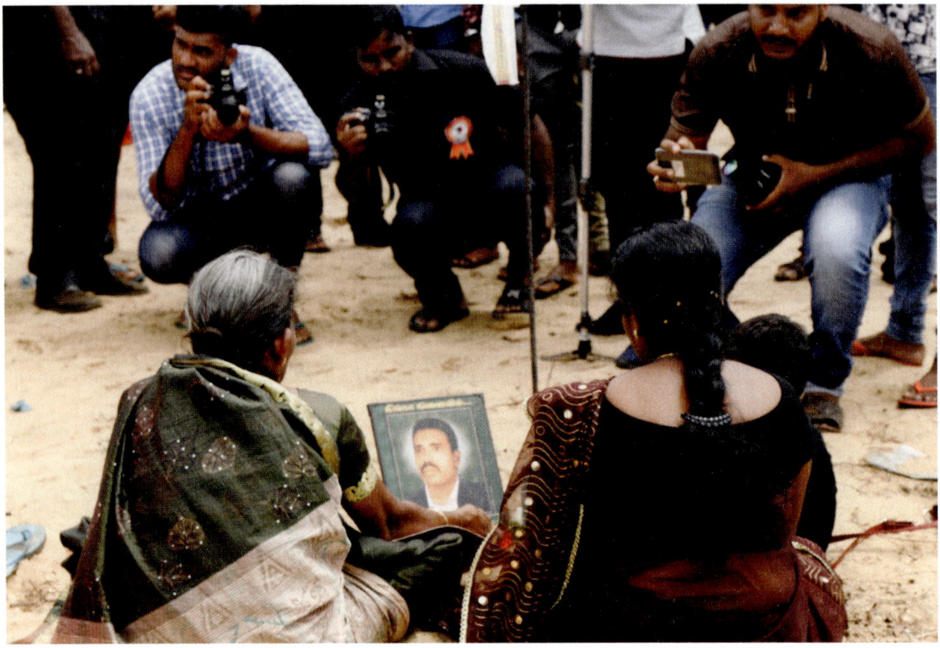

1.13 Photographers gather around a mourning family. Mullaitivu, May 18, 2018. Photograph by Vindhya Buthpitiya.

global constellation of hundreds of images posted on Instagram, Facebook, and Twitter. They constituted, through virtual iconographies and cartographies at least, a legible nation-state, as it was imagined by hundreds of thousands of Tamils scattered far from their homeland.

A buzzing media drone upset a few elderly mothers, reminding them of the hum of falling shells. Local photographers, media workers, citizen journalists, and activists congregated around grieving families, looking for the most arresting of potential photographic evocations that would in the days that followed the event circulate around the local mediascape (figure 1.13). Little children cried over parents they had only known for a few months of their short lives. Graying mothers wept over dead sons and daughters who had not survived past their teenage years or had disappeared upon surrender to the state. A father bore in his arms a large picture frame enclosing multiple faces: a family tree of death. A mother mourned a photoshopped memorial portrait of her son, two images flanking a text that spoke to his memory (figure 1.14).

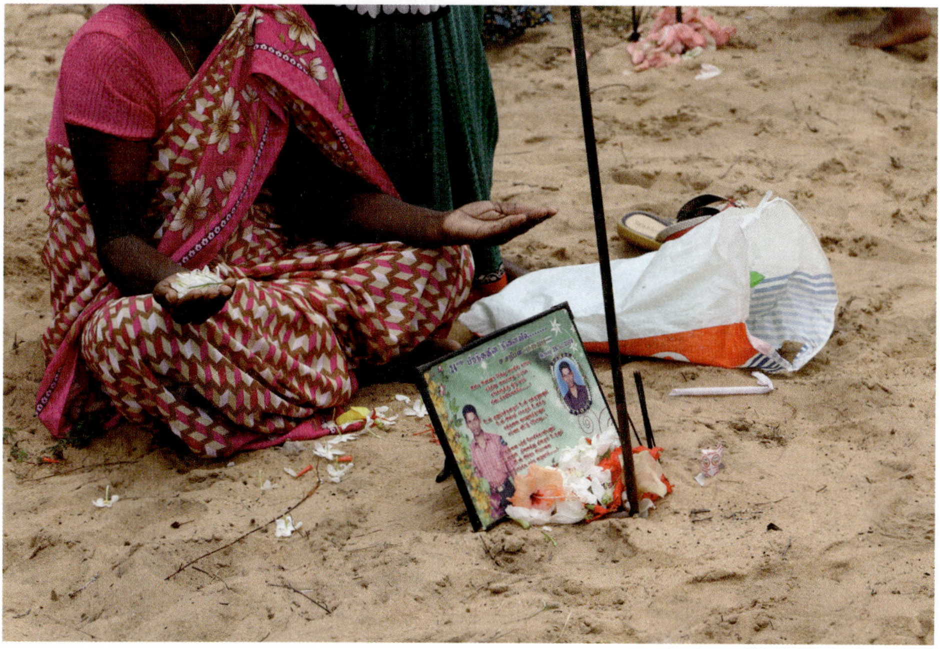

1.14 A mother mourns her son, pictured in a photoshopped memorial portrait. Mullaitivu, May 18, 2018. Photograph by Vindhya Buthpitiya.

Elsewhere in the northeast of Sri Lanka, the use of photographs in the yearslong demonstrations of the families of the disappeared was also notable (figure 1.15). Photographed extensively for the international press, images of the protests had become a visual trope for the failures of Sri Lanka's transitional justice processes.[67] Protesters themselves understood the ambivalence of photography, both wielding and containing its powers to make visible. In a context of heavy militarization, swift extrajudicial retribution by the state security apparatus, and impunity for human rights violations by state actors, visibility served as an unpredictable source of political esteem and political precarity. As protest leaders became recognizable by way of media coverage, visibility sometimes even afforded tenuous protection.

However, over many months of public demonstrations, their relationship to photography grew more complicated. What was once seen as a means of enhancing visibility, nationally and internationally, was sometimes also seen as a way in which their struggle might be co-opted or misused, politically, finan-

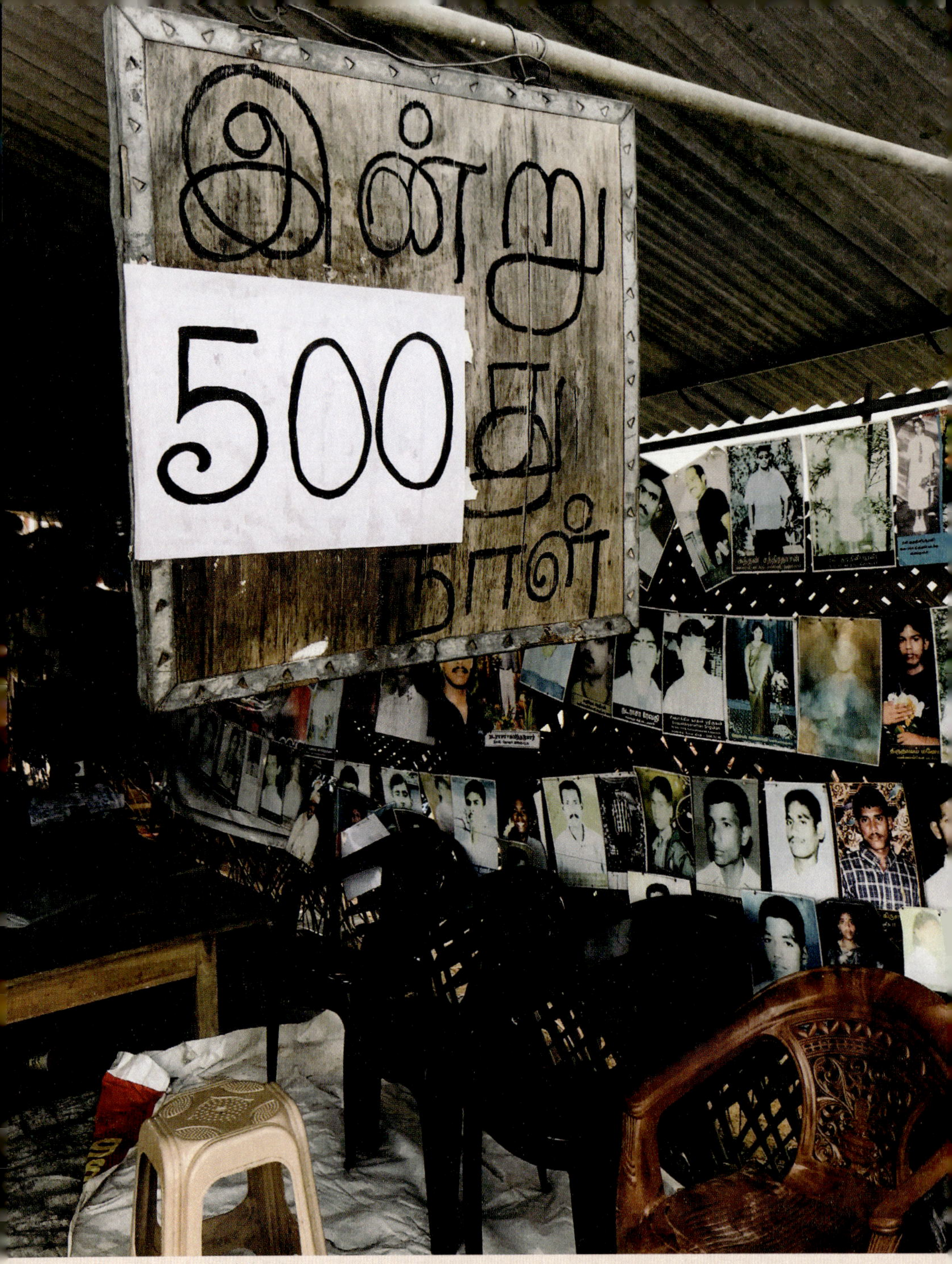

1.15 Protest tent of the Tamil families of the disappeared. Kilinochchi, June 2018. Photograph by Vindhya Buthpitiya.

cially, and otherwise, by photographers and other actors, including fraudulent immigration brokers. Many of these anxieties were tethered to and shaped almost entirely by the war, its "victory" by the Sri Lankan state, and how it emphasized the inequality and vulnerability of the Tamil citizenry. However, photography's ambivalent potential for both exploitation and managing social and political contingencies was recognized by those who mobilized the medium in their protest and remembrance. A number of these families had also gathered at Mullivaikkal that day to mark their losses.

As the Mullivaikkal commemoration proceeded, a sharp cry cut through the hum of mourning. "Intha mannukulla tan unmai irukkirathu [The truth is in the soil]," an *amma* (mother) in a brown sari keened. During this lament and curse, she despairingly grabbed at the earth with her hands. Photographers bunched around her. Two women held her up as she, a postwar Sita, clutched at the soil desperately, as if the earth might open up to offer her answers.[68]

The disquiet of the Tamil postwar is thick with photography.

Anticipation Nation

Although the Tamil community's relationship to the authoritarian Tigers was fraught at best, the group's effort at contriving a Tamil nation-state and ideal citizenry left an impression on the vocabulary and aesthetics of Tamil political articulation. At first glance, it might be argued that the Tamil public's continuance of the image-based practices instituted by the LTTE affirms John Tagg's proposition that photography inevitably yields to ideological imperatives.[69] Against this, we might underline the unlikely ways in which photography, in its everyday improvisations and mitigations, illuminated the entanglement of the personal and the political. The medium was appropriated in everyday expressions of individual political choices and the securing of personal futures in the face of uncertainty. Where Tamil citizenship during the war has been described as "complex citizenship," how might the future of the Tamil nation and citizenship be understood through photography?[70]

For Tamils, Sri Lankan citizenship, loosely defined as the relationship between the individual and the state framed by the constitution through franchise and fundamental rights, remained unequal. The mobilization of photography illuminated the tensions in this "impaired" citizenship, affording insight into personal and day-to-day reckonings with the state.[71] What the social and political life of popular photography revealed was that the Tamil political future, in terms of nation/state/homeland and citizenship, cannot be easily parsed from the effects of conflict-induced transnational dispersal and a large deterritorialized population. The citizens of photography are now globally located.

In the postwar present, the intimate and the everyday refract the history and lingering possibility for a "national" future. For instance, the afterlives of those National Identity Cards (NICs) remixed as emblems of political protest echo Strassler's observations about the social life of the Indonesian *pasfoto*, but the politics of the Sri Lankan postwar rendered the uses of these photographs even more explicit and subversive. Strassler argues that in the Indonesian example, "ideologies and practices of documentation tied to state bureaucratic knowledge production also reverberate within the intimate realm of personal and familial memory."[72] This observation resonates in Sri Lanka, where the official and the intimate have been in constant exchange, as seen in the example of copying negatives turned into memorial portraits. At Mullivaikkal, NIC photographs took on a new political resonance, defiant of the category of "Sri Lanka" itself.

Where the Sri Lankan state persists as the perpetrator, the reorienting of its visual-material marker of citizenship in an explicitly Tamil space of memory and resistance announces a space of intense inversion (figure I.16). In this setting, the refiguration or dramatic translation of NIC photographs pointed to a citizenship that eluded the Tamil community. Expanding on James Scott's consideration of the tools of legibility employed by the state, Veena Das and Deborah Poole examine how the state makes the population legible to itself through documentation.[73] While identity photography and its role in citizenship registration may, following Tagg, suggest how the state sees its citizens through photography, this does not exhaust the potential of photography. The potential that the NIC images have to write an alternative or double history is a function of their underlying trace, and of their contingency. Rather than Tagg's conclusion that photography "as such" has no identity, the diversity of its incarnations in Sri Lanka points to the exorbitance of its "political ontology."[74]

Through acts of state terror and violence, the lives and deaths of the Tamil community were subject to literal erasure, as evidenced by Mullivaikkal. The materialities and visibility of Tamil culture, polity, and history were also rendered invisible, if not destroyed, in what my interlocutors repeatedly described as "cultural genocide." The repurposing of identity photography and its incorporation into acts of resistance and "national" articulation against the state served as a powerful and poignant evocation of a political absence and disparity (figures 1.17a and 1.17b). Here, the digital permits greater amplification, extending and consolidating the nation beyond the territorial limits of the state through a dispersed community as well as a network of hashtags.

In his study of transnational Tamil marriages, Siddharthan Maunaguru examines how the multiple involuntary displacements and voluntary migrations have formed the locally and globally dispersed Tamil social, economic, and political milieu.[75] The significance of "anticipation" in "the state of being Tamils have regarding movement, violence, social mobility" is also key to understanding photographic practices.[76] This observation offers an important way to reframe the category of risk and vulnerability saturating the language of conflict.[77] It points to the mitigation and maneuvering that are often overlooked in contexts where communities are positioned as passive "victims" or resilient simply in response to violence.[78] This sentiment resonated with a collective political outlook and aspiration, both past and present. It spoke to the desire for sovereignty and self-determination in anticipation of a future nation-state but also practical mediations of citizenship (figure 1.18).

1.16 Identity photographs used by the families of the disappeared in protest. Kilinochchi, June 2018. Photograph by Vindhya Buthpitiya.

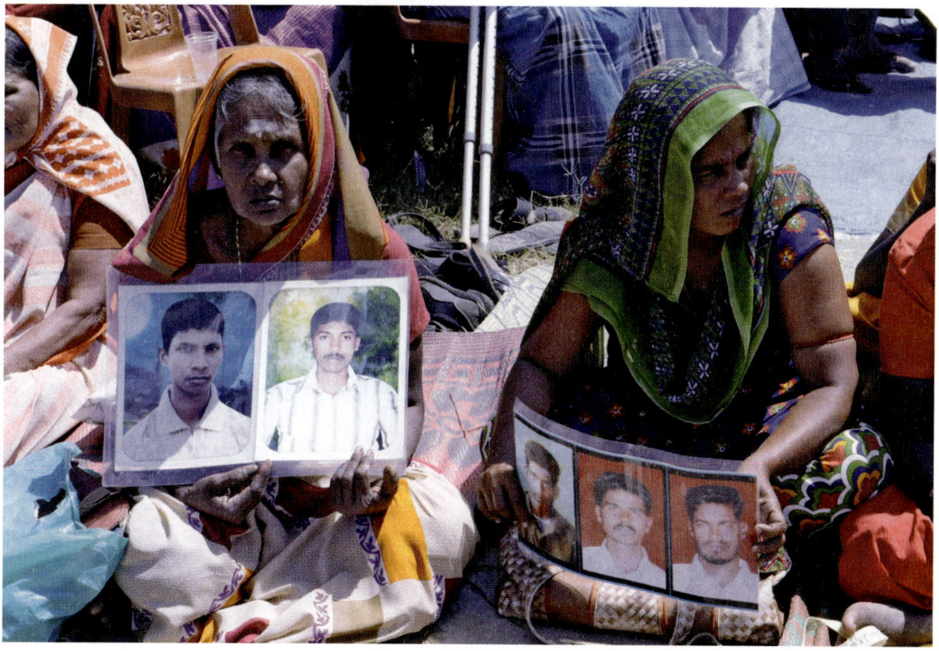

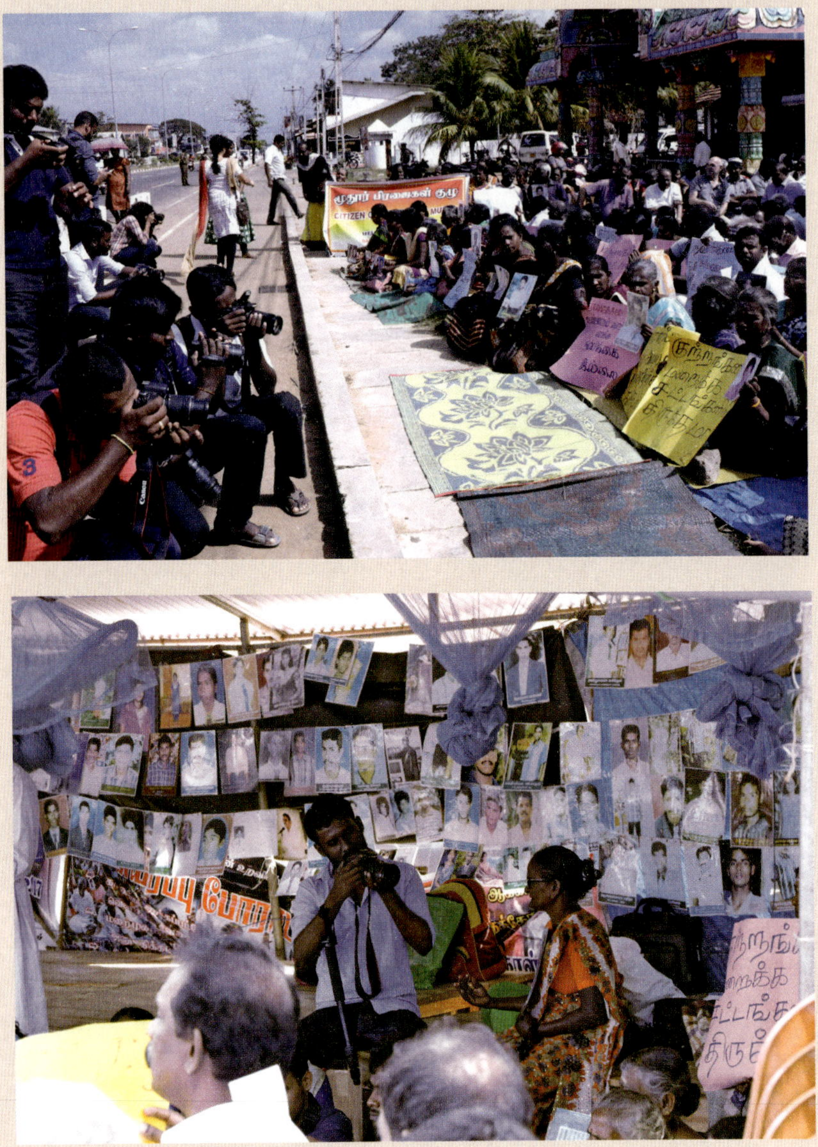

1.17a & 1.17b Journalists and activists photographing the protesters and rephotographing the portraits of the disappeared. Kilinochchi, June 2018. Photographs by Vindhya Buthpitiya.

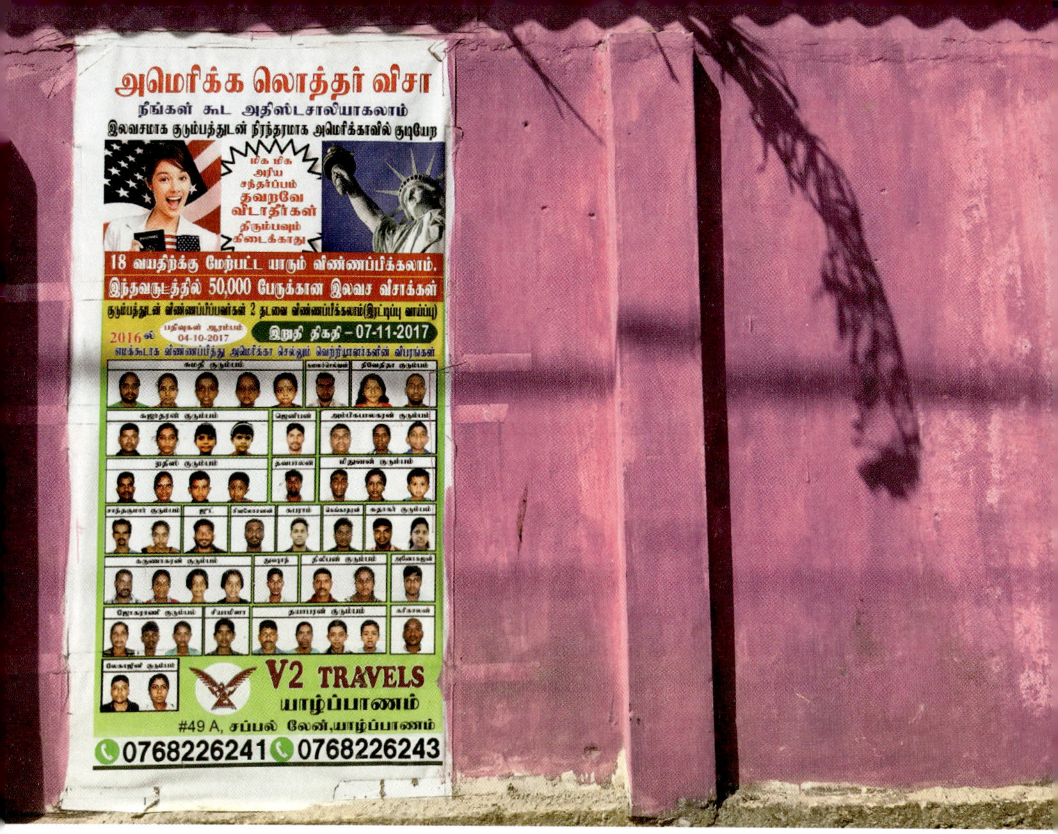

1.18 An immigration consultancy displays the visa photographs of those who successfully obtained American green cards. Jaffna, August 2018. Photograph by Vindhya Buthpitiya.

Examining the aspirations and liminality evoked in the photographs of Keralan migrants in the Arabian Gulf, Mohamed Shafeeq Karinkurayil notes how in the absence of formal means of citizenship, photographs, through their movement between spaces, provide pathways for "other modes of belonging."[79] Studio portraits taken to ornament transnational marriage proposals; elaborate wedding albums authenticating relationships; passport and visa headshots paving the way to new citizenships, prospects, and mobilities' images of loved ones held up in protest to confront the erasures of the state or in efforts to preserve histories; and expressions of a desire for a different political future on Instagram all serve as spaces for the imagining and articulation of a future where parity of citizenship might come to exist. Though steeped in a history of violence, the lively confluence of everyday photographic practices suggests the myriad ways in which the Tamil political imagination perseveres and how photography is oriented to the future.

Imag(in)ing Tamil Eelam

Truth is also imagined in digital "soil." Tamil Eelam is imagined through its eponymous geotag on Instagram, whereby the platform's globally dispersed Tamil users become linked to a map of photographs. Pradeep Jeganathan considers this early example of internet community formation as the "stretching, fragmenting form of the contemporary nation" to examine Tamil Eelam's relationship to "webspace."[80] Flagging the "rootlessness" of the LTTE, Jeganathan notes its placelessness "equidistant from everywhere, not quite anywhere," despite its hyperlocated claim.[81] "It cannot simply become an organization that intersects with 'Tamils' all over the world," he emphasizes, "for then it would lose that one idea, that so many of its supporters have died for and pay for: that small piece of land in north-eastern Sri Lanka—the nation as bounded territory."[82] Three decades later, with the advent of social media and user-generated capacities to augment online maps, Tamil Eelam found cartographic visual-political definition. It was made tangible by photographic accounts of "lived place" where largely young Tamils gave sociocultural and political texture to its virtual topography.

Posts include everyday photographs celebrating the beauty of the landscape, wedding and other family photographs, the victories of diasporic sporting teams, recirculations of protest and commemoration photographs, and selfies locating oneself in the homeland (figure 1.19). In this Instagram "country," bite-sized political histories and aspirations are mingled with personal recollections and tributes compiled by mostly young Tamils overseas. These are interspersed with the iconography and portraiture of Tamil Tiger heroes and martyrs. The history of the movement was often produced and uncritically glorified by Tamil youths abroad to cultivate communal learning and awareness. As Sharika Thiranagama notes, "The younger generations who grew up with the LTTE as a repressive quasi-state rather than a liberation group saw the LTTE not as a vehicle for meaningful utopianism but only as a pragmatic necessity. This means that they may not rush to resuscitate it now, unlike diasporic youth for whom it is utopian still."[83] The strains between those resident in Sri Lanka, for whom the stakes of political expression and negotiations of impaired citizenship are immediate, and those elsewhere, idealizing the political possibility of Tamil Eelam, played out in these compet-

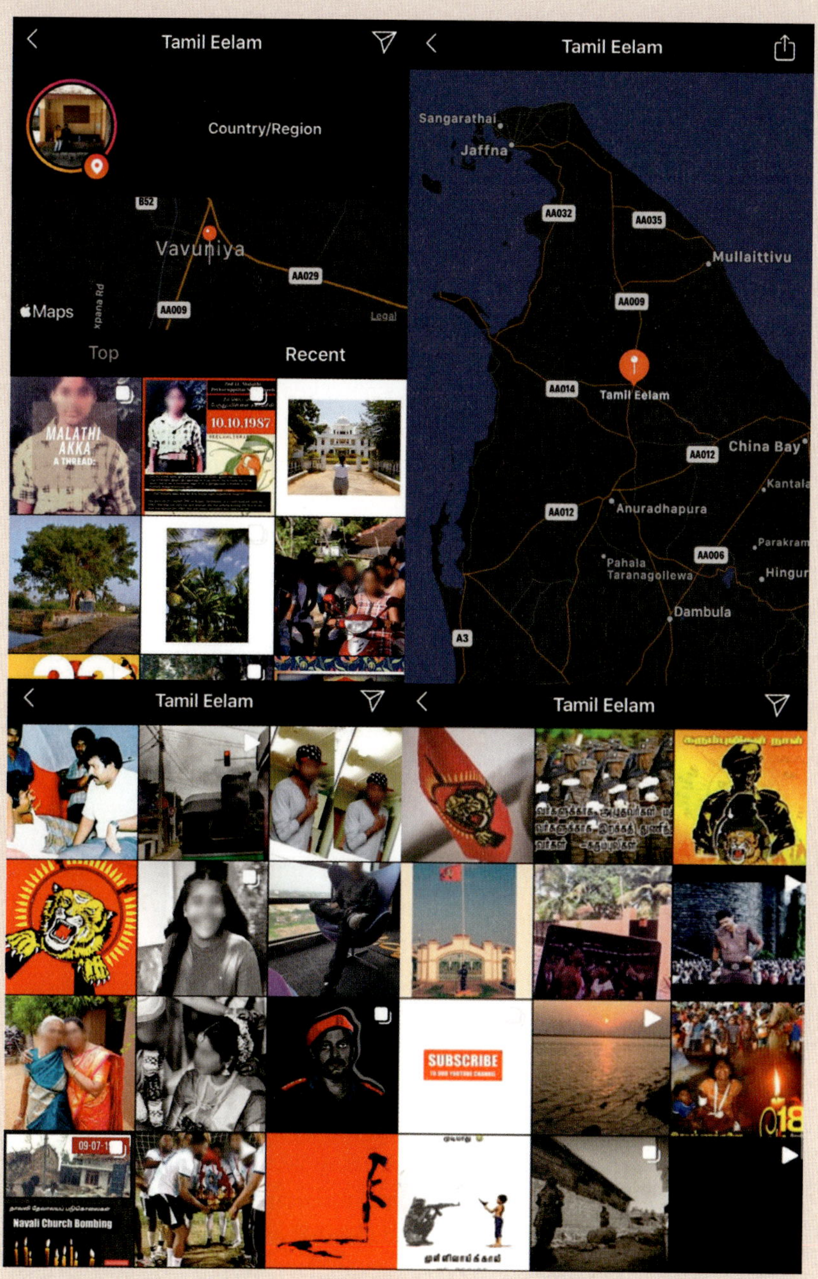

1.19 Screen capture of the public images tethered to the Tamil Eelam geotag on Instagram, 2020.

ing social photographies. These illuminate a diversity of political desires and a citizenship that is doubly split, not only between Sinhalese and Tamil but also between the global and the local.

For Komathy, a young woman who mostly grew up in the Vanni, photography through Instagram became a platform through which she was able to draw attention to the challenges of navigating the postwar as a young Tamil woman and highlight the "forgotten" beauty of her home that had for so long been associated with the horrors of conflict: "I want people to see that my hometown is beautiful and that it has a history that is not just defined by the war. I want to tell the stories of its residents and how proud they are of their land and their heritage," Komathy observed. Others, like Arunan and Sulaxan, young Tamil men in their twenties resident in Jaffna, trained their camera lenses on the scars of war and the ongoing wounding of Tamil bodies and the landscape by the state. Through their photographs and choice of hashtags and geotags that connected them to a tenacious aspiration for a homeland, their political sentiments and allegiances became clear. Captions critical of the status quo or expressing political desires that might be viewed as threat or subversion in Sri Lanka were posted in Tamil (as opposed to English) to conceal in plain sight. Posts with Tamil nationalist hashtags are often reported by their Sinhala nationalist counterparts and taken down as violations of Instagram's community guidelines. These too reemerged through various improvisations.

What Instagram permitted was the grain of these political differences to coexist and jostle in a heterogeneous visual discourse. The aspirant nation is realized in spite of borders that separate its photographic citizens. Digitized family photographs became global conversation pieces for reflecting on displacement and dispossession. Street scenes offered prompts to critique militarization and "Sinhalization." Photographs of LTTE cemeteries destroyed by the state were turned into anchors for #resistance and #remembrance. Though the photographs were situated in Jaffna, Batticaloa, Zurich, or Toronto, the located claim of the nation was pinned onto the virtual map of Tamil Eelam. This enmeshing with conflict spoke to the dispersal of the nation in a manner that vitalized its territorial claims—locality, as Arjun Appadurai noted, being built on global foundations.[84]

Future Citizens/Citizen Futures

Everyday photographs that were unremarkable in their making and mundane in their circulation still contained extraordinary political promise. This was apparent in their uses within spaces of resistance but also in their mediation of the social and bureaucratic processes that paved the way for new citizenships. Images were often produced to fulfill the requirements of the state or state-like actors for registration, securitization, and immigration. Ghastly images of atrocity circulated in equal step with studio portraits, family photographs, and identity card headshots, their political work diverse but no less central to the possibility of emancipation—whether personal or political.

During the war years, photography played a central role in the mediation of not only state and citizenship relationships but interpersonal relationships. Identity photography projects, the registration of persons, and immigration and humanitarian documentation regimes undertaken by state actors were central to the making, demarcating, and mobility of existing or aspiring citizens. For Tamils, vulnerable in the face of the state security regime, this bore significant implications for their corporal well-being and survival. Personal photographs commemorating birthdays, weddings, and other life events took on new significance. These were treasured and exchanged among families displaced and dispersed across faraway borders. Grand studio portraits became integral to securing marriages that permitted safety, opportunity, and new beginnings elsewhere.[85] Even as personal devices with cameras grew more common, young men and women visited studios to have their photographs taken to be circulated by marriage brokers. The most desirable marriage for many was to someone with "status," that is, permanent residency or citizenship in the West, which enhanced one's prospects and mobility where Sri Lankan citizenship was "impaired." While a quarter of the Tamil population lived abroad as a consequence of war, transnational marriage constituted an important migration strategy whereby "homeland" might be re-created in their host countries.[86] Here, photographers played an important role in authenticating relationships through a series of visual markers, including intimacy between couples, the presence of family members, and the portrayal of Tamil traditions for the benefit of immigration officials (figure 1.20).[87]

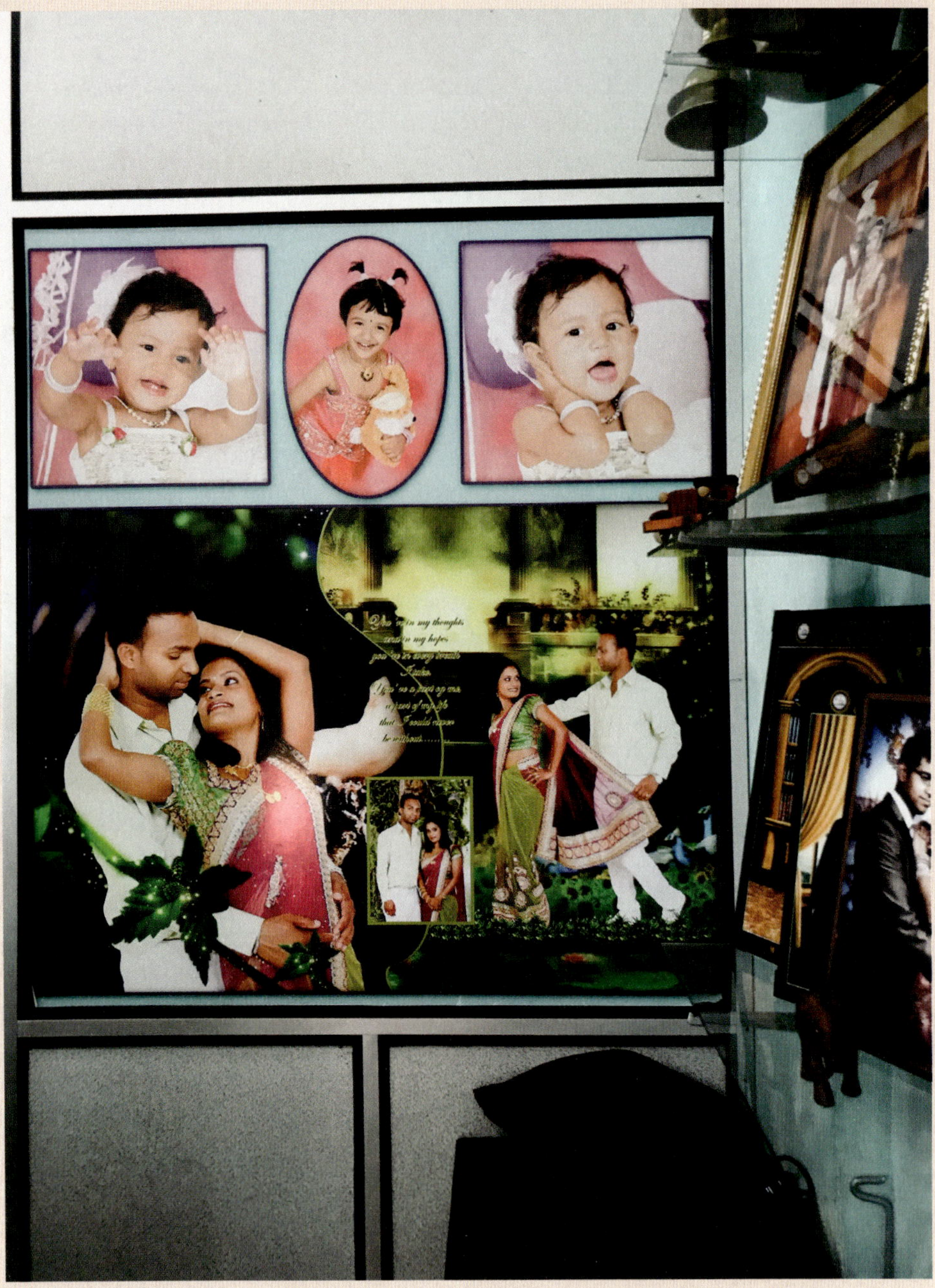

1.20 Sample wedding album page display. Jaffna, August 2018. Photograph by Vindhya Buthpitiya.

Conclusion

Against the backdrop of a political demand for emancipation in the form of a new nation-state, photography endured as a powerful mode of personal and communal political expression, solidarity, and imagining.

The photographies of competing nation-states in Sri Lanka, ranging from propaganda to public art and cultural production, shaped the local visual cultural environment and public sensibilities during the war. The state mandate for the "registration of persons" and associated photography also transformed the spaces, technologies, and capacities of studios, laying the basis for future materializations, conjugations, and circulations. Whether in the form of identity card photography remediated as ornate memorial portraits or the role of wedding photography in mediating new kinds of citizenship aspirations, the war continued to underpin the worlds of photographic production in extraordinary ways.

Notable was photography's uses within contexts of civilian protest and political claim making, echoing the medium's potential to foster borderless solidarity and civic duty.[88] Met with concerted efforts by the state to recast and erase counterhistories and narratives of the war, resistance also extended to remembrance and commemoration. Here, photographs evidencing individual lives and state-sponsored violence served an important political purpose. The visibility afforded and amplified by the visual was integral to the formation of transnational Tamil solidarities and political socialities and in contesting hegemonic projects of history making. Especially significant were the communal efforts within online spaces to navigate how Tamil political histories, identities, claims, and futures in the postwar might be expressed and imagined through images. Photography paired with social media platforms such as Instagram offered a compelling means to grapple with, interrogate, and respond to a convoluted past and present, and form and consolidate communities. These enabled the expression of belonging and un/belonging with respect to place and community.

The multitude of nations, states, and sovereigns and the competing registers of atrocity point to a fragmented world that contrasts with the space within which Azoulay calls for the spectator to "take part."[89] Where aspirations of nation and state were both conflicted and multiple, the categories of the "governed" and the "oppressed" were also problematized. In such a context, photography, even (or especially) in its "democratic" guise, became a medium through which political claims, as well as politically generative violence realizing acts of nation/state/citizen making, were stimulated and sustained.

Photography's capacity for producing and rationalizing violence, especially where ethnno-nationalist claims were at play, was also dramatized.

Photographic practices have been shaped by, interpreted through, contradicted by—and have contributed to—conflicting claims to citizenship and nation. Mapped against a war centered on a demand for political self-determination and the building of a nation-state, photography and related practices offer new insights into the lived experiences of conflict and the articulations of personal and political futures. The visual also serves as a lens through which to examine what being Tamil as a project of future *becoming* might entail. Here, photography serves as a dynamic means for making visible, claiming, demanding, and imagining in the wake of war and enduring oppression. The medium reveals, importantly, its role in the disruptive formation of borderless Tamil political socialities and solidarities that have, in turn, strengthened located claims of a homeland.

Notes

Interviews in this chapter were carried out between 2017 and 2018. Names, locations, and contextual information have been altered to protect interlocutors' identities out of concern for their safety. I am immensely grateful to those whose words, photographs, experiences, reading, and generosity informed this chapter.

1 In the epigraph, *Mullivaikkal* refers to the Karaiyamullivaikkal and Vellamullivaikkal areas located in the southern end of the Mullivaikkal peninsula in the Mullaitivu District where the third "No Fire Zone" was demarcated by the Sri Lankan state during the final weeks of the war in 2009. The strip of land spans about fourteen square kilometers bordered in the north by Valayanmadam and the sea and the Nanthikadal Lagoon and Vadduvakal (International Crimes Evidence Project [ICEP], *Island of Impunity*, 20).

2 See Frances Harrison's important contribution to documenting survivors' accounts in *Still Counting the Dead*. The Vanni is the mainland area of the Northern Province spanning the Mannar, Mullaitivu, and Vavuniya Districts and a portion of the Kilinochchi District. Forming the backdrop for the final phases of the war between 2006 and 2009, the Vanni was among the hardest hit in terms of war-related casualties.

3 Human Rights Watch, "Protect Civilians."

4 Between December 15, 2008, and May 2, 2009, Human Rights Watch recorded no fewer than thirty attacks on permanent and makeshift medical facilities in the Vanni that received hundreds of patients every day, even though their GPS

coordinates had been transmitted to the government by the doctors to ensure their safety (Human Rights Watch, "Shelling of Hospitals").

5 Estimate based on UN observations. See also International Truth and Justice Project Sri Lanka, "Death Toll."

6 See Haviland, "Sri Lanka Government."

7 *Hartal* is a South Asian term for a mass protest in the form of a shutdown of shops and businesses.

8 Weaver and Chamberlain, "Sri Lanka Declares End to War."

9 The prohibition on public mourning was relaxed following the unexpected electoral victory of the United National Party (UNP) and Sri Lanka Freedom Party (SLFP) coalition government led by common candidate and former president Maithripala Sirisena (2015–19). This marked a relative improvement to freedom of expression and civilian protest in comparison to the previous regime, led by former president Mahinda Rajapaksa (2005–15), under whose tenure the war ended. The Rajapaksa-led Sri Lanka Podujana Peramuna (SLPP) returned to power in 2019 with the election of Mahinda's brother and former defense secretary, Gotabaya Rajapaksa, as president. Restrictions on public mourning have been reimposed.

10 See Stokke, "Building the Tamil Eelam State"; and Natali, "Building Cemeteries." *Iyakkam* is used in everyday conversation as synonymous with the Tamil militancy.

11 Pinney, "Introduction" (this volume).

12 Azoulay, *Civil Contract*, 14.

13 Azoulay, *Civil Contract*, 25.

14 I use post/war as an abbreviation to combine the period of war and postwar.

15 Cf. Azoulay, *Civil Imagination*, 15.

16 See Tambiah, *Ethnic Fratricide*; Tambiah, *Buddhism Betrayed*; de Mel, *Militarizing Sri Lanka*; and Venugopal, *Nationalism, Development and Ethnic Conflict*.

17 Following Varzi, *Warring Souls*, 4.

18 Strassler, *Refracted Visions*, 23.

19 Benjamin, "Little History of Photography" (1999), 510.

20 Roland Barthes describes the "punctum" of the photograph as the "tiny shock" of a "partial object" that haunts an individual viewer (*Camera Lucida*, 43, 49).

21 Strassler, *Refracted Visions*, 23.

22 Kalantzis, *Tradition in the Frame*, 82.

23 See Lubkemann, *Culture in Chaos*; and Thiranagama, *In My Mother's House*.

24 Bronisław Malinowski's "imponderabilia of everyday life" comprised "a series of phenomena of great importance which cannot possibly be recorded by questioning or computing documents" (or in this case the visual analysis of photographic images). See Malinowski, *Argonauts*, vii.

25 Pinney, "Seven Theses on Photography," 150.

26 Salt and rice porridge was the only sustenance available to those trapped in

Mullivaikkal and has subsequently become part of communal commemorative practice. Inspired by the Jewish holiday of Passover, partaking in Mullivaikkal kanji has been adopted by the global Tamil community to honor those who died.

27 While it remains challenging to categorize photographers by affiliation given the ways in which everyday photography practices were appropriated and administered by the LTTE, I have used the term *civilian photographers* to describe studio and other professional photographers, including photojournalists, who were not directly employed by or did not wish to be identified as having been directly tasked by the LTTE.

28 Azoulay, *Civil Imagination*, 14.

29 See Schalk, "Resistance and Martyrdom"; Schalk, "Revival of Martyr Cults"; and M. Roberts, "Saivite Symbols." The section title is inspired by Mbembe, *Necropolitics*.

30 See Natali, "Building Cemeteries"; Perera, *Violence and the Burden of Memory*; and Perera, *Warzone Tourism*.

31 See Linfield, *Cruel Radiance*; Sliwinski, *Human Rights in Camera*; and Phelan, "Atrocity in Action."

32 The language of eradication relating to "anti-state subversion" evoking disease and pestilence features prominently in the vocabulary of the Sri Lankan state and security apparatus.

33 Thiranagama, *In My Mother's House*, 26.

34 Human Rights Watch, "Shelling of Hospitals."

35 TamilNet has been the subject of anthropological inquiry and described as a site of "popular anthropology" by Mark Whitaker, who suggests that the website, although often presumed to be pro-LTTE, only shared a similar Tamil Nationalist ideology. The website remains banned in Sri Lanka. See Whitaker, "Some Reflections."

36 TamilNet, "Source Files."

37 Benjamin, "Little History of Photography" (1999), 510.

38 In 2021 the monument to remember the lives lost at Mullivaikkal on the Jaffna University premises was demolished by the government, which stated it was a threat to the country's unity. As a result of widespread outrage and a series of hunger strikes by students, a new "peace" monument is expected to be built in its place.

39 Pinney explores the studio practice of postmortem photography in Central India, where the subject was not photographed during their lifetime; the deceased would be photographed surrounded by family. See Pinney, *Camera Indica*, 205–7.

40 TamilNet, "LTTE Announces Unilateral Ceasefire."

41 Arunasalam, *Paper*.

42 Cf. Benjamin, "Little History of Photography" (1999), 510.

43 See Mookherjee, "The Aesthetics of Nations."

44 "Bird of freedom" refers to the LTTE women's wing. See Brun, "Birds of Freedom."

45 Tagg, *The Burden of Representation.*

46 See Linfield, "Syria's Torture Photos"; and Smith and Siobhan, "Capturing Genocide on Their Cellphones."

47 Kleinman and Kleinman, "The Dismay of Images," 1.

48 See Brun, "Birds of Freedom"; and Thiranagama, *In My Mother's House.*

49 Journeyman Pictures, *Truth Tigers—Sri Lanka.*

50 See de Mel, *Militarizing Sri Lanka*, 13; and Perera, *Warzone Tourism.*

51 See International Truth and Justice Project Sri Lanka, "War on Civilians Exhibition"; and Sri Lanka Campaign for Peace and Justice, "'Tamils of Lanka.'"

52 Azoulay, *Civil Contract*, 24.

53 Azoulay, *Civil Contract*, 25.

54 Azoulay, *Civil Contract*, 25.

55 Azoulay, *Civil Contract*, 25.

56 Azoulay, *Civil Contract*, 26.

57 See Schalk, "Resistance and Martyrdom"; Schalk, "Revival of Martyr Cults"; and M. Roberts, "Saivite Symbols."

58 See Schalk, "Resistance and Martyrdom"; and Schalk, "Revival of Martyr Cults."

59 McDowell, "Symbolic Warfare," 27.

60 M. Roberts, "Saivite Symbols"; Natali, "Building Cemeteries."

61 M. Roberts, "Saivite Symbols," 77–80.

62 The poisonous Gloriosa superba or karthigai flower also has an unfortunate local association with suicide due to the plant's toxic root. The flower's resemblance to a flame served as a symbol of the "flame of sacrifice" that featured in the Maaveerar Naal ceremony.

63 Azoulay, *Civil Contract.*

64 Ferme, *The Underneath of Things*, 2–6.

65 Ferme, *The Underneath of Things*, 2.

66 See Tagg, *The Burden of Representation*; and Azoulay, *Civil Contract.*

67 See Buthpitiya, "Absence in Technicolour."

68 Sita is a principal character in the Hindu epic *The Ramayana*, attributed to Valmiki. Sita is believed to be the daughter of the earth goddess Bhoomi. During her marriage to Rama, the prince of Ayodhya, they are exiled to a forest when she is abducted and imprisoned by the king of Lanka, Ravana. Following her rescue by Rama, Sita is asked to prove her chastity by way of a test of fire, which she does. In the *Luv Kush Kand*, the final book of *The Ramayana*, which has not been attributed to the original writers, Sita, plagued with continued questions about her purity, finds refuge in an ashram, where she gives birth to two children, Luv and Kush. In a final challenge by a detractor, overcome with emotion, Sita prays to Mother Earth. The earth opens up beneath her and she disappears. The legend of Ravana pervades the Sinhalese and Tamil nation-

alist and popular political imagination in Sri Lanka (Sanmugeswaran, Fredricks, and Henry, "Reclaiming Ravana in Sri Lanka"; Witharana, "Ravana's Sri Lanka").

69 Tagg, *The Burden of Representation.*
70 Brun, "Birds of Freedom," 401.
71 Azoulay, *Civil Contract*, 14.
72 Strassler, *Refracted Visions*, 23.
73 Scott, *Seeing like a State*; Das and Poole, *Anthropology in the Margins of the State.*
74 Tagg, *The Burden of Representation*, 118; Azoulay, *Civil Imagination*, 11–18.
75 Maunaguru, "Brides as Bridges?"; Maunaguru, *Marrying for a Future.*
76 Maunaguru, "Brides as Bridges?," 61.
77 Jeganathan, "On the Anticipation of Violence."
78 Cf. Nordstrom, *A Different Kind of War Story.*
79 Karinkurayil, "Reading Aspiration," 10, 15.
80 Jeganathan, "Eelam.com," 515.
81 Jeganathan, "Eelam.com," 525.
82 Jeganathan, "Eelam.com," 525.
83 Thiranagama, *In My Mother's House*, 40–41.
84 Appadurai, "Disjuncture and Difference," 297.
85 See Buthpitiya, "Naveena Camera."
86 Maunaguru, *Marrying for the Future*, 4.
87 Maunaguru, *Marrying for the Future*, 87.
88 Azoulay, *Civil Contract*, 23.
89 Azoulay, *Civil Contract*, 144.

2

Visual Citizenship in Cambodia

FROM APOCALYPSE TO VISUAL "POLITICAL EMANCIPATION"

SOKPHEA YOUNG

Prologue

In Kon Kriel commune, Siem Reap–Oddar Meanchey, in 1989, close to the last stronghold of Khmer Rouge, Anlong Veng district, I can recall the presence of Vietnamese soldiers, the Khmer Rouge and *para* (armed people wearing army fatigues). These armed groups visited our village very often and on many different occasions. During the daytime, the Vietnamese soldiers came to our village, catching our dogs and collecting edible vegetables. At nighttime, the para stole our rice and livestock. No one dared to confront the para, and they were notoriously violent toward villagers, especially women. I heard of the Red Khmer (Khmer Krahom), which were Khmer Rouge guerrillas, but we didn't see them very often, although they resided near our village, along the border with Thailand. I once found some para clothes and uniform in the dense forest about five kilometers away from our home when I, together with other young adults, was herding our cattle.

While the People's Republic of Kampuchea's government—installed by the Vietnamese government—was controlling the major part of the country, we felt unsafe. I could not understand why, after the Khmer Rouge was defeated, my parents chose to return to their home village, Ktom, so close to so many kinds of armed forces, rebels, and guerrillas. We lived on the borderline between the Khmer Rouge, the Vietnamese soldiers, and other rebel forces. From our village, we often heard the noise of mortar rockets. We sought refuge at the bunker when we heard firing between the Khmer Rouge and the Vietnamese forces. From what I have observed, many villagers lived in fear since any of these armed forces could raid the village at any time. We survived by our own efforts, cultivating rice. We had never seen new technologies such as cameras and photography; we only had radios. We had rarely seen the government or the state exercise its responsibilities. Occasionally, we saw officials coming to our village to buy rice, and sometimes they offered animal vaccinations. Elders said that by selling rice to the state, we were supporting development and the economy. I can still remember that my grandmother's brother-in-law was a commune chief. He told villagers to collect anti-tank mines from the forest when returning from herding. Often in the evening, I would see young adults returning from herding, carrying a big green anti-tank mine. We were living in danger and fear for we could not predict what would happen the next day. While working in the paddy fields, some villagers were kidnapped, and our cattle were often slaughtered or rustled by unknown armed forces for ransoms in baht (Thai currency) and rice. Our village was easily raided at any time by these groups. We had civilian guards at night, but only some of them were armed (with rifles), while others were not.

In the village, everyone recognized each other based on their face-to-face relationship and regular contact with one another. We did not have any specific ID card and were not identified by any photographs or portraits. Our village was quite remote, being close to the Dang Rek mountain bordering Thailand. It was a five-hundred-kilometer trip to Phnom Penh, which required at least three to four days of traveling, at that time. We lived in relative isolation because our village was surrounded by paddy fields and dense forest. I recall that anyone who visited their relatives in my village had to report to the group leader, village chief, or commune chief, as we could not identify whether a person was a spy from the various armed forces. None of the visitors or any villagers had ID cards with a photo. Their identity could be manipulated easily.

Being a child and a citizen of the village, I recognized neighbors as the result of regular day-to-day contacts in the community. We were in a community characterized by a fragile citizenship. We did not know which armed groups we were claimed by, but of course the Phnom Penh government claimed our village as part of their territory. Our communication with the outside world, or even with those in the neighboring villages and communes, districts, provinces, and the country, was extremely limited. I rarely heard about TV, video, cameras, and other forms of communication. I knew only about radio communication since I saw some Vietnamese soldiers contacting their base station. I heard older people listen to the Thai radio, the Voice of America, the Voice of Free Asia, and the Khmer Rouge Radio from Anglong Veng. The Khmer Rouge radio broadcasted warnings that "the Vietnamese will kill or gut you if you return inside Cambodia." This was propaganda to prevent their "citizens" or soldiers from defecting and joining the government installed by the Vietnamese government.

In the 1990s, my parents decided to move to the district's center, Samrong, which is about ten kilometers from my natal village. I started to learn about the outside world in this crowded town. There, I learned about Barang soldiers (foreigners from the West: the United Nations Transitional Authority to Cambodia [UNTAC] soldiers). I saw their camp fenced with barbed wire. I saw they had lots of food such as fish, eggs, bread. Every evening, we stood by the earth road waiting for those UNTAC soldiers to drive their truck around, throwing snacks, noodles, cheese, and chips. We sometimes crawled into the Barang camp to collect trashed food: they threw away good food.

Sometime before 1993, I learned that people were lining up at my primary school to vote. I became aware that my parents had ID cards with their portrait. From that, I learned that there was a device called a camera. After the first general elections, I started to see video "cinema" (a thirty-inch TV screen installed in our village). The owner had a VHS player connected to a monitor screen installed in a big hall of about fifty to eighty spectators. Once a week, we watched a movie there. We enjoyed Hong Kong, Indian, and Chinese TV series. I remember my parents bought their first TV in 1996, and we connected with an antenna to watch Thai and Cambodian TV programs. However, the electricity was limited with frequent load shedding. We sometimes were able to use a generator to light our home in the evening, but often it was a complete blackout illuminated by a hurricane lamp. It appeared that our village had started to communicate with the outside. I saw army trucks transporting goods between our village and others in other districts and provinces. We were becoming connected.

A Wider History

To understand visual citizenship and its relationship to political emancipation in Cambodia, one needs to grasp the history over the past half century of a country that has been characterized by dramatic changes. I hope that the brief history of my encounters with media communicates something of the material and experiential dimensions of this.

Visually, Cambodia became known to the West by way of Angkor Wat, a structure that not only emerged as an iconic representation of antiquity but also became the visual identity of the nation. This identity was initially brought to the rest of the world by Henri Mouhot (a French artist), who sketched Angkor Wat in the 1860s. John Thompson, a Scottish photographer, made an expedition from Singapore to become the first to photograph the astonishing temple, in 1867, a few years after Cambodia signed a treaty to invite France to be its protector. The photographs of Cambodia were then published in Edinburgh (where Thompson lived), inaugurating a European tradition of visualizing Cambodia that would prove tenacious. In the same year, 1867, the photographer Émile Gsell was commissioned by French officials to photograph Indochina. In Cambodia, he photographed Angkor Wat and the royal family, contributing to the Western understanding that Cambodia embodied antiquity and royalty (figure 2.1). As early as the first decade of the 1900s, Cambodia's identities and livelihoods were revealed in postcard photos printed in Germany and France, and many other French photographers captured Cambodia's landscape, culture, polity, and economy until the Japanese occupation.[1]

The dissemination of images of Cambodian Hindu temples, its royalty, and the Orientalist preoccupations of postcards were nation making. The ways these images were produced and consumed by the West were very much Orientalist, constructing Cambodia as "other." However, these images also came to constitute the main body of an emergent national identity and self-recognition in Cambodia. As these images traveled across physical boundaries and spaces as well as times, they aesthetically invoked the identity and citizenship of the nation that had not been visualized or seen before by the West. These images manifested colonial "ambivalence," reflecting the split in the identity of the colonized Cambodian other.[2] Reflecting this "ambivalence," these images struggled to impose any normative French colonial power and authority over the Cambodians. As these images were circulated outside the country's physical boundary, they established the infrastructure for the recognition of a future Cambodian citizenship and nation. Not only did the images of the massive Angkor Wat built in the twelfth century amaze West-

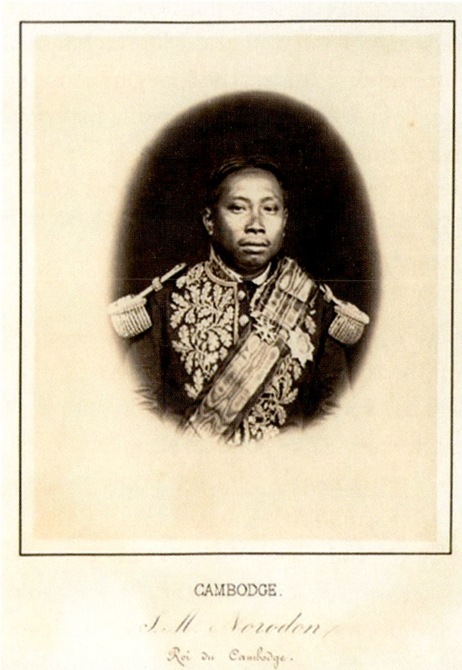

2.1 Portrait of King Norodom by Émile Gsell, 1870s.

ern viewers; they also illustrated the prowess of Cambodians in building such a monument.

These images, paradoxically, established the foundation of Cambodian identity and the nation. Photo postcards of Angkor Wat, the Royal Palace, and Cambodian people sent from Cambodia to France described Cambodians and the country to Western people.[3] The ability to describe or to identify Cambodians and their nation was based on visual representations, without which one may not be able to identify and describe Cambodia. Following the defeat of the French in 1953, the country developed its popular visual culture, through film and photography, but these were scarce and subsequently largely absent due to regime change and civil war from 1970 to 1998. In the aftermath of the Khmer Rouge, photography and other visual media have flourished and rapidly penetrated the country. Visual representations are now abundant.

Given this transformation, how do the absence and presence of images across time and space, from scarcity to atrocity and from atrocity to abundance, transform our understanding of citizenship, polity, and emancipation? These questions engage difficult theoretical puzzles concerning the relationship between photography, visual representations, citizenship, and polity. Many have analyzed visual images and photographs produced in periods of conflict without considering how citizenship evolved politically, economically, culturally, socially, and digitally across time and space. The inclusion of time and history into our analyses forces us to address the changing economics and technologies of the image and photography, encompassing the transformation from the camera obscura to smartphones.

Precarity and the Emancipation of Citizenship

In photography, the study of citizenship has been profoundly influenced by Ariella Azoulay's seminal works on the Israeli occupation of the Palestinian Territories.[4] The division of two regions invokes two interrelated notions of citizenship: noncitizen and citizen. Influenced by political theories, citizenship is defined as one being part of, or recognized by, the community, and the citizen being entitled to the state's services and protection. As a citizen of the occupying power, one enjoys recognition and rights, but not the noncitizens (i.e., Palestinians). Based on this, Azoulay proposes the idea of a "citizen[ship] of photography," arguing that everyone involved in photography, be it the photographer, the photographed, or the viewer, is subject to its "civil contract."[5] Azoulay's proposition is a result of examining atrocity photographs in the conflict zone made by photojournalists.

In *Regarding the Pain of Others*, Susan Sontag suggests: "Photographs of an atrocity may give rise to opposing responses. A call for peace. A cry for revenge. Or simply the bemused awareness, continually restocked by photographic information, that terrible things happen."[6] Azoulay proposes a much more definite potential outcome: viewers do not merely gaze at the abject in photographs; they shake off their bemusement and take action, either expressing sympathy or calling for preventive measures to avoid future atrocity.[7]

The nation-state is the interplay between "nation" and "state," between national identity and political autonomy, and between national integration and political sovereignty.[8] A "nation" is the consciousness of shared identity and culture, whereas the state is about territory and sovereign power.[9] Focusing on the national identity and culture, Benedict Anderson sees a nation as an imagined political community where everyone within a specific place shares, through the agency of print capitalism, their identity among that nation and its people.[10] A nation reflects a national identity in part determined by physical and political borders, and within which everyone identifies themselves as part of the same community. A nation, as an imagined community, cannot be formed without media as a catalyst, Anderson argues.

Print media (books, newspapers, and other disseminatory technologies) play an essential role in the imagined community. These print media allow individual members of the community to share experiences and to establish relationships of commonality without directly interacting with each other. Anderson, who has a great deal to say about newspapers and novels, does not pay much attention to the role of visuals, however. He was also writing before the advent of the borderless photograph and the establishment and dominance of the platforms for their circulation in an era of digital technologies and social media.

Neither Anderson's nor Azoulay's arguments engage the reality and complexity of the generation, circulation, and reception of contemporary photographic and visual representations in the era of digital technologies and social media. The technologies of visual and image productions have radically transformed, and so have the polities and economies within which they are embedded. In a postwar society like Cambodia, digital photography and smartphone cameras have rapidly democratized photography at the level of image production and simultaneously the means of circulation, as Facebook and other platforms have penetrated society. While many have been concerned about reading and writing literacies (i.e., conventional markers of "literacy"), these do not matter—they have been rendered irrelevant—when it comes to the use and consumption of smartphone cameras and social media.

So, how is citizenship generated and mobilized? In the digital age, citizenship and community take forms and assume trajectories beyond those suggested by Azoulay and Anderson.[11] Unlike the top-down vision of Anderson's print capitalism (where the citizen is always a consumer of someone else's media), citizens are now involved in their own (re)production of digital photographs without relying extensively on print enterprises capitalized by the elites. In contrast to Azoulay's focus on a citizenship of photography made possible by photojournalism, citizens of the digital camera and smartphone have the ability and authority to make and reproduce their photographs and media.[12]

With digital photographs flowing across digital and social network sites, the ability to rapidly build and expand memberships of online communities and networks goes beyond physical and preexisting political boundaries. The globalization of visual identity and recognition across borders provides citizen photographers with the rights to claim new kinds of citizenship. Citizenship is thus borderless, and it presents possibilities anywhere that the technologies, internet and social media, are accessible. The rapid enlargement of the membership of these communities and networks leverages individual citizens' power—including noncitizens'—over their rights, identity, and sovereignty. Rather than the sovereignty being defined by the rulers, photographic productions through selfies by smartphone cameras allow citizens to express their own rights, identity, and authority. They become an agent rather than a subject of photography.

Underrepresented communities are increasingly connected visually, although their rights may not be recognized by the state's service deliveries. Photographic production, circulation, and the online communities through which they flow, facilitated by Facebook and Instagram, establish a form of "emancipation." Emancipation involves the ownership and structure of power and the ability to escape the authority of others.[13] To emancipate one from the authority of someone (e.g., the state) is to become free and independent.[14] The photographic emancipation of citizens entails the exercise of power and rights against the ruler's authority in the hope of demanding freedom and sovereignty through a form of visual recognition. This emancipation exemplifies the willingness of citizens to contest the spectacular disciplinary power being constructed by the rulers, in this case that of the prime minister (PM), Hun Sen, who has for thirty-five years ruled Cambodia, since the end of the Khmer Rouge.[15]

Citizen photographers exert a capacity to influence when their images move from private space (cameras and smartphones) to the public space, that is, online social media platforms.[16] Not only do these platforms expedite circulation and interaction (through other citizens' comments); they also create common spectatorship (a social media "imagined community") in the public space.[17] Such spectatorship leverages contractual responses, especially to iconic atrocity images, images of the pain of the others, and those that document the extreme precarity of noncitizens in times of emergency.[18] While this is good for the underrepresented citizens of an oppressive and authoritarian regime like Cambodia's, involvement in online communities renders citizens prone to surveillance by the regime.[19]

An online community is managed by a machine that can process, store, and circulate images, and that machine "knows" and controls everything relating to the human online community. Friedrich Kittler argues that "machines take tasks—drawing, writing, seeing, hearing, word-processing, memory and even knowing—that once were thought unique to humans and often perform them better."[20] Machines, such as smartphones and cloud devices, are light-processing devices, reading and seeing everything, including images and personal data. Our smartphones, internet, and cloud devices are modern panoptic surveillance tools. Surveillance, indeed, is incubated in our photographic system of image production, storage, transfer, and circulation. Although individuals privately own them, these devices are better viewed, following Michel

Foucault, as akin to prison cells (which contain prisoners and their identity and visibility) that can be observed panoptically by the prison guards, and by the ruling regime and media capitalists in the digital age.[21] By viewing a photograph online or offline, everyone is covertly censored by another. Citizens' privacy, rights, space, and sovereignty are encroached and infringed by others.

Once a photograph is transmitted across digital media and platforms, it moves from a private space (analog; personal archives) to the public space (online media). The photographed may not know who has seen his or her photographs, but the internet machine has the potential to serve as a panopticon. These machines allow everyone to view each other with or without knowing each other. The ability to do so aligns with the state mission, controlling and disciplining their constituents using panoptic visual means. As identified by Foucault, the panopticon allows an agent to see everything without ever being seen. This optical media machine echoes the observations of Sontag and John Tagg on the alliance between photography, surveillance, and evidence.[22]

Sontag argued that "photographs became a useful tool of modern states in the surveillance and control of their increasingly mobile population."[23] This prophetic statement, posted before the globalized era of digital machines and social media, has been affirmed by recent works on smartphones, digital images and media, artificial intelligence, and the co-optation of global media within the state's surveillance and panoptic system. The number of Cambodian smartphone subscribers, whose figure increased exponentially from just 2.5 million in 2007 to 8 million in 2010 and reached its peak at 20 million in 2015, is highly vulnerable to cyber and technological surveillance.[24]

Focusing on digital data, and to some extent also images, Shoshana Zuboff argues that the digital community is exposing itself to great risk.[25] It is a risk of losing rights to privacy, rendering our private space visible to corporate giants. Our behavioral data and information, including our imagery and photographic identities, are being captured and analyzed by corporate media capitalists such as Google, Facebook, YouTube, Instagram, and Twitter. This data is exploited by artificial machines' algorithm (the synergy of light and machines, in Kittler's conception) and made available to private clients and, indeed, politicians and the states, at the expense of user communities.[26] Digital platform users are no longer "clients" but raw materials appropriated for commercial prediction and other commercial purposes.[27] While Zuboff's arguments are North American centric, they have implications for many (elected) authoritarian rulers in the Global South, including Cambodia. Hun Sen has openly threatened his critics by exploiting smartphone technologies to locate and arrest

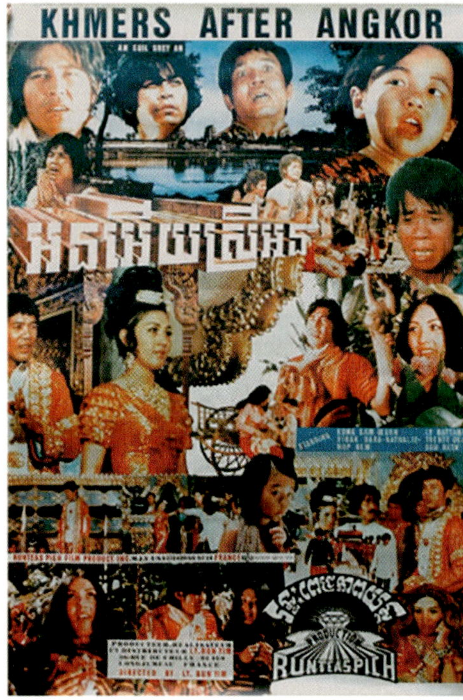

2.2 A poster of the Sangkum period by Ly Bun Yim, illustrating the vibrancy of pop music and culture. Originally from Ryum database. Screenshot from Sarah Richardot, "Cinema Reborn."

dissidents who post comments and imagery against the PM.[28] Millions of citizens have invested themselves in platforms that facilitate state surveillance.

Visual Culture as a Means of "Western" Civilization

Having secured independence from the French in 1953, King Norodom Sihanouk went on to found Sangkum Reask Nyum (Popular Socialist Community), which would endure after his death in 2012. Through his promotion of the arts, audiovisual materials flourished in urban areas and a booming film industry not only competed with the regional markets but also brought Cambodian visibility on the international stage. Remarkably, this small country produced more than three hundred films during this period.[29] Screening not only in Cambodia but also internationally, the films and a vibrant musical culture disseminated a form of Khmer popular culture, arts, and indeed identity to a wide audience (figure 2.2).

The period of modernization, progress, and prosperity was widely considered a "golden age." Photo studios flourished in urban areas where upwardly mobile consumers aspired to Western-style backdrops and makeup. Among the many photographs in the 1960s collected by Found Cambodia is one of a graduate school teacher (a well-paid and privileged public job) who was pictured in a studio in Phnom Penh.[30] Her dress and makeup very much echo those of France in the 1950s (figure 2.3).

As Cambodian cinematography developed, the visibility of King Sihanouk was promoted among the citizens of Cambodia, both rich and poor. Visibility was usually evidence of wealth and modernity, and consequently it was the poor who were not made visible through the medium of photography. While the urban population enjoyed access to public services, including education, transportation, and health care, as well as a Western "civilized" pop culture, the rural population was increasingly left behind and unseen. Cambodian rural communities were at the margin of the state's or regime's services and remained largely excluded from photography's field of visibility. However, there are some important exceptions. Photographs by the American political and cultural anthropologist Michael Vickery, for example, documented the condition of rural and indigenous communities in the uplands of Cambodia. Images like figure 2.4—in which the subjects' expressions suggest that this was their first encounter with the camera—dramatized the colossal divide between the country's elites and its subalterns.

2.3 A photograph taken in a studio in Phnom Penh in the 1960s. Photograph by Found Cambodia, http://www.foundcambodia.com.

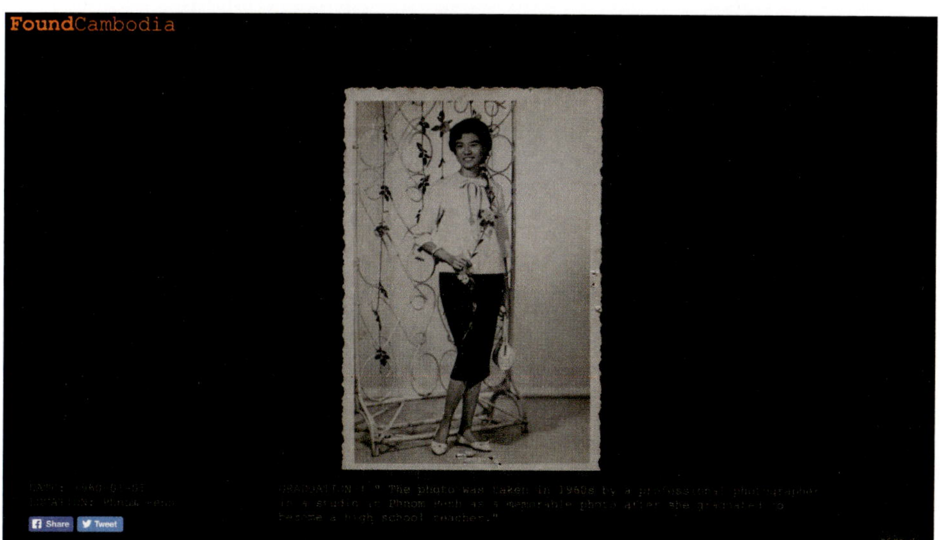

2.4 Indigenous communities in northeast Cambodia, circa 1950s. Photograph by Michael Vickery.

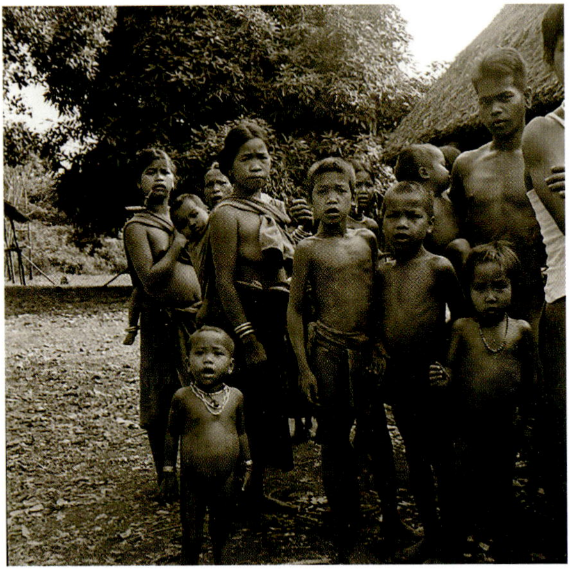

The gap between the rich and the poor was vast, and the welfare system—built for the benefit of the urban bourgeoisie—stoked class and hierarchical divides within society. This emerging disjuncture led to resistance from the Prachea Chun (Citizen Party)—founded by, among others, Pol Pot—which advanced an egalitarian and utopian society inspired by Marxism-Leninism and Mao Zedong's communism. The party then resorted to an armed rebellion against the bourgeois society entrenched by the Sangkum regime, which, in due course, was overthrown by General Lon Nol's coup d'état in 1970.

From Bourgeois Regime to Apocalypse

After defeating the Lon Nol regime, on April 17, 1975, the Khmer Rouge (KR) renamed the country "Democratic Kampuchea" and evacuated the urban population, consisting of about 2 million citizens, to the rural areas. The aim was to destroy what it saw as a corrupt, urban bourgeoisie and associated lifestyles, and reduce them to the status of the wider peasantry. After the invasion by Vietnam in 1978, it is estimated that about 1.7 million people died and more than three hundred mass graves were found throughout the country.[31] In addition to being characterized as revenge for the class inequalities intensified by the previous sociopolitical regime, the killing also demonstrated a complete absence of common citizenship or "khmerness."[32] Khmerness is a long-standing auto-valorization and collective identity of the Cambodian people. This involves self-essentializations such as being polite, helpful, respectful, and calm as part of a collective community. Being nonviolent and noninvasive was widely seen to reflect the centuries-old Buddhist values of the country.

Having seen how the KR cadres targeted wealthy elites, people understood that they had to strip themselves of the accoutrements of what were now considered privileged occupations—teachers, skilled workers, businesspersons, and officials—and divested themselves of materialistic belongings that suggested wealth. Possession of these could put their lives at risk under the new policy of the KR. To avoid being identified, people destroyed photographs and other forms of identity, or buried them in the ground, either before or during their enforced sojourn to the countryside.

The KR cadres watched citizens day and night. They spied on and listened to every conversation taking place. One interlocutor, Sineh Siv, recalled how a guard raided her hut and questioned her mother about the location of her father. Her mother lied to the guard, saying that "we were divorced because we did not get along." The guard then asked, "How did you not get along but have four children?" As the guard disappeared in the dark, she recalled, "My mother asked me to burn the photographs and to boil a kettle of water on the fire. I did not know why my mother asked me to burn those priceless photographs." Later, Sineh realized that it was to destroy evidence of the family lineage.[33] Having photographs of any sort at that time was evidence of a dangerous identity. The expense of photography could easily lead to accusations that one was a bourgeois beneficiary of the Sangkum or Lon Nol regimes.

Photography's subjunctive, or "as if," nature opens an ideal space for aspiration, consumption, and modernity, which in this context was dangerous.[34] It allowed a photographed person to celebrate and participate in modernity through the use of backdrops in the studio. Traveling by plane, owning a vehicle, speaking on the telephone, viewing TV, and living in a mansion were all possible in the proleptic space of the studio, but the desire of people to participate in a consumption-led modernity also produced tokens of potential incrimination under the KR. Aspirations and fantasies that photography promoted were treated as achieved facts by the KR, for whom every celebration of prosperity pointed to a harsh underbelly of deprivation. And the very fact of having economic access to the photo studio confirmed one's position on the side of the oppressor. Viewed by Pol Pot as an impediment to the creation of a new and equal society, Western modernity became an object of vilification. As the KR took over Phnom Penh and other major cities, it also burned books to expunge what it claimed were the corrosive ideas of Western intellectuals.[35]

The surviving photographs that Sineh has were from her father, whom she believed had been in France but had, in fact, returned to Cambodia. (The KR lured intellectuals studying and living abroad to return for the betterment of the country.) Hiding his biographical background, he secretly kept a few photos of his family hidden until the regime collapsed (figure 2.5). Together with his photographs, her father then returned to Battambang province to reunite with surviving members of the family.[36]

During the KR regime, a black-and-white photograph like figure 2.6 could cost the lives of the entire family and relatives. Taken in the 1960s, this photo records the identity of the entire family lineage, which could have been easily identified and exploited by the KR. The photo was retrieved from a person who was living in Battambang and was then digitized in the United States. It is now being used by a child in the photo (now sixty-seven years old), not only to trace and identify any surviving siblings but to recall the past. This photograph survived, but of the forty-nine siblings in this photo, sixteen were either disappeared or killed by the KR. Since it has been digitized, the photograph is now enlarging the visible space it occupies from analog to digital space, where the ability to gaze overcomes the physical boundaries of where the survivors live in Cambodia, the United States, and France. While the digitization of the surviving photograph preserves memory, it also ensures the transgenera-

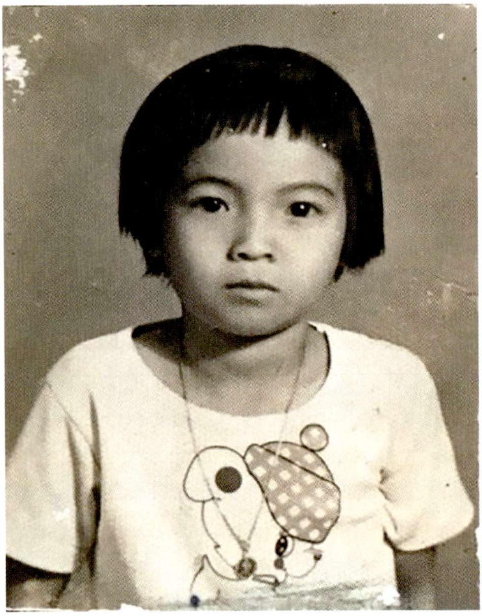

2.5 A young Seneh Siv, 1970s. Rephotographed by Seneh Siv, 2018.

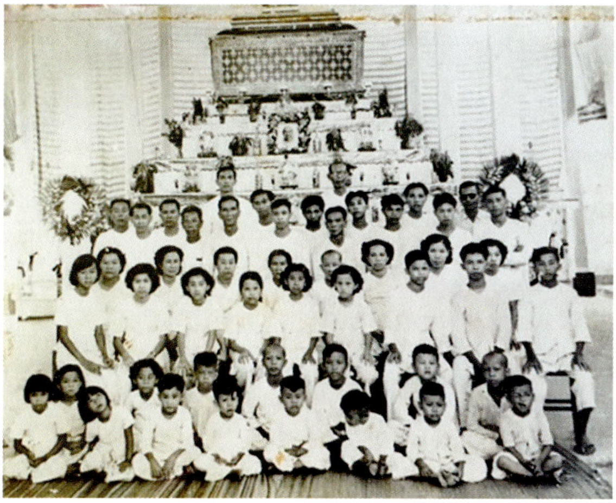

2.6 A photograph depicting the lineage of a family, taken on the occasion of a grandfather's funeral, in the 1960s.

tional transmission of trauma as a force that endures in Cambodia's politics of postatrocity.[37]

Using photographs for visual identity during the KR regime was, however, comparatively rare. A former KR comrade said, "We had only some notes written by the group leaders mentioning names of anyone wishing to travel to and from anywhere. We recognized one another based on written text, and everyday contact, not photographs."[38] Nhem En, a photographer for the KR regime and for S-21 (Security Prison 21, the infamous site of interrogation and torture by the KR in Phnom Penh), said that experts from mainland China provided their photography training and that cameras were used either to document the communist party's leaders like Pol Pot, comrades of the KR, and the visits of Chinese delegates, or for propaganda magazine production.

Cameras were, nevertheless, important tools in the political ideology of the KR Angkar and for the organization of power and administration.[39] Since many of the KR cadres—often poor farmers who did not have the opportunity to attend school—were illiterate, visual imagery inspired them to remain loyal to the party. Photographs envisioning a utopian society, depicting collective farming, building, and manufacturing, were published in the Angkar magazines, such as *Yuvachun-Yuvaneary Padevath* (Boys and girls of the revolution), January 1974 to November 1978; *Tung Padevath* (The revolutionary flag), January 1975 to September 1978; and *Tung Krahorm* (The red flag), 1975 to 1978. The aim was to inspire the youth to collectively build a utopian society. Photographs, including landscapes with citizens working hard in the paddy fields and factories, were reproduced in these magazines to demonstrate the effort of nation building (figures 2.7–2.10).[40] The photographs allowed the cadres to

2.7 Khmer Rouge's model houses being constructed. Photograph by Documentation Centre of Cambodia.

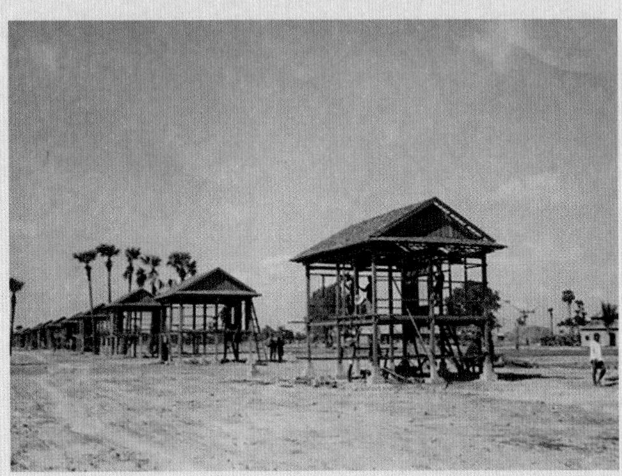

2.8 Khmer Rouge soldiers transplanting rice. Photograph by Documentation Centre of Cambodia.

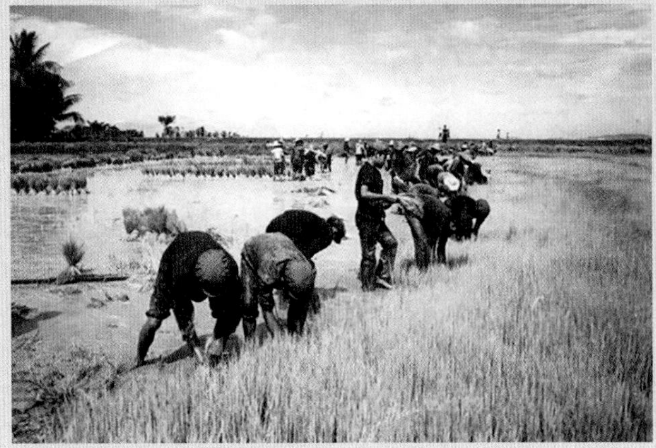

2.9 Female Khmer Rouge cadres working in a textile factory. Photograph by Documentation Centre of Cambodia.

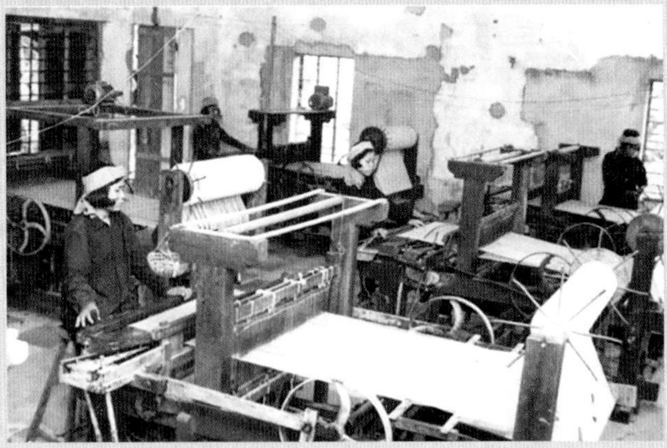

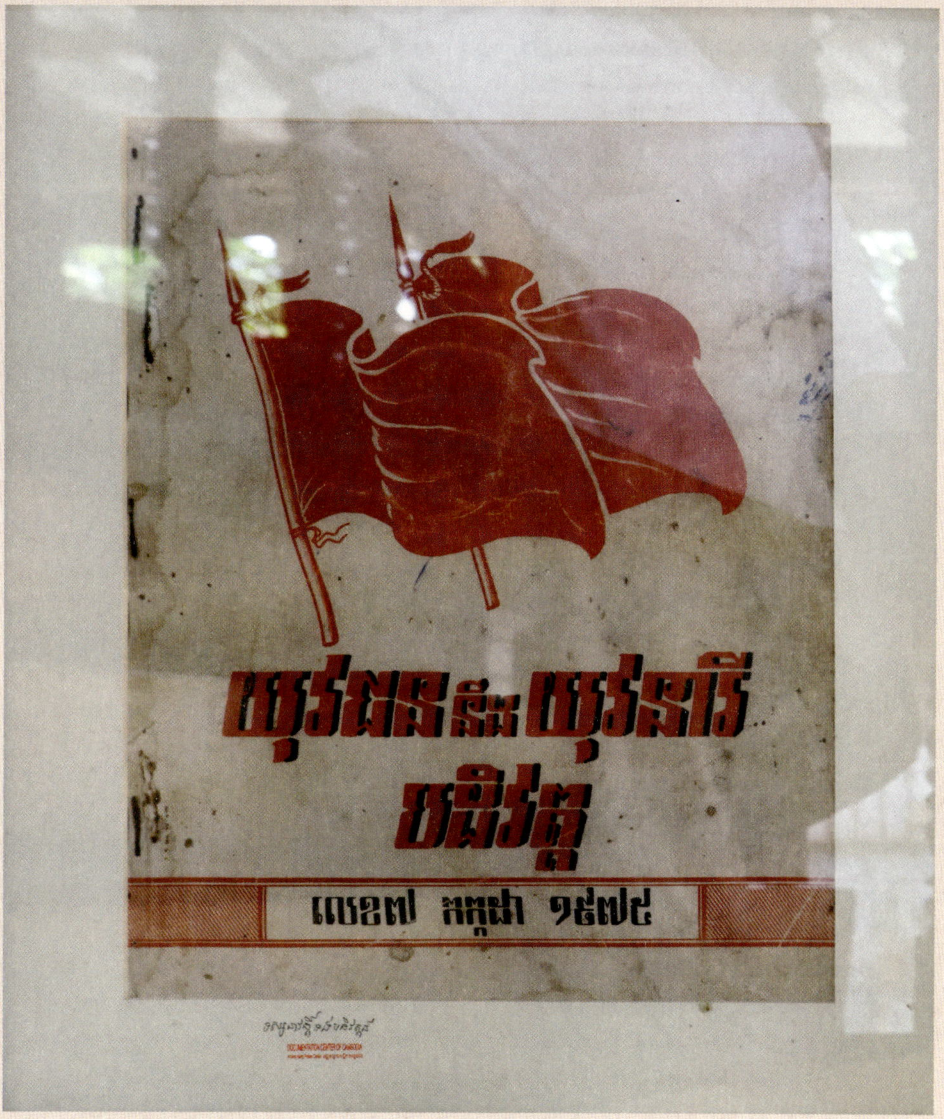

2.10 Khmer Rouge's youth revolution flag and magazine.

envision the future that was being promised to them. A photo of equally sized model houses being built for all Cambodians by the KR was likely intended to instill an egalitarian expectation and to motivate the cadres to strive to achieve collective goals, having the equal status of citizenship, no differentiation between rich or poor, but adequate shelter and sufficient food for all to consume. In the end, however, there was dystopia, not the revolutionary prosperity that was also promised by Mao Zedong's cultural revolution.[41]

Photography was used to identify and provide a record of citizens viewed by the KR as their enemies. In 1978 the KR launched a purging program to exterminate spies from Vietnam, and Vietnamese soldiers (who had been in Cambodia during the US–Vietnam war and did not return to their country after the collapse of the Lon Nol regime) and people who were accused of being CIA or other foreign agents who had served under the Lon Nol regime. The purge started in the eastern areas of Cambodia, and as the purge spread, a number of the former KR's militants or members, including Hun Sen, the present-day PM, defected and fled to Vietnam. Suspects from around the country were rounded up, with some sent to prison for interrogation and some killed immediately. When a suspect was arrested, the KR cadre would say, "The organization is sending him or her to be reeducated," and the person in custody was sure to realize that he or she was about to die. Unlike the Chinese cultural revolution, during which culprits were executed publicly to discourage others, the KR executed its victims secretly.[42] These killings were also a punishment orchestrated to intensify a terror that helped ensure citizens' obedience to the KR. In addition to those killed elsewhere, at least twenty thousand prisoners were photographed at a prison called S-21.[43] Once victims were photographed, they knew that they were "about to die."[44] Being photographed in S-21 signaled impending death.[45] The photo IDs, taken as victims were about to die, exert a chilling power. The subjects of the images were then sent to the killing field at the Cheung Ek graveyard, located on the outskirts of Phnom Penh. These S-21 photographs have become an icon of Cambodia's experience of atrocity. These emblems of the spectacular power of "punishment" (in Foucault's terms) not only left their mark on survivors but also morphed into disciplinary icons for the young generation. The former prison S-21 is now a genocide museum that exhibits the "pain of others," attracting millions of tourists from all over the world (figure 2.11). It is a highly recommended and top-rated tourist destination, but it is less attractive to survivors of the KR and the Cambodian populations in general, for it symbolizes a threat that still haunts Cambodia.

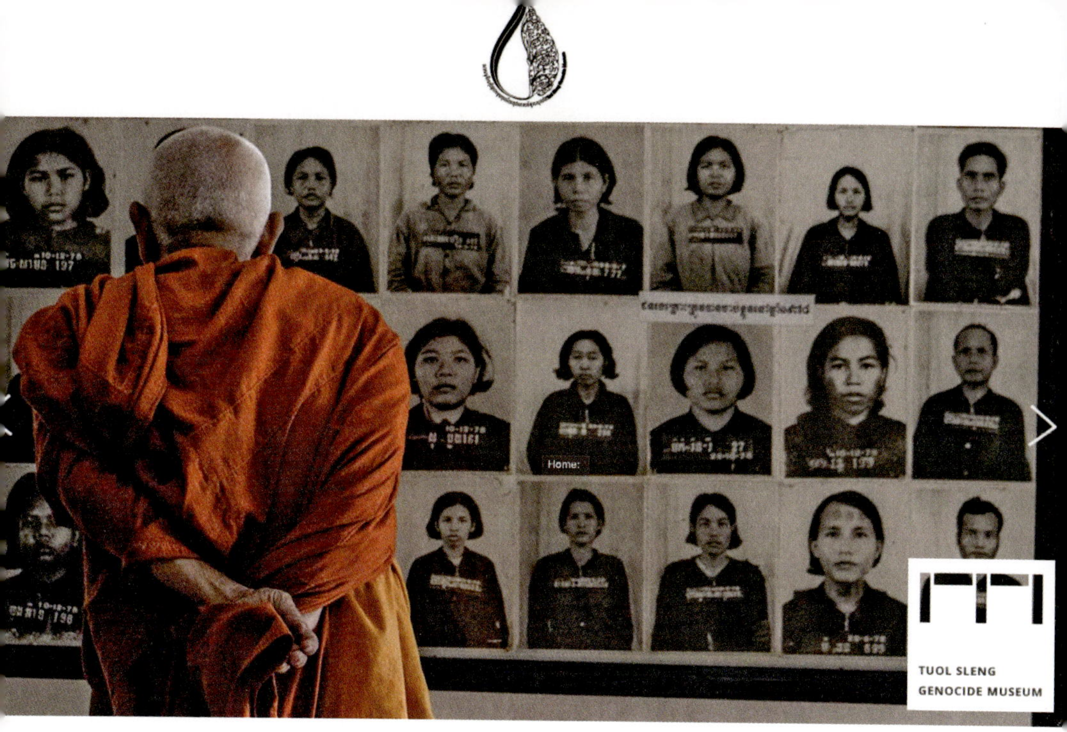

2.11 A Buddhist monk gazing at the ID photographs of S-21 prisoners. Screenshot from Toul Sleng Genocide Museum's website.

Contingencies of the Past, Present, and Future

In the aftermath, photographs of the KR have served as a locus of the politics of collective memory and disciplinary citizenship in Cambodia. Photographs from S-21 and other locations have reappeared in Cambodian society as vehicles for both remembrance and traumatization. Not only have these recalled atrocities and trauma, but they also serve as mediums for the transgenerational transmission of trauma from one generation to another.[46] The S-21 photographs transformed from analog to digital, expanding their sphere of circulation to create a common spectatorship. However, the transformation of atrocity images is contested, since they are, on the one hand, used politically to traumatize the victims or survivors of the civil war and KR. On the other hand, different spectators have provided different—contingent—readings for these photographs, using them to learn, remember, and prevent further atrocity. In the postapocalypse, atrocity images are used by politicians and rul-

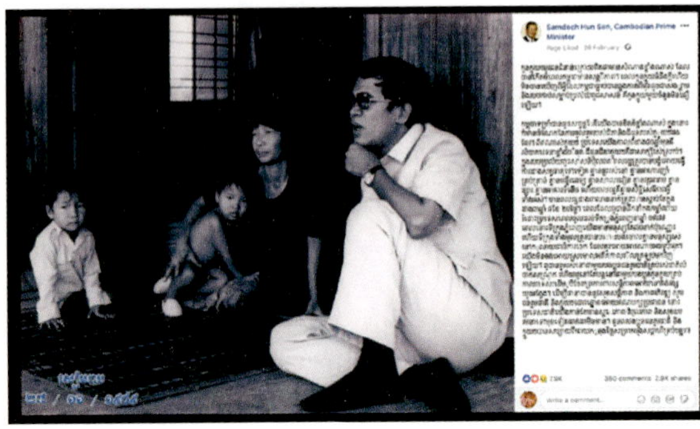

2.12 A screenshot of Prime Minister Hun Sen's photograph posted on his Facebook page, April 2019.

ers to discipline citizens. They have become part of an effective disciplinary strategy, traumatizing ordinary citizens or electorates to support the ruler's grip on power. Many contemporary visual art pieces that aim to heal the trauma of the KR haunt the "broken courage" of the present generation.[47] These images, which appear annually on social media, are deployed as part of a panoply of repressive measures used against liberal critics.

Black-and-white photographs of Hun Sen, from before, during, and after the KR, have been repeatedly circulated. He (or his agents) posted these photographs on his Facebook page (which has more than 12.8 million followers) with the intention of stoking collective memories of the darkness of the KR regime and cementing memories of his role (with Vietnamese support) in the liberation of the country. Typical of many examples, on May 18, 2018, he posted a photograph taken in 1989 showing him sitting with a family in Siem Reap province (figure 2.12). Circulated before the general election in 2018, it was intended to underline the differences between the current state of development and the past atrocity, and called for the electoral support of the Cambodian People's Party (CPP) to maintain peace, stability, and the prosperity of the nation.

The messages and the aesthetics of the photograph directly evoke the KR period. The caption says, "To assure peace and development, all our compatriots, nephews and nieces need to vote for CPP. Our nation will, definitely, gain even more stability, prosperity and happiness." This message resonates with Roland Barthes's hypothesis that "electoral photography is therefore above all the acknowledgment of something deep and irrational co-extensive with politics."[48] Hun Sen's portraits and photographs posted on social media not only aim at mobilizing electoral support but also clearly discipline constituents through a self-interested "Never Again," the perpetual invocation of a horrific past.

Photographs like those shown in figures 2.13a and 2.13b, screenshots from a long video narrating the PM's plan for national salvation, are used in propaganda warning of the dangers of returning to the killing fields.[49] These types of photographs are posted on his page throughout the year but come thick and fast in the lead-up to January 7 (Victory Day), when the ruling party celebrates national salvation. Additionally, every year on May 20, in places where mass graves were discovered, the event called Tngai Chong Kom Hoeung, or Day of Anger, is organized and featured on social media and almost all of Cambodia's television channels. In this event, students, youth, and military personnel wear black clothes and play the roles of KR cadres as they perform the violent torture of victims, beating and killing if one is accused of making a mistake, stealing food, or betraying the Angkar (figure 2.14). The day reenacts the suffering and vulnerability of the Cambodians, with the intention of sparking hatred against the KR regime (figure 2.15). As people view the events either on screen or in person, the reenactment transmits trauma, pain, and suffering to the younger generations. As Ulrich Baer claims, those who view photographic scenes of trauma internalize a responsibility for the evidence of atrocity embodied in the image.[50] The reenactment of atrocity events goes far beyond the act of (re)witnessing history so that the transgenerational transmission of the wound inflicts further pain and suffering.[51] The reenactment of the Day of Anger also opens up the subversive dangers of repetition and iteration, provoking popular comparisons of human rights under the present ruling regime and under the KR (1975–79). Figure 2.14, a Facebook meme juxtaposing images from 1979 and 2019, aligns the current regime's soldiers torturing ordinary citizens during a demonstration against land grabbing (*right*) with a similar image of a KR soldier killing innocent citizens in 1979 (*left*).

The circulation of these black-and-white images of KR atrocity in the early twenty-first century produces effects more complex than the redemptive "cruel radiance" expounded by Susie Linfield.[52] While ostensibly on the side of liberation and freedom, in practice these images are mobilized as part of a disciplinary politics whose aim is the suppression of dissent. During my fieldwork, many interlocutors agreed that we should learn about past atrocities, and that, for instance, a KR app should be developed to educate students. However, others demanded strict ethical principles that avoid exacerbating adverse impacts on the victims. As I visited Toul Sleng museum, it was clear that not many Cambodians wish to visit there, and the museum recently launched a fundraising program to mobilize and motivate Cambodians to visit so they could witness the photographs of their compatriots who were "about to die." The S-21 prisoner photos and the images from the Day of Anger point,

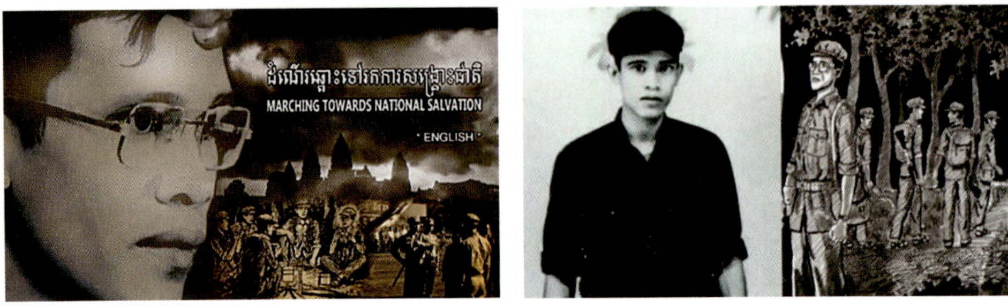

2.13a & 2.13b Screenshots of Prime Minister Hun Sen's national salvation film, showing his use of archival images.

for many Cambodians, not only to a past that they hope never to repeat but also to a future that hovers in the near distance. Images of past atrocities are mobilized by political elites like Hun Sen and have played a key role in securing his hold on power for more than three decades, along with other strategies, such as controlling the army, alienating the opposition, and co-opting other challengers. However, the control and manipulation of images, and especially photography, is of great importance to Hun Sen. It is well known that he cares very much if anyone harms or burns his photographs.

Creating a close relationship with Hun Sen is the route, for many, to fortune and power; many wish to ally with him. Being close to the PM would help protect anyone from being intruded on or harmed. We can observe this in everyday practices in which photographic portraits of the PM and other powerful people are installed at street corners, in offices, and in the home. A photograph showing oneself standing next to the PM allows the subject to claim a closeness to the PM, and that generates the authority to influence (or even to intimidate) less-favored clients in entrenched patronage networks. Photographs with Hun Sen were often taken at special events, including the conferring of awards, medals, or prizes to those who contributed to Cambodia's development. "It was very rare to have a photograph with the premier unless you have a strong connection," said a photographer. Those fortunate enough to appear in such photographs would then have the image printed at a large size with an expensive frame before hanging it in their office or at home to evidence how closely the owner was connected to the fountainhead of power.

The desire to be photographed with the premier is evident in everyday practice. In graduation events, we can see how proximity of Cambodian youth

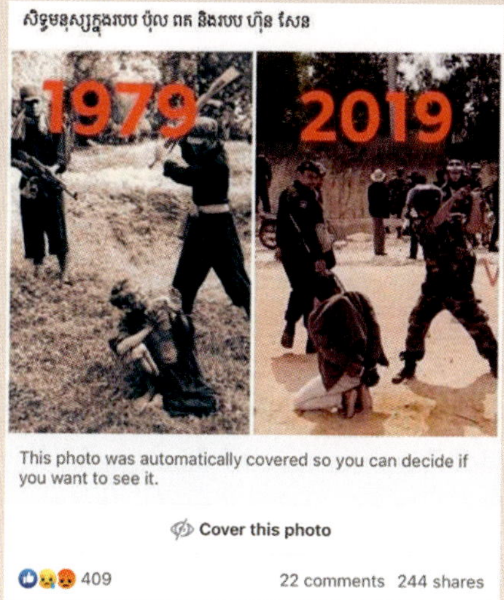

2.14 A Facebook meme comparing human rights in 1979 and 2019.

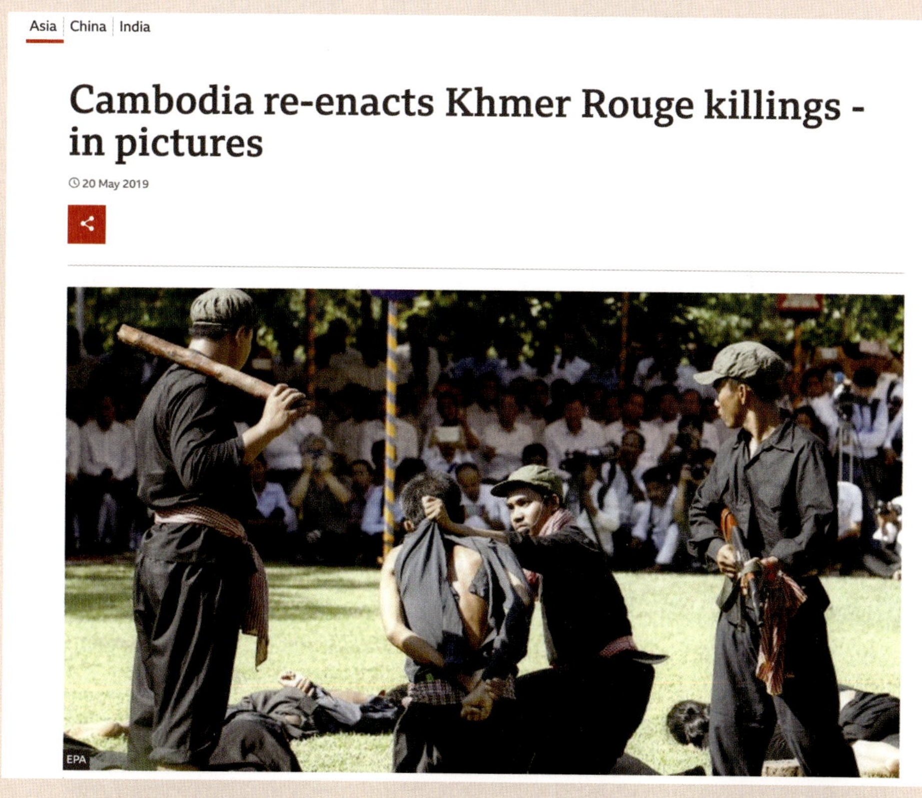
Asia | China | India

Cambodia re-enacts Khmer Rouge killings - in pictures

20 May 2019

EPA

2.15 The reenactment of Khmer Rouge torture and execution. Screenshot from BBC.

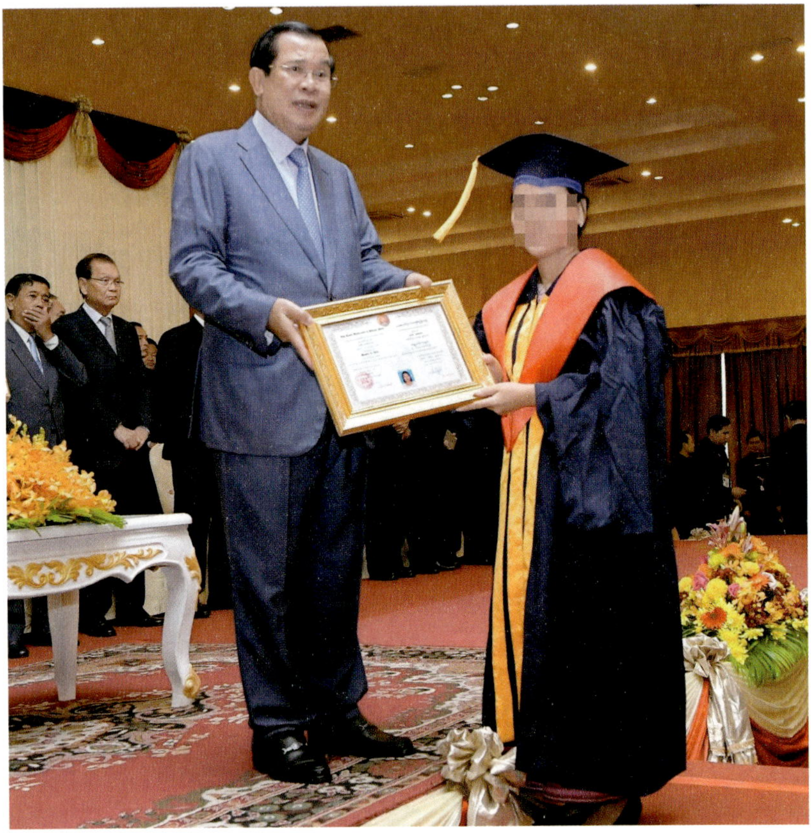

2.16 Photoshopped with Prime Minister Hun Sen. The graduate did not actually receive the degree directly from the premier.

to the PM helps envision a bright future after university. Outside the ceremony hall, commercial photographers covering the event would ask, "Would you like to photoshop your graduate photo with our prime minister?" Before 2014, most graduates chose this option: one photographer said "80 percent" of those he asked. The price was as low as $2.50 per photo. Having a photograph with Hun Sen—through whatever means—"manifests how powerful the owner is!" said a photographer. Such photos were displayed in different ways: hung in the home or office, or posted on Facebook as evidence of the power of a contagious magic that connected the humble graduate to the highest power in the land (figure 2.16).

In domestic settings and elsewhere, photographs of Hun Sen, sometimes with his wife, are hung on walls and held as protective talismans during protests (figures 2.17–2.19). "You can even see his portrait in someone's watch," Sopheap says.[53] His presence recalls that formerly enjoyed by images of Pol Pot or Mao Zedong. The multiplicity of images and his treatment as a king or even a god perversely echo the KR's notion that Angkar (the apparatus of the regime) has eyes like a pineapple.[54] In this powerful metaphor, the KR Angkar has eyes that can see in all directions, giving it a panoptic vision. In the same way, Hun Sen's portraits spy on his subordinates, officials, citizens, activists, opponents, and anyone else who crosses his encompassing field of vision. Almost all schools, pagodas, streets, and bridges bear his name and face. His presence through his photograph colonizes space and proclaims him as the only hero capable of rebuilding Cambodia's nation-state, after overthrowing the Pol Pot regime. Whereas the KR regime was marked by the invisibility of photographs as their anxious owners hurried to bury and hide them, in contemporary Cambodia, the more photographs are displayed or the higher they are displayed on the wall, the more power is acquired. Displaying photographs of Hun Sen and his wife just slightly underneath the royal family's portraits (Norodom Sihanouk and the queen) manifests how Hun Sen competes with the authority of the royal family (figure 2.17). Many see Hun Sen as a modern incarnation of a peasant king, Sdach Korn, who, five hundred years ago in Cambodia's history, assassinated an unjust king. Hun Sen's new era of leadership is even named "Cambodia's second kingdom" in recognition of this mythic echo.[55]

In contrast to the billboards illustrated by Strassler in Indonesia, where party billboard photographs are erected for the dissemination of political charisma and as part of election campaigns, Hun Sen's billboard and other photographs around the country are much more concerned with embodying and exercising power through demanding respect from (or in some cases, worship by) ordinary citizens.[56] They are more like photographic supplements to KR's panoptic pineapple. Some Cambodian citizens and officials do undeniably treat him like a god, as can be observed during his inaugurations and other special occasions. Officials are expected to bow down and *sam peah* (putting palms together as one does while worshipping Buddha). Some senior officials have to kneel and sam peah while speaking with him on the stage. If you are below the stage in the audience, you will need to stand up and sam peah when the supreme leader mentions his or her name.

2.17 Portraits of Hun Sen and his wife displayed just beneath the royal portraits at Anlong Veng district office. Photograph posted publicly on Facebook.

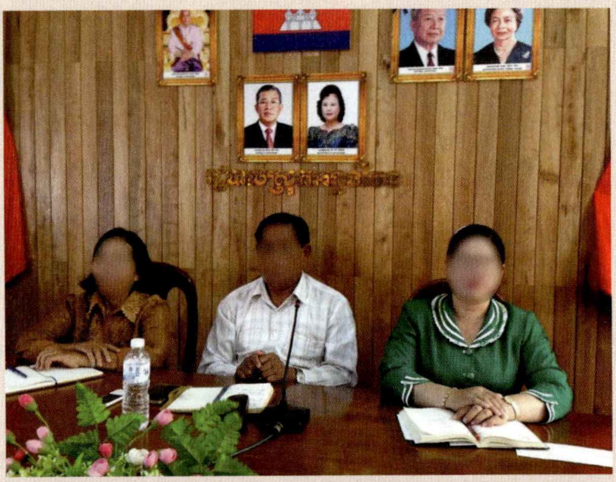

2.18 Hun Sen's photograph on the street. Photography by Sokphea Young, November 2017.

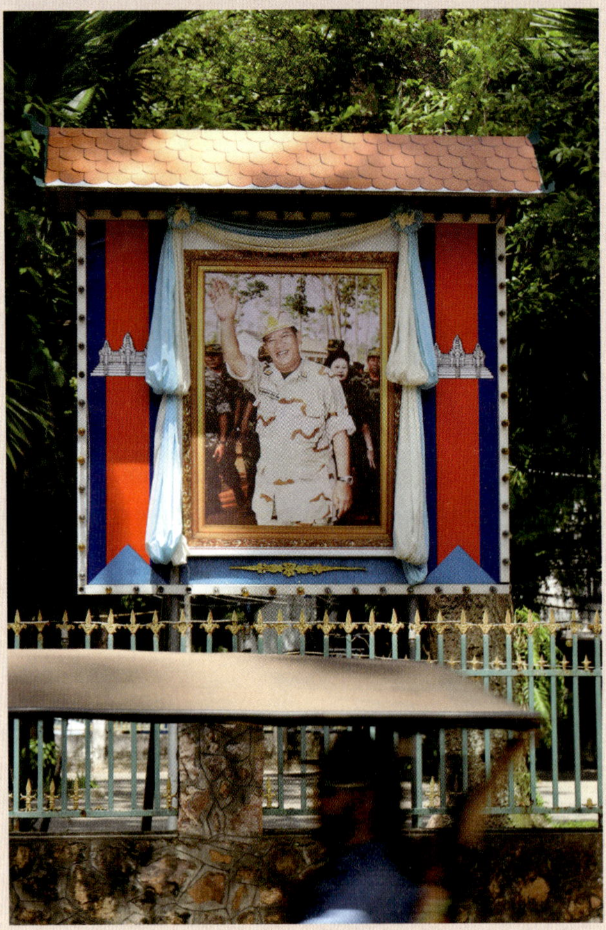

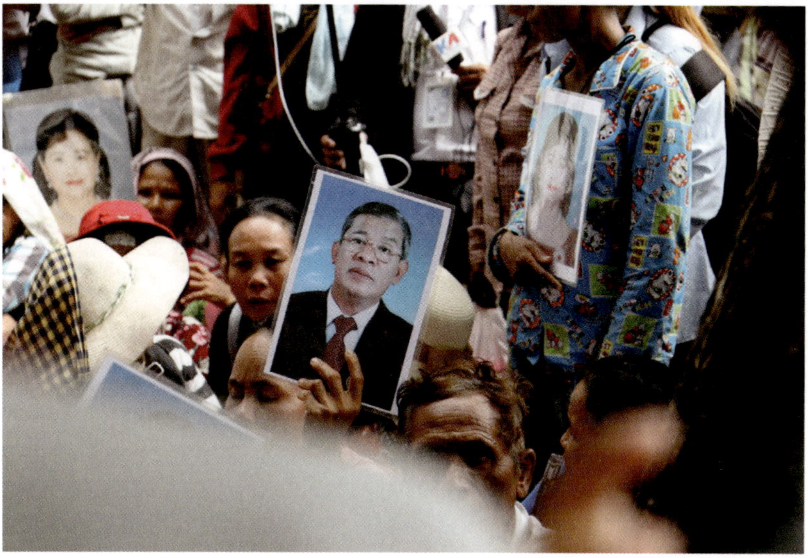

2.19 A protester holding portraits of Hun Sen and his wife as protective talismans during a protest against land grabbing. Photograph by Sokphea Young, May 2018.

From Scarcity to Abundance: Enlarging Space

While photography was a scarce resource during the war and the apocalyptic KR period, this is no longer the case given the burgeoning of photographic devices in the postwar economic liberalization. Even in very remote areas and among indigenous communities, affordable smartphones and camera phones have sharply increased and with this the circulation of images has grown hugely. The circulation of digital photographs across social networks has entirely replaced conventional chemical photographic production. The online social networks construct imagined platforms of visibility both within and beyond the nation-state. In 2017 Cambodians uploaded at least 1.2 million photographs daily onto Facebook from smartphone cameras.[57] As of now, the number of uploaded photographs vastly outnumbers the country's total population of 16 million people, of which 8.8 million subscribe to Facebook and 0.72 million are on Instagram.[58] However, in the act of posting on social media, the images' owners accept the authority of the media corporations that provide these platforms.

In the past, as an indigenous woman in a northeastern province of Cambodia explained, "to take a photograph, we needed to travel to the [district or provincial] center where photo studios are located." Sovy Lam, an indigenous woman who is now working for a local NGO in the province, said: "Before 2006, photographers were invited to photograph people in the village once in a while, especially during ritual events."[59] From 2010 onward, everything has changed since a laterite road, even though not very smooth, has connected her village, and mobile phone services have become available following the erection of a transmission tower covering the entire village. In 2014 internet connectivity became available. The community began learning about new modes of communication such as Facebook.

Given the low rates of literacy in the region, one may wonder how Facebook could be mastered. This was no obstacle at all since the rural practice of Facebook mostly involves uploading and sharing photographs taken on camera phones. The mobile phone sellers taught the users, and they then began learning from each other in the village. Sovy said, "Now, I can see many young adults in my community go online. They *bong hors* [post or upload] and share videos and photographs they produced by their smartphones." "I do not know what these mean to them, but everything is in the circle and connected. I sometimes do not want to be friends with them because they keep tagging their photographs every post," Sovy added. She is an indigenous woman with about five thousand Facebook friends in a village of fewer than one hundred families (figure 2.20).

The rapid adoption of modern communication technologies, such as smartphones and social media, by the young generation newly emerged from civil war underlines the hunger and desire to participate in modernity by marginalized and underrepresented people. The hunger and desire for advanced technologies testify to the older generation's belief in the Buddhist prophecy of possessing "magic ears and eyes," the ability to see and hear each other from afar, in the near future. Smartphones and social media offer a "magical" means of communication, proving the reality of the prophecy. Together with the reasonable price of internet 3G or 4G, networking through photography and social media platforms has thoroughly penetrated the indigenous communities of northeast Cambodia irrespective of literacy rates. For Cambodians as well as the indigenous people, seeing is more important than reading, and seeing is more important than hearing. This resonates with John Berger's argument: seeing comes before words, and the child looks and recognizes before speaking.[60] Nonliterate users find seeing and picturing more central in their lives. The ability to see on Facebook without meeting in person is the realization of Buddhist prophecy.

In Bo Keo district of Ratanakiri province, a young Jaray (a member of an ethnic group) who barely reads the Khmer language scrolled Facebook on an

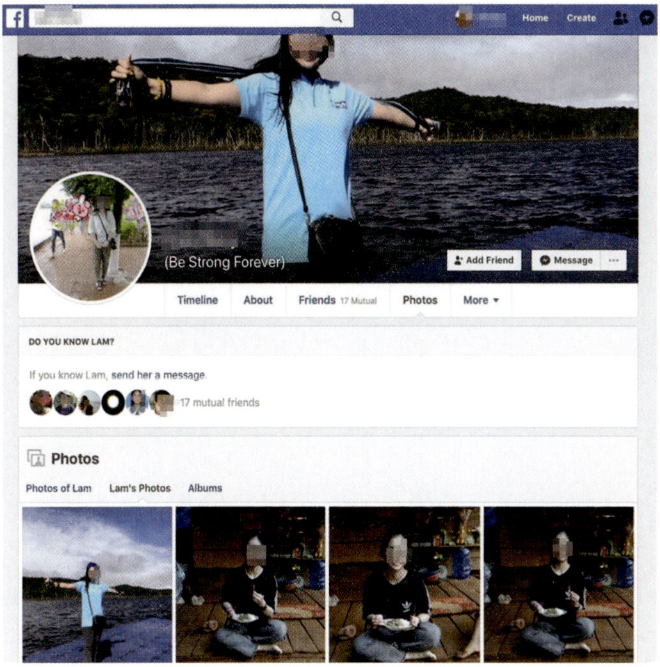

2.20 Sovy Lam's Facebook profile. Screenshot from Facebook, October 2018.

unknown brand smartphone. She was texting and sending images on Facebook Messenger to her friends. With a beautiful camera, this 100,000 riel (US$25) smartphone connects to internet cellular 3G. She could post and share an unlimited number of photographs: images of herself and wider communities and social worlds (figure 2.21). Considering space as a social relation where different spectators, including the state, interact in visibility, the endeavor to produce one's own photographs and identity within this space resists the photographic subjectivity of the state, including the legacy of the KR.[61] While citizen photographers exert their agency, through the production of selfies, portraits, and photo IDs, they serve, to a certain extent, as a "reminder" of the S-21 photo IDs. Commissioned to take photo IDs of high school students, Khvay Samnang, a Cambodian artist-photographer, comments on the similarity of contemporary S-21 photo IDs (figure 2.22). This work, titled *Reminder*, testifies to the way deeply ingrained trauma and memory can resurface through everyday visual practices.[62]

Affordable smartphones and digital cameras allow everyone to make their own photographs. This democratization has transformed the practice of Cambodians' vernacular photography. In the earlier period of scarcity, one interloc-

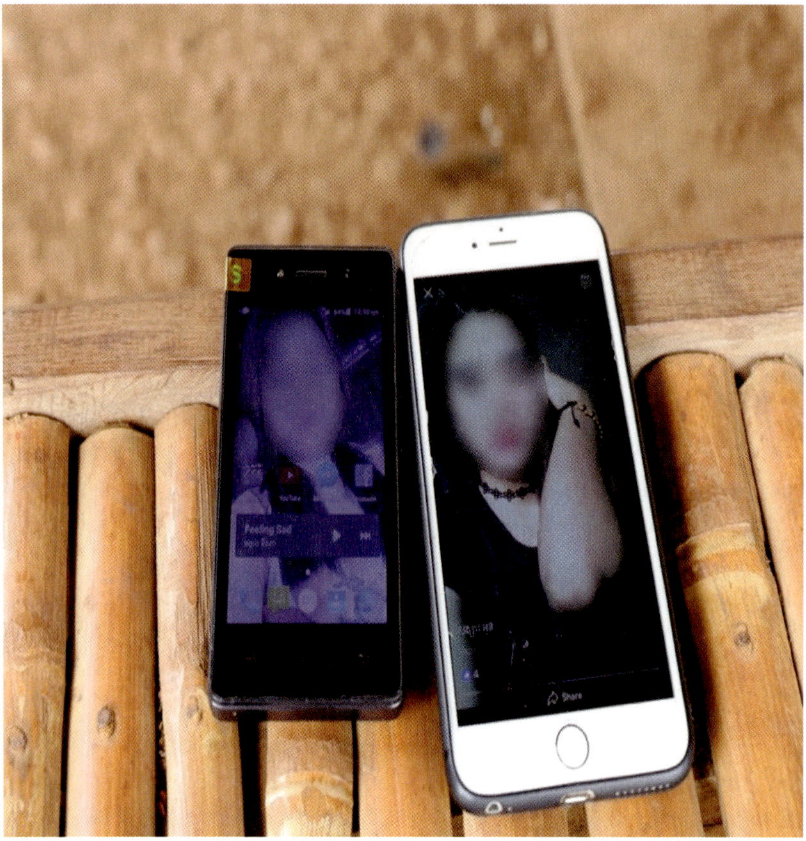

2.21 An indigenous woman's selfie on her Facebook profile. Photograph by Sokphea Young, October 2018.

utor demonstrated how he had reprinted an existing photograph and extracted his face to make a photo ID for a job application in the early 1980s (figure 2.23).

Emancipation: Reclaiming Citizenship, Rights, and Sovereignty

Before the war, the state and rulers claimed sovereignty over citizenship, yet Cambodians, in the aftermath, battled for their sovereignty by enacting citizenship and rights through photographic media. Eased by the advanced mediums of photography, Cambodian citizens are ever-present on the internet and social media. On these platforms, they constitute a new force that aims to deviate from authority. Cambodians have performed their citizenship and rights through photographs that already embody power or performative potential—usually known as the "contract" in the *civil contract of photography*, that is, the ability of photographs to affect spectators.[63] The proliferation and circulation of photographs online, as is the case with the subject of figure 2.20, is an exercise of power demanding interaction and recognition among the subject's community and beyond. Underrepresented communities, who can be considered as noncitizens and who have differential access to the state's social services, exploit photography. This can be photography by themselves or by photographic brokers: photo-activists or citizen journalists.

This photojournalism covers the most newsworthy issues, such as protest over land expropriation by the political elites and companies (figure 2.24). Citizen journalists face significant challenges and intimidation. Frequently intimidated by the police and violent contractors (or private company guards or those employed by the state or local authority), they can be easily labeled as part of the opposition that visualizes the irregularities and violence of the

2.22 Khvay Samnang's *Reminder* (2008), in which school photo IDs evoke memories of S-21 photo IDs.

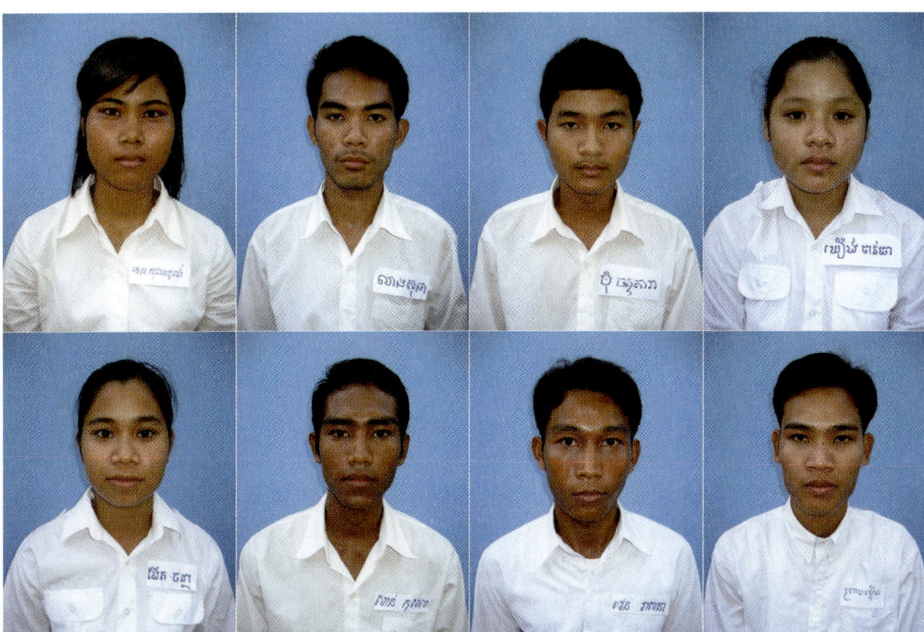

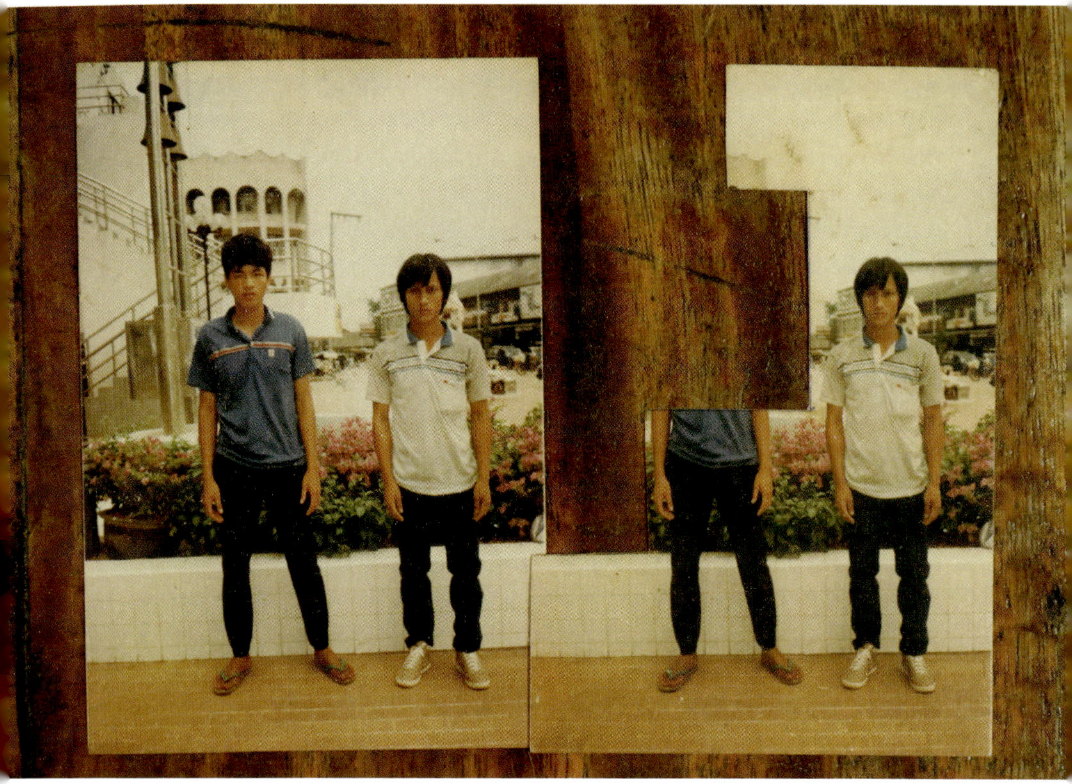

2.23 Preserving the original when reproduction was scarce in the 1980s. Rephotographed by Sokphea Young, October 2018.

state rather than the positive side of it, performing something similar to the X-ray of corruption in India, as described by William Mazzarella.[64]

A leading citizen photojournalist was recently summoned by the municipal court of Phnom Penh for questioning about his involvement with a deputy of the Cambodia National Rescue Party, Khem Sokha, and was accused of plotting a "color revolution" to overthrow the regime. Despite the allegation, his photographs and video recordings circulated on social media, especially Facebook, and became a weapon to evidence and counter the oppressive state or agent thereof. As the photojournalist's slogan goes, "I am a citizen journalist, I always share Cambodia's news to the world." In one of his posts on Facebook, he warned, "If you do not do anything at all, you will be victimized [by the state or elites] one day; it is not yet your turn." This was a message intended to mobilize citizen journalists and other people to act for and on behalf of those who are victimized and denied full citizenship and rights. Inspired by Kem Ley, the outspoken activist slain in broad daylight in 2016 in Phnom Penh, he traveled widely around the country to take photographs, which he shared on social media. This type of photographic work invokes the viewers and ordinary populace to take action collectively and to demand justice for the affected communities. Such activism is beyond the definition of Nicholas Mirzoeff's visual activism, the interaction between pixel and action.[65] The aesthetic contents enact a form of citizen power, provoking action that ultimately aims at influencing the state to redress its failure.

2.24 A citizen photojournalist. Screenshot from Facebook, July 2018.

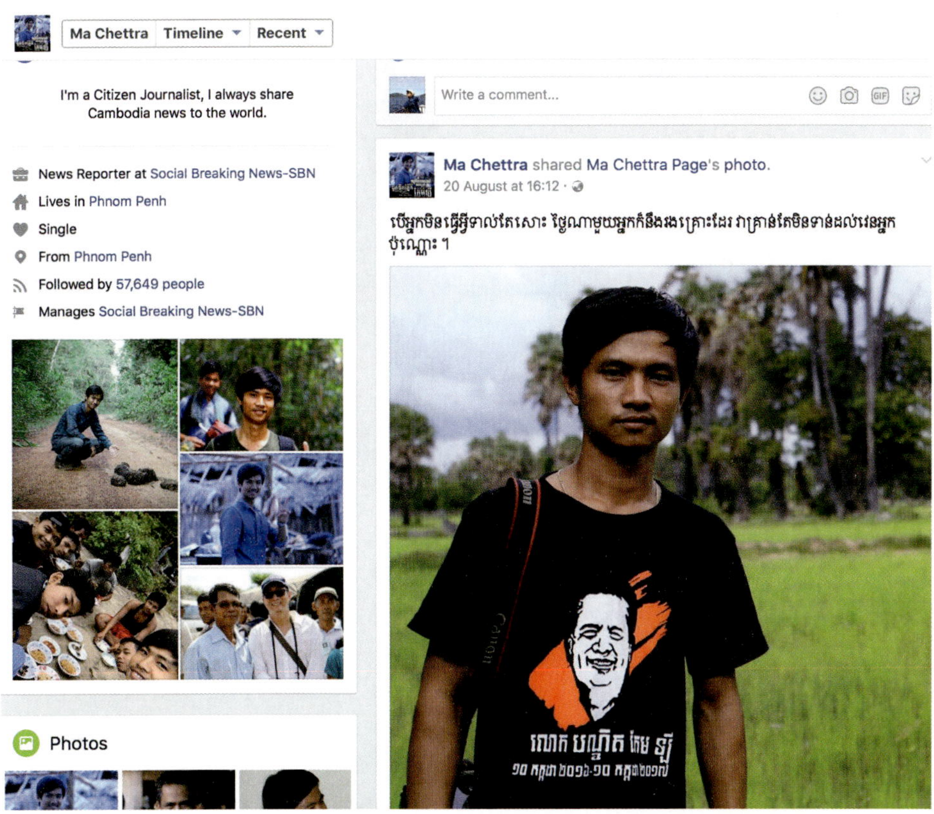

The population enjoyed the freedom of making and producing photographs, either for the promulgation of their own identity or on behalf of other underprivileged groups, this being facilitated by affordable smartphone cameras. However, once circulated on social media, they proved fluid and uncontrollable. From the activist and underrepresented community perspectives, photography on social media is a double-edged sword. On the one hand, the photographs are able to demand recognition and express citizens' rights. On the other hand, as photographs are released from the personal space of the private smartphone to the public space of social media platforms, they are subject to surveillance by the ruling regime. It can be dangerous.

Just as during the KR regime, Angkar enforced visual surveillance, so the current authoritarian populist regime enforces disciplinary surveillance on those who use photographs and audiovisual materials to amplify citizens' critical visions, including illustrating malfeasances and irregularities of the rulers. The posting of photographs and videos on Facebook is considered a legitimate act by most citizens, but many have come to appreciate the true costs that can attach to such actions. Those posting images that are critical of the supreme leader or the king will face arrest following the amended section of the penal code dealing with insults to the country's leader. Endorsed in February 2018 by the National Assembly, it is a "lèse-majesté" law similar to that adopted by Thailand's monarchic system. However, Cambodia's version includes nonroyal and nondivine figures such as the PM. This amendment singles out "word[s], gesture[s], writing, picture[s] or other media which affect the dignity of the individual."[66] The law is reinforced by an efficient state machinery. Hun Sen has been reported as saying along the lines that, "We can see what you are doing and speaking. . . . We can find you [those speaking or acting against the regime] within a short time."

Many people have been arrested and sentenced. Among many examples, in 2017 a woman throwing her shoes at Hun Sen's portrait on a party billboard (figure 2.25a) fled the country for Thailand, where she was arrested and then repatriated to Cambodia.[67] Like the man who threw his shoe at President George Bush during a Baghdad press conference, she was imprisoned under the "lèse-majesté" law. In February 2018, a man who called the government "authoritarian" in a Facebook video was arrested on his wedding day.[68] In May 2018, a male barber was arrested after he shared photographs of the current king, Norodom Sihamoni, in a car, and PM Hun Sen and his wife, posted on Facebook by another account (Khmer Thatcher). He, however, confessed

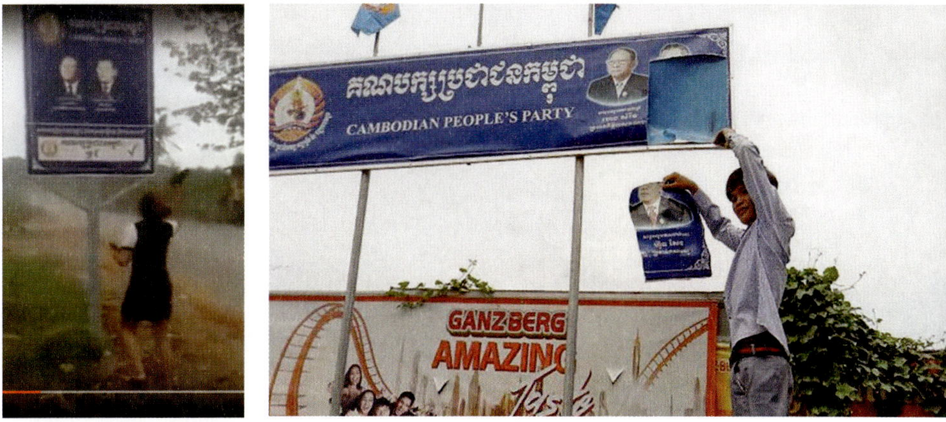

2.25a & 2.25b Citizens' reactions to the prime minister's party billboard portraits. Screenshots from YouTube, September 2019.

that he simply shared the post to a group to express his discontent with the current king. Along with the video of villagers affected by flooding, the post shows that villagers argued with the authorities who restricted their movements (while escaping the flood). The allegation was that the post unfavorably compared the current king to Cambodia's former kings, who cared more about citizens' concerns.[69] Likewise, a young man cutting a portrait of Hun Sen from the party billboard was arrested (figure 2.25b).[70]

These arrests are often provoked by the belief that photographs embody the soul of the person they represent. There can be no doubt that Hun Sen firmly believes that photographic portraits of him contain his soul. His belief is similar to the animism attributed to the Wa-teita of eastern Africa by the early anthropologist and mythographer James Frazer. When they encountered the camera for the first time, they believed that the photographer was a magician who tried to capture their souls by taking and making photographs of them.[71] Likewise, PM Hun Sen confirmed in a public speech that "Cambodia believes in omens or animism. If you make an effigy and burn photographs . . . you violently harm someone's body."[72] This was a public response to those diasporic Cambodians and migrants living in Australia who planned to burn Hun Sen's photographs and effigies in their protest at his visit in 2018 (figure 2.26). He threatened that he would follow the protesters and beat them in their homes. Activists defended the burning as freedom of expression. But there is a paradox: as photographs are digitally printed and circulated rapidly in the era of social media, Hun Sen is losing his sovereignty and power. The

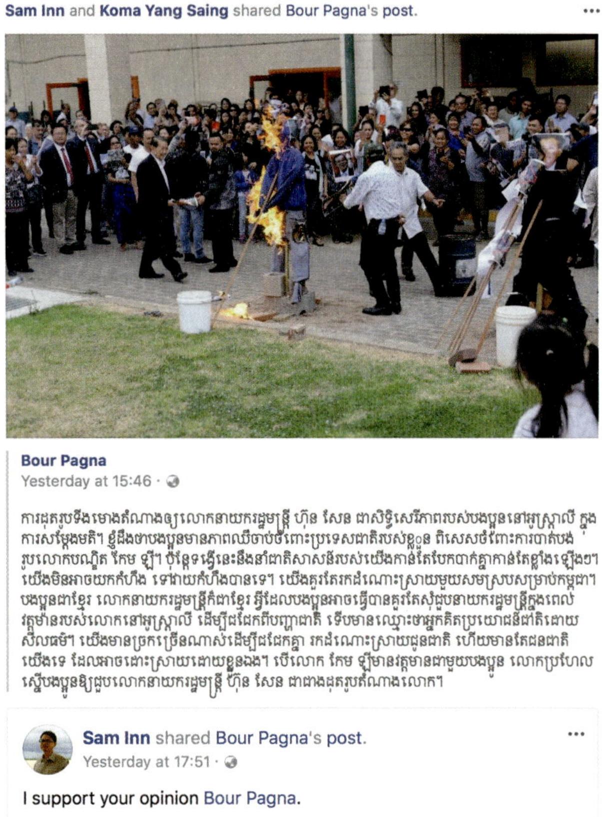

2.26 Australian Cambodians burning Prime Minister Hun Sen's photographs and effigy. Screenshot from Facebook, February 2018.

very abundance of images that would appear to consolidate the pineapple-eye surveillance of Angkar also renders him vulnerable. Images that appear to proliferate his power through endlessly repeated embodiments also render him vulnerable to defacement. The "magic eyes and ears" of Buddhist allegory also render his multiply disseminated body subject to attack. Dissidents can inflict damage on Hun Sen through photography from afar. The circulation of his images, as well as proclaiming his power, also exposes him to opponents who wish him ill, or even death.

These destructive actions suggest that in addition to the concept of the civil contract of photography, we also need to develop a notion of the "political contract" of photography that can illuminate the "work of politics in the age of mechanical reproduction."[73] The circulation of photographic images online and in public space jettisons them into the space of political contestation. In an authoritarian context such as Cambodia, this involves a complex and dialectical dynamic centered on the information that photographs contain but also on their material afterlives. Hun Sen propagates his own image as a way of disseminating power. Citizens, for their part, also demand a competing visibility, which renders them subject to surveillance: citizen photographers find their photography used as a means to identify, locate, and arrest them. But Hun Sen's endlessly replicated images, in turn, render him materially vulnerable as citizens engage in acts of rebellious defacement that cut through from the surface of the image to the body underneath.

Notes

I am grateful to all interlocutors whose stories and photographs form parts of this chapter. Unless otherwise stated, all names and places mentioned in the chapter are pseudonyms.

1 Montague, *Picture Postcards of Cambodia*. Tracing the photographic history between 1867 and 1953 is not the aim of this chapter. For more historical detail, refer to Montague, *Picture Postcards of Cambodia*. This work depicts the popular representation of different cultural, economic, and political activities during the period. Other photographs of Cambodia during these ninety years are available at the French School of the Far East (http://www.efeo.fr), which collected and archived more than 26,000 images.

2 Bhabha, *The Location of Culture*, 53–54.

3 Montague, *Picture Postcards of Cambodia*.

4 Azoulay, *Civil Contract*; Azoulay, *Civil Imagination*.

5 Azoulay, *Civil Contract*, 17.

6 Sontag, *Regarding the Pain of Others*, 13.

7 Sliwinski, *Human Rights in Camera*; Linfield, *Cruel Radiance*.

8 Rejai and Enloe, "Nation-States and State-Nations," 140.

9 Ichijo, "Sovereignty and Nationalism," 159–60.

10 Anderson, *Imagined Communities*, 37.

11 Azoulay, *Civil Contract*; Anderson, *Imagined Communities*.

12 Azoulay, *Civil Contract*.

13 Inglis, "Empowerment and Emancipation," 4.

14 Biesta, "A New Logic of Emancipation," 41.

15 Young, *Strategies of Authoritarian*, 38.

16 Levin, "Performative Force of Photography," 329.

17 Möller, "Photography after Empire," 506.

18 On contractual responses, see Hariman and Lucaites, *No Caption Needed*.

19 Möller, "Photography after Empire," 506.

20 Kittler, *Optical Media*, 11.

21 Foucault, *Discipline and Punish*, 197–200.

22 Sontag, *On Photography*; Tagg, *The Burden of Representation*.
23 Sontag, *On Photography*, 5.
24 Young, "Citizens of Photography," 64.
25 Zuboff, *Age of Surveillance Capitalism*, 14.
26 Kittler, *Optical Media*.
27 Zuboff, *Age of Surveillance Capitalism*, 69–70, 202.
28 Young, "Internet, Facebook," 73–74.
29 Richardot, "Cinema Reborn."
30 See Found Cambodia, accessed February 18, 2019, http://www.foundcambodia.com.
31 Tyner, "Dead Labor," 70.
32 Hinton, "Head for an Eye," 369.
33 Interview with Seneh, October 18, 2018.
34 Strassler, *Refracted Visions*, 20; Zelizer, "Atrocity, the 'As If,'" 155.
35 Mehta, *Cambodia Silenced*.
36 On some occasions, photographs were buried in the ground or hidden elsewhere to protect them from being seen by the Khmer Rouge. Kim Hak's "alive" photographic works revive the buried photographs and objects in the space of the art gallery. See Kim Hak, "Alive," accessed September 20, 2020, https://www.kimhak.com/works/alive/. Found Cambodia, the online archive run by Charles Fox, also illustrates how the photographs survived the Khmer Rouge by burial.
37 M. Hirsch, "Generation of Postmemory," 202.
38 Interview with a former Khmer Rouge comrade, October 10, 2018.
39 Tyner, Kimsroy, and Sirik, "Landscape Photography," 578. Angkar refers to the KR as a whole led by the Communist Party of Kampuchea.
40 Tyner, *Nature of Revolution*, 110–11.
41 See Li, *Red-Color News Soldier*.
42 Li, *Red-Color News Soldier*.
43 These prisoners and their ID photos are not always those of ordinary Khmer Rouge citizens but members of the KR organization.
44 Zelizer, "Atrocity, the 'As If,'" 156.
45 Zelizer, "Atrocity, the 'As If,'" 155.
46 M. Hirsch, "The Generation of Postmemory," 203.
47 Ly, *Traces of Trauma*, 39.
48 Barthes, *Camera Lucida*, 91.
49 The video posted by the Government Agency press located the Council of Ministers: "Marching towards National Salvation," accessed April 8, 2019, https://www.facebook.com/PressOCMOfficial/videos/1387636501364451/.
50 Baer, Spectral Evidence.
51 Caswell, *Archiving the Unspeakable*, 11, 21.
52 Linfield, *Cruel Radiance*, 1.
53 Interview, September 20, 2017. Sopheap is a pseudonym.

54 Ly, "Devastated Vision(s)," 72.
55 Norén-Nilsson, *Cambodia's Second Kingdom*, 1.
56 Strassler, *Refracted Visions*, 17.
57 Joseph Soh, "Cambodia's 2017 Social Media and Digital Statistics," Geeks in Cambodia, February 9, 2017, http://geeksincambodia.com/cambodias-2017-social-media-digital-statistics/.
58 Chloe Ang, "Cambodia's 2019 Social Media and Digital Statistics," Geeks in Cambodia, July 16, 2019, http://geeksincambodia.com/cambodias-2019-social-media-digital-statistics/.
59 Interview, November 5, 2019.
60 Berger, *Ways of Seeing*, 141.
61 Lefebvre, *Production of Space*, 32; Azoulay, *Civil Contract*, 21.
62 Vuth, "Cambodian Photographers."
63 Azoulay, *Civil Contract*, 17; Levin, "Performative Force," 328; Young, "Citizens of Photography," 2.
64 Mazzarella, "Internet X-Ray," 473.
65 Mirzoeff, *How to See the World*, 291–92.
66 Chheng and Nachenson, "Lese Majeste Law Now in Effect."
67 Chheng and Kijewski, "Woman Who Threw Shoe at CPP Sign in Video Sought."
68 Mech, "Man Held after Calling Government 'Authoritarian' on Facebook."
69 Chheng, "Second Man Charged under Country's Lese Majeste Law."
70 Seangly, "Billboard Cutter Held."
71 Frazer, *Golden Bough*, 47.
72 Based on a video clip posted publicly on Facebook by Hun Sen.
73 Benjamin, "The Work of Art in the Age of Mechanical Reproduction."

3

Photography, Citizenship, and Accusatory Memory in the Greek Crisis

KONSTANTINOS KALANTZIS

The Flag That Might Not Disappear

Our scene opens at the anniversary of the 1944 Distomo slaughter, on June 10, 2018. The ritual commemorates the 1944 invasion of the Greek mainland town and the murder of some 223 civilians by the SS troops. For locals, the event is the ultimate manifestation of Nazi (often seen as characteristically German) bestial violence. But the recollection also breaks down along the left–right axis. Rightist, anticommunist interlocutors say it was retaliation for a leftist guerrilla attack on a German battalion. The narrative is ferociously disputed by leftists who invoke historical sources showing that the slaughter was not connected to the attack and celebrate the defiance against occupiers. The commemoration event is taking place at a highland vista overlooking Mount Parnassus, with participants gathered around a modernist white monument displaying engraved slaughter scenes (figure 3.1). The ritual features the formulaic language and solemn tone emblematic of such commemorations throughout Greece. It is attended by residents as well as local, national, and German political representatives, a few Greek antifascists, representatives of associations claiming German compensation money, and German antifascist activists of the AK-Distomo collective who visit the village annually and assist the municipality with the ongoing lawsuit concerning German compensations to the town's victims.

Though the commemoration has been taking place since the 1940s, its political relevance has been renewed following Greece's 2010 bailout deal with the European Union (EU) and the International Monetary Fund (IMF), formally presented as addressing its huge debt and budget deficit.[1] Since the ensuing austerity phase, the event draws a large audience and receives ex-

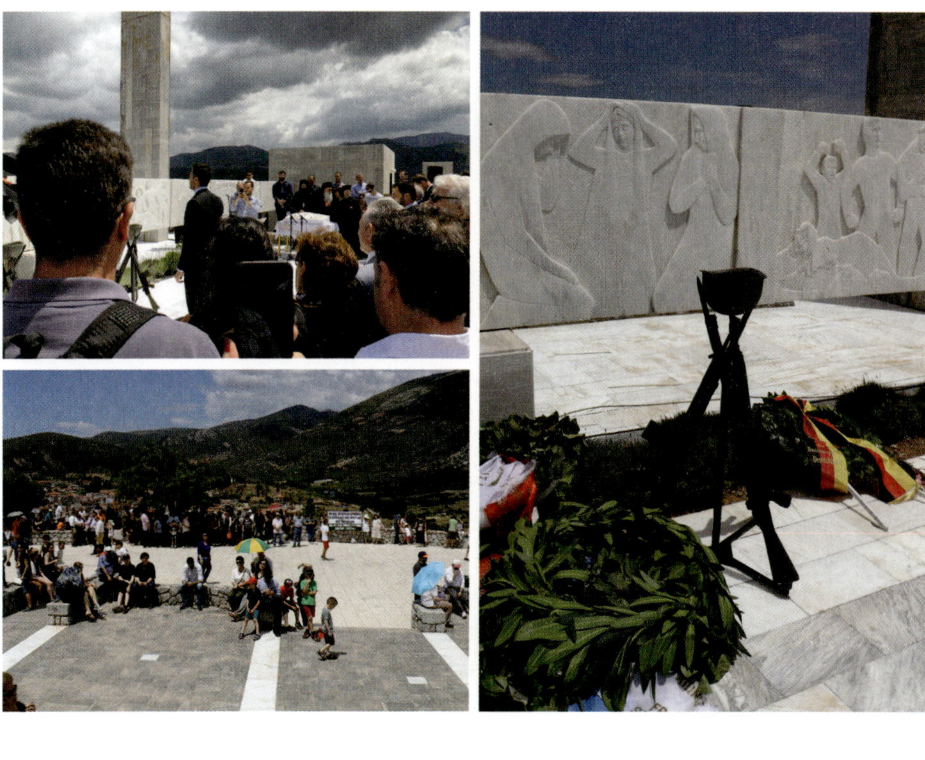

3.1 Carved figures at the Distomo memorial depict scenes from the slaughter and a wreath features the German flag (*right*), which many interlocutors deemed undesirable. Locals call the memorial "the mausoleum," as bones from the massacred population are stored inside a special room. The memorial was inaugurated in 1978. Photographs by Konstantinos Kalantzis, 2018 and 2019.

tensive media coverage. As I am photographing the event, various politicians and other bystanders discern my digital single-lens reflex (DSLR) camera as an indication of professional status and ask me to take their picture (these politicians are often seen locally as capitalizing on the slaughter for their self-promotion). But everyone is vexed by a laurel wreath featuring the German flag in the backdrop, and they want me to edit it out of my frame. The wreath had been deposited by the German ambassador. Some German attendees said he left it apart from the other wreaths, hoping that its visibility would highlight Germany's desire for atonement. Pointing to the continued denial of Germany to provide compensations or reparations for war crimes, these interlocutors scorned the ambassador's gesture as superficial.[2]

The undesirability of the flag may also be understood in the light of Greek public representations of the harsh austerity measures and the political monitoring of Greece as a form of violence perpetrated by Germany and evocative of that exercised by German troops during the occupation. Several ethnographers have emphasized the tendency among Greeks to invoke deeply felt past historical experiences as prisms through which to make sense of the present.[3] That tendency adds a culturally specific complication to Marianne Hirsch's argument that the definition of the present in relation to the past pertains to a particular traumatic moment in post-Holocaust Europe.[4] In Greece, embodied evocations of the past are constant and not just about the cross-generational transmission of trauma through representations (what Hirsch calls postmemory) that, as I describe here, my interlocutors reject as false. In the Greek post-2010 period, the 1940s continually come up and Germans become perceptible as executors of austerity descending from historical executioners. The emphasis on this historical parallel was pronounced among particular groups (e.g., people involved in associations fighting for Germany to pay compensations), a fight that has at times been depicted by centrist liberal commentators as irrationally intransigent, an accusation leveled against those who refuse to forgive in other contexts of "irreconciliation" and one that repeats dismissive views of Greek anti-austerity protests by conservative northern European commentators in the early bailout years.[5] But the evocation of the German occupation also characterizes a sensibility that is palpable more widely in the post-austerity phase, beyond seemingly stable political oppositions. Thus a leftist academic commentator compared scholarships given to Greeks to study in Germany to the internment of Greeks in concentration camps during the 1940s and a populist rightist radio host drew a parallel between austerity-related pension reductions to German dive-bomber aircraft attacks. In keeping with its anti-colonial, nativist appeal, the demand for reparations by Germany was adopted by the SYRIZA-ANEL coalition government that was elected in 2015.

There is an even more culturally specific disdain for the German wreath to unpack here, as residents of Distomo and Kalavryta, the two towns that suffered massacres explored in this chapter, are especially concerned about official German donations and so-called soft diplomacy.[6] They fear that these policies aim at silencing compensation claims and eroding the memories of German brutality. Concern is especially strong among leftists, some of whom observe closely the Distomo compensations trials (currently taking place in Rome), but it is also shared by most residents, who fear that with the passing of local witnesses, the German narrative that downplays the slaughter will be harder to dispute.

Thinking through photography, these two towns constitute examples of the "horrific sublime"—Nayanika Mookherjee's term for the visualization of female rape victims during the Bangladeshi 1971 war.[7] Historical representations of these towns have focused on black-clad bereaved widows and their deprived children.[8] Kalavryta interlocutors in fact remember the women in black visually dominating the town's public spaces after the slaughter and say that boys' nicknames began deriving from the mother's rather than the father's side. The enhancement of a performative maternal register is captured in a photograph taken by a Greek reporter in the 1940s where mothers/widows (pictured as a surveying Greek chorus) cast their pained but powerful gaze over their children (figure 3.2). The image of abjection and pain also applies to less disseminated imagery, like the photo on the mirror of a barber shop in Distomo. The photograph was taken during a Red Cross mission and portrays the now-senior owner, Giorgos Vlachos (figure 3.3), in the company of other children. Many old interlocutors in Distomo, in fact, own photographs of themselves (taken by such missions) as starving, orphaned children.

As is the case with other iconic images of deprivation and pain (e.g., Dorothea Lange's *Migrant Mother*, Nick Ut's *The Napalm Girl*), an important question concerns the extent to which the circulation of such imagery can amount to anything more than harmless normative tokens of pain and to thus mobilize political processes.[9] It is useful here to think through the work of theorist and activist Ariella Azoulay, who argues that photography's political efficacy ought to be addressed beyond "the pain of others" (the commonplace discussion about images of pain anaesthetizing viewers).[10] For Azoulay, photography altered the ways in which those subjected to domination realized themselves and allowed the opening of an empowering civic space for them. Drawing on this proposition, I argue that it is important to investigate the kinds of (civic or

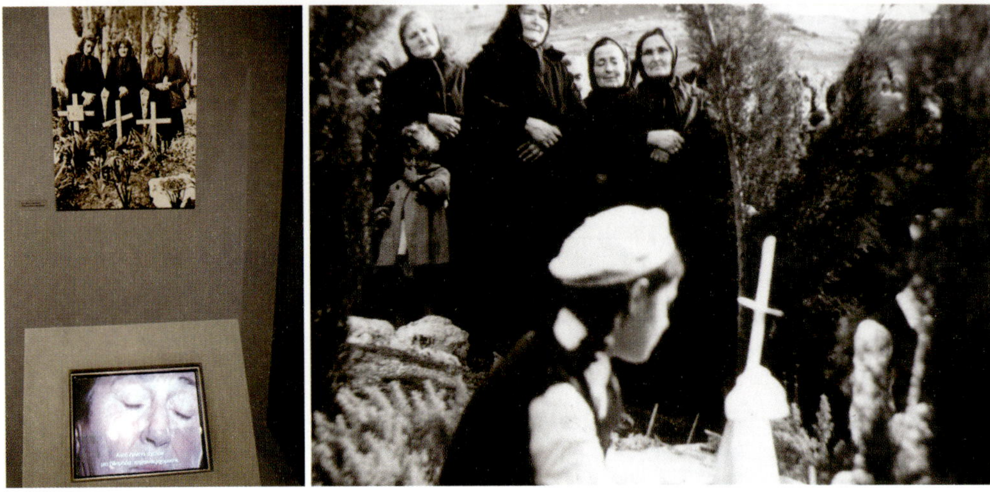

3.2 *Left*: Detail inside the Municipal Museum of the Kalavritan Holocaust, where an image of mourning women is displayed over a video wall featuring interviews with survivors. *Right*: Photograph taken by a Greek photojournalist visiting Kalavryta during a commemoration of the December 13, 1943, slaughter. Many interlocutors note that following the massacre, Kalavrytan public spaces were visually dominated by black-wearing women. Left photograph by Konstantinos Kalantzis, 2018. Right photograph by unknown photographer, likely a member of the Agency of United Photojournalists, ca. 1945.

other) subjects that become possible through and around photos in their contemporary uses. I further suggest that the emotional and psychological aspects of picturing subjects—photography's "affective and tactile dimensions"—determine the kinds of politics possible (Azoulay seems to be separating the psychological from the civic).[11] To understand this zone of the political-cum-affective, one ought to investigate people's embodied responses to imagery and to ethnographically test photography's potential to open up civic spaces by grasping what happens with photographs in daily practice.

The tone in photographic emblems of the Distomo 1944 slaughter would be a starting point for understanding the work these photos do for people. Take an elementary school student's comment on a photograph depicting a senior couple with their (orphaned) grandchildren (figure 3.4, right), taken by professional photographer Voula Papaioannou, working for the United Nations Relief and Rehabilitation Administration (UNRRA) in 1945. When asked during a 2019 municipal event to comment on what the depicted subjects might be experiencing, the student said, "They look sad." The picture evokes Greek Orthodox representations of Virgin Mary and associations between motherhood and suffering.[12] In the 1950s, Papaioannou visited the

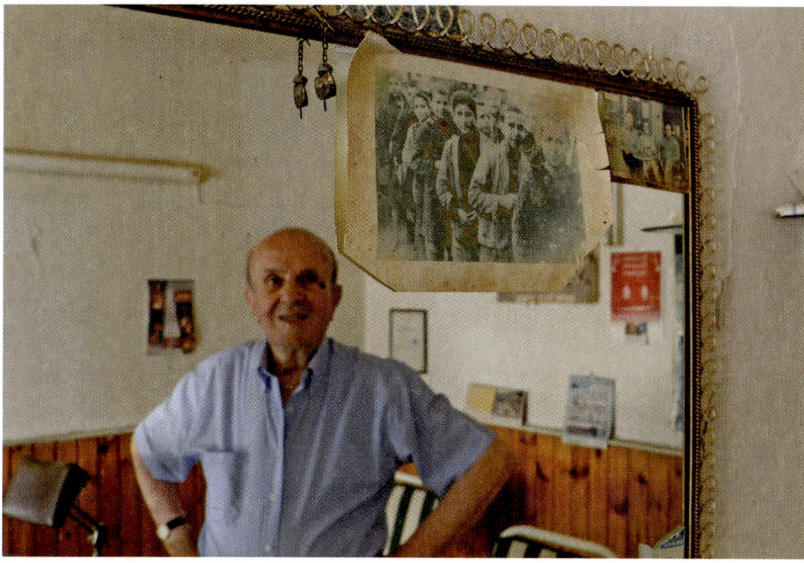

3.3 Giorgos Vlachos staring at a photograph of himself along with other Distomo children taken by a humanitarian mission that occurred following the slaughter of the local population by German SS troops in June 1944. The photograph has been ornamenting the mirror of his barber shop for decades. Photograph by Konstantinos Kalantzis, 2018.

mountainous and coastal Sfakia region in southwestern Crete (figure 3.5), where I have been doing fieldwork since 2006. The tone of her Sfakian images supplies another key subject of the "national family album." I am using Time Warner's term about emblematic US photos as a way to think about photographs' social resonance via perceptions of kinship.[13] If Distomo enables the envisioning of the nation as a mourning female, Sfakians are called upon to fulfill the fantasy of a fighting male striking back. Though the gendered imaging of the nation is long-standing, "the crisis" has generated a considerable volume of gendered projections of Greece's relationship to the West (including the masculinist representation of the West as a female tourist).[14] Voula Papaioannou's Sfakian pictures are slightly less monumental than those taken by Nelly in the 1930s, but they continue her predecessor's picturing of the region as a male whiskered figure in traditional attire, thus drawing on but also reinforcing the national imaginary whereby Sfakia constitutes the epitome of rugged nativism.[15] Representations of the Cretan man as an archetypical figure of native resistance accommodate different political investments in the post-2010 period. The trend encompasses the photojournalistic coverage of the 2016 Cretan farmers' clashes with the Athenian police (invested with antigovernment sentiments from both left and right) through Sfakia's own ex-mayor's representation (and self-representation) as an opponent of colonial/surveying forces, impersonated by figures such as the EU health commissioner who reprimanded the ex-mayor for smoking during press conferences in 2018.[16]

Sfakians partake in this semantic climate, and in my post-2010 visits I often heard people critiquing the area's and the nation's surveillance and tutelage by Germany. Many expressed this disdain as the fatigue of offering hospitality and a desire to put limits on invasive guests.[17] These guests, who, as Sfakians claim, have enjoyed this hospitality for years, were now seen as abusing locals' generosity by overstepping in practices such as land buying or by adopting offensive manners, hence the local resonance of a nationally oft-cited story of Germans declining to pay for service on account of Greece owing "them" money. In an instance showing how the trope of hospitality is used across

3.4 Two images taken by professional Athens-based photographer Voula Papaioannou in autumn 1945 in Distomo, Greece. In archives and published editions, the subjects appear anonymous, but recognizing and naming them was my local interlocutors' main priority. *Left*: Orphaned children Maria and Takis Sfontouri with their grandmother Maria Karouzou at the graveyard. During fieldwork in 2018, I heard that following both of their spouses' recent passing, Takis told his sister, "It's now just the two of us, again," referring to their orphaned state that followed the 1944 slaughter. *Right*: Orphaned children (Chrysoula, Argyris, and Kondylia) of the Sfontouri family with their grandparents (Panagiotis and Kondylia). These children are still alive. Photographs by Voula Papaioannou. Copyright Benaki Museum Photographic Archive.

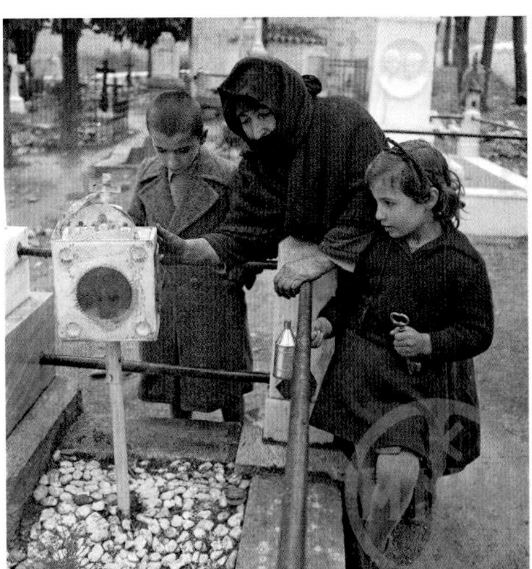

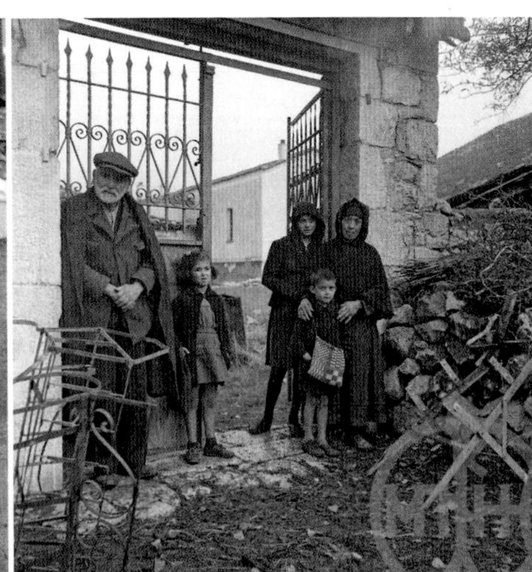

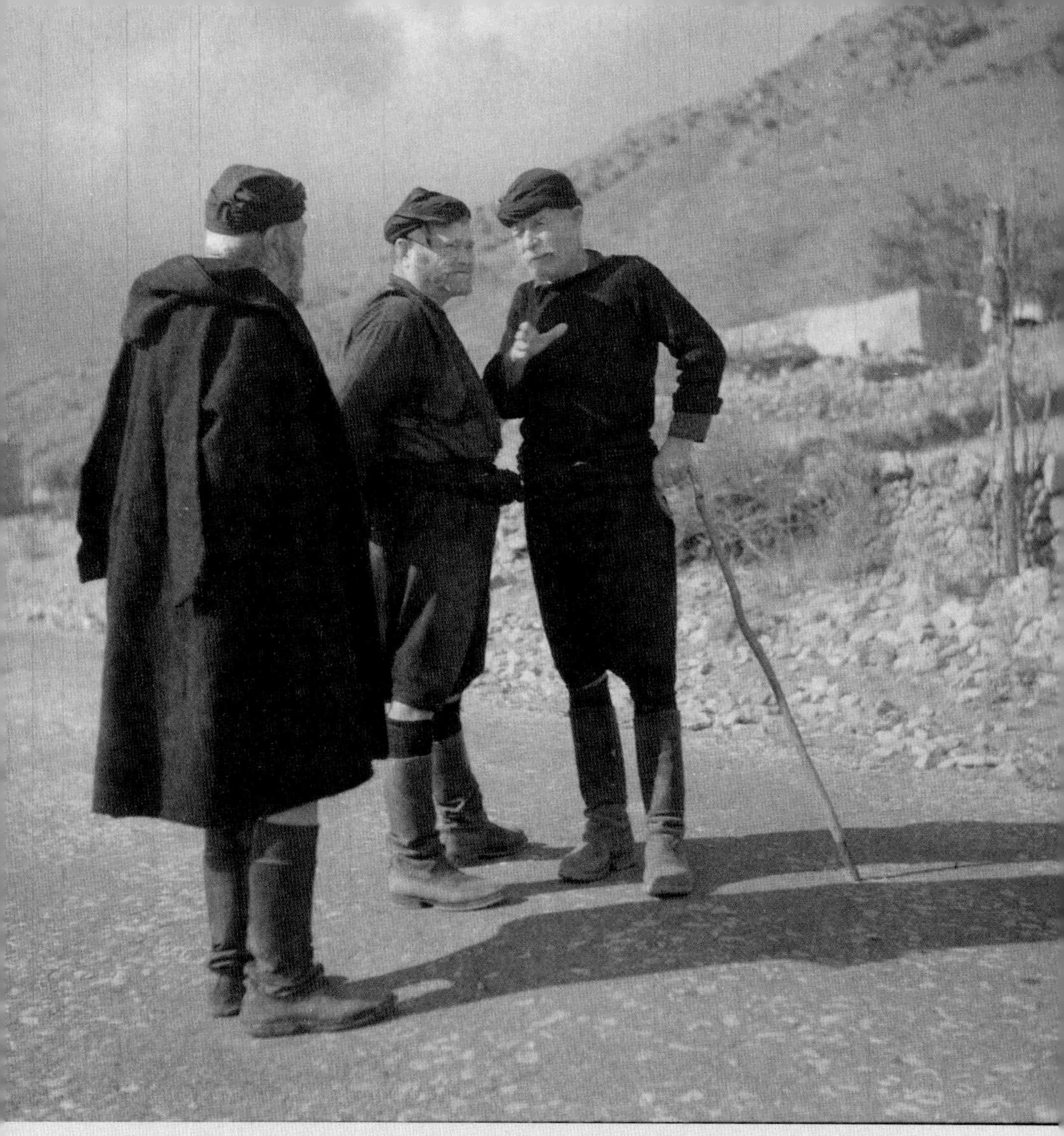

3.5 Voula Papaioannou, *Men from Sfakia*, ca. 1955. My interlocutors, eager to identify the subjects in historical photos, recognized them as representing the Varis (*left*), Tsapas (*center*), and Tsiridanis (*right*) patrilines. Photograph by Voula Papaioannou. Copyright Benaki Museum Photographic Archive.

scales (nation/village, etc.) and how German visitors can be seen as spokespeople of their country's demands for austerity, locals suggested that hikers who found themselves in need of transportation because they had underestimated the challenges awaiting them should be subject to the charges that under such circumstances apply in Europe.[18]

At the same time, many returning tourists from Germany and other parts of Northern Europe (middle-class people interested in "tradition") not only have been adoring the area as a rugged enclave but have also offered local households photographs of their ancestors that they took in the past. These images are often the only available photos of deceased ancestors. The incidents reflect the deep asymmetry in the encounter between a rural society and those representing it (whose images locals must get hold of in order to envision themselves) and reveal the cyclical process whereby the presence of the observing photographers enhances the idioms they record by virtue of their presence and of the pictures' local recirculation.[19] Importantly, the photographers gifted such images in gestures of reciprocity and gratitude. Here, "the German" is no longer the sovereign (whose flag is considered out of place in Distomo) but a subject in a complex zone where Sfakians appear as affectionate, generous hosts. The different subject positions in which Greeks situate themselves vis-à-vis the German Other are encapsulated in an instance of algorithmic display on my Facebook wall. A post by a Kalavrytan leftist woman featuring one of Papaioannou's Distomo photos with a caption about Germany's unpaid debt to Greece was followed by another post by a Sfakian hotel owner welcoming two German guests with an image of the trio clinking glasses at his establishment.

This chapter investigates the role of photography in imaginaries and experiences of conflict, and parity during a moment in contemporary Europe defined as a "crisis." I engage Azoulay's provocation that photography may enact citizenry in a way that defies official mandates and the medium's own hierarchical and objectifying capacities.[20] Eschewing the term's normative, teleological connotations, I treat "the crisis" as a historical phase that started with Greece's 2010 bailout deal (and it can be further divided into sub-phases).[21] Among Greeks, even middle-class Occidentalist liberals, the phase is marked by a heightened sense of anxiety regarding their position in Europe (many liberals counter the painful realization of asymmetrical citizenship by emphasizing the necessity for more structural adjustments). This cuts to the core of a resilient challenge of modern Greece, explored by Michael Herzfeld and others: the endorsement of (classical) Greek heritage by European nation-states coincided with demeaning suspiciousness (albeit occasional fascination) over the country's European status, while Greeks themselves viewed the prospect of being granted this status with ambivalence.[22] Thus, from the perspective of the anti-colonial nationalist sensibility, which is characteristic of the post-2010 period, liberals' pro-Western stance amounts to obsequious mimicry. This anti-colonial constituency recruits Cretans as ideal protagonists of native resistance to Western orchestrators of tutelage. Drawing on ethnography in three field sites (organized in two case studies), my chapter explores different possibilities of (a photographic) "citizenship" between the parties involved: tourists and locals, hosts and guests, perpetrators and victims, powerful and peripheral nation-states. I present two idioms of engaging photographs through which people reconstruct the past and imagine the future. In the first section, I explore the relationship between tourists and Sfakians in Crete, as mediated through photographic imaginaries of nativeness and tradition. While tourists, who insist on gifting back images to the subjects, are often incorporated into local sociality, Sfakians look at these images in an idiom of authorial displacement that forgets the photographers and the asymmetrical dynamics that inform the pictures, thereby limiting the sharing of a common social space with photographers. The second section explores the mainland towns Distomo and Kalavryta, where photography relates to modalities of witnessing, flagging pain and moral protest, which I describe as accusatory memory. Germany here is no longer tangible in dialogues with tourists and is addressed via concerns with Realpolitik and victimhood, and photography emerges as a surface that offers undeniable information and as a medium expected to capture the horrific past and assign the subject positions of victim and perpetrator, which become stark reminders of the impossibility of a shared civic space with Germany today. These case studies present complementary and also different forms of ancestor veneration and (gendered) national imaginaries, and they illuminate divergent possibilities of photography in creating but also denying spaces of exchange and coexistence.

Celebrated Warriors

HOSPITALITY AND THE ACCOMMODATING AVENGERS

Our next scene takes us to Kallikratis, the rocky Sfakian village and execution site during the German Occupation that features dispersed semi-abandoned hamlets among sparse trees. Inside a coffeehouse with quasi-domestic atmosphere, the elderly owner who hadn't seen me in years is iterating formal versions of village history, concerning its 1943 destruction by Nazi troops. Behind him, I notice some visual additions: portraits of himself and a photo collage dedicated to his childhood experience of fleeing the Nazis. His wife and son are present too, and when I ask about the sources of these images, they all casually reply that they had been taken "by a German." This is a common retort in the myriad Sfakian households and coffeehouses whose walls and cabinets are replete with photos of family members (often male ancestors). This kind of photography emerged in the 1960s when Sfakia became popular with European tourists, particularly Germans, attracted to the area's sensorial qualities (e.g., the proximity of mountains to the sea) and the reputation of authentic, hospitable, but also dangerous locals (involved in blood feuds and a masculinist public culture). The socially generative power of this attraction is indexed by the number of Northern European women who married local men in the 1970s and 1980s. The visual component of this libidinal entanglement is evident in a video I was shown by a German woman. It was originally shot by her father during his Sfakian trips; in it, she appears as a small child in the company of a local boy, whom she ended up marrying some decades later.

The pictures tourists took and later sent back to Sfakia reflect the asymmetrical flow in the local imagination economy, whereby representations of rural subjects are crafted and imported by powerful outsiders (e.g., folklorists and botanists).[23] Locals did not, as a rule, possess cameras (until the 1990s or so), which meant that their visual memorialization depended on outsiders, sometimes even on commercial photographs (e.g., postcards), which Sfakians reused and reframed as family photos in their own spaces.[24] Images by travelers open up dialogical cultural investments between subjects and photographers around the idea of (male) Sfakianness as a visually distinctive category, related to a perceived Doric descent and putatively manifested in elements such as sharp facial features and blue eyes. At another nearby village, a senior man showed me an image of himself taken in the 1950s by "a German" (figure 3.6). He recalled he was originally reluctant to be photographed, as he was mourning (hence the beard in the photo), but his submission to the camera, which he performed bodily by mimicking the shooting of a rifle, was worth it as this was "a good photograph" and of a time from which he has no other images of himself. The rifle metaphor situates photography in the context of hunting, preying, and blood feud practices.

When locals are asked about the impact of tourism in the abstract, they describe it as a corrupting force of modernity that destroys the Sfakian ethos. However, the omnipresent photographic traces of tourist presence complicate matters. People describe tourism and land buying by foreigners as a betrayal of devotion to family property, ancestry, and pride in the village and as moral corrosion by money. Land buying in particular can be understood as hospitality whose temporality rules have been reversed: the guest now controls the stay. In the post-2010 phase when these ideas were enhanced, tourism was further conceptualized as an object of judgment by an imagined ancestral jury. Jokingly one man said that if Sfakians' ancestors came back to life, they would slap contemporaries for having degraded themselves to make money "out of serving omelets" (signifying here a cheap, fast food). In another "animistic" version of this scenario, an old friend in his sixties imagined that the trees nourished by the blood and bones of deceased Sfakian warriors buried in the rocky gorge that we were crossing were casting a disapproving glance on contemporaries, whom he described as money-chasing proprietors and no longer fighters molded by a harsh mountainous landscape. Yet the very same man engaged in warm exchanges with tourists. The pictures they took of him were featured in his house in various locations. As with the coffeehouse proprietor whose portraits "taken by a German" filled the walls, one can think of these photos as points of entry into an optical unconscious, to recall Walter Benjamin's observation about the tacit, unimaginable, worlds that photography may open up.[25] Their presence speaks to emotional and material exchanges

3.6 Manousos Nikiforakis (Patsoumas) showing me (the photographer) a framed photograph of himself taken when he was nineteen by a German traveler. Manousos attributed his initial reluctance to be photographed to the fact that he was mourning (apparent in his beard) and described the photographic act by physically mimicking the shooting of a rifle, thus placing photography in the context of hunting and preying. Original photograph (*left*) by unknown photographer, ca. 1955. Photograph with Manousos by Konstantinos Kalantzis, 2017.

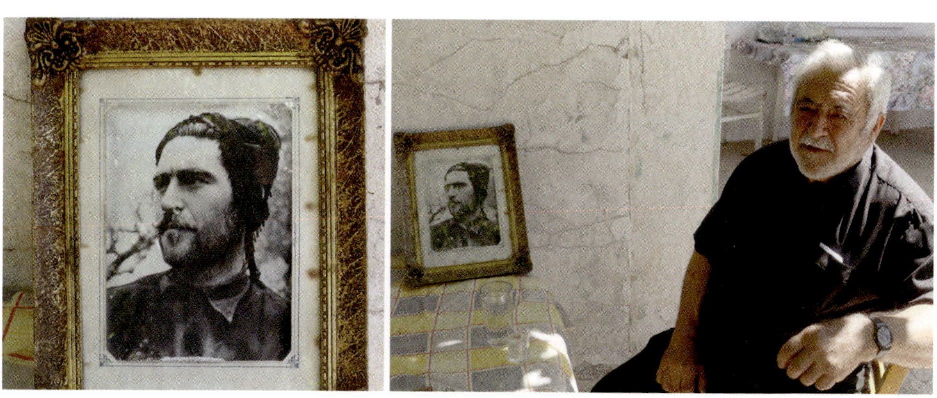

that have little place in formal narratives about the relations between Sfakians and tourists.

A certain tension thus emerges between the (national and international) representation of Cretans (especially Sfakians) as resisting warriors and the daily accommodation of German visitors. In fact, in various proto-tourist accounts I collected, Germans were amazed by the fact they were treated generously in the 1960s and 1970s despite the historical proximity to World War II. A relevant narrative I heard in Sfakia concerns a 1960s incident whereby an old local woman comforted a young German tourist crushed by guilt over the war crimes committed in the area. She is said to have held him in her arms and told him, "Don't cry, my child, it was warfare" (*min kles pedhi mu polemos itan*; i.e., something beyond his control). Moreover, in the spirit of the emotional dynamics between early tourists and Sfakians, she cast him in a filial role. But Sfakians are imagined nationally as avengers. For example, mainland Greek interlocutors who were guest workers in Germany in the 1960s told me they admired Cretans because of the occupiers they had killed and gleefully remembered that sometimes their German factory coworkers attributed their injuries to service time in 1940s Crete and particularly in the event, celebrated throughout Greece as the high moment of spontaneous resistance to Nazi parachutists, known as the "Battle of Crete."[26] The figure of the Cretan is recruited imaginarily here as a reply to the question posed by a Greek woman at the Kalavryta memorial for victims of the 1943 massacre by the Nazis: "wasn't there anyone to kill the killers?" which speaks to how the envisioning of Cretans as figures of resistance assigns them a reparative imaginary capacity of stopping invaders and avenging for national injury, in keeping with the nonforgiveness they putatively practice in their blood feuds that other Greeks learn about in popular representations (e.g., TV series, the news and novels).[27] Communist guerrillas of the Greek People's Liberation Army (ELAS, Ethnikos Laikos Apeleftherotikos Stratos) are also seen as avenging figures, for instance in stories that celebrate how they targeted Greeks who collaborated with the Nazis, but, unlike Sfakians whose evocations cut across the spectrum, their endorsement pertains mostly to leftists.

But Greeks' expectations are often in tension with Sfakians' daily practice. For instance, a leftist urban interlocutor proudly said that Eleni, a middle-aged woman from a village that had been burned down by Germans, caused through her loud retort the shamed departure of a German visitor who wanted to buy land where Germans had burned down houses in 1943. Yet my knowledge of Eleni's exchanges with German and other tourists at their family establishment differed starkly from that ascription. In a special box where she keeps photos sent by visitors, images depicted herself and her husband in rural labor or in preparing meals, which visualizes the fantasy of the rural subject as rooted in place and taking care of the guest. On the back of these images and in letters, tourists wrote how often they think of the Sfakian couple during the winter while sipping the raki she gave them, and they shared personal details about their own relationships to their family and friends. Though Eleni was fond of these images, she was also somewhat bemused as to how their limited verbal communication (as they didn't speak the same language) gave rise to such strong emotional investment. Photography emerges here as a mode of affective communication that exceeds language.

The son of another Sfakian man who was widely photographed by professionals and tourists throughout his life explained to me that his father's contacts with guests built on the nonverbal communication of "eyes and hearts." In an image taken in the 1970s by a German visitor, we see that the old man's living room is replete with pictures from prior interactions with visitors (figure 3.7). The image illuminates the return of photos to the subject as an act of reciprocity, while also visualizing the basic scene of these interactions: domestic and public hospitality. Described by Herzfeld as a way of containing and reversing the symbolic threat visitors from affluent countries pose locally, hospitality in Sfakia still provides a framework in which locals receive admiration by guests and experience moral satisfaction out of offering.[28] Throughout highland Western Crete, people tell stories about puzzled Northern European visitors who assumed that the feasts in which they accidentally found themselves participating cost money only to hear the hosts' amused response that (their) money wouldn't work there. The flip side of this story is provided by Northern European semipermanent residents of Crete, who frequently sketch their fellow Europeans' imprisonment in a disenchanted, joyless life, causing their own desperate desire to escape.[29] They juxtapose their compatriots' fixation with punctuality, money acquisition, and lack of spontaneity to the high value attached to spending time eating and drinking with friends in Crete. A group of expats to whom I showed some photos I had shot in Sfakia in 2007 identified one image, showing a senior man sitting by the table he prepared for his guests, as the most moving (figure 3.8). In the words of a Dutch woman, it shows exactly what Northern Europe lacks. Hospitality encounters are characterized by performative nonchalance, evident in Eleni's own statement, while looking at tourists' images, that she can never remember their names. This obliviousness, common among Sfakians, is premised on the perception of tourists as nameless members of transitive masses whom Sfakians contrast with their own rootedness.

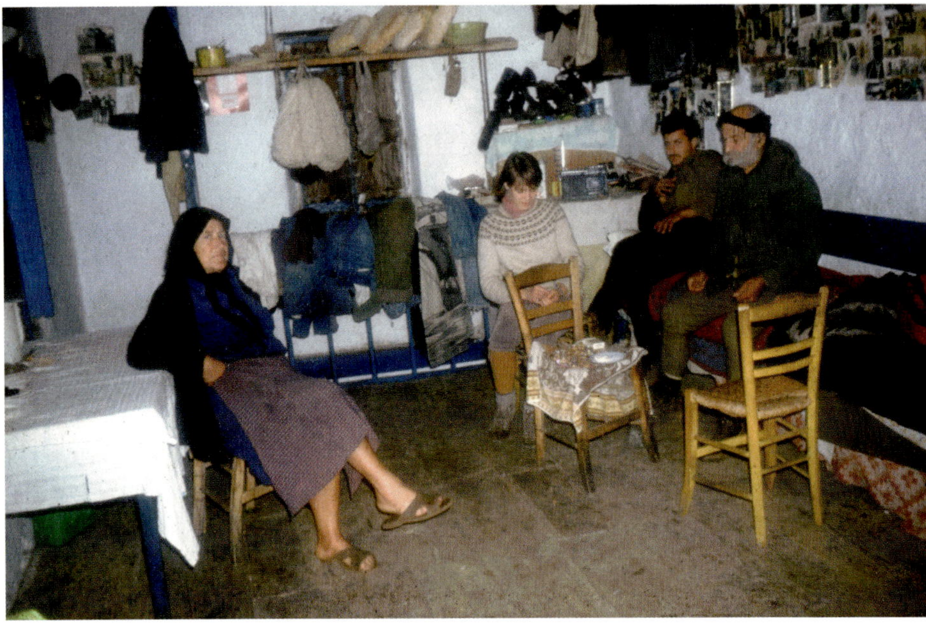

3.7 Photograph portraying Manolis Nikoloudis with his wife and son hosting a couple of German travelers. Nikoloudis, shown here at an old age, has been photographed by tourists and professional photographers throughout his lifetime (see Kalantzis, *Tradition in the Frame*, 86–114). Note the photo wall behind Manolis, featuring images that his guests have returned to him over the years. Photograph by Wolf Lustig, ca. 1978.

Monetized hosting such as that occurring in commercial tourism introduces tensions into locals' moral claims to hospitality.[30] Sfakians from highland villages, for instance, who pride themselves on offering true (not commercialized) hospitality, attribute coastal Sfakians' servitude to tourists to either financial need or a morally questionable drive for profit.[31] Monetized engagements with tourists began historically in nonmonetized spheres (like the one depicted in figure 3.7). Decades later, the old man's sons started a hotel near where he hosted passing travelers. Photography played an important role as a mode of communication and a way for guests to express gratitude. Thinking with Pierre Bourdieu, both tourists and Sfakians are invested in an exchange (hosting guests, gifting back photos, etc.) that through careful performances conceals the aspects that would make it appear "economic," that is, subject to self-interest and calculation.[32] For Sfakians, the downplaying of *the economic* makes possible the claim that hospitality (as in offering food for

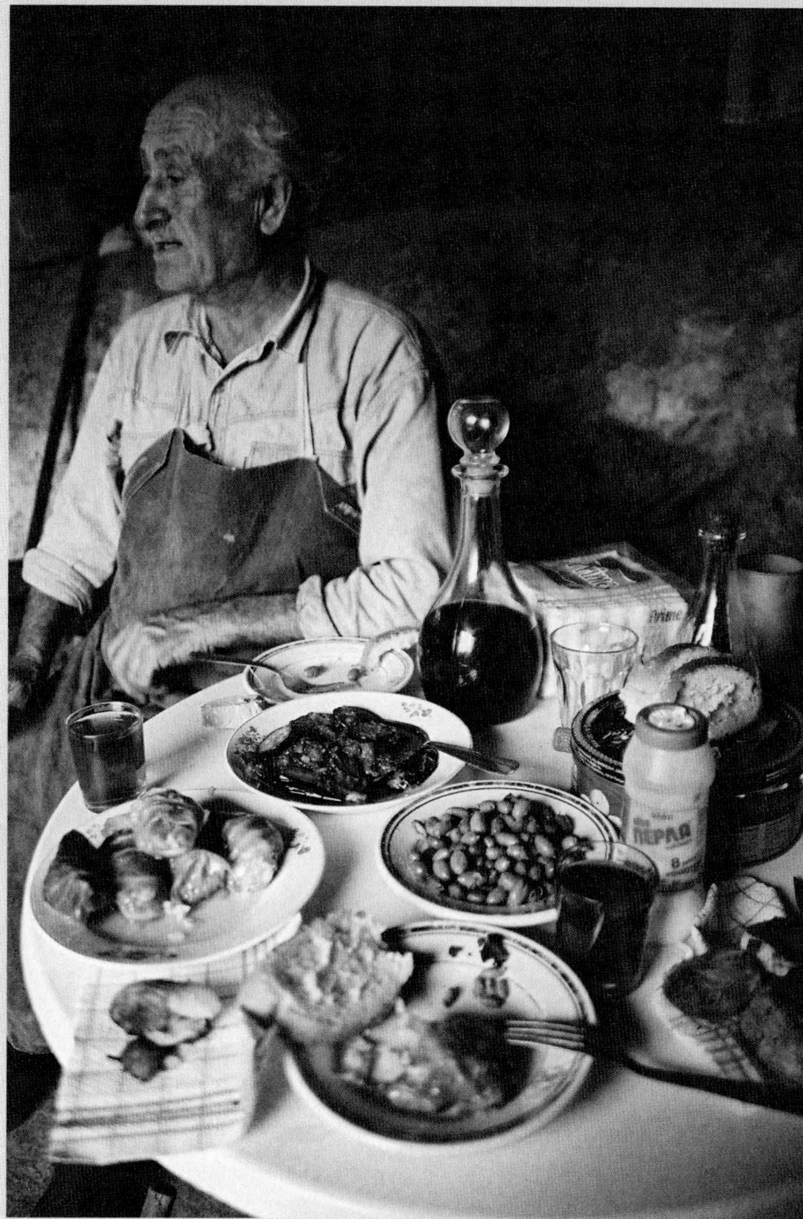

3.8 Photograph of Frixos Giales that I took during an impromptu feast he and his wife, Maria, prepared while locals and I were visiting his raki distillery at a highland Sfakian village. The image was discerned by non-Greek residents of another part of southern Crete, in my 2018 conversations with them, as encapsulating the ethos of hospitality that they find Northern Europe to be lacking. Photograph by Konstantinos Kalantzis, 2007.

free) is possible despite an advanced tourist infrastructure, while for returning tourists it allows the sense that they participate in local sociality regardless of their status as customers. These photos additionally trigger emotional responses, as in the Sfakian expat who reportedly wept upon encountering the portrait of his father sent to the coffeehouse that the old man used to patronize, by a German tourist (figure 3.9). These exchanges assign a key role to photography in the dynamics of social segmentation, by which I refer to how social differentiation is based on shifting criteria, while boundaries of insideness and outsideness are continually negotiated through the contextual emergence of division and reconciliation.[33]

Segmentation, Herzfeld has recently argued, explains the seeming paradox of an agonistic society (Greece) expressing solidarity with other (often precarious) populations within Greece against Europe/Germany who, as external surveyors and enforcers of austerity, trigger alliances against them.[34] And the same logic arguably extends to particular German guests in Sfakia who through fields of exchange and affect may become "our Germans" vis-à-vis "Germany" despite formal rhetoric. This stance is enhanced by a point Sfakians make frequently: that "insiders" (and not foreigners) are the biggest enemy. This was the retort of the sitter of figure 3.6 when I asked about his encounter with a German photographer so soon after the war. He explained that Greek traitors did greater damage during the occupation than Germans. Besides, Sfakians commonly approve of the ability to coexist with an enemy in public spaces without exposing one's sentiments, if an inevitable encounter in a particular context demands it, another sign of how animosity and agreement are constantly negotiated.

PHOTOPHILIA, AUTHORSHIP, AND THE CITIZENSHIP OF ADULATION

The images taken by Sfakia's tourists attest to the visitors' cultural investments and to the kinds of themes that attracted them and were available for their cameras. Especially in the case of villages that suffered losses in the 1940s occupation, the Germans who offered these pictures to locals performed a form of pilgrimage that draws on genealogical imagination. It is intended to undo the evils of one's ancestors, identify with those they fought against, and establish a community with them that may qualify as what Azoulay calls citizenship.[35]

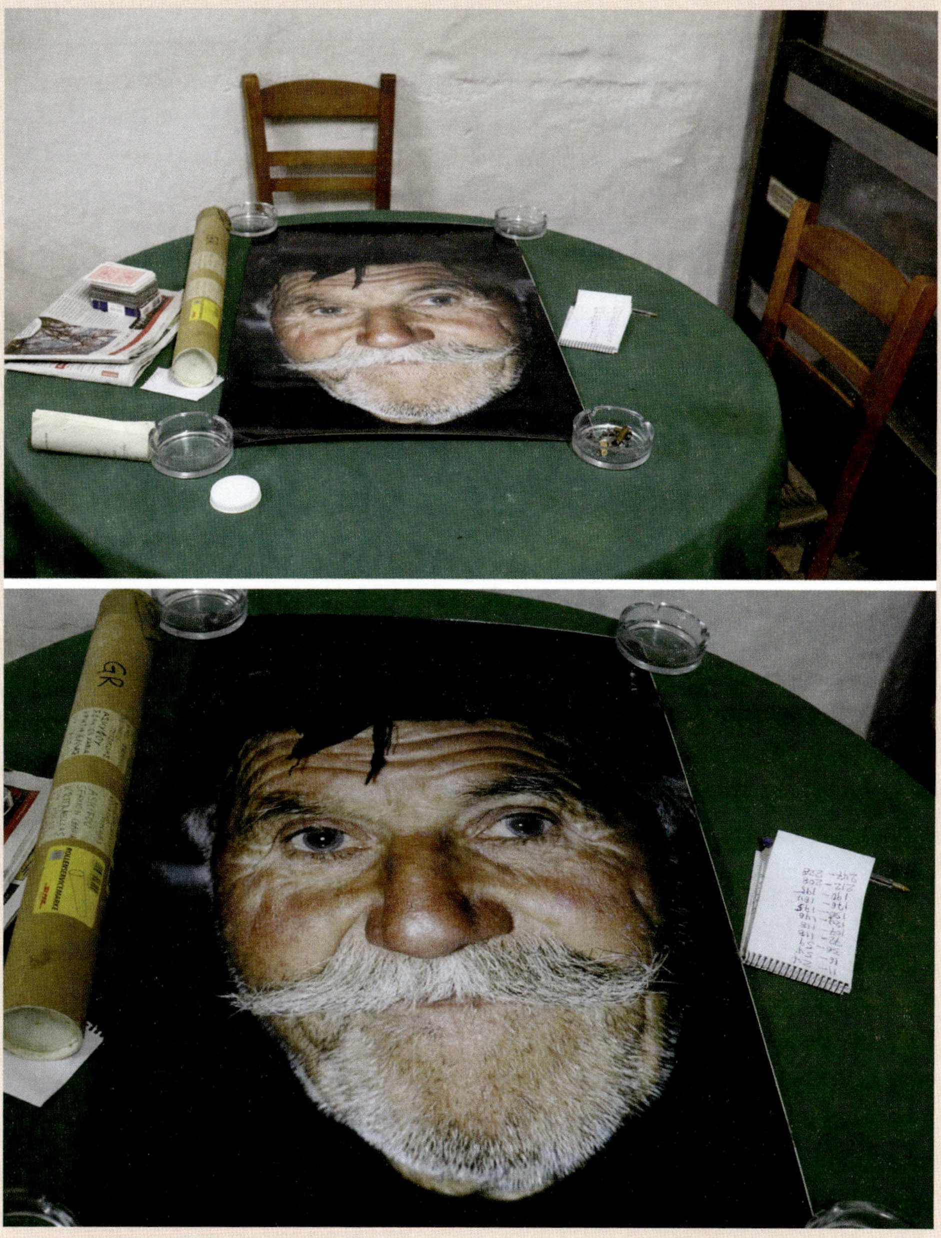

3.9 Photograph of Yannis Mpouhlis sent in the mid-2000s to the proprietors of the coffeehouse adjacent to where it was originally taken by a German tourist. The photographer, who returns periodically to Sfakia, signed the parcel and accompanying letter with a Greek version of his German name. Original photograph by Johannes Lange, 1979. Photograph with table by Konstantinos Kalantzis, 2017.

This might be one possible reply to the question of why German (and other) tourists take these photos of Sfakians and why it is important for them to bring them back. In many ways, photography was the only form of skill and labor Sfakians allow their urban guests who are otherwise deemed incapable in realms that locally matter (like hunting and pastoral activities). This recalls Peter Rivière's account of the Amazonian Trio who defined him as a guest because they thought he was inept at being anything else.[36] At one level, the sending back speaks to a moral prerogative: "it was the most natural thing to do" in response to locals' hospitality, as a long-term returning visitor told me. She was giving back what she was capable of.

Through reciprocity, these guests seek to attain subject positions that partly resonate with those of an ethnographer. They wish to partake in intimate local knowledge, for instance, by furtively asking about blood feuds and illegal activities. They strive to be accepted by a rough society that nevertheless treats them softly. They emotionally invest in locals as a surrogate family, stressing metaphors of care through food given by doting hosts (recall the old woman comforting the crying man like a grandmother).[37] This fantasy of familial belonging is complemented by a desire to disseminate and insert oneself into the Sfakian social landscape through photographs. It recalls Nancy Munn's account of how the person among the Massim in New Guinea is dispersed via acts of hospitality, here echoed by the guests' reciprocating hospitality via photography.[38]

Death plays a key role in this dispersal, as the passing of Sfakians makes visitors' images especially valuable and allows the photographers to feel that their practice is important to locals. Take Jean-Jacques Strahm, the Swiss man who took his photo booklets containing images from the 1960s onward to local establishments. After the recent death of a local fisherman, he immediately posted his image of the deceased man online to express his condolences. His booklets furnish image-events. During the birthday gathering of an Anglo couple coming to Sfakia since the 1970s, the local proprietor brought Jean-Jacques's booklet to the table. People passed it around, noting who the subjects were, and they stressed the fact that no other images of these men were available locally.

The photographers' intentions notwithstanding, it is important to grasp which of these images of ancestors and of themselves Sfakians consider successful and why. I argue that Sfakians' way of looking at these pictures constitutes a certain kind of politics. Consider people's responses to a 1978 image portraying Sfakian men outside the coffeehouse at the village that was burned down in 1943 (figure 3.10). It had been taken by a German semipermanent resident in Sfakia who was originally involved in a real-estate project and who knew people and the region well. Given Sfakians' aversion to foreigners' land buying, the project had been controversial from the start but became additionally so in the post-bailout-deal phase when foreigners' purchases came to be viewed in parallel with news of national resources sold cheaply to Greece's creditors. I included this image in the exhibition *The Sfakian Screen: Looking and Living in the White Mountains of Crete*, which I curated in 2018, exploring what digital photographic practices mean in a society that has until now been represented only by scholarly outsiders.[39] The photographer of this image had recently digitized and shared with me his rich visual archive of the region (a hint to contemporary digital exchanges of archival photography of Sfakia happening online), while his semipermanent/insider status offered an opportunity for me to open up the question of who can be considered "Sfakian" today.

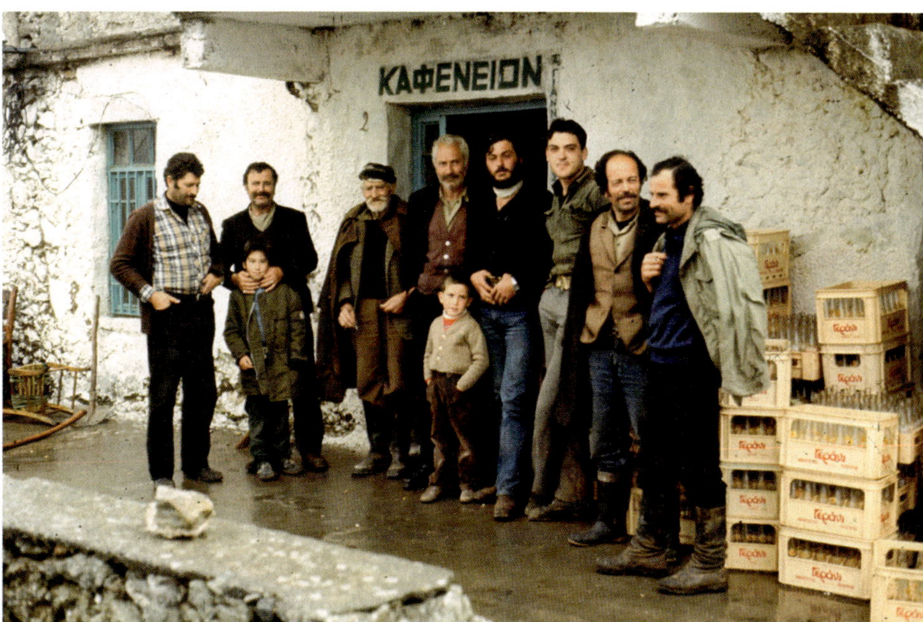

3.10 Photograph depicting Sfakian men at a highland village. This image was a favorite among Sfakian viewers of the 2018 exhibition *The Sfakian Screen: Looking and Living in the White Mountains of Crete*. The image was taken by a German man, resident in the region. Ignoring questions of authorship, Sfakian spectators focused on recognizing the subjects and discussing Sfakian lifeworlds of the past. Photograph by Wolf Lustig, ca. 1978.

None of my local interlocutors at the show, however, mentioned who took the photo (despite the caption naming him). Instead, they focused on recognizing the sitters and providing personal stories that were sometimes interspersed with imitations of their voices.[40] This reflex pertains to every image taken by nonlocals in Sfakia. It was familiar to me, as in previous work I explored Sfakians' emphasis on recognizing sitters in commercial photographs as a critique of the typology that treats these sitters as anonymous rural specimens.[41] Those interlocutors would challenge commercial photographers' exploitative tactics, resembling at some level the complaints uttered by the sitter of the famous *Migrant Mother* photo against the photographer Dorothea Lange.[42] And there were also locals who criticized their co-villagers for falling prey to the photographers due to their desire for self-promotion. Sfakians in the exhibition now personalized this historical photograph and also eschewed any political issues that would come up if I asked them about the photographer in relation to Germans' land buying.[43] Their practice of recognizing and naming the subjects was accompanied by emphatic affirmation of the importance of the appearance of these old men—a form of "ancestor worship" hinging on the visual. This worship is also expressed in embodied ways. A popular genre of locally produced images that has exploded after the use of smartphones concerns the embodiment of the ancestral archetype of the warrior on the mountain (drawing on nineteenth-century iconographies), and it treats the mountain as a transcendental zone where an idealized past may be enacted.[44]

In *The Civil Contract of Photography*, Ariella Azoulay argues that bourgeois/nationalist ideas of intellectual property are foreign to photography, which inherently exists by virtue of a community of producers, subjects, and spectators with equal roles.[45] Though Sfakians do not utter this egalitarian vision, their obliteration of photographers' details breaks with the tradition of authorship and copyright that Azoulay critiques. In particular, Sfakians are not targeting the asymmetry between photographer and subject as such, but they obliterate it by iterating the primacy of the subject. They adore the aura of those photographed (accompanied often by narratives idealizing these ancestors' perseverance in harsh conditions), displace the authorship of the image, and neutralize the ability of photographers to inscribe themselves in place. The photos I have been returning to people since 2006 follow a similar trajectory. They are frequently reposted online but never with reference to their photographer despite the warm, close ties I have with those who repost them.

The stance is embedded in a local perception of authorship that may be viewed as the patrilineal, hierarchical version of Azoulay's civil contract. "Someone's photograph" refers for Sfakians to the person it portrays and never to the photographer. When I told a local participant in the *Sfakian Screen* exhibition that *he* might travel to the United States, meaning the show might be displayed there, he found my claim puzzling and said that this isn't really *his photo*, as he isn't portrayed in it. The old anthropological solution would be to attribute this sensibility to people's lack of familiarity with a literate tradition wherein copyright and citations are fundamental conventions.[46] But, I argue, Sfakians' obliteration of authorship is comparable to forgetting aspects of the colonial past in Madagascar, as reported by Jennifer Cole.[47] It is an active process of imagining the present by negotiating the fact that, rather than being the producers, locals have been historically the anonymous subjects of powerful outsiders' photographs.

Sfakians' approach is purificatory and hierarchical as they distinguish between images of their ancestors (especially in black and white) and colorful photos portraying scenes with tourists. Like the people who complained about the wreath at the Distomo commemoration, Sfakians mostly want their ancestors to be displayed as singular subjects, not mingled in transcultural ties with the photographic community that Azoulay considers constitutive of the "civil contract." This sensibility translates into other domains too. When I organized the 2018 exhibition, a few (mostly male) interlocutors expressed their disappointment that the show concerned contemporary colorful images their co-villagers took with their smartphones and not old, archival images of deceased Sfakians (such as figure 3.5) like those I had circulated in the past. Thus the coffeehouse photo (figure 3.10) provided an antidote to that disappointment as it allowed people to admire the (predigital) past, without acknowledging that past's mediation by a German photographer. That some Sfakians preferred the old archival images to those that co-villagers produced in the present complicates the liberal assumption that the digital ("new") media offer liberation from past hierarchies and create an egalitarian civic space; such hierarchies may in fact be exactly what is desirable for some people in old aesthetic domains.[48]

And it's not just transculturation that is being negated through the preference for singular portraits but also a rejection of being captured by a tourist. In keeping with their understanding of cameras as weapons (figure 3.6), Sfakians describe cameras as "spies" and "traitors," which, especially in the social media era, can expose sensitive information to a wide public. Visibility is associated with risk more generally, as when people sketch the danger of accidentally witnessing illegal activities in the region. But the disavowal of cameras competes with the desire for having a portrait taken, hence my friend Nektarios's threats that he would break my "traitors" were undermined by his careful display of photographic portraits of himself that I and other travelers had taken in the past. Visual pleasure competes with the rejection of cameras as spying instruments, and in a similar fashion, the normative disavowal of Germans as colonizers competes with an accommodating, even affectionate stance. Further, images by tourists are easier to celebrate because by coming from the outside, they eschew the severe critique of self-promotion that applies to any Sfakians who publicize themselves or their patriline.

The suspicion of cameras also needs to be contextualized in Sfakians' perceptions of Germany as the prime agent of modernity. Archetypical technological artifacts (e.g., cameras or trucks) that appear in the village are often assumed to be "German." And that modernity is seen by Sfakians as both necessary and oppressive.[49] Modern artifacts have a particular connection to Germany's assumed knack for military exploits. People thus share stories about German camera-bearing spies who surveyed Crete before World War II in order to facilitate the subsequent military invasion. During the crisis, this notion of Germany's surveillance has been enhanced with Sfakians often joking during feasts that scenes of entertainment and affluence will make (surveying) Germans propose harsher austerity measures for Greece.

Sfakians' suspicion of exploitation and surveillance is mitigated by amicable guests who claim to want to know the region and its people more intimately, while providing locals with photos that suit their self-image as hospitable and traditional. This is an image that emerged as a result of the interplay with Western travelers, since at least the eighteenth century.[50] In fact, there's an analogy between Sfakians' own exaltation of the mountains as sublime regions of freedom and mystical energy and tourists' adoration of Sfakians as Romantic subjects. Tourists consistently affirm Sfakians' mythologized self-conceptualizations as pure descendants of the Dorians and as products of a history of armed resistance.

Paraphrasing Azoulay, what motivates Sfakians to look is *not* the *res publica* but a desire to see and possess their most celebrated traits in photographs.[51] Sfakians generally deny having common experiences with tourists as a basis for a shared (civic) space. At the same time, these images furnish interactions (as when the photographers return them to the sitters) that exceed a categorical notion of incompatibility and clash between the guests (Germans) and the hosts (Sfakians). Tourists, on the other hand, are motivated by participation in a community that suits the fantasy of a rugged traditional enclave. Their commitment to returning photos suggests a desire for reciprocity with locals, even aspirations that locals be grateful for these photos. Among foreign property owners, efforts to establish connections with locals (e.g., by buying farming products) are further linked to hopes of navigating tense relationships (e.g., to neighbors whose animals may destructively graze in their gardens). Sfakians are fond of images (especially old, black-and-white ones depicting their ancestors) as part of their conviction that Sfakianness is a visually distinctive category, and they enjoy these interactions with tourists in spheres where the performative reworking of the insider/outsider boundary allows visitors temporary positions inside local sociality. The importance Sfakians give to offering hospitality as a moral gesture, which these photos become ultimate proofs of, further enhances their photophilia. Victimage by Germans, like that framed in relation to Distomo and Kalavryta, wouldn't constitute a locally approved image as it would override the warrior–host subject position.[52] This is the position that visitors are so keen on articulating in this photographic citizenship characterized by adulation.

Embittered Eyes

MARTYRDOM AND THE VISIBILITY OF TRUTH

The final hall of the Municipal Museum of the Kalavritan Holocaust is filled with a group of Austrian middle-aged men and women. They are gathered around octogenarian Giorgos Dimopoulos, listening to his firsthand experience of the December 13, 1943, massacre perpetrated by the Wehrmacht and its translation by the group guide. The audience is sighing in commiseration as the speaker emphasizes the brutality, injustice, sadism, and horror of the massacre and the period that followed the murder of more than five hundred men and the burning of most of the town's buildings; he also explains that adjacent (smaller) villages suffered similar losses. Giorgos addresses his audience in their national capacity and expresses bewilderment at the fact that a country (Austria) known for its "civilization" (he cites Mozart, as an example) would create such an atrocity. Conjuring scenes of terrified women and children fleeing, amid burning houses, the school in which they had been held captive, while all males approximately over thirteen were taken for execution, he alludes to the impossibility of words ever doing justice to the experience.[53] Like Renato Rosaldo, he seems to think that narrative is no substitute for personal experience.[54] Some of Giorgos's descriptions of the slaughter feature the formulaic tropes that one encounters in local and national accounts of the event, like the one about a frozen piece of bread soaked with the blood of an executed man that becomes the only sustenance for his starving children.

Such representations, with their allusions to Christian iconographies of pain, have a certain stylistic rigidity reminiscent of what Maurice Bloch described as "arthritic" ritual discourse.[55] In fact, visitors traveling to the monument dedicated to the murdered residents of Kalavryta tend to utter things that don't formally qualify as ritual but still feature formulaic and repetitive elements. Under the reverberating solemn female voice heard through the memorial's speakers making references to the Germans' bestial violence, many Greek visitors identify with the victimization of a small resisting place (and by extension, nation) by a cruel, robotic military system.[56] Some leap to the present to what they perceive as the brutalization of Greeks by German austerity policies or they highlight the putative contradiction of having suffered at the hands of Germans yet enjoying German products or traveling to Germany for pleasure. The responses emerging at the monument (and to a degree at the museum) tend to privilege the nation as unchanging essence (brutality as a perennial German trait targeting Greeks as victims-cum-heroes). In other words, they critique power differentials and Greece's "colonization" within the EU, through an emphasis on the nation (and its ostensibly broken sovereignty) which in the post-bailout years did not offer protection against economic violence or effect accountability for Germany's past crimes. For residents, the monuments in both Kalavryta and Distomo open up a kind of ancestor veneration hinging on vision. Several people told me that looking at the monuments from afar puts them under the eyes of their pained ancestors and empowers them to keep struggling for German compensations to happen and to persevere in life more generally.

The museum is housed in the school building where women and children were held captive by the Germans on December 13, 1943. Its final hall is filled with black-and-white portraits of the murdered men, their names in columns for the viewer to connect, and a digital platform that supplies short biographical information for each man (figure 3.11).[57] As with an image of local schoolchildren before the war, encountered near the entrance, these portraits' power stems from what Roland Barthes described as photography's double temporality: "this will be and this has been."[58] As is the case with Alexander Gardner's 1865 portrait of conspirator Lewis Payne, who had been sentenced to death, when the viewers encounter these faces on the wall, they know they are already dead. Poignantly, the Kalavrytans didn't know at the time that they would soon be killed.

Dimopoulos is occasionally invited by the museum director to give tours on account of his firsthand experience of the slaughter, which adds reliability and vividness to his testimony. Locals refer to Dimopoulos as one of the

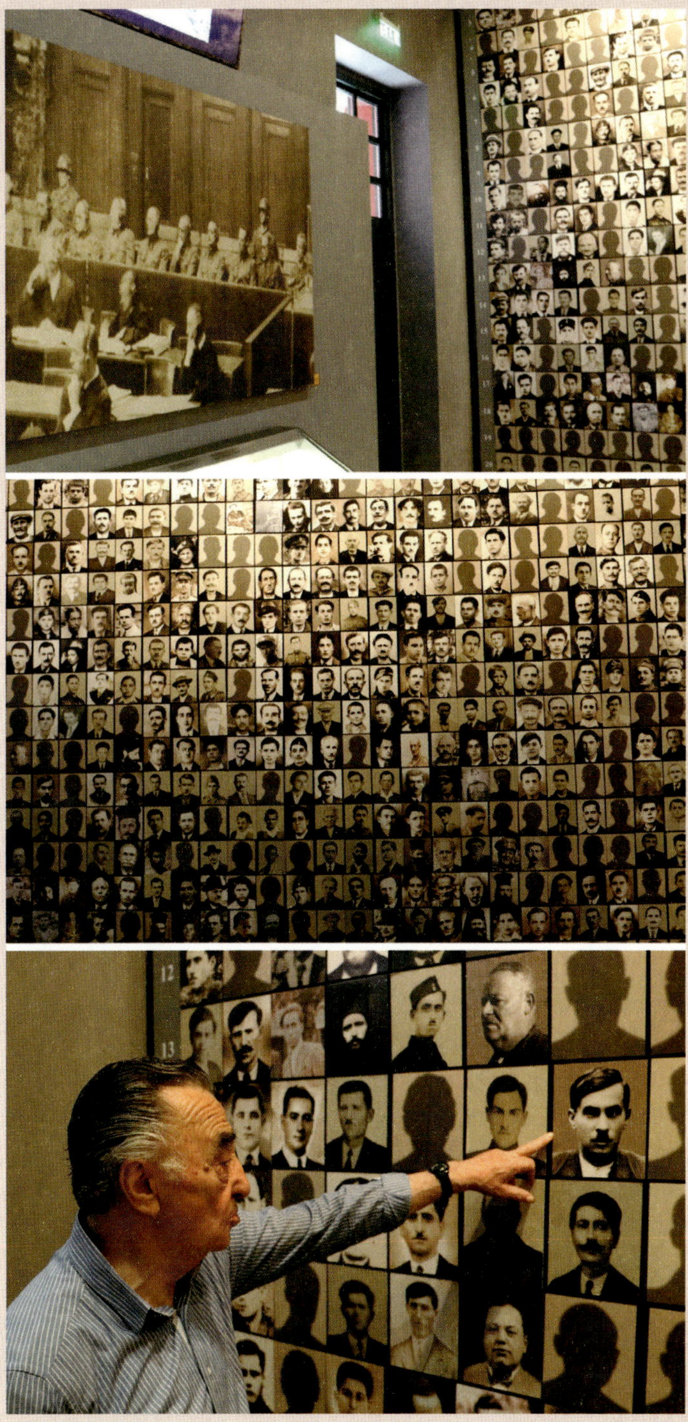

3.11 Images in the final hall at the Municipal Museum of the Kalavritan Holocaust. Note in the visual pantheon of murdered residents the silhouettes used for those victims whose photos could not be retrieved. *Top*: An image from the Nuremberg trials placed to the side of the photo wall. *Bottom*: Survivor Giorgos Dimopoulos points to his father's portrait. Photographs by Konstantinos Kalantzis, 2018.

last slaughter survivors. The idealization of witnessing as a modality that is at play in both towns needs to be considered here. In the local hierarchy of value, to have witnessed the slaughter (particularly the actual execution) is seen as affording an immensely important subject position. Locals claim there is a need to record the stories of the very few survivors who are still alive. In Distomo, a middle-aged man who voluntarily gives moving tours to visitors in front of black-and-white portraits of the murdered residents refers to survivors' testimonies as "holy scripture." Anthony Pagden, writing about European encounters in the Americas, underlines the importance of witnessing in Christian cosmology by pointing to the etymological connection between martyrdom and the Greek word *martyras* (witness).[59] There is a certain privileging of vision and immediate presence here: having seen horror (as Bartolomé de las Casas claimed to have done) gives one a special position vis-à-vis non-witnesses.[60] These photos on the walls then display the eyes that saw horror and are thus different from the eyes and bodies of the next generations, who lack personal experience of the slaughter and may, in locals' view, compromise their political stance vis-à-vis Germany.

The aura with which both leftist and nonleftist interlocutors surround survivors goes along with skepticism toward the views of others who have no firsthand experience of what happened. But accounts of the slaughter and their different allusions to the subsequent 1946–49 Greek civil war are strongly divided along leftist and rightist positions.[61] Local leftists typically claim the German attacks were decided in advance and that resistance to the occupation was a moral prerogative that the Greek People's Liberation Army rightly engaged. Some commentators nationalize the point further by saying that without resistance "we would still have Turks ruling," referring to the Ottoman dominion, which the early nineteenth-century Greek War of Independence disrupted (of which Kalavryta is nationally emblematic as an alleged place of origin). Rightists, on the other hand, blame the communist guerrillas for attacking German troops and thus provoking retaliation. Some rightist commentators push the polarity further by claiming that the leftist guerrillas purposely provoked the retaliation so as to punish the town folk for being too complacent and bourgeois. Further, leftist interlocutors emphasize the role played by Greek collaborators, often from the same villages that the Germans attacked.

At stake here is the binary between collaboration and resistance that resurfaces today in the context of the opposition between Greece and its creditors. For leftists, presenting resistance as a moral imperative, the historical parallels are clear: past collaborators are comparable to contemporary officialdom, receiving money from German institutions such as the Deutsch-Griechischer Zukunftsfonds that "rewrite history" and blame communist guerrillas for the Nazi atrocities, thus undermining the compensation claims. For many rightist interlocutors, that suspicion is exaggerated, while some self-proclaimed centrist liberals even assert that they prefer foreign guardianship (as transparent and efficient) to the putatively corrupt local/national political forces. Some leftists claim to find the Kalavrytans' 1940s surrender to the German aggressors embarrassing, thus highlighting the tension between heroism and victimage/passivity that underlies national narrations of the slaughter. One Kalavrytan interlocutor added a gendered visual component to notions of resistance as he extolled the combative iconography of a memorial in the Distomo area (featuring male warriors in arms) compared to his home-town monument's aesthetics of weeping motherhood. This man otherwise spoke in admiration about the endurance of women in the 1940s, but at a memorial level the image of bereaved mothers signified loss rather than struggle. For him, as for most leftists, it is the Greek People's Liberation Army that provides an image of resistance to the occupiers, one disputed by rightists. This is where Crete comes into play nationally as it supplies an imaginary figure of resistance and revenge for a wide constituency not restricted to leftists.

It is in the light of the unresolved tension concerning different agents' responsibility in the 1943 slaughter and its position as an unfathomable horror scene in people's social imagination that locals value witnessing. I argue this can be fruitfully understood by thinking through film and photography as modalities. What is valued through witnessing is empirical proximity to the subject and the notion of unmediated sight, which is why the most esteemed survivors in Kalavryta are those who saw the actual execution on the hill by being among those who were shot at (they weren't just present in the town when it happened). According to a rumor that circulated in Kalavryta for a considerable amount of time, German soldiers *shot* the entire execution on film and kept the footage in their archives. If true, the incident would be a perfect example of the visual as a colonizing apparatus and at the same time a means of recording self-incriminating evidence that may damage those same colonizers.[62] The rumor was so strong that I heard the museum's final hall (the room with the black-and-white portraits) had a dedicated case that remained empty in anticipation of the video footage's return to the village, once the amateur researcher who claimed to have found it brought it back from the German archives. The rumor speaks to a series of important issues in local understandings of the event: the Germans emerge as modernity's surveyors (some said the footage was shot from an airplane) and their surveillance is linked to both social control and (sadistic) pleasure; the (filmic) visual is invested with the hope that it will resolve all discussions about what happened; the visual is seen as the ultimate form of the historical. As Paul Valéry put it in the late 1930s, for something to constitute "historical knowledge," it needs to have been photographed first.[63] In fact, both the Distomo and Kalavryta museums display silhouettes for those victims whose images weren't available. In other words, a visual figure is still necessary on the wall so that the victims constitute history (figure 3.11). During a session that he requested, where I filmed the steps he took while fleeing the school, survivor Giorgos Dimopoulos confirmed expectations of cameras as instruments that provide definitive historical answers.[64] He repeatedly told me that his difficulties in describing the scenes would have been resolved "if only there were cameras back then."

The value placed on autopticism also comes out in the views of a man who has been involved in a personal project of photographing traces of the 1943 slaughter in the landscape (an archive that he never publicizes). He told me that it was only after the passing of a particular (leftist) survivor that rightist "imposters" began blaming leftist guerrillas for the slaughter. They waited for his death, that is, so that their falsities wouldn't be disputed by a witness of historical reality. In many ways, the privileging of empirical/visual immediacy disavows what Marianne Hirsch describes as postmemory, the inter- and intragenerational transmission of memories of a traumatic event via stories, images, and other representations.[65] In a quasi-Platonic fashion, people in Kalavryta and Distomo disqualify those (mediated) representations as figments (at best misguided, at worst manipulative) and seek to locate the primary, raw evidence, or lament its impossible recovery. The appreciation of the witness as an ideal figure and related cultural expectations of the camera may be thought through the history of cameras in anthropology. Drawing on an idea by David Tomas, Christopher Pinney has argued that with the professionalization of the discipline in the early twentieth century through the establishment of ethnography as its prime methodology, ethnographers themselves came to metaphorize and embody the qualities of the camera. Ethnography constituted a tripartite process (preparation at home, exposure to the field site, and return home to write) that duplicated the photographic procedure, such as exposure to light and subsequent development at the studio.[66] Thus the power to capture the (cultural) truth, with which the camera was endowed during the early, nonprofessional phase of the discipline, was later displaced onto ethnographers. Similarly, my interlocutors hope that film can capture the truth and dispel the ambiguities about 1943, but they also accept that such footage is impossible to retrieve and project their hopes onto witnesses as figures who captured the impossible sight. Let's now delve further into the kind of work that the few existing photos from the 1940s do for people.

DOWNCAST, NOT SURVEYING EYES: ON ACCUSATORY MEMORY

The first local public events to ever address the slaughter in Distomo and Kalavryta revolved around photography and involved the collection and display of images of the murdered men, women, and children. Leftist interlocutors stress that this could only happen after the fall of the 1967–74 Colonels junta that marked the end of rightist/royalist hegemony within which any positive references to (leftist) guerrilla resistance were penalized. In Distomo, the exhibition process brought up what we might call animistic investment in photographic portraiture. I was told that no local man or woman wanted to store the collected images of the deceased in their house before the first exhibition for fear of these images' effect. One can infer that these photos were seen as capturing the presence and soul of the depicted subjects, as something more than two-dimensional paper.[67] According to locals' descriptions, those in charge of the first exhibitions were later accused of capitalizing on the deceased for their own publicity or even for monetary profit. The critique reminded me of Sfakians' dismissals of anyone claiming to represent the area to outsiders, and of their conviction that local writers self-servingly obscure the area's true "history" in order to inflate particular families' roles.[68] The suspicion of mnemonic mediators is entangled in Distomo and Kalavryta with the dismissal of *postmemory noise* that, in this view, misrepresents the raw, primal event of the slaughter. It is in the role as mitigators of such suspicions that we ought to understand Distomo's and Kalavryta's museums' function. Both museums are officially designed by ministry-based museologists (a plan is currently under way for Distomo), but both build on previous efforts by expats and locals to assemble historical materials. By virtue of their state–public character, they are deemed the only appropriate spaces for displaying the slaughter in ways that would not raise suspicions of self-serving motives, such as self-glorification. Self-glorification refers here to overstressing the losses of particular families compared to others (a competition that also informs relationships among the afflicted villages on the whole). And though certain local scholars may complain that their co-villagers don't visit the museums as often as they should, these spaces become quasi-domestic depositories of ancestors' images, which residents visit especially on the commemoration days. One Distomite man in his sixties told me about a dream he once had of his murdered father scolding him for not having been married yet. He said his dad "looked exactly like his photo at the museum." He said he had no real recollection of his father as he was too young when he was killed in 1944. His local peer with whom he also shared this story affirmed the significance invested in photography as presence and memory (and in the museum as its holder) by replying, "So you dreamt of the photograph!"

In this narrative, the father becomes an ancestral witness, judging the (inadequate) actions of his son. My interlocutor thus conjured an imagined male, photographic version of what C. Nadia Seremetakis described in the Peloponnese as the female chorus that laments the dead while assessing the roles the bereaved played in their lives.[69] It is important to grasp the work assigned to this imagined jury, especially as we think of the more politicized version of affect generated in public uses of such photos. Take how this affect operates spatially in both museums, where a specific wall is dedicated to images of the German perpetrators with captions stressing their impunity. It is as if the eyes of the ancestors (on adjacent walls) stare out at their killers (in Kalavryta, defendants at the Nuremberg trials face these ancestors sideways; see figure 3.11). In tours given by local volunteers or museum employees, emphasis is given to pausing in front of the perpetrators' portraits and elaborating on their responsibility, which elicits most visitors' aggravation. Thus, for many Greeks, the visit to the museums becomes a way of embodying the position of the exasperated (national) subject and further sharing it with others. One is reminded of Sarah Gensburger's exploration of French visitors of Holocaust museums, who recognize each other as people sharing particular principles.[70] In this vein, some Greek visitors (I heard schoolteachers) placed flowers at the bottom of a gigantic portrait of Maria Pantiska, originally published in a 1944 edition of *Life* magazine (we might call her the Greek version of Lange's *Migrant Mother*), at the Distomo museum (figure 3.12). Their gesture indicates a pilgrimage to the deceased and shows one possible operation of these emblematic photos. Pantiska remains unnamed here and embodies a symbolic Ur-sufferer, which feeds into normative ideas of the rural Greek woman as a figure of pain and endurance. For my local interlocutors, however, engagement with this photo also draws on the particularities of the image (what we might call indexicality), which is further enhanced by their knowledge of her biography. Local interlocutors thus noted that in the photograph she was mourning her mother, who was killed along with female kin while preparing a mortuary ritual for a nephew murdered by another German battalion some forty days prior (this comment implicitly compares her to Distomites who lost more than one parent). These observers also commented that her headscarf's position indicates the photographer's staging, and they recall that this image triggered a marriage proposal by a Greek American reader of *Life* magazine that her father averted.

In the locales under discussion, public use of imagery involves a constant interplay between the *emblematic/iconic* (the lamenting woman as symbolic Ur-mother, the Sfakian man as Ur-traditional) and the *indexical* (the depicted as a remembered individual, subject to personal affect).[71] An important as-

3.12 Dmitri Kessel's image of Maria Pantiska, originally featured in a 1944 edition of *Life* magazine headlined "What the Germans Did to Greece." This image is reused in various editions, posters, brochures, and related materials, locally and internationally. The photo is used here as a poster at the entrance of the Distomo Museum of the Victims of Nazism. Original photograph by Dmitri Kessel, ca. 1945. Dmitri Kessel collection, ELIA-MIET Photographic Archive (Hellenic Literary and Historical Archive-Cultural Foundation of the National Bank of Greece). Photograph of the entrance by Konstantinos Kalantzis, 2018.

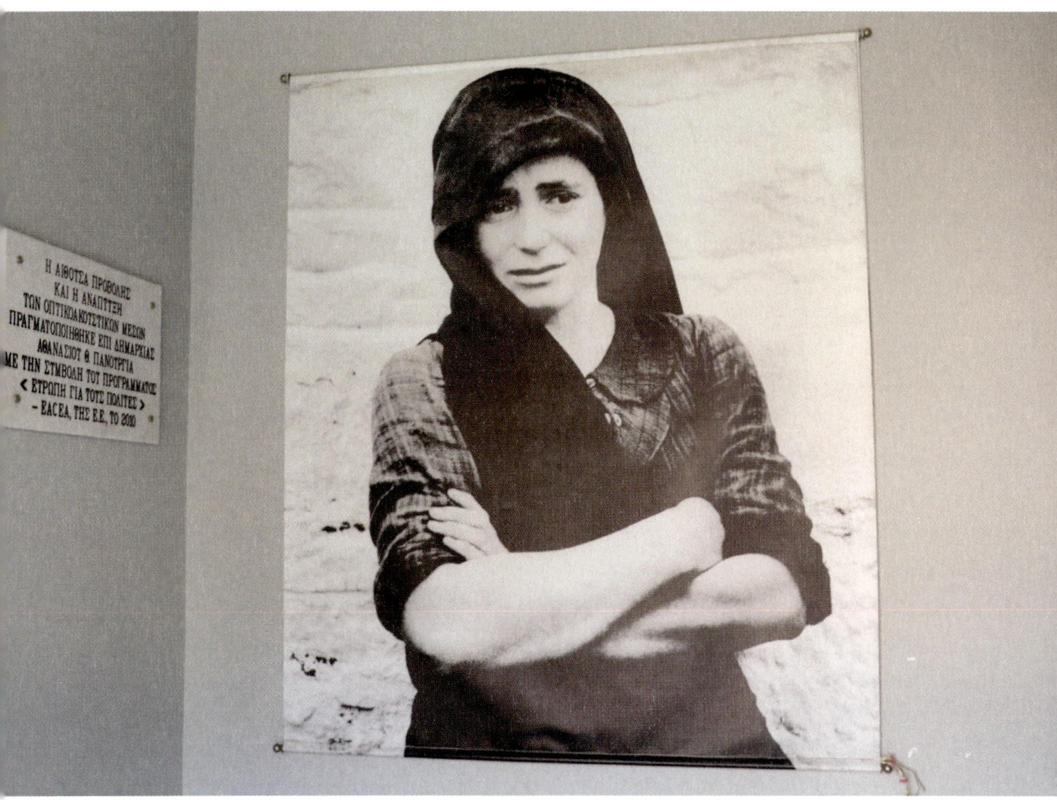

pect in the literature about emblematic imagery concerns the extent to which widely circulated photographs are, in Barthes's terms, "tame," that is, neutralized and entirely absorbed into hegemonic narratives, or whether they entail political potential and the capacity to be "indelible image[s] of terror."[72] However, the indexicality of Kalavryta and Distomo photos extends beyond locals' ability to recognize the depicted subjects as individuals. For one, locals are subject to national pedagogy and may often describe the subjects in the formulaic nationalist language deployed in the media. Most importantly, the emotions that even nonlocal visitors project on these photos speak to indexicality in Margaret Olin's terms, that is, as pertaining to the viewer's desire to recognize and be touched by the image rather than to an inherent quality of the photograph.[73] This is what happened, for instance, when a Russian middle-aged visitor in Kalavryta encountered the famous photo showing ax-bearing Nazi soldiers smiling in front of burning buildings that was possibly taken in Distomo and was reportedly discovered by photographer Spyros Meletzis inside a German's camera confiscated by Greek communist guerrillas (figure 3.13, bottom left). The display of this photograph on the wall of a shop in Kalavryta selling "traditional" products (supposedly determined by the shop's urban decorator) might seem to evidence the photograph's taming and the obliteration of its indexicality, since the particularities of the image are lost. Yet the Russian man stared at the image for long, spoke of his grandfather's role in fighting against the Germans in World War II, and remembered the old man's medals at which he marveled as a child. This scene also concerns the capacity of historical imagery to evoke a certain familial modality whereby viewers cast themselves in the role of (grand)children of the deceased.[74] A common dynamic I observed in the Kalavryta memorial involves Greek parents reading the ages of young executed individuals and telling their own children, "He was like you!" For some visitors, this animates a sense of discord with Germany today. Certain university-educated interlocutors who offer guides at the museum dismiss this discord as all-too-easy anti-Germanism, which they claim to encounter often among Greek visitors who allegedly ask insistently about German visitors' reactions to the exhibits.

Many of the instances related here recall Azoulay's description of photography's employment as "grievance," by which users become civic subjects (she is referring to disaffected subjects deprived of official citizenship).[75] This modality extends beyond the museums and underlines a ubiquitous moral desire in Distomo and Kalavryta. What is this grievance about? There are dozens of instances where people display images as a moral protest, a practice that exceeds the left–right axis that otherwise produces divided readings of

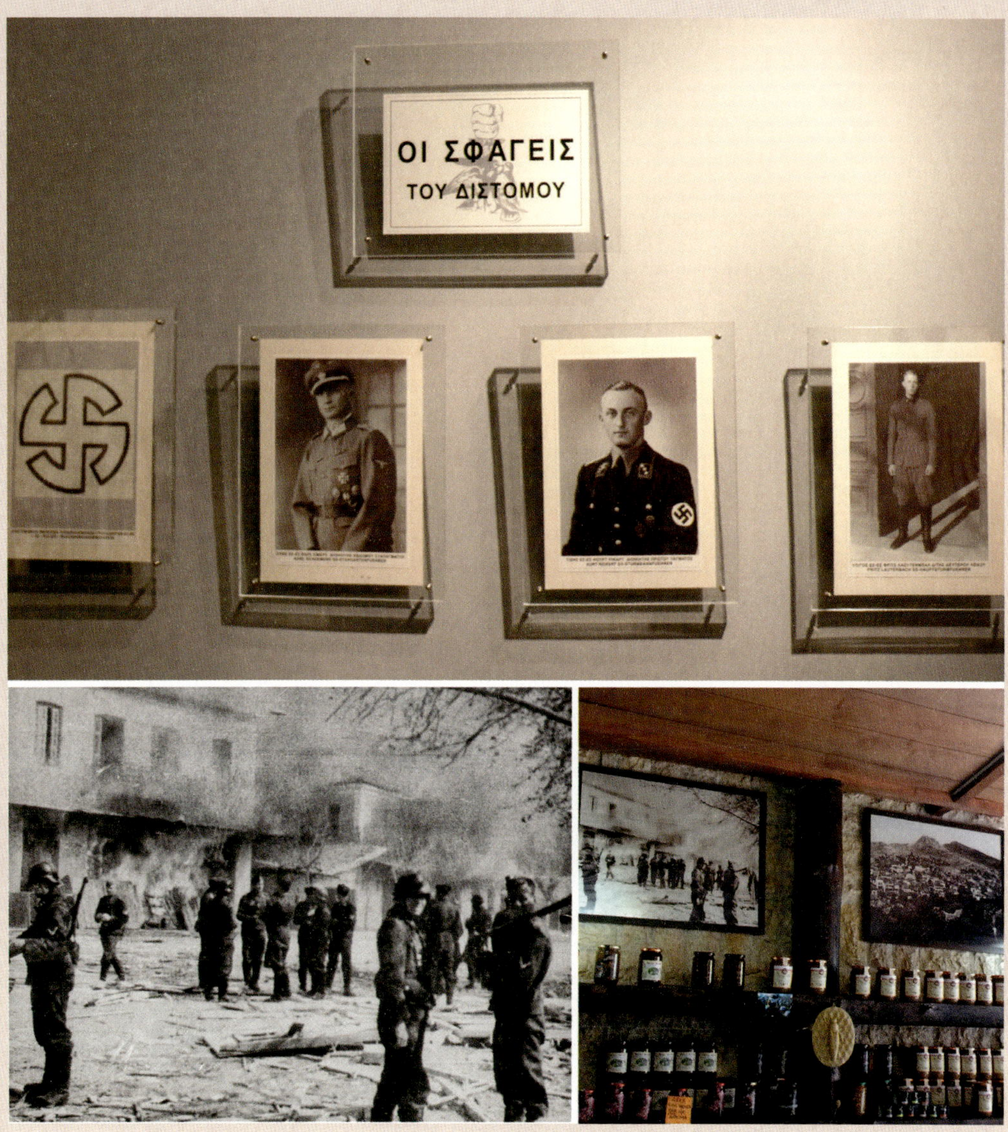

3.13 *Top*: Photographs of Nazi officials as displayed at the Distomo Museum of the Victims of Nazism with the caption “Distomo’s butchers.” *Bottom left*: A famous photograph that allegedly depicts a scene from the 1944 Distomo slaughter and was reportedly found by photographer Spyros Meletzis inside a German soldier’s camera confiscated by a Greek (ELAS) guerrilla. Note the image’s reuse (*bottom right*) inside a Kalavryta shop selling “traditional” edible products, a choice that the owner attributed to the shop’s professional decorator. Original photographs by unknown photographer, 1944. Contemporary photographs by Konstantinos Kalantzis, 2018.

the past.[76] Thus the owner of a shop in Kalavryta frequented by tourists has put up an image of his uncle who was killed. The caption explains that he was killed by "German fascists" of the regular army and that "we never forget him nor do we forgive—his memory is eternal." This man is loudly involved in the claim for Germany to pay reparations to Greece and consistently targets Greek collaborators ("past and present") of the Germans. But also consider the elderly woman Nitsa Sfontouri from Distomo, whose position was a far cry from the activist leftist profile of the aforementioned man and who frequently hosted European (especially German) journalists and social scientists at her home. During these visits, she told her guests in her distinctive bitter, eloquent style the story of her grandfather's, parents', and two sisters' murders, which she partly witnessed, and narrated her orphaned childhood under the care of her strict grandmother.[77] She also showed her guests the composite image of her murdered relatives (figure 3.14). Visual assemblages of this kind reflect a common iconographic motif found in Kalavryta and Distomo homes. They were made in professional studios using portraits of the murdered kin, which the relatives brought to the proprietor. When I asked Nitsa why she still gives interviews, against her sons' advice to avoid revisiting the slaughter as it wears her down emotionally, she instructively replied: "It's a small form of punishment, to narrate *their* barbarism—to say how unjustly they destroyed us. [. . .] What kind of soldier picks up a machine gun and murders a young woman, aged twenty-nine, with her kids?"

This is a modality we might describe as accusatory memory. It speaks primarily to a moral desire that transcends the compensation claim (the claim, which mostly concerns Distomo residents, attracts divisive commentary). Vision has a central place in this desire as my interlocutors want to shame the perpetrators' descendants and have them display what Martin Jay called, in a different context, "downcast eyes."[78] If Germany is the arch metaphor of modernity's surveyor (a notion resurfacing today with Greece's monitoring in the crisis), accusatory memory demands that the shamed German spectators look down and listen; their gaze no longer commands or surveils. This desire further explains the disdain for the German wreath with which I opened this chapter. A key misgiving against its orchestrating role relates to an idea I heard often by Distomo and Kalavryta interlocutors: that the potential existence of a plaque acknowledging sponsorship of local institutions by Germany would be the greatest humiliation. Accepting this gift, in this view, would grant Germany the role of a powerful orchestrator, even if it concerns the display of its own crimes. Thus two outspoken critics of German soft diplomacy in Kalavryta underlined that the perpetrators' descendants' eyes ought

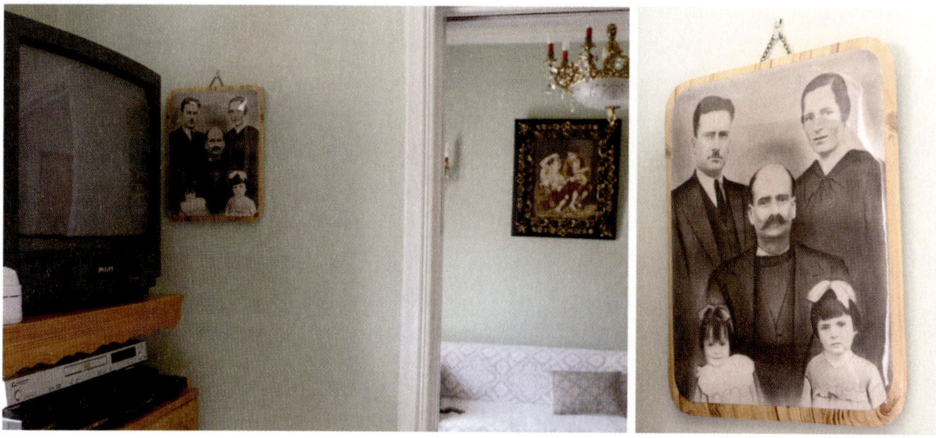

3.14 Composite studio photograph in which portraits of family members murdered by the SS troops in Distomo have been reassembled. It represents a common pictorial practice found in Distomo and Kalavryta. Sitters (*top left to bottom right*): Miltiadis and Kondylia Nikolaou, Dimitris Kailis, Katerina and Maria Nikolaou. Courtesy of Nitsa Sfontouri. Photograph of interior by Konstantinos Kalantzis, 2018.

to look down in shock. On different occasions, they both told me that they are skeptical of German educational excursions to the area as long as these do not include visits to the local cemetery. These men expected that the cemetery's materiality (with tomb engravings attributing deaths to the 1943 slaughter) will enhance the students' sense of moral obligation and guilt.

Like other visceral engagements with the past, accusatory memory practices anticipate a particular kind of future.[79] It is a future in which the memory of German violence is alive and one where the line separating the victim from the perpetrator is clearly visible. Thus leftists are particularly angry at the argument that 1940s guerrillas' actions caused the Nazi retaliation, as such an idea blurs who the actual perpetrators were and equalizes responsibility among groups with vastly different moral commitments.[80] Accusatory memory is simultaneously skeptical of any postmemory apparatuses. In Azoulayan terms, my interlocutors deny the sharing of a common civic space with the perpetrators and their descendants, particularly as the latter refuse to acknowledge their crime and offer an effective apology, though it is often ambiguous in local conversations (and it differs among the various actors) whether this apology means monetary compensation, a set of radically different political gestures, or more. In keeping with the anticolonial sensibility of Distomo and Kalavryta critics, actions such as the German embassy's sending of a wreath or small sponsorships to the municipality are offensive gifts (akin to "cheap beads and mirrors offered to the Indians," as different interlocutors have said), that is, inadequate gestures that aim to misguide people into thinking that Germany's responsibility is over. Their accusatory memory shares with other aggrieved communities of survivors globally an objection to the inadequacy of reconciliation and justice processes that fail to address people's own concerns with injustice and reparation in contexts ranging from Northern Ireland to Canada and Sri Lanka.[81] The photographic component of the desire to distinguish victim from perpetrator is apparent in how Germans and Greeks inhabit distinct visual realms in the museum halls (in Kalavryta, the dead ancestors look out at the perpetrators). During a discussion in Kalavryta about a published group photo from the 1950s showing local orphans at a German boarding school with their supervisors (part of a humanitarian program recruiting local children and sponsoring their studies in Germany), one interlocutor said emphatically that the kids were "surrounded by a bunch of fascists!" Coexistence with German authorities here can only mark containment, surveillance, and humiliation. The same interlocutor later invoked a published historical work with information from "German archives" about a particular local boy in the group as being incurably defiant and disdainful of everything German. My interlocutors then remembered the man's playful manners and amusedly celebrated the disorder he created at that German institution when he was a child.

Conclusion: Sentimental and Instrumental Realism

This chapter has explored photography and the act of looking as embodied practices that articulate moral/political visions and set up particular possibilities of imagining and coexisting with others. Sfakians, who are expected to embody the nation's resistance to occupiers, turn out to warmly accommodate German (and other) tourists. This dynamic is enhanced by these tourists' glorification of Sfakian hospitality, which feeds key local self-images and also relates to Sfakians' constant (segmentary) renegotiation of boundaries of insideness and outsideness and their deep aversion to the figure of the internal enemy, which weakens the devotion to animosity against the foreign enemy. Sfakian self-images of resistance, unique (male) appearance, and hospitability are enhanced by photographs supplied by tourists who have thus historically fed a Sfakian photophilic "ancestor worship." Parity is key to the tourists' gesture of sending these images back. In wanting to reciprocate and participate in locals' lives, they venerate notions of ruggedness and tradition, thereby augmenting Sfakians' own idealization of old photographs: a stance we might call sentimental realism, borrowing the term from Alan Sekula.[82] Yet Sfakians also engage the asymmetry involved in this visual economy (that they are never the producers of ancestors' images) by *forgetting* the authorship of these photos and by privileging visualizations of their ancestors as singular subjects. Their idealization of the ancestors' aura, though it is fed by tourists' photos, partly counters these visitors' desire for a common civic space and removes their agency.

At the other end of parity, I explored Distomo and Kalavryta residents' experiences and practices of displaying the 1940s, during which they suffered immense damage by German occupiers. In my analysis, the visual extends here beyond particular images into perceptions of witnessing as a modality hoped to resolve uncertainties about the past against the *postmemory noise* of the past's multiple representations. These representations become suspect in these two locales where interpretations of the past are divided along the left–right axis and where the display of historical images outside the museums is accompanied by intralocal critiques of exploitation. In Sekula's terms, we are dealing here with an *instrumental realism* that demands the visualization of the occupiers' atrocity, thereby making a political and moral request, which I describe as *accusatory memory*.[83] It is about emphatically remembering the atrocity against the pervasive fear that this memory is being diluted today. Accusatory memory partly plays into the claim for Germany to financially compensate Greece for the slaughters, but it also expresses a wider moral position and sets up a particular kind of future. The position seeks a reversal of Germany's role as surveyor and perpetrator, which has been enhanced in the context of Greece's post-2010 bailout deal and its EU/German-derived monitoring. Photography as well as other practices of remembering here inscribe the line that separates victim from perpetrator and ask that German onlookers look down in shame.

In both Sfakia and the mainland, photography emerges as an affect-generating sphere but with different political potential. Under the rubric of ancestor veneration and the dynamics of hospitality, Sfakians reverse the asymmetry of the encounter and forget the bellicosity against Germany that they are expected to enact nationally. Yet, though they forge affective relationships mediated by images in the sphere of hospitality, they also obliterate the authorship of travelers' photos, thereby introducing new boundaries and hierarchies between photographers and subjects. A more politicized disdain of Germany's role in authoring and dictating what is to be remembered characterizes Distomo and Kalavryta. Photography here conjures the victim that stares its perpetrators in the eye and demands moral justice against the European-derived universalist vision of common citizenship, which in the postausterity moment becomes visibly broken anew.

Notes

I am grateful for feedback and conversations with colleagues and students during my 2022/23 fellowship in Comparative Cultural studies at the Harvard Center for Hellenic Studies in Greece. Previous work on Crete was supported by the Arts and Humanities Research Council, University College London, the University of London, and the Seeger Center for Hellenic studies at Princeton University. I am thankful to my PhotoDemos colleagues Chris Pinney, Naluwembe Binaisa, Vindhya Buthpitiya, Ileana L. Selejan, and Sokphea Young for their fruitful comments throughout the years. I am very grateful to Alexandra Bakalaki for her valuable feedback on an earlier draft of this chapter. I am hugely indebted to Kostas Chritis for creating the image collages and his general help with photographs. I am also grateful to Tina Gericke for sharing ideas on the Greek-German constellation. Many thanks to Amalia Papaioannou at Distomo for her comments and for facilitating image permissions as well as the Municipal Museum of the Kalavritan Holocaust staff for their general help and for enabling access to materials. My thanks also go to the staff of the Benaki Museum Photographic Archive and the ELIA-MIET archive who eagerly facilitated access and gave me permission to reproduce visual material. I am especially thankful to all my interlocutors in Sfakia, Kalavryta, and Distomo for welcoming my inquiries and engaging with me over the years.

1 For a critical account of the bailout deal, see Varoufakis, "Being Greek."

2 Technically, compensations to victims fall under different legal categories depending on whether the plaintiffs are individuals (compensations) or state entities (reparations). Following many interlocutors, I use these terms interchangeably here to refer to any kind of compensation to victims (states or individuals) that evokes a wider question of reparation as a moral stake. Official organizations (e.g., "The network of martyr towns") make more technical distinctions among the different categories of compensation.

3 Sutton, *Memories*, 143; Stewart, *Dreaming*; Knight, "Cultural Proximity."

4 M. Hirsch, "Generation of Postmemory," 205.

5 On "irreconciliation," see Mookherjee, "Introduction," 21.

6 Cf. Papagaroufali, *Ipia diplomatia*.

7 Mookherjee, "Raped Woman," 382.

8 For a material reworking of portraits of Kalavrytans post 1943, see the artwork

About 1500, by Fotini Gouseti, http://www.fotinigouseti.com/index.php ?page=the-present.

9 Hariman and Lucaites, *No Caption Needed*, 188; Mookherjee, "Raped Woman," 390.

10 Azoulay, *Civil Contract*, 89.

11 Brown and Phy, "Introduction," 7.

12 See Hirschon, *Heirs*, 152; Sant Cassia, *Bodies*, 136; and Seremetakis, *Last Word*.

13 Hariman and Lucaites, *No Caption Needed*, 2. See also Hirsch, "Generation of Postmemory," 225–26.

14 Kalantzis, "'Fak Germani,'" 1051–57.

15 See Kalantzis, *Tradition in the Frame*, 72–76. Nelly was the professional name of Elli Sougioultzoglou-Seraidari (b. 1898, Aydin, Asia Minor; d. 1998, Athens).

16 See Kalantzis, "Proxy Brigands"; Kalantzis, "Picturing," 73–75.

17 See also Shryock, "Breaking Hospitality," 30; and Candea and da Col, "Return," 1.

18 On the trope of hospitality, see Candea, "*Derrida*."

19 See Kalantzis, *Tradition in the Frame*, 191–201.

20 Azoulay, *Civil Contract*, 85, 88, 97, 103, 106.

21 Roitman, *Anti-crisis*, 4, 70.

22 Herzfeld, "Absent Presence"; Herzfeld, *Cultural Intimacy*; Gourgouris, *Dream Nation*.

23 Kalantzis, *Tradition in the Frame*, 191–201.

24 Kalantzis, *Tradition in the Frame*, 101–9.

25 Benjamin, "Little History of Photography" (1999), 512.

26 See Kalantzis, "Proxy Brigands," 26–27.

27 See Kalantzis, *Tradition in the Frame*, 59–76. By "injury," I am hinting at Melanie Klein's notion of reparation (originally concerning the infant-mother constellation), that is, the restoration of positive properties of the figure on which one depends. The term is taken up in recent critical scholarship concerning the relationship between colonizers and those they colonized historically. Though its application to Greece needs careful consideration, the anticolonial imaginaries encountered in post-bailout Greece open up themes of injury and repair especially as regards Germany, though responses may at times be unlike the "decolonizing" activism encountered in certain postcolonial settings in their perceptions of gender and nationhood. See Klein, *Love, Guilt and Reparation*; Eng, "Colonial Object"; Huard and Moser, "Editorial Introduction."

28 Herzfeld, "'As in Your Own,'" 86.

29 See Latour, *We Have Never*, 114.

30 See Candea, "*Derrida*," 34.

31 See Shryock, "Breaking Hospitality," 23.

32 Bourdieu, *Outline*, 171–72.

33 Herzfeld, *Anthropology through the Looking-Glass*, 156.

34 Herzfeld, *Subversive Archaism*, 77–78. See also Papataxiarchis, “O adianoitos ratsismos,” and Rakopoulos, “Solidarity.”

35 Azoulay, *Civil Contract*, 104.

36 Candea and da Col, “Return,” 3.

37 Cf. High, “Melancholia.”

38 Candea and da Col, “Return,” 9.

39 *Sfakian Screen* exhibition catalogue, https://citizensofphotography.org/wp-content/uploads/2022/11/Konstantinos-Kalantzis-Sfakiani-Othoni.pdf. See also the short video “*The Sfakian Screen* local photo exhibition” featuring viewers’ responses to some of the images, including to the one discussed here: https://youtu.be/vuG1e3S7rso.

40 Cf. Edwards, “Photographs.”

41 Kalantzis, *Tradition in the Frame*, 93–113.

42 Azoulay, *Civil Contract*, 101; Hariman and Lucaites, *No Caption Needed*, 52–67.

43 It should also be noted that over the years the photographer cultivated ties with a number of locals and made an effort to bring the German buyers in touch with different Sfakians who live in that part of the region.

44 See Kalantzis, *Tradition in the Frame*, 165–69.

45 Azoulay, *Civil Contract*, 103.

46 Cole, “Work of Memory,” 612.

47 Cole, “Work of Memory,” 612.

48 See Hirschkind, de Abreu, and Caduff, “New Media,” 4.

49 Kalantzis, *Tradition in the Frame*, 219–24.

50 Kalantzis, *Tradition in the Frame*, 191–97.

51 Azoulay, *Civil Contract*, 131.

52 For a visual account of the two subject positions (warrior and victim), see the trailer titled “Photography, Ethnography and Political Imagination in Greece: A Film Preview by K. Kalantzis,” https://youtu.be/9DGrXwKMm8s.

53 This is why I named the short film I shot with him, reenacting his experience of the day of the slaughter, *The Impossible Narration: Memory and Photography of the Kalavryta Slaughter*. The film can be accessed at https://youtu.be/2KAkIlqAXcA.

54 Rosaldo, “Introduction.”

55 Sant Cassia, *Bodies*, 133; Bloch, “Symbols,” 64.

56 For a glimpse into the monument and the role of sound in it, see the short video *Place, Sound, and Image at the Kalavryta Holocaust Memorial*, https://youtu.be/fJESY_U4O_o.

57 These portraits can be accessed at the Municipal Museum of the Kalavritan Holocaust website, https://www.dmko.gr/i-germaniki-stratiotiki-epichirisi-kalavryta/ektelesthentes/ektelesthentes-kalavryta/ (last accessed November 5, 2022). They can also be found at a specialized section of the website titled “The Pantheon of the Murdered,” which features a representation of the actual photo wall of the museum. These pages include images of the survivors as

well as of women and children who had been locked up at the school (the latter organized per family). Last accessed November 5, 2022, http://pantheon.dmko.gr/.

58 Barthes, *Camera Lucida*, 96.
59 Pagden, *European Encounters*, 67.
60 Pagden, *European Encounters*, 67.
61 See also Droumpouki, *Mnimeia*, 352–400.
62 See Didi-Huberman, *Images in Spite of All*, 20–23.
63 Valéry, "Centenary of Photography," 195.
64 *Impossible Narration*, https://youtu.be/2KAkIlqAXcA.
65 M. Hirsch, "Generation of Postmemory," 205, 208.
66 Pinney, "Parallel Histories," 81–82; Pinney, *Photography*, 61–62.
67 On such repressed animism in Western Europe, see Wright, "Material," 76–77; and Pinney, *Photography*, 34, 140–45.
68 Kalantzis, *Tradition in the Frame*, 139.
69 Seremetakis, *Last Word*, 105, 126.
70 Gensburger, "Visiting History," 14.
71 For a visual account of one interlocutor's response to such imagery, see the video "Photography and Memory of the Distomo Slaughter: A Conversation with Images," https://youtu.be/BiFE6c_KX2I.
72 Barthes, *Camera Lucida*, 119; Hariman and Lucaites, *No Caption Needed*, 188; Mookherjee, "Raped Woman," 390, 392.
73 Olin, "Touching Photographs."
74 M. Hirsch, "Generation of Postmemory," 213.
75 Azoulay, *Civil Contract*, 132.
76 For images mobilized in/as protests, see also Buthpitiya, "Absence in Technicolour."
77 Nitsa Sfontouri, who died in August 2021, appears in the trailer titled "Photography, Ethnography, and Political Imagination in Greece: A Film Preview by K. Kalantzis," https://youtu.be/9DGrXwKMm8s.
78 Jay, *Downcast Eyes*.
79 See also E. Hirsch and Stewart, "Introduction," 262; and Moser, "When Photographs Fail," 15.
80 On the equalization of blame in Northern Ireland, see Josephides, "Being Held Accountable."
81 See Mookherjee, "Introduction"; Josephides, "Being Held Accountable"; Buthpitiya, "Absence in Technicolour"; and Moser and Huard, "Editorial Introduction."
82 Batchen, *Burning*, 9.
83 Batchen, *Burning*, 9.

4

Insurgent Archive

THE PHOTOGRAPHIC MAKING AND UNMAKING OF THE NICARAGUAN REVOLUTIONARY STATE

ILEANA L. SELEJAN

Imaginings

"We are living the end of the Sandinista Revolution," Juan exclaimed with a sigh as he leaned back in his seat.[1] It was a torrid July afternoon as we sat on his terrace, going over the weekly news and contemplating the imminent arrival of the fortieth anniversary of the revolution in just a few days. Birdsong and the sound of children playing in the schoolyard next door interrupted the otherwise motionless air. Like many of his peers, Juan began his career as a photographer in the aftermath of 1979, the year when the Sandinista Revolution—led by the Frente Sandinista de Liberación Nacional (FSLN, Sandinista National Liberation Front)—succeeded in ousting dictator Anastasio Somoza Debayle. The dynastic regime of the Somoza family was thus triumphantly unseated and the Guardia Nacional (National Guard) dismantled after decades of authoritarian rule.[2]

It was a momentous event in the history of the country. The Sandinistas rose to power with the quasi-unanimous support of the population and that of a broad coalition of forces across a historically divided political spectrum. In the immediate aftermath, the great experiment of the revolution, which took up the following decade, drew mass participation, mobilizing the general public toward accomplishing the promises of a revolutionary movement that was widely perceived as self-made. Cultural producers, photographers, filmmakers, artists, writers, and educators enrolled in the project, enthusiastic in their support. Before the 1978–79 insurrection, many had been active members of the FSLN covertly or in exile, later to incorporate into the *lucha armada* (armed struggle). After July 1979, at peacetime, they began working for various Sandinista organizations and institutions, many of which they helped found, as part of an integrationist nation-building process.

Throughout the 1980s, there was a constant need for workers and professionals in all economic sectors, with government-sponsored offices permanently understaffed and underfunded. Despite having a mixed market economy in place, the Sandinista state was highly centralized, greatly limiting the private sector. Most professional photographers were employed by governmental organizations—two large areas were the press and the Departamento de Propaganda y Educación Política (DEPEP, Department of Propaganda and Political Education)—while others kept intermittent assignments with oft-censored independent media channels such as the newspaper *La Prensa* or maintained studio-based practices. Photographic studios and traveling photographers continued to thrive, albeit limited by economic restrictions and the on-and-off availability of photographic materials.

Claudia Gordillo, to take one prominent photographer's example, was employed by the official newspaper *Barricada* and assigned to the war correspondents' division. Her differences with the Frente eventually led to her leaving the newspaper. She then shifted her focus toward a more introspective practice, at a remove from revolutionary politics and ideology. Even while at *Barricada*, she had continued to work independently, pursuing a long-term ethnographic project of documenting Nicaraguan society, religious syncretism, and the interweaving of ritual and everyday life (figure 4.1). Later, she became a staff photographer and member of the Centro de Investigaciones y Documentación de la Costa Atlántica (CIDCA, Center for Research and for the Documentation of the Atlantic Coast). Working with a team of anthropologists, she documented ethnically diverse communities living on Nicaragua's Caribbean Coast. Many of her photographs illustrated the pages of *Wani*, the center's multilingual publication, starting in 1984.[3] "Wani is not only a symbol of a past we need to eradicate but also of the history we are in the midst of making," the editors of the journal boldly proclaimed in their introduction to the first issue, which featured a cover image by Cordelia Dilg (figure 4.2).[4] "*Wani* seeks to express and analyze the reality of the Atlantic Coast, thus contributing to the task of forging national unity."[5]

Wani was representative of the type of cultural programs the Sandinista government was pursing throughout the country, yet especially in relation to the Atlantic Coast. This region had historic differences with the Pacific Coast of Nicaragua and had been forcefully annexed in 1894 during the government of José Santos Zelaya. Furthermore, indigenous and Afro-descendant communities strongly resisted centralization, seeking to preserve autonomy and their ties to the anglophone Caribbean. Integrationist initiatives, including mass literacy campaigns, were meant to secure and solidify the country's identity as a revolutionary nation. Photographers played an important role in bringing these projected identities to light, by contributing to a range of widely circulated publications and visual materials that included posters and billboards, even murals, which often reproduced recognizable photographic imagery.[6] Nonetheless, some practitioners were critical of this programmatic approach to the medium, reluctant to produce ideological work, as was Gordillo's case.

There was a greater context to this. In the aftermath of the Cuban Revolution, from the 1960s to the 1980s, photographers, documentarians, and filmmakers in Latin America sought imagistic means to engage the public politically. While documenting revolutionary advances in a regional and transnational context remained a priority, the production of images was underwritten by a profound idealism. As *fotógrafos comprometidos* (engagé photographers) and producers of *cine militante* (militant cinema), they sought imagistic means to bring about revolution, activating the political imagination of *el pueblo* (the people).[7] The Sandinista Revolution, from 1978 to 1989, occurred at an opportune moment, as utopian prospects and dreams of a world revolution were otherwise winding down. In a region marred by military dictatorship and civil war, Nicaragua became a cause célèbre, inspiring countless solidarity movements and actions around the world, parallel to the Non-Aligned Movement. This resulted in the accumulation of a vast image bank, an informal archive, currently scattered in personal and institutional archives in Latin America and beyond. The perception of Nicaragua as a revolutionary nation, like Cuba, Mexico, Russia, or France—in reverse chronological order—and the profound identification of Nicaraguans as an insurrectionary

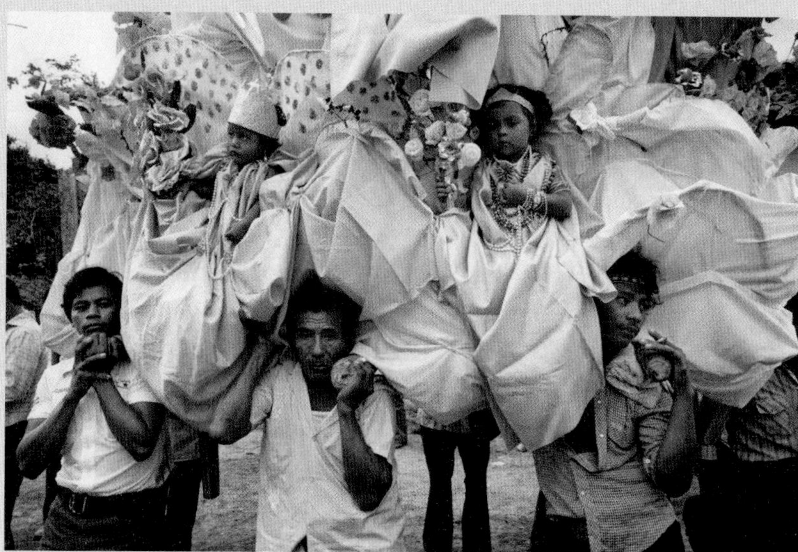

4.1 Claudia Gordillo, *Angelitos de Catarina* (The little angels of Catarina), Meseta de Los Pueblos, 1981.

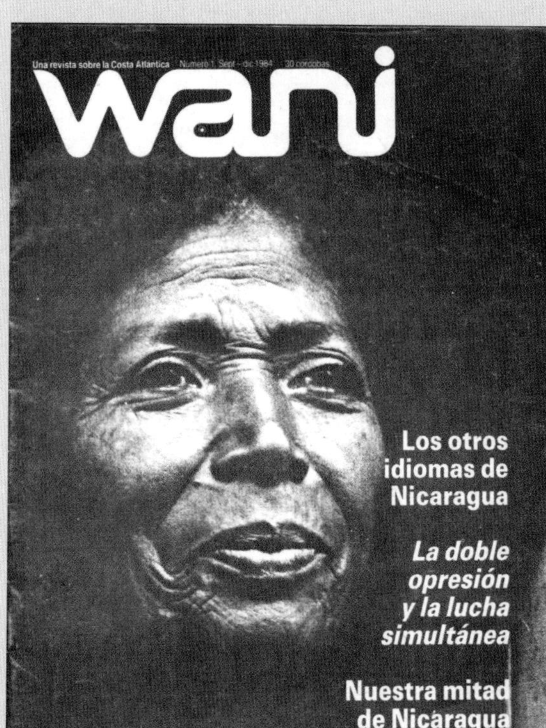

4.2 Cover of the first issue of *Wani* (1984), with a portrait by photographer Cordelia Dilg.

people, coupled with this extensive visual record, activated long-term attachments. These enabled a type of revolutionary mythmaking that has been, to this date, deeply immersed in and connected to the everyday.

Contemporary accounts vary, yet many previous cadres who returned to civilian life have reflected on the gradual ideological fallout from within the party and among its supporters. Unsurprisingly, some carried the standard higher than others; and, especially with the onset of the Contra War, divisions deepened. By the end of the decade, severe economic hardship, enhanced by pressures of a United States–imposed embargo and the introduction of a mandatory military draft in 1984, made the revolution lose much of its initial momentum. Furthermore, a number of catastrophic internal conflicts and crises—including escalation into civil war with indigenous communities on the Atlantic Coast—were consistently downplayed by the Sandinista leadership, which, with the support of Cuba and the USSR, was determined to advance the revolution against all odds. By the mid-1980s, the "romance" that many of my interlocutors had highlighted as their prime motivation during the years of resistance, and in the immediate aftermath of the victory, was fading. While discussing iconic images of the Sandinista Revolution, for instance, former *New York Times* correspondent Alan Riding highlighted the capture of the National Palace by Sandinista militants on August 22, 1978, which preceded the 1978 armed insurrection: "I think that photographically perhaps the *toma del palacio* was [significant], because you had a charismatic figure like Edén Pastora who was built up so he became sort of the Che Guevara of the moment, just because there were iconic images of him; then that helped in the romanticization of the revolution, which is a very important factor." Emphasizing this aspect, he continued, "Any analysis of the revolution has to be of how it captured the idea of romance, and it did even among leftist intellectuals who were already disenchanted with Cuba."[8]

Nonetheless, that utopian idealism had lasting effects and has endured as part of a foundational myth of the nation, passed on across generations. Paradoxically, despite many important developments that unfolded during the four decades in-between "then" and "now," current political imaginaries appear to be still anchored within the memory of those foundational years. This break, or discontinuity, within the story of the Nicaraguan nation-state is further reinforced by a strong nostalgia for the irrecoverable past. Former Sandinistas often expressed a profound disappointment with the corruption of the state, the party, and, concurrently, a collective sense of loss—the antipode of the comradery they previously shared. This sentiment was already felt during the last years of the revolution, and especially after the electoral defeat of 1990.[9] Several memoirs by leading revolutionary figures touch upon this issue, whereby the defeat at the polls was interpreted symbolically as being equivalent to a loss of the original ideals of the struggle. "We spent our entire youth building that dream, working day in and out, often without pay," photographer Margarita Montealegre shared. "It's been hard to let go ever since."[10]

On the other hand, what happened within that discontinuous "in-between" only figures marginally in terms of Nicaraguans' self-representation as citizen revolutionaries, whether veterans or heirs to a revolutionary past. Hence it is significant to interrogate how revolutionary idealism mutates, as it is configured and reconfigured within the popular imagination by visual means; how the contemporary Sandinista state has sought to reroute historic allegiances, affect, and *memoria histórica* (historic memory), redeploying the symbolism of the past in order to maintain power; and how those vertical movements are continually challenged from below, across an insurgent horizontal axis that unsettles image-power relations, projecting this utopian idealism of the past into an unforeseen or *yet to-be-seen* future.

The Sandinista Revolution was conceived as a cultural movement from its very beginning and had a long-term, profound impact on Nicaraguan society. It created visual forms that contributed to the construction of political, national, and transnational identities following the fall of the Somoza dictatorship (1937–79). Recent studies have sought to investigate the legacy of the revolution locally and from a transnational perspective. However, little to no attention has been paid to the significant amount of photography and popular visual culture that was produced within its scope.[11] I argue that the consideration of political aesthetics is essential to understanding the history of the revolution as well as its impact on the present—especially with regard to shifting notions of citizenship and belonging. Recent protests have shown that the revolutionary iconography created during that period continues to be consequential, shaping the contemporary political imagination. Contemporary "image wars" evoke and reflect on those earlier moments, during the Cold War, when Nicaragua became a global hotspot of popular insurrection. Here we might consider Serge Gruzinski's reading of colonial America as "a fabulous research laboratory" where "images, image systems and *imaginaires* of the conquerors" were confronted "in successive and uninterrupted waves," a process that has continued to *recur* in the present.[12]

The arc of this chapter's narrative (and of its corresponding monograph) thus spans the forty-plus years since the start of the popular insurrection of 1978, and until the onset of the 2018 uprising, culminating with the 2019 anniversary of the Sandinista Revolution.[13] While keeping this important historic context in mind, the chapter nonetheless focuses on the recent protest movement that began in April 2018 in Nicaragua. Its primary purpose is to analyze how photography was used within this context, advancing theoretical notions about documentary formats, digital activism, and (social) media in relation to memory. After briefly setting up the backdrop, in the sections that follow, I trace the paths of transmission and circulation of key images and tropes, the proliferation of images via photographic technologies in an insurrectionary/revolutionary context, reflecting on what makes photography particularly powerful and effective in an activist sense, spurring audiences into action. This discussion revolves around the use of phone cameras and social media as tools for demanding justice as well as for witnessing and documenting "live" history.

The group of *autoconvocados* (self-assembled citizens) that coalesced around the Movimiento Estudiantil 19 de Abril (19th of April Student Movement) during several eventful months in 2018 constituted the largest social movement to develop in the country since the Sandinista Revolution. Indeed, the violent events that took place in Nicaragua in 2018, the subsequent extreme punitive measures of the state, and the ongoing human rights crisis seem to have reactivated a public that has previously been perceived either as stuck within a Cold War partisan/reactionary paradigm or, by contrast, as apathetic and complacent. Parallels between the historic insurrection and these contemporary events were established almost immediately, by people who had experienced episodes both firsthand and cross-generationally. The latter category is a case in point with regard to the transmission of historic memory, ideas around nationhood, and their representations. Photographer Oscar Navarrete began his career as an embedded army photographer during the Contra War and has worked as a photojournalist since. As one of the main photojournalists for the newspaper *La Prensa*, he documented the 2018 protests in depth, and he has created a substantial photographic archive, intended to be used as evidence for the future. Reflecting on parallels with historic events, Navarrete commented: "Para mí fue vivir una especie de Déjà Vu. Escuché otra vez el vívido rugir de los fusiles y las postales sangrientas de la guerra de los ochenta" (For me, it was like living some kind of déjà vu. I was hearing the vivid roar of guns once more, seeing those bloody "postcards" from the eighties again).[14] Indeed, the gap of the "in-between" seemed ever-present (figure 4.3).

Rebelión en Abril (The April Rebellion)

On April 19, 2018, the streets of Managua erupted in protest. What began the day before, as a *plantón* (sit-in) to contest a controversial tax increase that was meant to rescue the insolvent National Social Security Fund, escalated quickly in response to clashes between peaceful protesters and government supporters, accompanied by violent repression by the police.[15] The hashtag #SOSINSS multiplied, scribbled hastily on walls, offline and online—where INSS stands for Instituto Nicaragüense de Seguridad Social (Nicaraguan Social Security Institute). Word of "el pueblo insurrecto" (the insurgent people) and "la insurrección" (the insurrection) spread within a matter of days in Managua, and soon throughout the country. While students occupied universities, citizens took to the streets, engaging in civil disobedience acts and reacting against the perceived generalized corruption and abuse of the Ortega-Murillo regime. Indeed, students assumed a prominent role in the protests and, together with large sections of the population, formed a movement of *autoconvocados* also known as the Movimiento Estudiantil 19 de Abril, honoring the day when the first citizens were killed.[16]

4.3 Oscar Navarrete, "Mi déjà vu," 2019. Web-based multimedia presentation, with toggle bar moving between photographs taken on the frontlines of the Contra War and during the 2018 protests in Managua. Fundación Violeta Barrios de Chamorro, 2019.

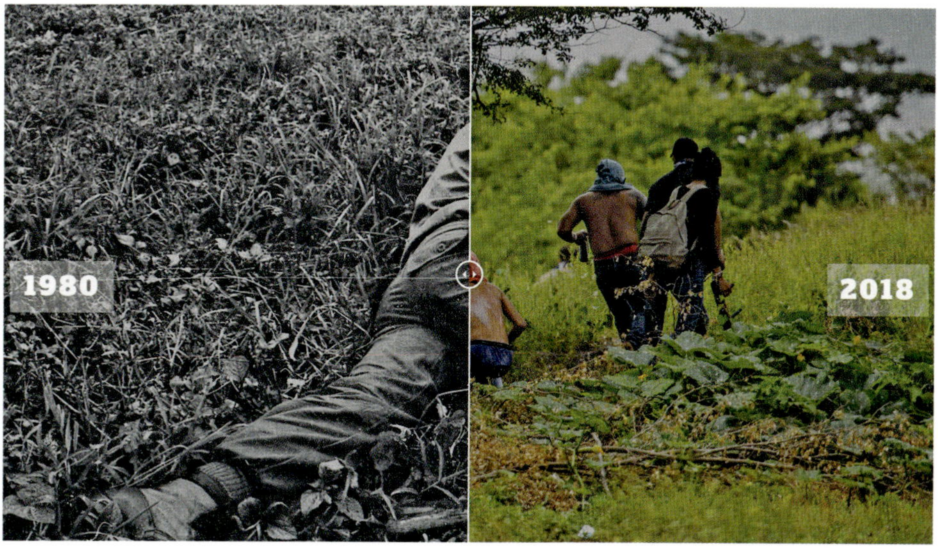

During the first days of unrest, while TV channels were censored, citizens used mobile applications and online platforms such as Facebook and WhatsApp to organize themselves and to share documentation of confrontations with antiriot police and government supporters. Photograph*ing* served multiple functions, best described by the Spanish verb *grabar*, meaning "to capture" or "to inscribe": (1) to view and record happenings that were exceptional, and perceived as such; (2) to bear testimony and serve as evidence, which was something that people realized was immediately necessary since the government was denying all responsibility, seeking to manipulate facts, while continuing to repress; (3) to deploy online, in order to call the citizenry to action.

The images, videos, and "stories" (on Instagram and Facebook) that were crossing the feed also served to reactivate memory, even if unintentionally. Scenes from the Sandinista Revolution appeared to be replayed on the streets, as identified by numerous observers. People frequently described their experiences with reference to photographs from the past, including Susan Meiselas's iconic image—colloquially referred to as the "Molotov Man"—which was taken in July 1979, on the last day of the popular insurrection. Millennial youth sought to reclaim the symbols of dissent that their predecessors had deployed during the late 1970s and 1980s. "It felt like looking through a window onto the past," a man who was too young to remember the historic revolution told me, as though one insurrection overlaid the memory of another. The statement resonates with Roland Barthes's reading of photography as "an emanation of *past reality*: a *magic*, not an art."[17] Photography has the ability, as seen here, to summon the past. Well-known visual vocabularies and established repertoires of protest collided with the discontent of the present. Such leaps within the past were nonetheless turned or projected toward the future while being enacted and embodied in public space.

The sudden appearance of new images in the visual public sphere manifested itself as an overflow of content, against a backdrop of prolonged silence due to censorship. Correspondences with well-known photographs from the 1978–79 insurrection were tested, as the memory of the historic revolution was actively engaged with in the streets. This effervescence nonetheless spurred iconoclastic acts, and here one is reminded of Bruno Latour's thesis concerning the generative potential of such actions, their accelerated movement, jolting perception out of stasis, summoning, calling to action.[18] The "feed" on mobile apps and online platforms became the primary locus where a Latourian "cascading" of images manifested itself. One example illustrates the type of *galvanizing* procedure that I observed in use between the street and the screen during the weeks of unrest. I am interested in how visual tropes were made and remade, picking up reference points from previous visual-political constellations, sampling from along a loosened spatiotemporal timeline of events. Starting on April 21, an increasing number of photographs of students in violent, warlike scenarios started to be circulated on social media and in the press (figure 4.4). Young men and women were seen battling the riot police, among streets strewn with rocks and fragments of glass. Molotovs were flying one way, tear gas in response, rubber bullets, and the occasional live round. A caricaturist picked up a particularly heroic image (figure 4.5), and so did the online community, from where it started moving around the digital realm, reshaped in multiple memes.

The speech bubble "Libertad!" invokes Eugène Delacroix's *Liberty Leading the People* (1830), although the gesture draws further connections. A range of responses appeared online, from historic photographs of the Sandinista Revolution and comments relating the two to visual references from outside the local context, for example, images from the Paris student revolt of May '68 or a "vandalized" Banksy (figure 4.6). Using the "story" feature on Instagram, a young photographer shared a complementary, even more graphic image by Flores, taken moments apart from figure 4.5, with the caption "Esta foto no es de los 80's es del 21 de abril del 2018" (This photo is not from the '80s but from April 21, 2018). These images appeal to global imaginaries of resistance, identifying moments of overlap. Can we speak of a repertoire of unrest, of constellations of images and tropes constituted out of mutually referential, and perhaps mutually reinforcing, images? Or is there an immediate fall into cliché?[19]

People compared the students' struggle to the tale of David and Goliath, a common reference in recent protests around the world—as seen in the case of a "viral" photograph taken by Mustafa Hassona on October 22, 2018, of a protester slinging a rock during a protest against Israel's blockade of Gaza. In Nicaragua, the parable carried deeper resonances due to its repeated visual iterations in association with national hero Andrés Castro, who fought against the invasion of US filibuster William Walker in 1856 (see figure I.23, in the introduction to this volume). During the following weeks and months, this "image" of a figure throwing a rock, or rather its defiant pose, was recurrently identified online as a key trope within a range of pictures and illustrations. Finally, the gesture was turned into a stencil, multiplying on the city's walls. The example resonates with Karen Strassler's analysis of post-Reformasi image cultures in Indonesia. As she writes, "Appealing to possible futures through

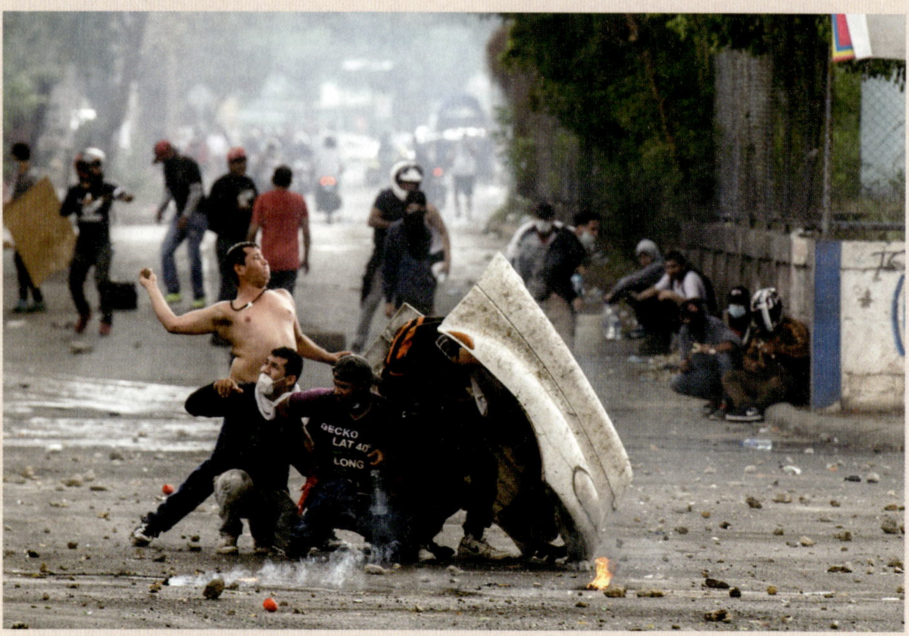

4.4 Jader Flores, "At Upoli and its vicinity, police repression and violence intensified over the weekend," *La Prensa*, Managua, April 21, 2018.

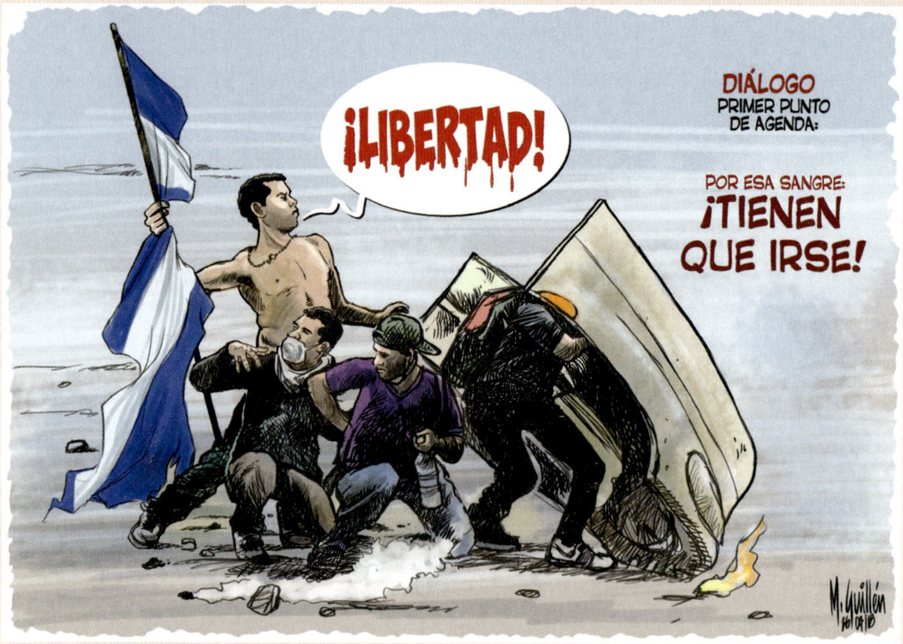

4.5 Manuel Guillén, "Liberty! [National] Dialogue, first on the agenda: For this [spilled] blood, they must go!," *La Prensa*, April 26, 2010.

reworked icons of the past, [political stencils, memes, etc.] suggest how making, circulating, and responding to images has become a pervasive mode by which people enact their political agency."[20]

There is a further, future-oriented sense in which this visual trope can be interpreted, not least due to its association with this range of images that belong to a global repertoire of struggle. The gesture was identified out of a range of actions and procedures that were enacted spontaneously, even when repeatedly, in response to an immediate situation. Yet it was noticed, perceived as a déjà vu, drawn out as part of an intuitive process of selection that nonetheless validated it, thereby granting it further weight and significance, elevating it from the everyday. Georges Didi-Huberman notes that "before affirming themselves as *acts* or actions, uprisings arise as *gestures*, corporeal forms"; yet these gestures are "transmissible, they survive despite us, and despite all" in close manner to what Aby Warburg would characterize as *Pathosformel* within the *longue durée* of history.[21]

4.6 Pedro Molina, *Banksy "Vandalizado"* ("Vandalized" Banksy), 2018.

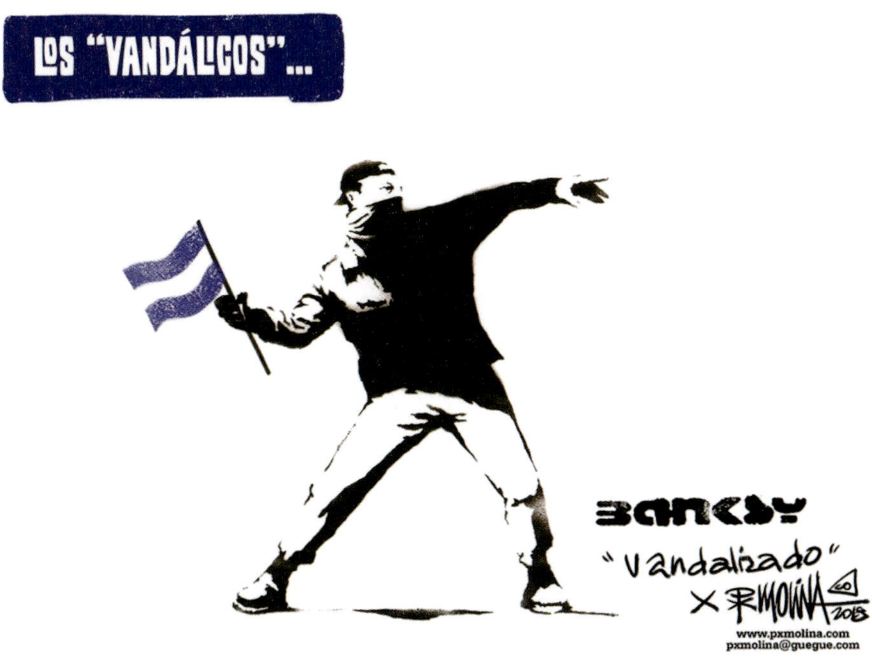

We might consider the gesture of "throwing" by comparison to Delacroix's painting, which gave French citizens an image of themselves as agents of history, and reflect upon Siegfried Kracauer's hypothesis that in the eyes of the viewing public, the picture wasn't just a representation of the past "but that it also lifted a corner of the veil that hid the future" (see the introduction to this volume).[22] Here, monumentalizing the unknown citizen is achieved, procedurally, within the lateral space of social media. Yet this also unavoidably triggers further recombinative processes, which are impossible to predict, from below. In a more literal sense, the figure of the student, a harbinger of change, intervenes upon the present—and, at the same time, upon its photographic event.[23] His physical movement from left to right in the frame halts the sense of movement through time into a perpetual advancement, indeed an acceleration toward the future, a push toward change. We cannot see what lies outside the frame; nonetheless, "the veil that hid[es] the future" is lifting.

Here, one encounters an immediate connection to Meiselas's "Molotov Man," which has likewise mutated into multiple forms and formats, having experienced a number of appropriations and transformations throughout its "social life."[24] That procession of images and the intermedia collisions that yielded them, applied across the span of four decades, appears to have accelerated in virtual space and time, causing present iterations of the image to "burn out" and dissolve into the informational stream rather prematurely. Nonetheless, the "Molotov Man" as a prototypical, vectorial image enables fecund, future proliferations. Within this context, it is important to consider the accidental or unintentional aspects that pertain to the story of Meiselas's image, its *becoming* an "icon" of the revolution. Archived contact sheets (black and white) and color slides reveal her searching for the picture, her attempts at finding the best way to frame the character and his actions, within the setting at hand. There is a sense of suspense and buildup, although one can hardly predict what might happen next. Then follows the capture of the throwing action, and of the few brief moments in its aftermath, its drawback, so to say. Within that forward thrust, a suite of iconographic details are brought out, piercing the picture plane: the figure's likeness to Che, the rosary around his neck, the barricades behind, the "Pepsi" label on the Molotov bottle, etcetera. Their coincidence enables a potent exchange with the future audience of this image, in a manner similar to Barthes's theorization of the "punctum" and "studium" by relation to Koen Wessing's photographs of the insurrection, taken the year before in the same town, Estelí.

The frame of the "Molotov Man" was isolated out of multiple possible shots, which resonates with Ariella Azoulay's notion of the "untaken photo-

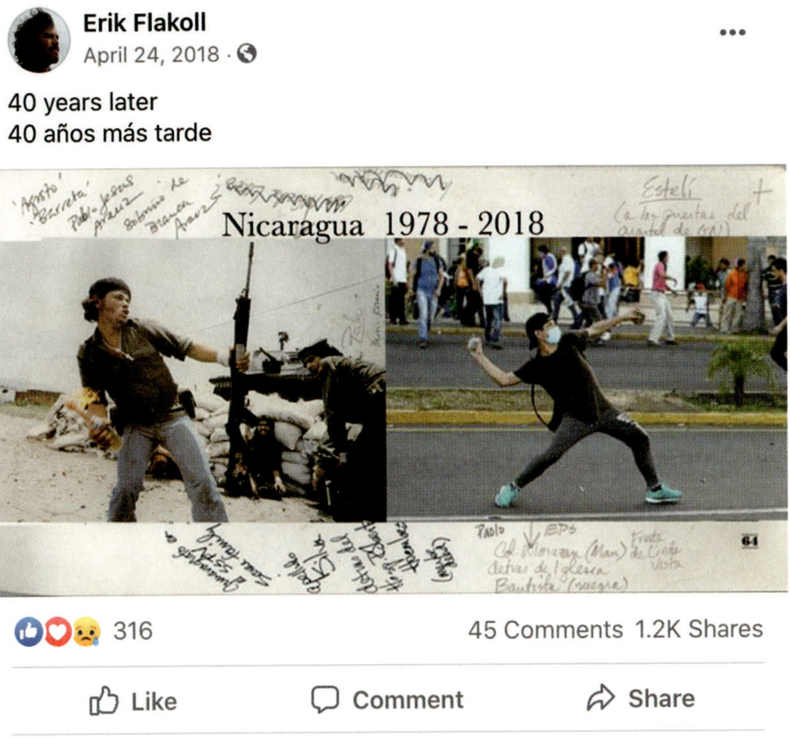

4.7 Facebook post showing a digital collage of Susan Meiselas's "Molotov Man" photograph from the historic Sandinista insurrection taken in 1979 in the town of Estelí, and a contemporary image taken by Jairo Cajina during the April 2018 protests in Managua. The collage is inserted onto a page from Meiselas's book *Nicaragua, June 1978–July 1979*, which includes her annotations, an image that promptly appears when one searches for the "Molotov Man" online.

graph" or the "unphotographed event."[25] The parallel between contemporary images and the "Molotov Man" did not escape protesters and online observers, who almost immediately turned this association into memes, through collage (figure 4.7). Despite having become a representative image for the contested regime, a logotype, resurrected especially during revolutionary anniversary events, Meiselas's picture held its ground. Even in this new context, it still contained all the referents for the struggle: behind the figure, the barricade, in his hand a Molotov cocktail or, in this case, a stone, the *boina*, worn in solidarity with "El Che," replaced by a hat. The composition functions almost like a reverse of Robert Capa's *Falling Soldier* from 1936. Eerie resemblances pertain to details such as the position of the weapon, of the body, and the way in which movement is halted in time. Yet as the Republican soldier recoils, the "Molotov Man" thrusts forward. One's fall is reciprocated by another's leap ahead.

I interpret these recent collages as deliberate attempts to reclaim the picture, or to reengage and reactivate it in the present context. Similar attempts to reclaim, repossess, or resignify the visual realm played out on the streets in the coming days. Citizens' engagement with visual materials produced accumulations, a layering of frames, images, and graffiti or *pintas* (tags), interchangeable in their symbolic content. Images, fragments, symbols, and visual tropes became raw materials for the making of new identities. The places where these accumulations started to appear were well known, excessively familiar perhaps, yet had barely been engaged with up until this point due to the government's policing of public spaces. With the protests came an urge to fill all surfaces, pavements included. However, this "spillage" originated online. In other words, there was a certain buildup on social media, until these accumulations started to be visible in the city. New visual configurations overlapped with sites of memory, some old, some new. Photography was the means through which many of these gestures were engaged; it was performative, made to be revisited, seen again and again, as trace.

HEAVY METAL

Grainy cell phone pictures and videos showed crowds of people cheering as monumental metal trees were being brought down, uprooted from the city's streets. The scene was one of ecstatic celebration, challenging the overall mood during days of indignation and rage. The first tree, a public sculpture, was cut down with chainsaws on April 20. The next day, this action was repeated, the fall not only expected but carried out with more precision, in front of an audience. Crowds had gathered around the rotunda Jean Paul Genie and held up protest signs, banners, and Nicaraguan flags, chanting and singing. Traffic passed by, car honks creating a continuous, deafening wall of noise. When the tree came crashing down, people first looked on incredulously, then rushed toward it, trampling the structure. Similar rituals were observed on following evenings around the city, as another fourteen trees were brought down. The crowds increased in size, the "cutting" method determining the length of the wait. Even when the crowds were smaller, these events were turned into public spectacles almost immediately through the presence of cameras and recording devices, streaming video content on social media sites.

The "live" feature on Facebook was used extensively during the protests. Protesters taught one another how to use it during protests and marches, which led to the immediate proliferation of uploaded content. As documented by the Grupo Interdisciplinario de Expertos Independientes (GIEI, Interdisciplinary Group of Independent Experts for Nicaragua), the usage of social media sites (especially Facebook, Twitter, and YouTube) increased manifold between March and June 2019—the main period during which antigovernmental protests took place. A peak in activity was seen between April 19 and 24, coinciding with the amplification of the protests, since this was when the first civilian deaths occurred. Further peaks were registered throughout this period, in correlation with marches and protests that attracted large numbers of people. An estimated three million tweets were generated in response to the protests, while more than ten thousand videos were shared across the three platforms.[26]

Initially installed as part of a city beautification project, the 140 metal *arbolitos* (diminutive for trees) were sarcastically referred to as *arbolatas* due to their monumental sizes, between seventeen and twenty-one meters in height, or as *Chayo palos,* as a mocking tribute to their creator, Vice President Rosario Murillo, nicknamed La Chayo. Inspired by Viennese Secessionist painter Gustav Klimt's 1909 painting *The Tree of Life*, these multicolored decorative light sculptures were initially planned for the celebration of the thirty-fourth anniversary of the revolution, on July 19, 2013. The anniversary has been a monumental affair since 1979, drawing numerous crowds to the city's downtown, an area that had remained undeveloped since the devastating earthquake of 1972. Eight trees were proudly displayed as part of the ongoing renovation of the Puerto Salvador Allende and the Paseo Xolotlán, a recreation area bordering the lake. Later, another 132 trees were installed moving outward from this symbolic, central location for the revolution, gracing Managua's main avenues and rotundas. At the center of this city-wide "installation" is a monument dedicated to Hugo Chávez, whose uniformed figure rests in an "orchard" of metal trees. During the protests, this was the most heavily guarded roundabout within the entire city, which led to speculations about its significance and even conspiracies about Rosario Murillo's engagements with witchcraft. The positioning of the structures and their concentration in the city's central areas amounted to a takeover of public space, to an extent that was considered invasive. The exorbitant costs for the project—close to US$3.5 million, with additional costs for illumination and maintenance—became a cautionary example of the habitual misuse of public funds.[27]

The *arbolitos* thus became an immediate target for the rebellious youth, a gesture of retribution but also one that saw iconoclastic vandalism as a redemptive strategy to reclaim public space.[28] The widely circulated videos of these events, the falling again and again within the frame, can be seen as acts of public exorcism, performed and then revisited as image. A witness told me he couldn't stop the scene from replaying in his mind, with images coming back, one after the other, in a tumbling succession of frames. An alternate reading could propose that such actions were *performed as image* from the very beginning, mimicking or acting in continuity with preexisting visual-performative templates, given the long history of revolutionary iconoclasm globally and locally. Such genealogies might include the destruction of monumental sculptures in revolutionary France, the Paris Commune, the generalized rage against Communist icons in the former USSR, and, more recently, effigies of Saddam Hussein; the occupation of Plaza Italia in Santiago, Chile; and the takeover and interventions on the monument of General Manuel Baquedano. Viktor Misiano reflected upon the removal of the statue of Felix Dzerzhinsky, Bolshevik revolutionary and founder of the Soviet state security, on August 22, 1991, in Moscow, as "a key moment which marked the end of the 'performance' and the start of the mechanism of history."[29] In Managua, direct comparisons were drawn almost immediately with the toppling of Anastasio Somoza's equestrian sculpture in 1979 and well-known footage of that event.

One commentator expressed: "Trato de imaginarme si así se sintieron los que derribaron la estatua ecuestre a Somoza, en julio del 79" (I try to imagine if this was how those who took down Somoza's equestrian sculpture felt, in July of '79).[30] Nicaraguans of different generations are familiar with this footage since it is frequently shown on television, especially in the context of the yearly celebrations of the anniversary of the revolution. In 2014 artist Alejandro de la Guerra staged a performance titled *La caida* (The fall), which reenacted the toppling of Somoza's statue in front of a crowd of bystanders and journalists. A video documenting the performance was later uploaded to YouTube, where some visitors expressed confusion as to whether or not the video showed the historic event.

On April 19, 2018, a rather unusual profile picture appeared on social media feeds and began to multiply (figure 4.8). The "sticker" revisited the removal of the equestrian monument of Anastasio Somoza in 1979 (figure 4.9) and juxtaposed it with an event yet to happen. The rendering of the image as a

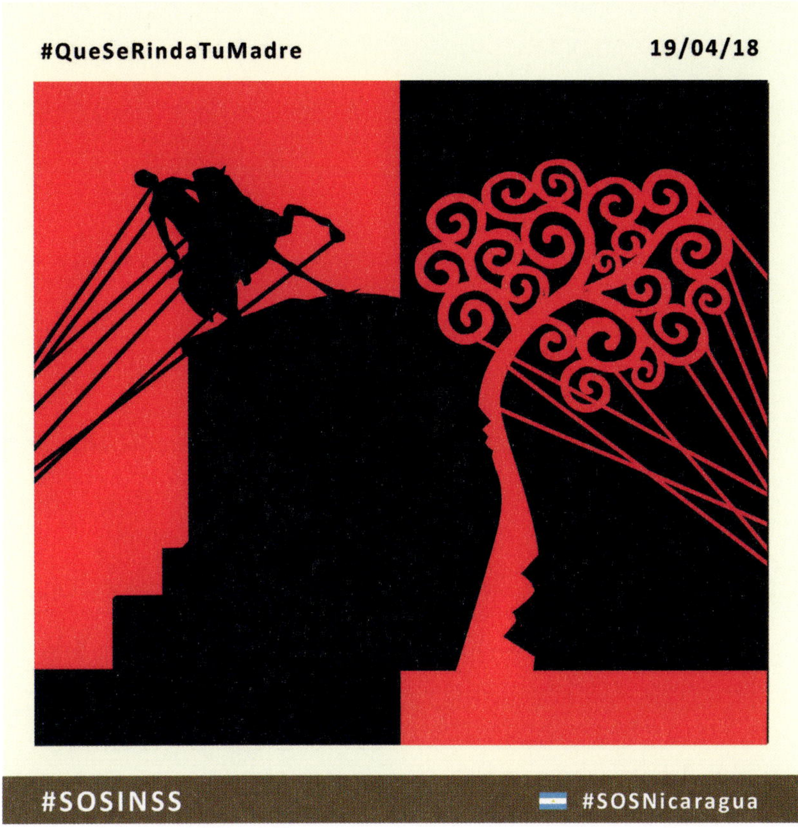

4.8 Anonymous, *Nadie es eterno* (Nobody is forever), #SOSNicaragua, April 19, 2018.

silhouette—instead of its well-known photographic equivalent—speaks to the symbolic significance of the gesture, which, as previously noted, resonated with the general public immediately. Transforming the toppled monument into a silhouette brought it onto the same plane and visual context as the metal trees, which were already rendered in 2D. Furthermore, the familiarity of Nicaraguans with the insurrectionist red and black was deployed here with a subversive end in sight: the revolution must be resignified.

That this image went viral, even before the first tree was taken down, prompts urgent inquiry into the potential of evocative image making to stir and provoke, especially within a context as heavily politicized at that of Nicaragua. A type of iconographic sequencing was thus set into play, one mon-

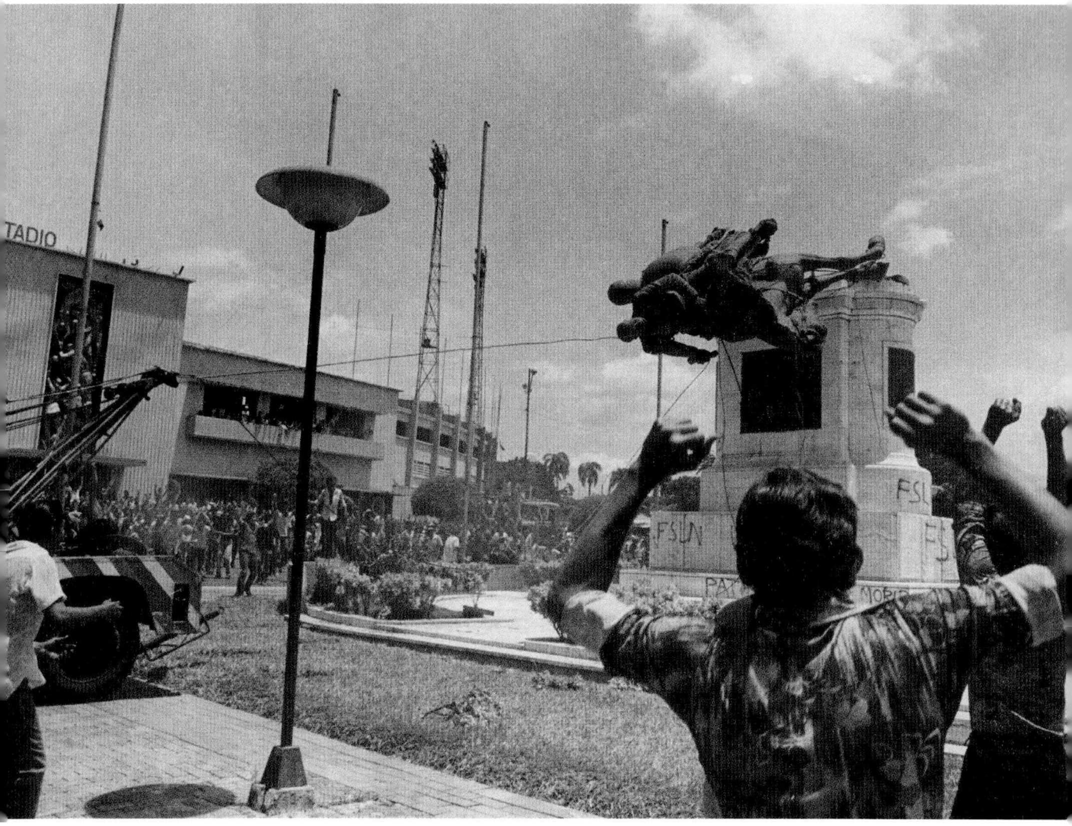

4.9 Equestrian monument of Anastasio Somoza García taken down in Managua, July 19, 1979. Photograph by Eddy Cruz Flores. From the archive of *La Prensa*, by permission of the Instituto de Historia de Nicaragua y Centroamérica (IHNCA).

umental artwork replacing or rememorializing another. Murillo's "forest of symbols" was, after all, an attempt to supplant another monumental sculpture in Managua, which had become synonymous with the revolutionary past. The silhouette of Sandino, designed by Ernesto Cardenal, was installed in the Parque Histórico Nacional Loma de Tiscapa, the highest point in the city.[31] Given the saintlike cult around the national hero, the monument was impossible to decommission or delegitimize. The installation of a "tree of life" immediately next to Cardenal's Sandino sculpture is telling in this respect; likewise, the same construction techniques were used, which might point to the making of a symbolic double.

I first attempted to reach one of the occupied universities, Universidad Politécnica de Nicaragua (UPoli, or the Polytechnic University of Nicaragua), on April 25. We tried several routes to get through; however, all the streets were cordoned off by barricades. The deeper one went into the barrio, and the closer one came to the university, the more barricades could be seen. A former advertising board, covered in graffiti, now served as a roadblock (figure 4.10). A tire was left in front of it, ready to be set on fire, if needed, to deflect attackers. On the light posts behind, one could discern discoloring streaks of red and black paint, the signature of the FSLN. In numerous images that circulated online, I would later recognize the same types of billboards filled with graffiti and tags, sometimes used as backdrops for portraits and selfies.

Until April 2018, Nicaragua's visual landscape was governed by images of the presidential couple, a brooding personality cult, and ever-rising tides of commercial advertisements. In the 1980s, visual tactics to engage

4.10 Barricade outside UPoli, April 25, 2018. Photograph by Ileana L. Selejan.

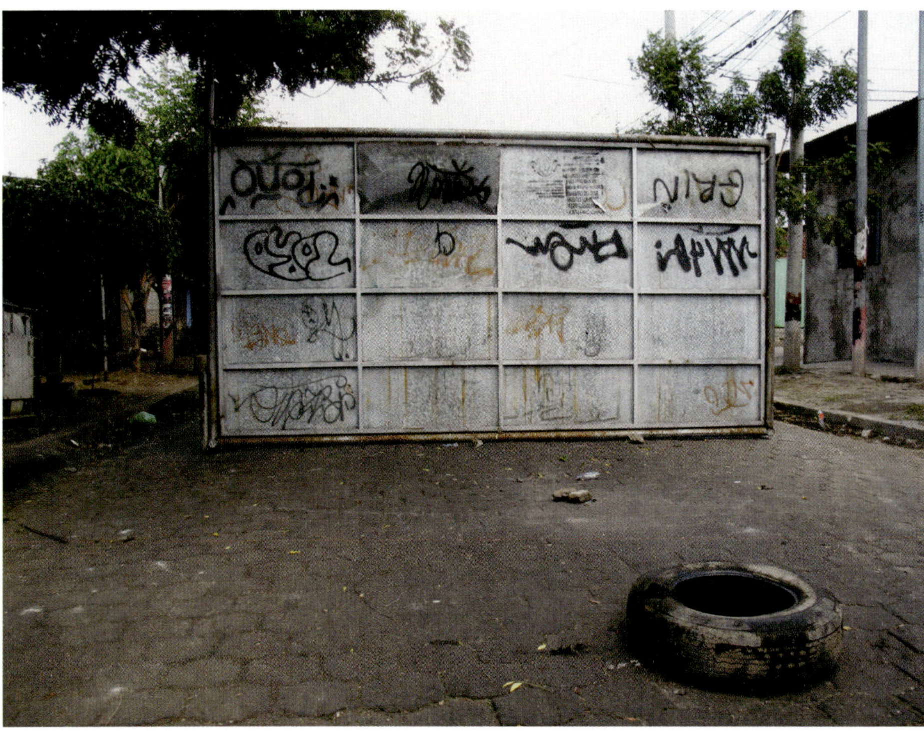

citizens in public space became widely used, as the Sandinista government sought to disseminate political imagery via posters, billboards, and murals as part of campaigns for social justice and revolutionary change. During the first weeks of unrest, the images were defaced, spray-painted or paint-bombed, and smeared in red and blue. Protesters climbed up on the advertising boards, peeling off the images, tearing them from the support. In many cases, empty frames were all that was left (figures 4.11–4.13).

"Art-destruction is art-making in reverse; but it has the same basic conceptual structure. Iconoclasts exercise a type of 'artistic agency,'" Alfred Gell argued in relation to the famous case of suffragette Mary Richardson, who defaced Diego Velázquez's painting *Rokeby Venus* with a kitchen knife at the National Gallery in London in order to protest the government's mistreatment of fellow suffragette Emmeline Pankhurst. "The *'Slashed' Rokeby Venus* by Richardson," Gell continued, endowing the iconoclast's persona with authorship, "is, without question, a more powerful image than the old one by Velázquez . . . because the image bears traces which testify directly to, rather than simply represent, the violence women endure, or believe they endure."[32] The Ortega-Murillo personality cult was built, at least in part, on the sacredness of the revolution, upon an expectation that their association with heroic events from the past conferred on the party and its leaders indisputable legitimacy and uncontested authority, rendering them "untouchable." The mass production and distribution of their image merely served to reinforce this idea, without threatening its "aura." Yet it was exactly the banality of their image, its ubiquity, that made its defacement even more powerful as a symbolic act, as something that everyday citizens exploited with "artistic agency."

It was not the first time that such actions would supersede one another in the visual history of Nicaragua. They evoke the photographic and filmic record of various iconoclastic gestures perpetrated against the figure of Somoza, his image and effigy, after the dictator's flight in July 1979 (see figure 4.9).[33] The photographic capture freezes the frame, condensing the continuous flow of the action into a quantifiable entity, concurrently monumentalizing the event and increasing its reproducibility by other means. Gestures and actions—perforation, smashing, breaking, rupturing—were performed for the camera, while bystanders engaged with the remnants and fragments in their aftermath.

In Managua, Masaya, and León, barricades were raised using the same type of cobblestone as in the insurrection against Somoza—as if people still knew exactly what needed to be done. An element most deeply engrained in the

Nicaraguan public imagination, the *adoquin* (cobblestone), became a symbol of resistance during 1978–79. Similar to its precedent, April brought about a revolt of basic means, and in plain clothes: young people covered their faces with masks and T-shirts and used a type of folding that resembled "armor," leaving only their eyes visible. As if fulfilling a prophecy, or performing an oft-rehearsed, never-forgotten task, people started building the barricades. Their actions were transgressive, moving both forward and backward in time, since, as these gestures unfolded, people started seeing parallels to past images almost immediately and brought them back into public debate via social media. Such was the case of the "Molotov Man." Additional pictures by Meiselas, and by other photographers who documented the insurrection of 1978–79, appeared on social media feeds, spliced onto present realities through powerful comparisons that were nonetheless soon discarded—image-events in the churn of social media move at higher speeds.

Yet the ways in which this particular image has been reused since 1979 are important to consider in relation to the repertoire of revolutionary imagery that emerged in Latin America, and worldwide, in the aftermath of the Cuban Revolution. Iconic pictures were essential to the revolutionary process, as was their repetition. Once established, the trope mutates, with gradations of realism (true to life) and abstraction (the stencil reduces the image to its basic elements, yet the procedure relies on the image still being recognizable, otherwise the sign would be void). The iterative mobility of the *sign* is rather astounding as it skips time and place, moving from walls to public plazas around the country. It has become an icon, a symbol of the revolution and a part of processes of memorialization, percolating through the public imaginary.

Iconic images such as Meiselas's undoubtedly hold great power over the public imagination. While the extent to which they can be reused again and again is impossible to foretell, such processes are illuminating as to the ways in which the revolution became part of the local vernacular and was incorporated into official culture. Meiselas's photograph is a pertinent example in this sense, resonating with Robert Hariman and John Lucaites's hypothesis that "there is much more than the ideological relay occurring when photojournalism does succeed at constructing an *intermediate* zone between hegemony and resistance, that is, when it creates a public culture."[34] One might consider as a point of comparison a recent collage by Nicaraguan artist Gabriel Pérez Setright that juxtaposes the image of the famous guerrillero with that of a storefront—the Pepsi bottle and a McDonald's, united at last (figure 4.14). It is part of a series that "parasites" other images by Meiselas that have

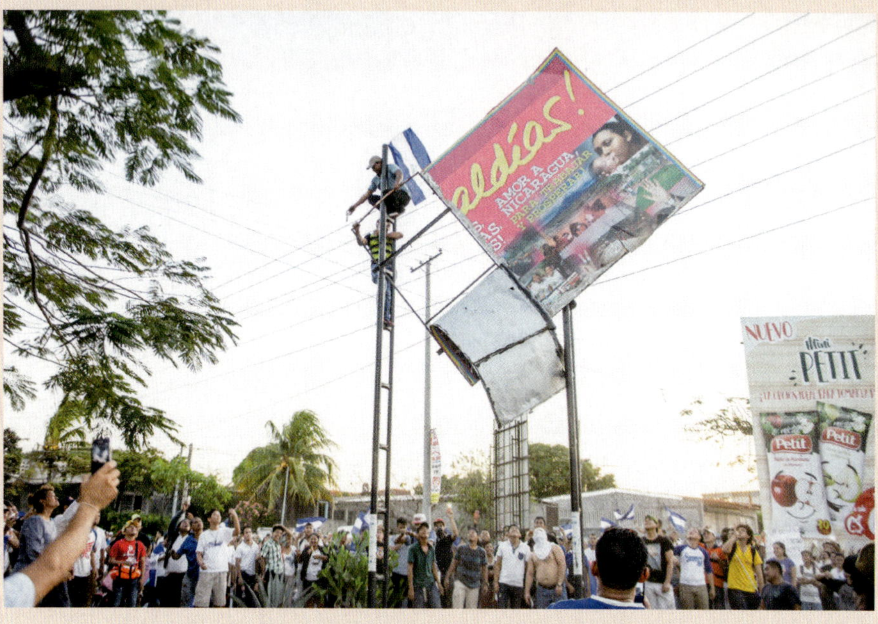

4.11 Protesters taking down government billboards in Managua. *La Prensa*, May 18, 2018. Photograph by Carlos Valle.

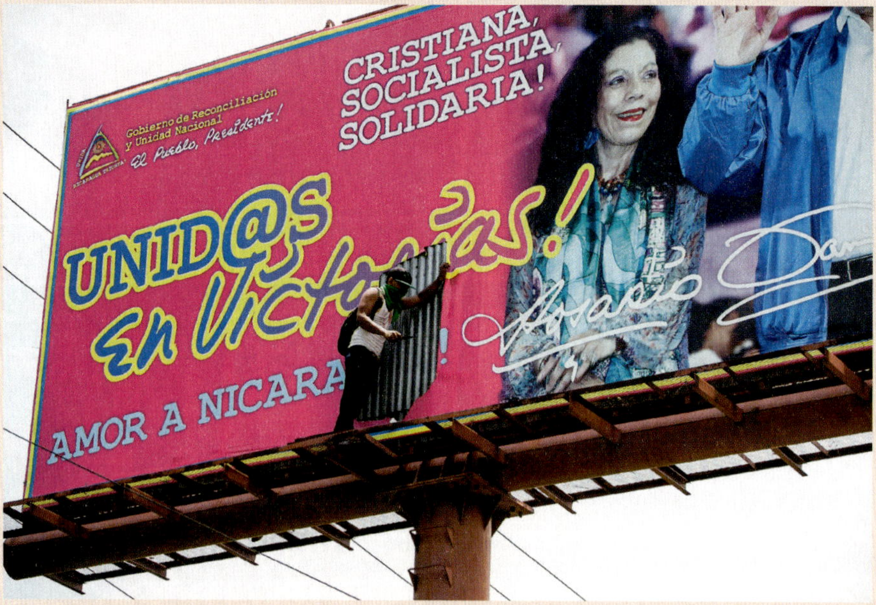

4.12 A protester tears a billboard along the highway as, below, a caravan in support of the town of Masaya moves past, May 13, 2018. Photograph by Jorge Eduardo Mejía Peralta.

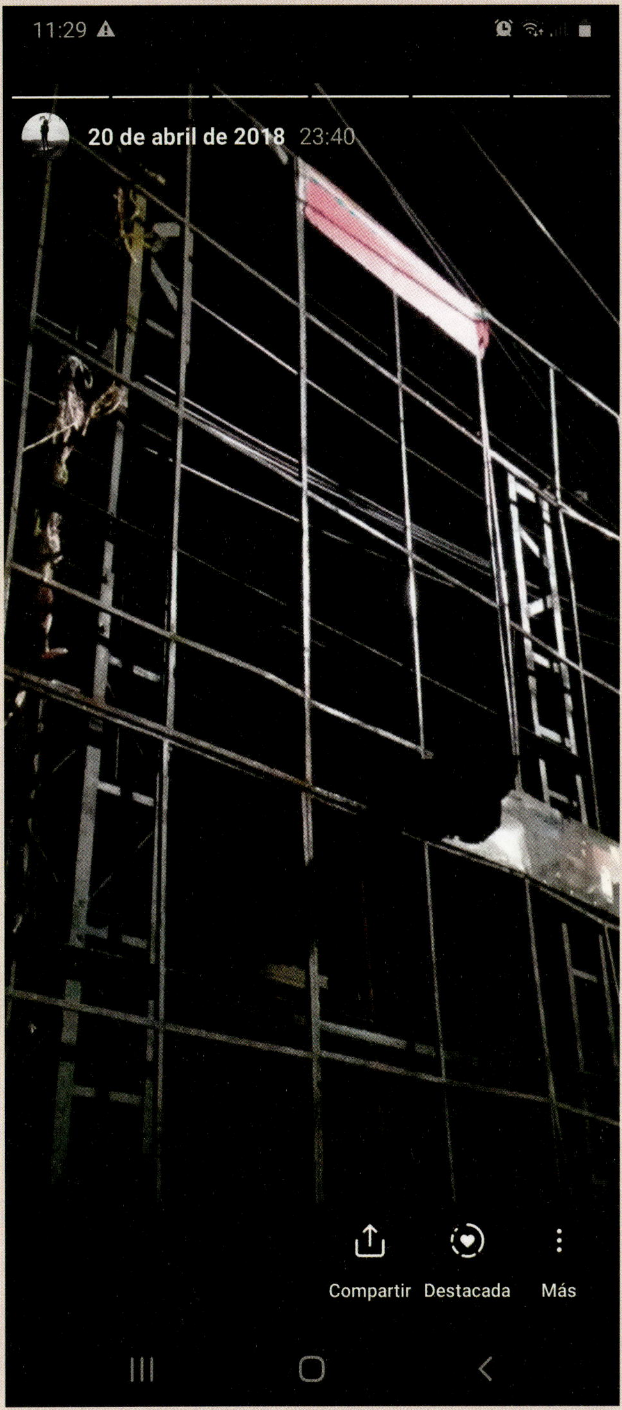

4.13 An Instagram "story" by photographer Álvaro Cantillano, showing the empty frames left after billboards were taken down, April 20, 2018.

become enmeshed in public memory. Visible marks from the literal cut-and-paste technique enhance the incongruity and perceived inadequacy between the memory of the revolution and the present. The shifting elements and deliberate mismatching prompt viewers to question how certain images, no matter how implausible, are normalized.

In response to making this series, Setright had spoken about the need for a new imaginary in Nicaragua, noting the "invasion" of commercial signage in public space, a phenomenon that makes clear Nicaragua's dependency on international capital and the government's adherence to top-down neoliberal economic models despite its participatory and socialist rhetoric. It was telling that the rebellion targeted precisely these advertisements as well as the Ortega-Murillo billboards. As became clear during the recent unrest, protests present opportunities to insert new images and image typologies in public space.

4.14 Gabriel Pérez Setright, *Molotov Man at McDonald's*, 2016.

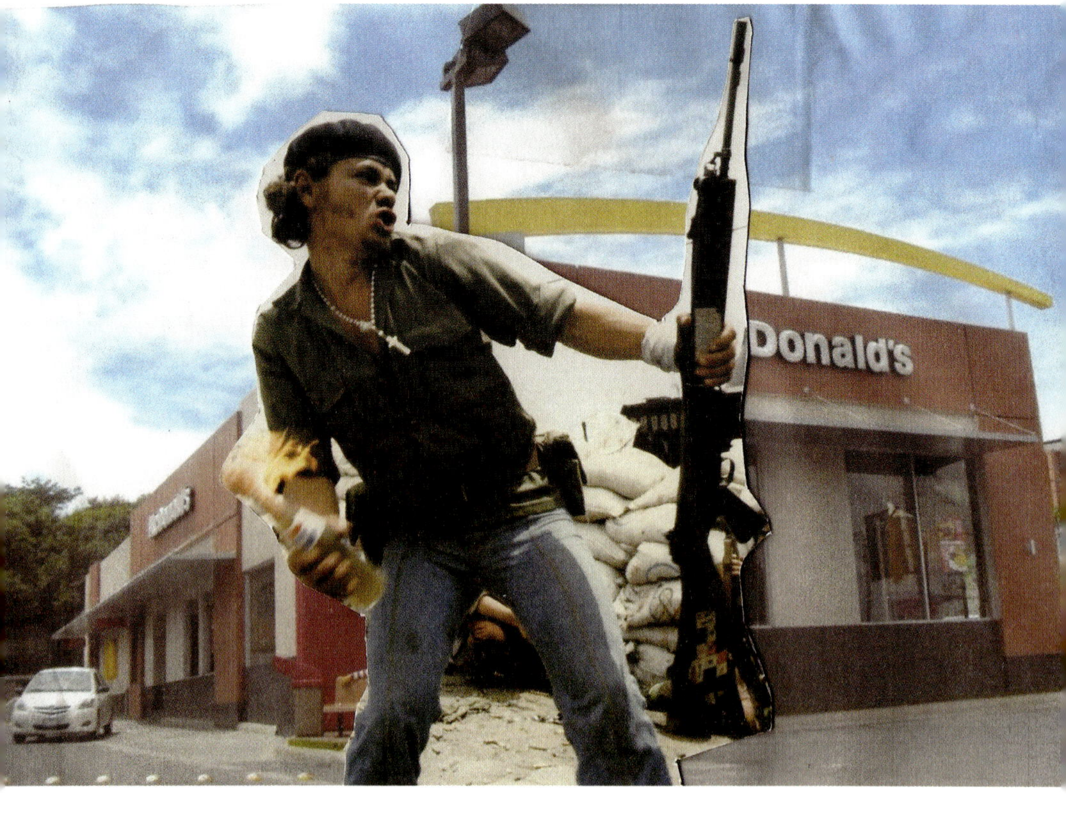

When it comes to iconicity, Nicaragua has a very clear example of a powerful homegrown national symbol: General Augusto César Sandino. The Sandinista movement was inspired by his rebellion against the US invasion and occupation of Nicaragua between 1927 and 1933. Drawn and stenciled onto city streets, Sandino's eponymous silhouette became a symbol of resistance against the Somoza dictatorship. The use of stencils is significant here, as the image originally gained power through the selective erasure of figurative content, a prime example thereof being the global image of El Che. The absence of documentary exactitude further reinforces the symbolic presence of the missing figurehead, monumentalizing it. Somewhat counterintuitively, through reduction, the silhouette achieves amplification—as shown by Ana Longoni in relation to the "Siluetazo" in Argentina, when during a civic action staged on September 21, 1983, "the Plaza de Mayo [in Buenos Aires] became, for several hours, a giant improvised workshop for the production of silhouettes." "The symbolic effect of the Siluetazo," she continues, "turned the production of silhouettes into a powerful, recurrent and public visual strategy. Silhouettes became a distinctive symbol for representing the disappeared."[35] In Nicaragua, following the victory of the revolution, Sandino's image was turned into an icon, ever-present. However, representations shifted along with the aesthetics of the Sandinista Front, from abstraction back into realism, in a style oddly reminiscent of academic Socialist Realism. In more recent years, Vice President Murillo has enhanced the cultlike memorialization of the hero.

During the 2018 protests, Sandino's image became a site of heavy contestation, bordering on violence and absurdity. The Nicaraguan national flag was hung around the neck of numerous Sandino monuments throughout the country, while the pedestals were repainted in white and blue. Once Operación Limpieza (Operation Cleanup) began in July 2018, government supporters and paramilitaries painted them back to red and black and replaced the flags with FSLN banners. Previously depleted by official discourse, the *auratic* potential of the national hero appeared to have been renewed, the *sign* resilient, hereby restored. The figure/icon/trope (Sandino, the Molotov Man) traveled through the city's formal and heterotopic spaces. It became embedded within the city's new material topographies and was layered, reconstituted with a certain sense of futurity, through visual (popular) media.

Before the protests, "old" symbols of Sandinismo were slowly withdrawing from view. Even the previously ubiquitous FSLN flag had more or less disappeared. The fading paint was no longer scheduled for renewal, since the

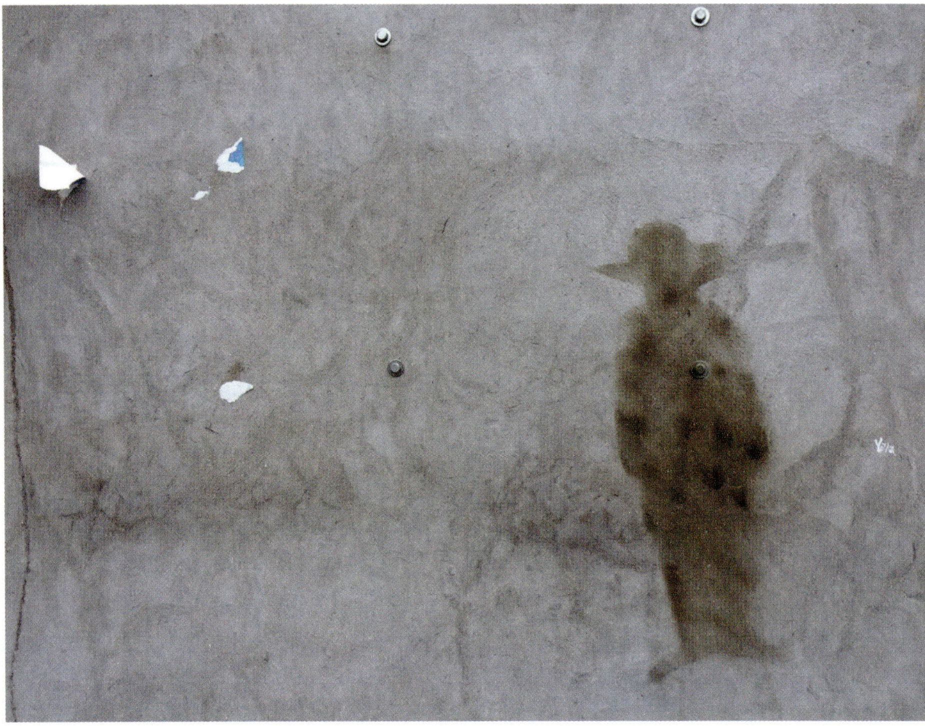

4.15 Sandino's silhouette etched in smoke on the side of a building in Bluefields, Nicaragua, October 2017. Photograph by Ileana L. Selejan.

party had officially changed its colors to a range of flamboyant pinks, yellows, and blues. Four decades earlier, their appearance in public space—constantly threatened with erasure or removal—marked dissent. Before April 2018, I interpreted this gradual erosion as symptomatic of the extent to which these indexical presences (the FSLN logo, Sandino's silhouette) were voided by current configurations of power. Their fading signaled their domestication, the dissolution of their subversive potential into a fatigued revolutionary status quo. Since April 2018, however, the FSLN logo and proregime slogans have reemerged, taking over the streets, their militancy enhanced. Heightened by recent confrontations, these signs no longer carried the seeds of rebellion. Rather, they aided the repression, reinforcing the government's absolute control over public space, the policing of all forms of protest. Thick lines in black paint were sprayed over dissenting views.

The silhouette of Sandino reappeared, however, time and again, yet unequivocally siding with the protesters. The "haunting" of the *original* revolution, despite or *in spite of* its current, official manifestations, rippled through such seemingly accidental scribblings and actions. As Mark Fisher has remarked, pessimistically, "What haunts the digital cul-de-sacs of the twenty-first century is not so much the past as all the lost futures that the twentieth century taught us to anticipate."[36] Yet here, within this present insurgency, we see a constant push toward not only revisiting those "lost futures" but also recomposing them anew. This instinct has not yet reached any form of finality—for many, like Cardenal, the revolution was "lost" in its path. It is what continues to trouble the waters, sending forth ripples, perturbances, and disruptions, which filter through, registering within the visual realm. Upon those shifting surfaces, fleeting images form.

Aftermaths

On the eve of the thirty-ninth anniversary of the Sandinista Revolution on July 19, after approximately three months of resistance, the protest movement was silenced through the use of disproportionate force by police forces and paramilitary loyalists. More than three hundred citizens were killed, between one thousand and over two thousand injured, and more than seven hundred arbitrarily imprisoned (Nicaragua's total population amounts to six million, with an estimated one million living and working abroad).[37] The United Nations High Commissioner for Refugees (UNHCR) reported that more than 150,000 Nicaraguans have gone into exile since the protests began, with the majority having requested asylum in neighboring Costa Rica.[38] These estimates are based on official figures and need to be complemented by a large number of Nicaraguans who remain clandestine.[39]

Throughout the months of protests, officials and the general public alike minutely recorded events on the streets in Managua and around the country, sometimes as a means to understand (perhaps in retrospect) those very actions that they were confronted with firsthand. There was a shared awareness that cameras became a continual presence once the crowds reached critical mass and converged at key sites. Different types of images were produced. "Citizen journalism" was practiced in the streets and was learned "by doing," while photojournalists were "hunting," to use a Flusserian term, for iconic or representative images.[40] The "people's" pictures were most striking due to their immediacy, trembling, blurred, uploaded raw, straight into the stream, from the intimacy of one's phone—Hito Steyerl's notion of the "poor image" could serve as an operative category here.[41] Caught within the flux of a "liquid temporality," much of this content was transferred online, where it "lived" and continues to linger—with a chance of becoming reactivated in perpetuity—until it is removed.[42] The press pictures, on the other hand, were more controlled, often illustrative. They seemed overtly focused on the dramatic, neglecting those very "elements of contingency" that Barthes held on to in his discussion of photographic semantics and affect.[43] Yet such distinctions fade when thinking back about those sleepless, momentous days and nights. Back then, they were all engulfed in the tidal sweep of the 24/7 feed, side-stepped by the tremendous mobilizing potential it brought in its wake.[44]

The distinguishing image-viewing format became the vertically framed smartphone snapshot or video, juxtaposed with the horizontal picture plane of the screen. Structurally, this vertical social media "stream" created a relationship of contiguity between viewer and witness, overlapping their gazes, since it replicated within the confines of one's home the position of the witnessing body in relation to the device and the scene. Experientially, viewers were so-to-say transported onto the scene. This "effect" was enhanced by the city's soundscape, since the noise of the protests—screams and chants, loud honking, and a choir of vuvuzelas—was audible throughout the night, fading in and out. On bleaker nights, the towering silence would only be broken by the sound of mortars, gunshots, and the sirens of police cars or emergency vehicles.

The "endless mirror effect" of social media, the repetition generated via sharing—picture within picture—was further amplified by the ubiquitous presence of mobile phones, alight screens reflecting each other in every frame. It is noteworthy that most of the videos and images shared during the protests were generated in clusters, populating, rather than invading, internet channels all at once. The occasion gave everyday citizens an opportunity to feel as if they were a part of a historic moment, and the mobile phone camera was their means of participation. Yet within this mass, a tremendous amount of noise was generated as well. Every scene that was deemed significant enough to warrant recording and sharing betrayed the presence of other camera phones, alight and held up high. This reflex developed almost immediately as more and more everyday citizens witnessed violent events firsthand. This reaction was possibly influenced by the regime's denial of its actions and the weaving of a parallel narrative that aimed to discredit the protest movement. These actions and formats speak to the tradition of documentary photography, which privileges the individual image, searching for the iconic. Here, the most powerful iterations emerged out of a sheer pixelated mass (still or in motion), in a manner similar to the modalities described by Rabih Mroué in "The Pixelated Revolution" (2012).

No individual image *captured* in this context works in isolation; rather, they are all mutually referential, and can potentiate, even reactivate, one another, or establish new relations (figure 4.16). This is perhaps where photography's potential to perform iconoclastically, to enable a *détournement*, ultimately lies, even when latent. The archive is more than a fragment, and ever short of complete, recursive, haunted. It is, in an imaginative, future-oriented sense, inexhaustible, while the repertoire (and I'm thinking here with Diana Taylor) may be reconstituted in perpetuity.[45] The very movements of the crowd that helped make this monument—people streaming up and down along its sides—also made it photographable, while the rest of protesters passed by *viewing* it, photographing it. The living monument, stationary if only for a brief moment as individuals stop and pose, is itself a picture (my image is only a trace), its power derived from its temporariness. Here, as in the case of the toppling of the metal trees, the image-event functions as a participatory structure.

I use the term *image-event* as an extension of Azoulay's observation that "the event of photography is never over," nonetheless while engaging with the rich discussion and conceptualization provided by Karen Strassler.[46] As Strassler writes: "An 'image-event' is a political process in which an image (or a constellation of related images) crystallizes otherwise inchoate and dispersed imaginings within a discrete and mobile visible form that becomes available for scrutiny, debate and play as it circulates in public." Furthermore, she adds, "each iteration of an image transforms the time and space of its emergence. Conceptualizing *all* images as unfolding events enables us to see them as contingent and politically consequential processes in their own right."[47] I argue here that the "image-event" begins to form before, in advance of the image; it precedes it, it prophesies it, while being shaped by it in turn.

An image ecology, or environment, a "visual economy"—to use Deborah Poole's phrase—emerges at the intersection of all lines of sight and is negotiated between participant subject positions (figures 4.16–4.18). In addition to investigating the production and circulation of images and image-objects, Poole writes that "it becomes important to ask not what specific images *mean* but, rather, how images accrue value."[48] This excess of vision—everyone's phone shoots and records continuously—has provoked a shift in the subject position. The selfie immerses the subject-viewer into the scene (figure 4.18). I would go even further and argue that a form of extreme reflexivity is at play, where the ultimate exchange of gazes happens in digitally interconnected space. Given the number of cameras switched on at all times, we might conjure such an imagined community as the physical, embodied environment of the street "cascades" into the online stream. While individual gazes will

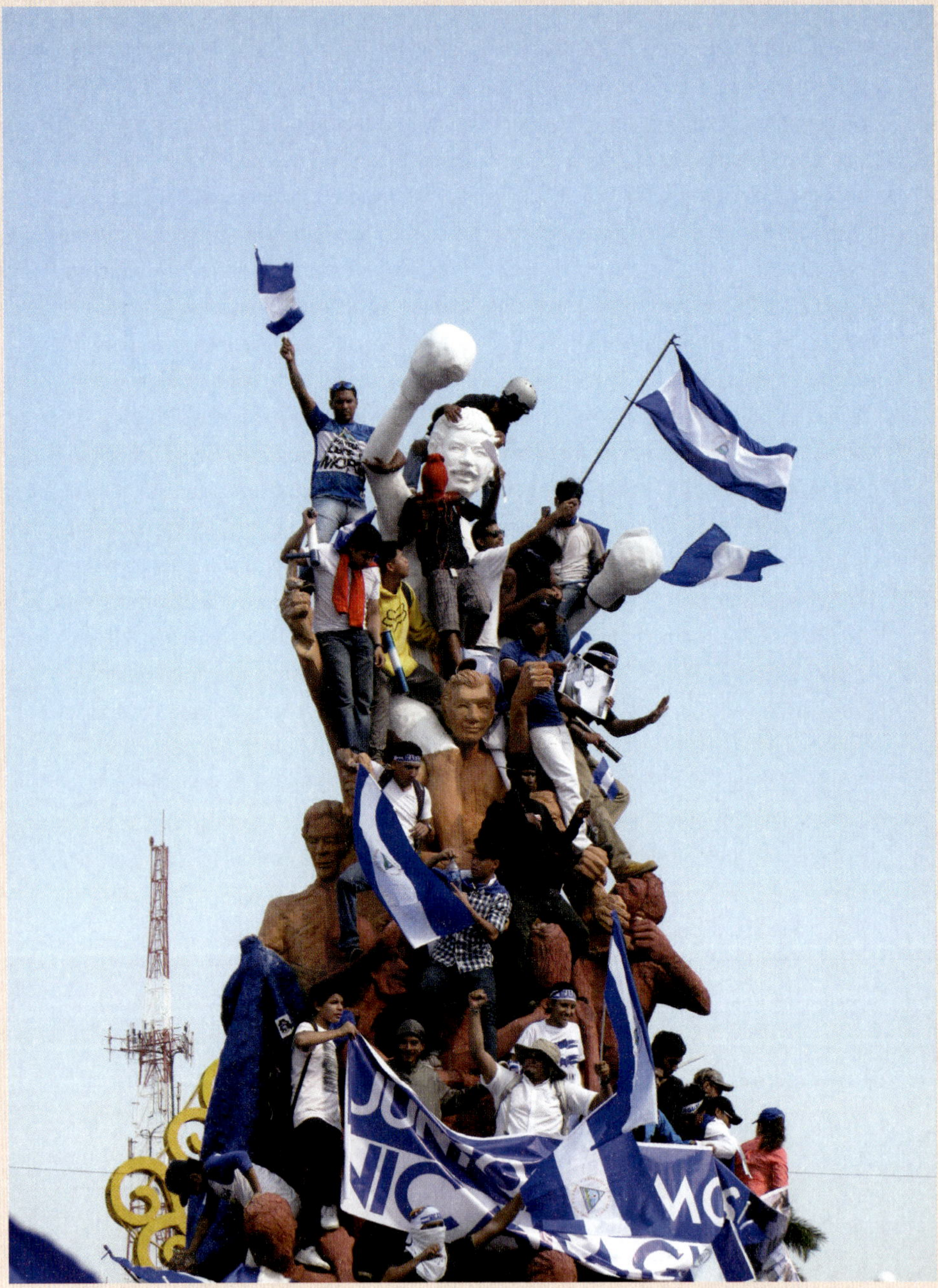

4.16 People climbing on top of the statue of Alexis Argüello, Managua, May 9, 2018. Photograph by Ileana L. Selejan.

never meet *in person*, their encounter is nonetheless made possible in absentia, along that theoretical horizon. The firsthand experience is therefore never complete. Rather, it is both lived and watched, inviting the revisiting of that moment from there on. As it unfolds in real time, experience is concurrently mediated and expanded by means of a complex technical apparatus—itself seen, felt (the camera held in one's hand), and imagined by means of a virtual network. This type of expanded visual environment—reminiscent of Gene Youngblood's theorized "expanded cinema"—might complement the extreme reflexivity that such monumental events have the potential to engender.[49]

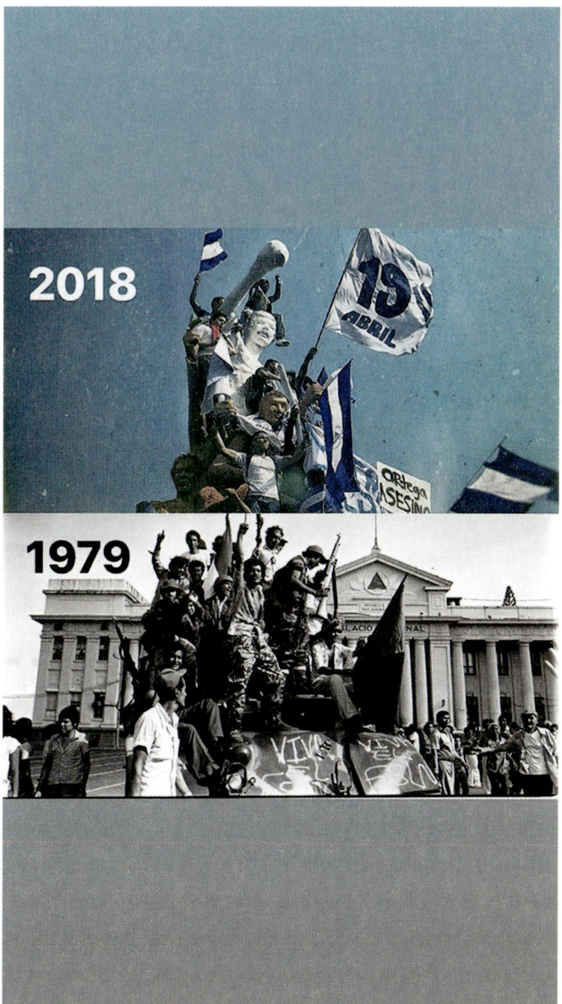

4.17 An anonymous Instagram "story" drawing a parallel between the 2018 protesters scaling the Argüello monument and the celebrations of the Sandinista victory in the Plaza de la Revolución in July 1979, photographed by Pedro Valtierra.

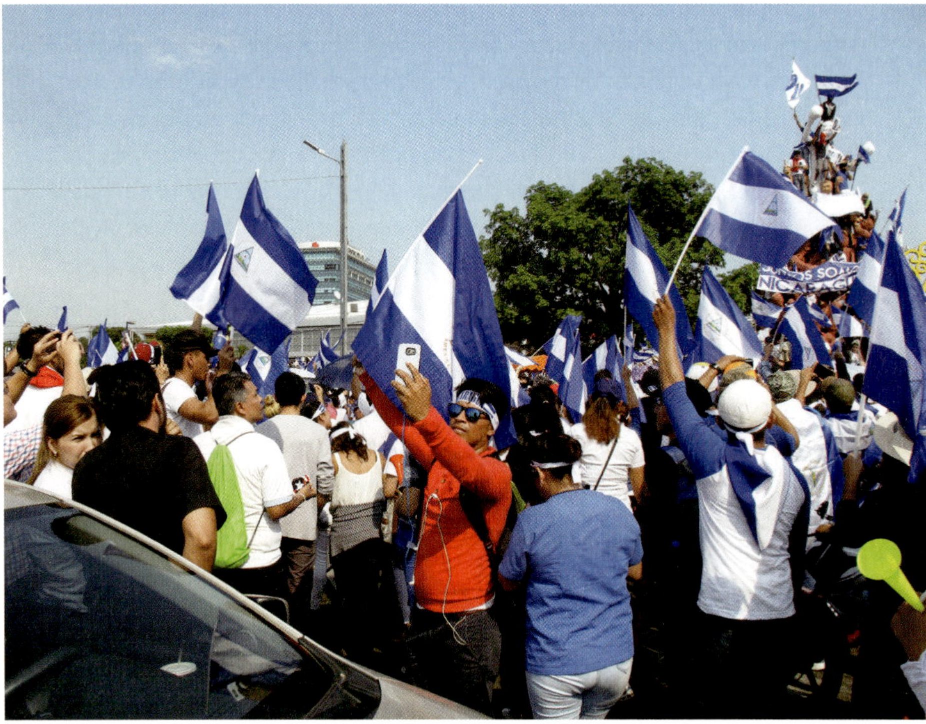

4.18 A man takes a selfie with the Argüello monument in the background, Managua, May 9, 2018. Photograph by Ileana L. Selejan.

One might argue that Nicaragua had historically experienced an overflow of political activism, manifested to a great extent within the visual realm and through the field of culture broadly defined as popular. As Ernesto Cardenal asserted in 1982, “La revolución es cultura y la cultura es revolución” (Revolution is culture and culture is revolution).[50] This refrain may have resonated with the generations that joined the underground resistance against the Somoza dictatorship and who participated in the revolutionary process that took up the entirety of the 1980s as well as with those who fought in the Contra War. However, the electoral defeat of FSLN in 1990 as well as subsequent neoliberal governments led to fragmentations and increased polarization within the country. Once the FSLN returned to power in 2006, the perceived monopoly over memory further corroded revolutionary idealism. Even the students who initiated the 2018 protests and who spoke out against the regime claimed revolutionary fatigue. Nonetheless, some of the “classicized” revolutionary iconography was reclaimed, in ways that speak to the political potential that the reversibility of signs holds within strategies of détournement.

The antigovernmental protests that began in Nicaragua in April 2018 generated a vast amount of photographic imagery, video documentation, visual graphics, and street art, which connected to local photographic histories while tapping into global imaginaries of dissent. Are we to read these photographic gestures as anticipatory, contributing to the making of a new civil contract, as suggested by Azoulay?[51] Does the Nicaraguan case constitute a clear example of photography becoming a key means for people to demand rights, in advance of actualized representation? Is this an instance of an *about to be* (or *about to become*) even more potent than Strassler's *as if* or the *not yet*?[52] Photographs are certainly participating in a process of renegotiating the public sphere that has already begun, yet which has been suspended by state power. It remains to be seen whether this temporary surge in image production will drive the public imagination and produce change or merely signal a repetition of the same. Albeit temporarily, photography has enabled the creation of a social space where the field of politics could be reconfigured anew.

From April 2018 and throughout 2019, the state of siege continued. By then, however, the "movement," if there was ever one, had fragmented. A number of diverse groups had joined efforts and forged alliances, such as the Alianza Cívica (Civic Alliance), which continued to push for dialogue with the regime. However, several splinter groups had been active alongside, mostly focused on issue-specific civil rights agendas, including campaigns for the release of political prisoners, the protection of women and LGBTQ individuals, the rights of rural workers, indigenous autonomy and environmental rights, and campaigns against sexual violence and *feminicidio*. Nonetheless, all these groups built upon or grew out of previous social platforms and initiatives, some long-term.

Citizens continued to rebel, although through slighter, more covert gestures, arising briefly, yet quick to draw back again, muffled by the sound of the everyday. Until 2019, I hadn't returned to the country in over a year, yet strong memories of the 2018 uprising were vividly playing in my head. Total chaos had set in within a matter of a few short days. Massive marches took over the streets, schools were closed, universities were occupied, and entire neighborhoods hunkered down behind barricades. The rhythm of the city had switched dramatically. More urgent routines hastily replaced regular ones: schedules were shortened, banks shuttered their windows, shops ran out of water and medical supplies, and people rushed back and forth to their jobs, only to retreat into their homes at night. It struck me how it all seemed well

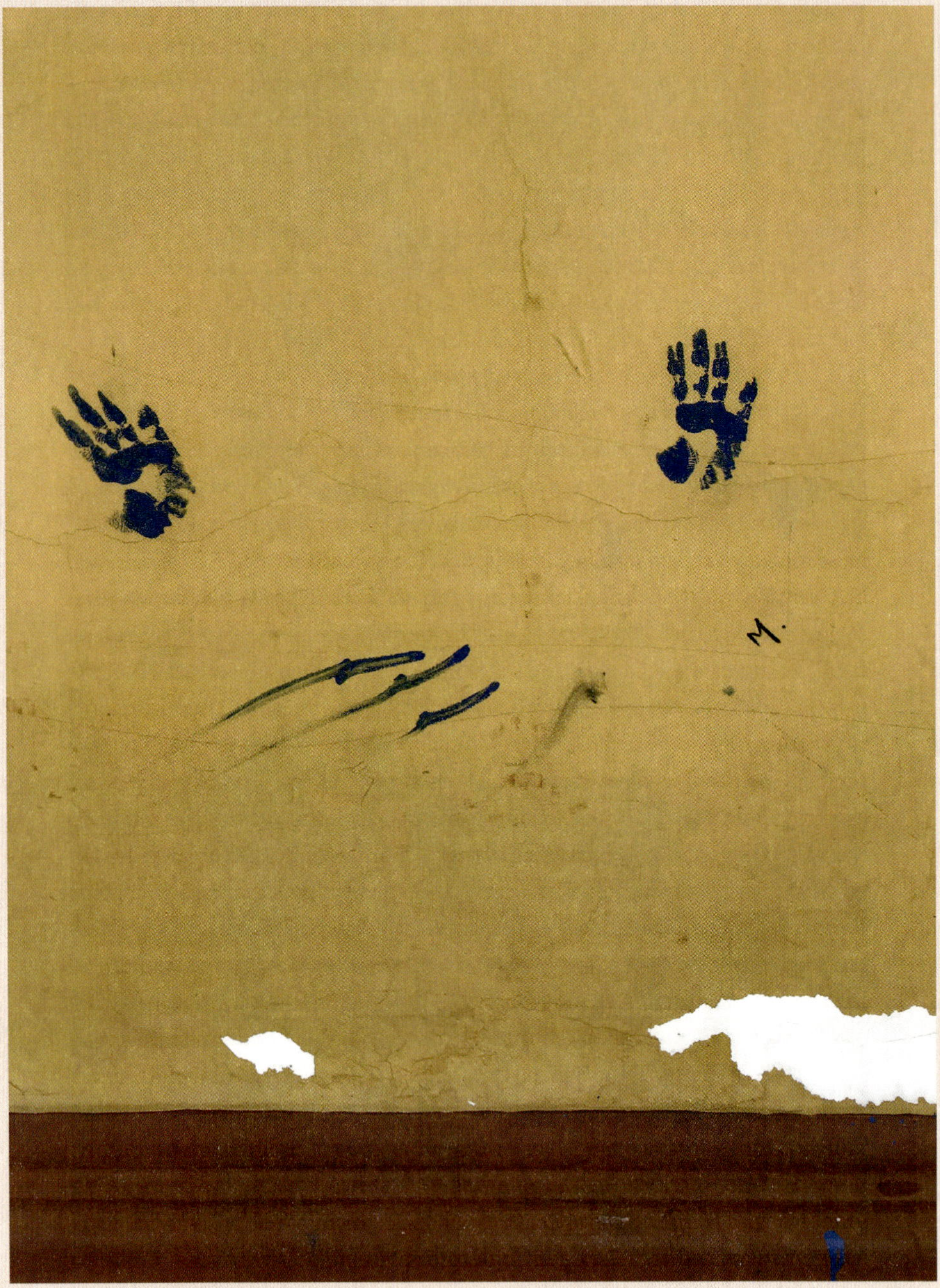

4.19 & 4.20 Erased wall markings, still visible under layers of paint, and "fresh" gestures hastily imprinted onto the street in León, July 2019. White and blue, the colors of the Nicaraguan flag, have become the new colors of resistance across the country. Photographs by Ileana L. Selejan.

rehearsed, something people were prepared for, or perhaps these were routines resurrected from the past. By nightfall, the city lay abandoned, almost everyone seemingly glued to their TVs, radios, or social media feeds, consuming the continuous flow of information coming in and out of the streets where, by all resemblance, there was a war.

I heard the word *normalization* often in July 2019. Yet while walking and driving around Managua, León, and Masaya, I could see traces of what had happened that previous year. Graffiti, *pintas*, stencils, and other types of markings were still visible under layers of painted-over red and black. The historic colors of the FSLN, which had been used to signal allegiance and to demarcate territories during the years of struggle against Somoza, were now used to suppress and censor dissent. Yet these patches of paint clumsily strewn around the city's streets drew attention to the inscriptions underneath instead of canceling them out, thereby granting them further power, turning them into icons of sorts (figures 4.19 and 4.20). Every trace and leftover fragment seemed to harbor something prophetic, operating as indexes and relics at the same time.[53] Anyone who had been there in 2018 could see right through these clumsily attempted cover-ups. They could read the dissident scripts and slogans, retrace the images that lay behind them.

"We are living the end of the Sandinista Revolution." Juan's words rang in my head once more. A few days later, I walked into the ebullient parade of the fortieth anniversary of the Sandinista Revolution. As on all previous occasions, it was a festive affair, loud, with food stands and street vendors everywhere, a multitude enveloped in red-and-black flags, T-shirts, and caps, most of them branded with images of Sandino, Daniel, and Che. Susan Meiselas's "Molotov Man" made his appearance on camo print, a saintlike revolutionary highlighted against a backdrop of reactivated militant red and black.

The seemingly endless crowds streamed along Managua's central Avenida Bolivar, from the Hugo Chávez roundabout, bypassing the Plaza de la Revolución, a few kilometers down toward the Paseo Xolotlán, bordering the lake. There, from the top of a colossal podium, the leaders of the FSLN presided over the assembled. Although it was an important landmark for the revolution, the anniversary did not manage to attract the star revolutionaries it had brought onto the stage in the past years. Daniel Ortega's most important ally, Nicolas Maduro, had more urgent matters to attend at home. Instead, there were a few foreign dignitaries and representatives, most prominently renowned political evangelists from the United States who stood alongside Ortega, Vice President Rosario Murillo, and several members of the historic FSLN. Revolutionary songs from the eighties updated to the rhythms of flamboyant pop and reggaeton blasted through rows and rows of concert-size speakers. Soporific anti-imperialist, anti-intervention speeches turned into a quasi-continuous surround sound, carrying through to the lake, immersing the already disassembling crowds.

Notes

It has been a privilege to be a part of the PhotoDemos team; our conversations have greatly contributed toward the development of this chapter and of related publications. Many thanks to Anooradha Iyer Siddiqi and Brian Larkin at Barnard College and to Jorge Ribalta and Ana Longoni at the Reina Sofía Museum for inviting me to present work in progress. I am grateful to Pablo Hernández Hernández, who kindly hosted me at the University of Costa Rica, facilitating invaluable exchanges with esteemed faculty and students. In Nicaragua, thanks are due to the Instituto de Historia de Nicaragua y Centroamérica, director Edwin Matamoros Chávez, former director Margarita Vannini, and the institute staff for their support. Claudia Gordillo and Margarita Montealegre have been especially generous in sharing their work with me throughout the years, and I am deeply grateful for their friendship and support. Any errors in reading or interpreting their work, alongside other photographs and statements included here, are solely mine. Thanks to all the photographers and artists who have contributed reproductions of their work toward this publication. For the writing of this chapter, I have benefited greatly from conversations with numerous scholars, photographers, artists, writers, journalists, activists, and members of the public, all of whom must remain unnamed out of concerns about their safety due to ongoing state repression in the country. My greatest sadness is not being able to share this work with you, not yet at least, in a context in which we can debate it freely. The events of 2018 in Nicaragua have profoundly altered the lives of many, including mine. As we witness their devastating aftermath, I remain hopeful, knowing that other possible futures are being imagined.

1 Juan, interview with the author, Managua, July 16, 2019.

2 The Sandinista Front (FSLN) assumed de facto leadership of the country after a nationwide popular insurrection toppled the regime of Anastasio Somoza Debayle in July 1979, effectively unseating one of the longest-lasting familial dictatorships in modern Latin American history. Daniel Ortega was elected president in 1984; however, he lost the following election, in 1990, in part due to the Contra War that was ravaging the country and an ongoing trade embargo imposed by the United States. Under his leadership, the FSLN finally returned to power in 2006. Rosario Murillo, his wife, became vice president following the November 6, 2016, general election, when the party won 72.44

percent of the vote. International observers were prevented from monitoring the elections.

3 The journal editors explained that the title *Wani* was a transliteration of the indigenous word *guani*, first mentioned in Diego de Porras's chronicle of Christopher Columbus's 1502 journey to Caray (now Puerto Limón in Costa Rica). According to this historic account, *guani* meant gold. The editors contested that narrative, arguing instead that this interpretation betrays the colonizers' desire. See *Wani*, "Por qué Wani?," 3–7.

4 Cordelia Dilg is a German photographer who traveled to Nicaragua for extended periods of time from 1979 to 1986. Between 1981 and 1984, she lived in the country as a solidarity worker. She documented the revolution, contributing editorial content and photographic work to a number of state-sponsored publications, including *Wani*.

5 *Wani*, "Por qué Wani?," 6.

6 See Kunzle, *Murals of Revolutionary Nicaragua*; and Craven, *Art and Revolution*.

7 The meaning of *el pueblo* (the people) in Nicaragua shifts during the revolutionary period, primarily through the wider dissemination of Marxist political theory and the influence of Cuba. In addition to local expressions, its usage speaks to the greater sense of transnational solidarity that developed during this period throughout Latin America in reaction to authoritarianism, as evidenced in cultural production. For instance, the song "¡El pueblo unido, jamás será vencido!" (The united people will never be defeated) was written by Chilean *nueva canción* group Quilapayún during the government of Salvador Allende and became widely popular as a protest song in the aftermath of the Augusto Pinochet coup in 1973. In Nicaragua, this song became one of the main revolutionary anthems, and it has remained embedded in collective memory as a key artifact from the revolution. It was used extensively during the 2018 protests. In addition to these political-ideological interpretations, the term *el pueblo* encapsulated historically relevant definitions of "community" and "the public." As in the rest of Latin America, *pueblo* can also refer to a village, a small town, or a community. See Eiss, *In the Name of El Pueblo*.

8 Alan Riding, interview with the author, Paris, June 7, 2017. Riding had published the first internationally circulated in-depth article on the Sandinista insurrection, which was illustrated with Susan Meiselas's now iconic photographs. See Riding, "National Mutiny."

9 See, for instance, Ernesto Cardenal, *La revolución perdida* (The lost revolution), first published in 2001. Throughout my years of field work in Nicaragua, I observed communal acts of "mourning" the revolution on several occasions, for instance, at book launches and other gatherings of former revolutionaries who continue to have public profiles, especially as members of a politically committed, intellectual middle class.

10 Margarita Montealegre, interview with the author, Managua, July 20, 2019.

11 Craven, *Art and Revolution*, and Kunzle, *Murals of Revolutionary Nicaragua*, constitute notable exceptions, as well as Buchsbaum, *Cinema and the Sandinistas*.

12 Gruzinski, *Images at War*, 3.

13 I enter the story circa 2011, when I decided to travel to Managua following a job as a photography archivist for an archaeological project in Egypt that was prematurely terminated by the onset of the Arab Spring. I planned to research Nicaragua, prompted by my PhD advisor's recollection of the momentum gained by the resistance movement against Reagan-era interventionist politics during the 1980s. He had mentioned that Meiselas's *Nicaragua, June 1978–July 1979* (1981) was instrumental in shedding light on local realities. I imagined the book with frayed edges, passed from hand to hand. Upon arriving in Managua, it became immediately apparent that access to photographic archives was going to be difficult, if not impossible, given the disputed memory of the revolution. I slowly started acquainting myself with local photographers and artists, mostly people who had participated in the revolution in various official and non-official roles, many of whom had meanwhile opposed the regime. Over the span of a decade, I extended my research into investigating so-called vernacular practices, analyzing the work of studio photographers and amateurs. I have thus sought to overcome the fractures and gaps within the public record, to work around the many silences encountered, through in-depth ethnographic fieldwork.

14 Navarrete received a journalism award from the Violeta Chamorro Foundation for his coverage of the protests; this interactive web-based presentation was created on that occasion. See Navarrete, "Mi déjà vu."

15 The *plantón* was organized after the government announced an increase in Social Security contributions and 5 percent cuts for pensioners. The vice president convened the Juventud Sandinista (Sandinista Youth) to stage a countermarch. Members of the Juventud and *turbas* (mobs) on motorcycles attacked the small crowd in the afternoon, which resulted in serious injuries. Journalists and photographers were also attacked and had their equipment stolen or destroyed.

16 The 2018 student movement was constituted ad hoc, first in response to the government's mishandling of a massive fire that engulfed the Indio Maíz biological reserve starting on April 3, charring five thousand hectares of rainforest. Social media played a key role in the organization of these protests, under #SOSIndioMaíz. See Rocha, *Autoconvocados y conectados*.

17 Barthes, *Camera Lucida*, 88.

18 Latour, "What Is Iconoclash?"

19 One might reflect here upon the etymology of the word *cliché*, which is synonymous with "stereotype" in French and refers to printing processes. A cliché is a reproduction matrix, printing block, or metal plate from which series of multiple prints can be produced.

20 Strassler, *Demanding Images*, 8.

21 Didi-Huberman, *Désirer désobéir*, 31–32.

22 Kracauer, *Orpheus in Paris*, 3–4.

23 See Azoulay, *Civil Imagination*, 26–27.

24 Christopher Pinney develops this notion throughout his in-depth analysis on photography in India, in dialogue with Arjun Appadurai's seminal edited volume *The Social Life of Things: Commodities in Cultural Perspective*. See Pinney, *Camera Indica*, 10.

25 Azoulay, *Potential History*, 782–83.

26 See GIEI, "Report."

27 Aguilar and Moncada, "'Árboles de la vida.'"

28 I have written about vandalism in the context of the 2018 protests, by relation to the Nicaraguan government's attempts to delegitimize the movement and prosecute protesters, and I have argued that in this case such gestures and actions might be interpreted as symbolically reparative. See Selejan, "Vandalism as Symbolic Reparations."

29 "Actions were based entirely on historical citation, of events from the past and images from the past, which are found in abundance in the minds of the Soviet people saturated as they are with ideology. As in all revolutions, a postmodernist mechanism, an aesthetic of citation was once again set in motion. All successful revolutions end with statues coming down. . . . Popov, the Mayor of Moskow, had signed a decree calling for the dismantling of statues which the people hated so much. So removing Dzerzhinsky was a key moment which marked the end of the 'performance' and the start of the mechanism of history, when the mechanisms of the new ideology began to work again." Viktor Misiano, interview in Lewis and Mulvey, *Disgraced Monuments*.

30 González C., "Así se vive la caída."

31 Augusto César Sandino (1895–1934) was the leader of an armed insurgency movement that opposed the US Marines' occupation of Nicaragua, between 1927 and 1933. After the Marines' withdrawal, following the signing of a peace treaty, he was assassinated under orders of General Anastasio Somoza García, who was then leader of the National Guard. Somoza became president of Nicaragua in 1937, thereby inaugurating the Somoza dictatorship. Sandino would inspire the foundation of the FSLN in 1961.

32 Gell, *Art and Agency*, 64.

33 The private possessions of the Somoza family met a similar fate, although interestingly some of their photographs survived. Hope Portocarrero Somoza's family albums are currently in the collection of a local historian in Managua. The photographic archives of Somoza's official newspaper, *Novedades*, which profiled the dictator and his family extensively, were found in a trash pile by photographer Margarita Montealegre and are currently archived at the Instituto de Historia de Nicaragua y Centroamérica in Managua.

34 Hariman and Lucaites, *No Caption Needed*, 10.

35 Longoni, "Photographs and Silhouettes," 10–11.

36 Fisher, "What Is Hauntology?," 16.

37 Arbitrary detentions have become a means to suppress dissent. See Amnesty International, "Nicaragua: Silence at Any Cost." On February 9, 2023, the Nicaraguan government released and exiled 222 political prisoners to the US, stripping them of their citizenship; 35 remain in custody.

38 UNHCR, "Number of Displaced Nicaraguans."

39 The most comprehensive report to date was published by the Grupo Interdisciplinario de Expertos Independientes (GIEI) on December 21, 2018, and addressed the violence that occurred between April 18 and May 30. The GIEI operates under the mandate of the Inter-American Commission on Human Rights and the Organization of American States (OAS).

40 "The act of photography is like going on a hunt in which photographer and camera merge into one indivisible function. This is a hunt for new states of things, situations never seen before, for the improbable, for information. The structure of the act of photography is a quantum one: a doubt made up of points of hesitation and points of decision-making." Flusser, *Towards a Philosophy of Photography*, 39.

41 Steyerl, "In Defense of the Poor Image."

42 Notion developed by Marianne Hirsch and Leo Spitzer in relation to Jeff Wall's 1989 essay "Photography and Liquid Intelligence." See M. Hirsch and Spitzer, *School Photos*, 13.

43 Barthes, *Camera Lucida*.

44 One might point here to Strassler's distinction between "evidentiary" and "ludic" images: "Evidentiary images promise to ground public truth claims in a technological guarantee of transparency," while "ludic" images "deploy remediation, repurposing, and reworking to generate new constellations of truth and modalities of revelation on the surface of the images." In the case of Nicaragua, I would argue, however, that this distinction is relative, and that the two categories are interdependent and cross-pollinate. Strassler, *Demanding Images*, 24.

45 Taylor, *Archive and the Repertoire*.

46 Azoulay, *Civil Imagination*, 25.

47 Strassler, *Demanding Images*, 13–14.

48 Poole, *Vision, Race, and Modernity*, 10.

49 Youngblood, *Expanded Cinema*.

50 Cardenal, "Revolución es cultura," 64.

51 Azoulay, *Civil Contract*.

52 In her book on popular photographic practices in Indonesia, Strassler theorizes photography's potential "to bring into material, tangible proximity a fantasy portrayed 'as if' it were real." Strassler, *Refracted Visions*, 77.

53 Religious symbolism had emboldened the protests; churches provided shelter from attacks, while secular altars were set up at sites of gathering within cities, within neighborhoods, and even alongside barricades.

5

"We Are Moving with Technology"

PHOTOGRAPHING VOICE AND BELONGING IN NIGERIA

NALUWEMBE BINAISA

Ìlá Òràngún: Locating the Citizenry of Photography

I sit outside Hajj Hammed's studio in companionable silence as we watch the bustle of market day pass along the main road and spill over into the narrow side streets of Ìlá Òràngún, an ancient rural city in Osun State, Nigeria. It is a hot, still day made bearable by the clarity of the air, in marked contrast to the stultifying heat of Lagos, the megacity commercial capital of the country. My focus on Ìlá Òràngún is in part inspired by Stephen Sprague's seminal essay "Yoruba Photography: How the Yoruba See Themselves" and his insistence that much can be learned if research into photography privileges "the cultural values and perceptions" of the societies we seek to understand.[1] This is a powerful yet flawed provocation because the term *Yoruba* has a multifaceted meaning representing a people, nation, language, and cosmology foregrounded in the ancient *Ifa* corpus that spreads far beyond the confines of West Africa to the Americas, Caribbean, Europe, and beyond. The flows embedded in the term *Yoruba* encompass a people who possess an array of cultural specificities that cut across subgroups and the borders of contemporary nation-states. Their visual and material culture marked by forced and voluntary incursions and dispersals, now at home across a global diaspora, grounds precolonial bonds of affiliation and fraternity established long before the making of present-day West Africa.[2] The intersecting mobilities of photography are captured in the concept of "image world" advanced by Deborah Poole in her work on the Andes, to draw attention to the social, economic, political, and cultural transfers that photography enables.[3] Yoruba photography might signal the recognition of an important branch of photography, yet expressed as a subset it revalidates center/periphery typologies and falls into the trap of ex-nomination that reinforces the sovereignty of Euro-American epistemologies.[4]

The politics of belonging are intertwined within the politics of location and vision. World system photography as a concept is one way out of this imperial cul-de-sac and enables us to "grasp the historical interconnectedness of practice and cease to ghettoize 'non-normative' practices."[5] It counters the opacities that stem from the forked tongue of simultaneous recognition and qualification as "other" based on the specificities of location.[6] This tried and tested script of recognition as confirmation of the periphery leads to the age-old question reframed another way, "Can the subaltern see?"[7] In this chapter, I explore different affordances of photography within legacies of violence, transformation, and modalities of belonging. It is in this combination that possibilities are present for gaining deeper insight into the global through a country as diverse as Nigeria, with its disputed and contested revisioning of nationhood. I take the quote in my title, "we are moving with technology," as a point of deep reflection on the multiple pathways and junctures that striate everyday lives in Nigeria. Uttered by Hajj Hammed (figure 5.1), a studio photographer in Ìlá Òràngún and the current president of its branch of the Nigerian Professional Photographers and Videographers Association, it is a commentary that I grew to realize evokes both stasis and movement, related to the imposed temporalities of colonial time and its narratives of development. It also reflects the wisdom of an indigenous cosmology and its enduring relevance in the digital age, referencing the Yoruba saying "Ayé nyí, à ntòó" (The world rotates and we follow it/We follow the world as it rotates), implying that change is constant and human beings are obliged to move with the trends or become irrelevant.[8] "We are moving with technology" is extracted

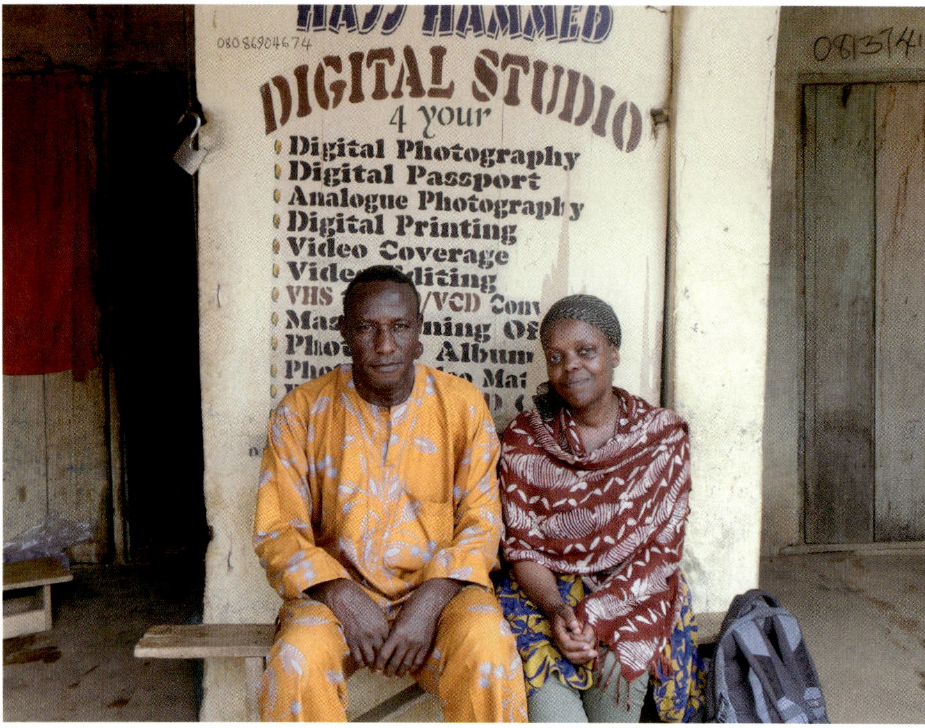

5.1 Hajj Hammed, president of the Ìlá Òràngún branch of the Nigerian Professional Photographers and Videographers Association, and Naluwembe Binaisa sit outside his studio. Rephotographed by Naluwembe Binaisa, August 2017.

from a longer recorded passage in one of my many interactions with Hajj Hammed. In the following, he responds to my specific question about what he understands as Yoruba photography. He rejects the prefix "Yoruba" as pertaining to a distinct photography and says:

> There is nothing like that [Yoruba photography]. There is not any difference because we are the same. Because this profession is the work of the God so there is no difference throughout the world. The work comes from God, yes! You know Yoruba says, "Olódùmarè made people in his own image." You know this is a work of God. So, there's no difference. We are together in the same pattern, we are one. It is the same changes. By the time

> we change with this technology, we are moving with technology. The *oyibo* [white people] are moving with it [photography] before our own here, they just introduced it to us, but we are still moving now. We are the same now, no difference.[9]

Hajj Hammed's invocation of Olódùmarè centers indigenous epistemologies where the aesthetic liberty of creation is conjoined to the moral authority of God, revisualized within the technics of photography. Here "we are the same" obliterates the specificities of location that scaffold difference and lays the foundations for the transparent coeval project of mobility and transformation that is the "citizenry of photography."[10] Despite the introduction of photography as a technology of progress and civilization through "othering" the indigenous, its globalization seems to heighten a counterpublics of solidarity, inclusion, and transformation. The call to Olódùmarè within an imagery of conjoined livelihoods and self-reflexive awareness of the politics of "divide and rule" brings to the fore the notion of two publics that differentiates between a moral and amoral public.[11] In his ground-breaking explanatory inquiry into the logics of the nation-state in Africa, Peter Ekeh proposes a bifurcated public sphere composed on the one hand of an amoral civil public that corresponds to the structures, violence, and exploitation of the colonial and postcolonial state and on the other hand a moral primordial public that reflects the enduring rights and responsibilities of people to one another. In key respects, the moral primordial public shares a conceptual space with the civil contract of photography that demands a relationality beyond the political orders of the nation-state.[12]

This chapter seeks to pose alternative sightlines into the lives of citizens by unpacking the layers of intersection between photography, self-representation, and political imaginaries. It is a multisited ethnography that draws on long-term fieldwork in South West Nigeria, gathering photographs from a broad range of sources and daily interactions, in family homes, employment settings, the street, the museum, the gallery, and the digital world of the ubiquitous mobile phone.[13] In these quite distinct spaces of display, retrieval, and at times abandonment, I trace different modalities of photography as it facilitates and invokes the potential of movement along material, spatial, and temporal vectors of belonging. I pay attention to these image-events within the intimacy of family albums and in the public sphere of the urban fabric dominated by the portraiture of religion, state, and the fluid effervescence of youth engagement through social media.[14] It was through these diverse environments that I came to pay attention to the resilience of indigenous cosmologies rooted in aesthetics that, as the prominent scholar Rowland Abiodun insists, are embodied through everyday practices of art and language to bridge the physical and spiritual dimensions.[15]

Dislocated Citizenship

Belonging, voice, and identity are claimed on a range of levels in the context of Nigeria, and the early association of photography with relations of power, aesthetics, and aspiration remains visible within the built landscape of the postcolony. Where previously portrait photographs of the British monarch and governor general held pride of place in public as visual shorthand of allegiance, in contemporary times we find photographs of the current president and state governor. The past remains a valuable reference point in the photographer's tool kit, deployed to ground as well as lay claim to the present and enunciate the future. In following these vectors closely, one can trace the entanglements between indigenous vernacular framings of the visual from the colonial to the postcolonial neoliberal geopolitical moment. What this provokes us to think about is the need to take into more careful consideration the relationships between power, aesthetics, and aspirations.

Election times are ones that draw on shared political imaginaries. This is evident in the large billboard poster placed during the 2018 election season at the main road just before one enters Ìlá Òràngún, as the road passes the roundabout in front of the palace of the king, the Orangun-Ila (figure 5.2). This busy artery acts as the main thoroughfare along which are found shops, general provision merchants, churches, the central mosque, and a plethora of dwellings for artisans and daily laborers, including the ancient city's studio photographers. Past this jumble of shops, and Ìlá Òràngún's only prestige hotel, the road reaches the villa residence of Chief Adebisi Akande, a former governor and major national political force. This brackets the two central seats of power in the city, one obtained by descent through the monarchy and the other through universal suffrage and the plebiscite ballot box.

This billboard promotes All Progressives Congress (APC), the national political party in power in Nigeria during fieldwork and up to the time of going to press (2018–23). Nine different photographs on the right-hand side portray the classic headline implementation goals that appear in serial election campaigns. These include the delivery of improved security, sanitation, roads, and health. The left-hand panel announces the slogan "Like Father, Like Sons" and skillfully allies the composite portrait of three political "sons" of Osun

State with their "father," the late Chief Obafemi Awolowo. He is visualized in authority through nostalgia-laden black and white as the successor to the "throne" of the Yorùbá progenitor, Odùduwà, thus striking an invocatory chord for a nation yet to be realized.[16] There is an explicit conjuring of a citizenry of photography that straddles the linear temporality of progressive time. This captures the future yet to come, the "as if" potentiality of photography that disrupts the long-standing center/periphery ordering of the world.[17]

Framing this poster as embedded and exemplary of world system photography makes space for the event of photography, where the relational unfixed

5.2 Political imaginaries anchored in past glory: This billboard mounted during the 2018 election season straddles the main road into Ìlá Òràngún, proclaiming the achievements of the ruling incumbent political party All Progressives Congress (APC), sponsored by the membership of the local constituency branches of APC. The visual narrative embeds the achievements of APC's "Every Step, a Promise Kept!" within the values of Chief Obafemi Awolowo, "the Father" and one of Nigeria's foremost independence fighters. His portrait in black and white appears on the extreme left of the three portraits that appear in color of political leaders who have followed in his wake (*left to right*): Chief Bola Ige, Chief Adebisi Akande, and Ogbeni Rauf Aregbesola. Photograph by Naluwembe Binaisa, May 2018.

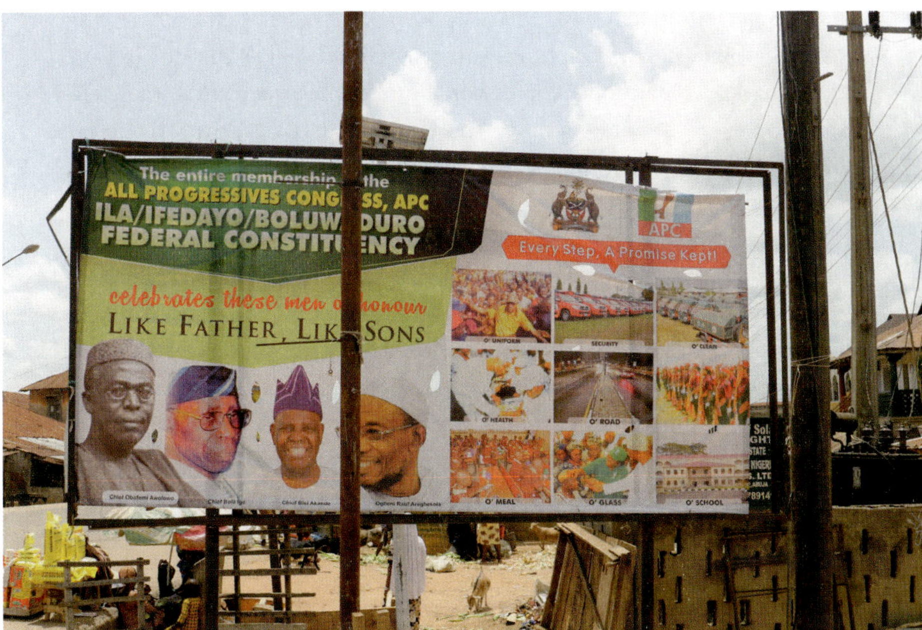

dynamism between the photographer, client, audience, and technics of photography is never sublimated. This counteracts the injunction that "under imperial rule there is no longer a common world to care for but only scattered enclaves to protect."[18] Instead there is a visual reveal of what is ordinarily obscured, namely, that imperial history remains intimately intertwined within the politics of the local. Two decades into the twenty-first century, we see the enduring visual potency of the late Chief Obafemi Awolowo, one of the main anti-colonial political agitators for Nigeria's independence. Despite never attaining the office of president of Nigeria, his complex legacy is co-opted within a party that aligns with the virtues of what has been termed Awoism or Awoness.[19] The iconic Awolowo portrait with his signature round spectacles and traditional *fila* (cap) is glimpsed daily on the crumpled 100-naira note exchanged in commonplace market transactions. Yet now remediated, it rises up to meet the public in this political campaign flex banner.[20]

Plural mobilities and temporalities are important concepts in this chapter, as are stasis and suspension. Through my various encounters in the field, I understand mobilities as physical movements and as circular multitemporal and multisensory experiences of insight, aspiration, and social mobility. Ìlá Òràngún, this small ancient city, is significant in the pantheon of kingdoms that grew out of the original migration of the sons of Odùduwà from Ilé-Ifè, the oldest Yoruba city traditionally regarded as the birthplace of all the Yoruba. Despite Ìlá Òràngún's geographical position outwardly off the beaten track in Osun State, this ancient city is important as the royal seat of the Yoruba Igbomina people, a substantial number of whom reside in neighboring Kwara State.[21] The redrawing of federal state boundaries left the ancient palace and their oba (king), the Orangun-Ila, within the borders of Osun State. In many ways, this highlights the dissonance between the political and affective bonds that stretch across the intimate space of the family to the community beyond. The depths of these ties are obscured when they are redefined through constitutionally mandated borders.

These slippages within boundaries of belonging reflect the tension between the ancestral, political, and individual assertions of affiliation. Part of these struggles is rooted in a colonial project that "created" Nigeria at the stroke of a pen. The future nation-state was famously bequeathed the name Nigeria by the journalist Flora Shaw, who later married Lord Lugard, the colonial governor of Nigeria.[22] The final unification at independence in 1960, of what was to become a new nation-state, was tortuously achieved through several contested iterations, giving weight to the famous remark by Chief Obafemi Awolowo that "Nigeria is a mere geographical expression."[23] The current constitutional federal structure recognizes all citizens of Nigeria as equal under the provisions of Section 318 (1) of the 2011 Constitution (as Amended). Concurrently, it recognizes the rights and privileges at the state level of indigenes who are designated as such through their patrilineal line of ancestry.

Photography plays a conscripted and privileged role in these legal silos of belonging since identity photographs attached to identity papers attempt to stabilize these shaky subjective boundaries. Standing at the junction where the poster is positioned, we glimpse the seemingly timeless nature of life in Ìlá Òràngún. The roofs are corrugated rusty tin, and market women with their children wait patiently for passing trade. Everywhere goats search for snacks from overlooked leftovers. There is heightened activity at this junction created by restless student groups, as some wait for lifts while others zip past on *okada* motorbike taxis, three perched on a seat to save money on their trip. Disdain and resigned weariness tinge the reception of these election posters as many interlocutors say, "It is just election season, this is what we do," implying awareness and public acquiescence with political promises that may or may not be met. The physical and imagined infrastructures of social mobility and immobility are the routes through which many of these aspirant image references are trafficked. Mobilities draw attention to the tension between photography as a set of local practices yet one that is responsive to the dynamics of a global technics. Voice and belonging emerge at times as contradictory valances through photography. They bring into view the accommodations and resistances that intersect different levels of framing the nation, the community, and individual quests for self-actualization.

Life is precarious in Nigeria, yet that precarity is rarely glimpsed in personal family archives. Instead, what one encounters are polished, immaculately dressed visions of calm or joy. What lies just under the surface of the photograph, the random odds of living or dying that accompany something as mundane as traveling from one city to another, is hidden. It was during my frequent lengthy travels (four and a half hours between Lagos and Ilé-Ifè, six hours between Ìlá Òràngún and Lagos, two hours between Ilé-Ifè and Ìlá Òràngún) that questions of mobility, conflict, and home became finely focused. It is an impossible journey to photograph or to fix. You lurch at top speed, carried by a bus transporter packed with twenty-four people, driving through sharp bends at breakneck speed as rumors of random kidnappings loom, and the driver swerves to avoid all who equally share his assumption that they are the rightful owners of the road.

One of my central contentions is that Nigeria is a context where what Walter Benjamin termed "contingency," that excess of photography that cannot be contained, permeates the visual lexicon.[24] This is a context where interlocutors insist that the photographs speak, that beyond the relations of photographer, audience, and client, an agency transcends the constraints and boundaries of daily life. This is not quite the utopian Azoulayean conceptualization of the "civil contract of photography" but is rather rooted in the "real politick" of everyday life.[25]

The sections that follow aim to give deeper insight into the three interrelated levels (nation/community/individual) where photography, voice, and belonging intersect. In the first part, I introduce studio photographers who are rooted in the rural economy of Ìlá Òràngún and Ilé-Ifẹ̀, in particular, the older generation: Simple Photo, Uncle Special, Hajj Hammed, and Dr. Lukson. Although their respective practices might differ, they reflect visual logics grounded in enduring communal norms that insist on the "liveliness" of the image-event, to frame the rhythm of life in these ancient cities. In the second section, I focus on the family where interactions with photography show women at the vanguard of gendered care responsibilities. Through this lens, photographs emerge as sites of resistance, continuities, and transformation. In the third section, I focus on youth stranded by precarity yet buttressed by the mantra of "self-help" that stands as a metaphor for the absence of government in everyday parlance. For many of these youth, access to smartphones is part of everyday life and social media brings the global ecumene within reach, opening potentially rich alternative border-crossing avenues to self-actualization.

Elder Studio Photographers: Tradition and Transformation

It is market day and people jostle for space with kid goats running among them on what is normally a very quiet sidewalk. Simple Photo, memorialized in Sprague's article for his excellent *ibeji* twin and triplet portraiture, has a studio close to the royal palace of the Orangun-Ila in the center of this ancient city. Market days in this part of the nation-state follow the Yoruba calendar. This means that market day rotates every five days, demonstrating the persistence of an ancient time frame, despite the imposition of the colonial seven-day calendar. Market days are the central dynamic pulse of the town, providing a stable rhythm that defines the vital economic activities of Ìlá Òràngún. This is a symbiotic system that balances with neighboring urban centers, so that market days never clash. Market day on Wednesday means that the next market day is on Sunday, irrespective of the fact that it is an observed day of worship for Christians. Similarly, Friday prayers at the mosque, the other persistent marker of the week, rarely interrupt the rhythms of the five-day market calendar. Market days are the days when the population of Ìlá Òràngún expands to accommodate itinerant traders, farmers, and visitors from villages near and far, as vendors, including photo studios, take advantage of the commercial opportunities provided by this day.

Ìlá Òràngún, as with many ancient towns in Western Nigeria, reflects the early urbanization of life among the Yoruba that predated the colonial project. These forms of urban living organized society around household clan neighborhoods as well as associations and guilds that represented different industries. Some scholars speculate that this indigenous precolonial adoption of urban organization favorably lent itself to the uptake of new technologies and skills such as photography and tailoring, within a preexisting model of industry and training.[26] Photography associated by Benjamin with the "age of mechanical reproduction" emerges in Nigeria to herald a less clear break.[27] Instead, photography joins an ascendant trajectory where the arts and material culture are assigned metaphysical properties in their interactions within society. This environment supports "a strong belief in the interface of the visible and the invisible, the tangible and the intangible, the known and the unknown [where] the act of looking and seeing . . . is much more than a perception of objects and the use of eyes."[28] This might go some way to offer a deeper understanding of why in Ìlá Òràngún, as Sprague notes, double-exposure photographs came to replace, for some clients, the wooden or stone-sculpted ibeji.[29]

The formalization of photography as a profession followed the long-established association structure for many trades and industries in Nigeria. Photographers formed associations and took on apprentices who ordinarily undertook three years of training before they were granted their "freedom" by their master and allowed to set up their own studio. This structure was in line with other apprenticeships such as tailoring and took its inspiration from older traditional guilds such as sculpture and bronze making. In his studio, Simple Photo is surrounded by portraits of early apprentices as they perform their freedom ceremony and enter the status of qualified professional photographers (figures 5.3a and 5.3b). His wall is dominated by photography and tailoring graduates as his wife was a master tailor, reflecting the proximity between these two professions.[30] It is still quite common to see a display of "freedom portraits" in a range of shop-front businesses, from tailors to stationery and office suppliers. Here the proprietor of the business, "the master," poses with apprentices who have successfully graduated and gained their freedom.

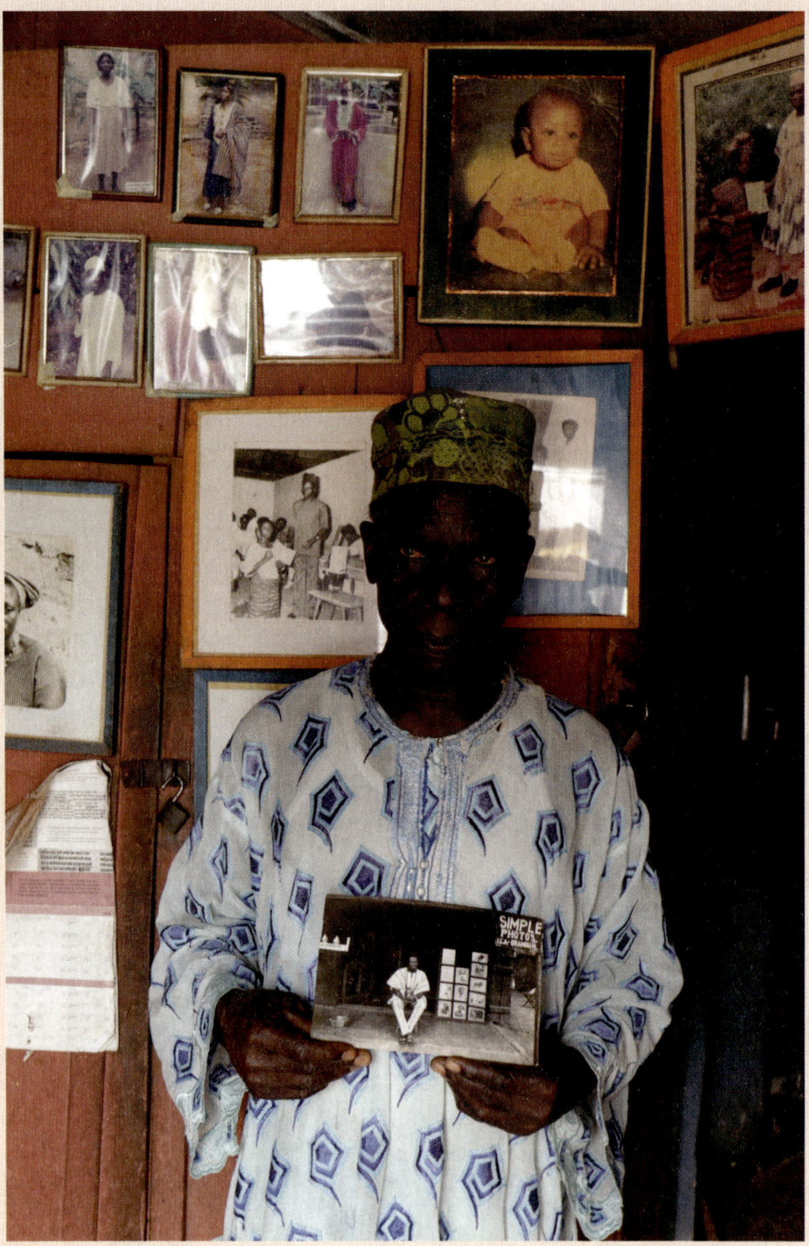
SIMPLE
PHOTOS

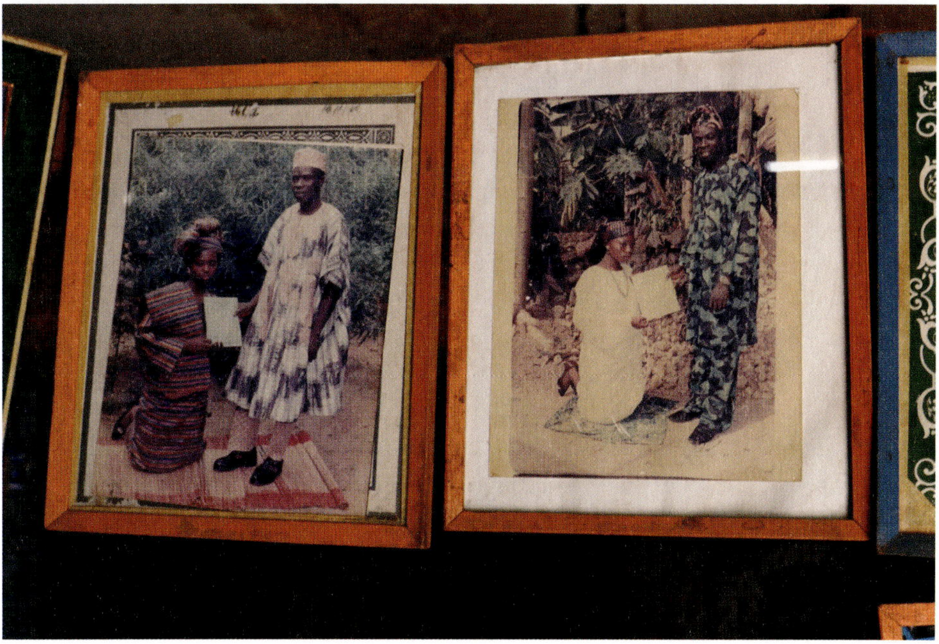

5.3a (left) Simple Photo inside his studio or "shop" as they are commonly known, holding the photograph taken in the 1970s by Sprague. To his left, the door leads to his inner studio, bereft of old-style backdrops. **5.3b (above)** A close-up of some of the "Freedom" photographs of students who graduated from various apprenticeship schemes. The portraits are taken in the favored pose, with the apprentices kneeling before their masters as a sign of respect while receiving their certificate of accreditation. Photographs by Naluwembe Binaisa, July 2018.

In all these photographs, the apprentices kneel in front of their master and receive their certified freedom. This is the preferred composition as apprentice and master framed together visually stabilize continuities as the baton is passed to the next generation.

The elder studio photographers with whom I had the most interaction—Uncle Special (known as Sir Special in his younger days), Simple Photo, and Ade de Love—were based in Ìlá Òràngún and appeared in Sprague's publications, while the fourth elder photographer, Dr. Lukson, was based in Ilé-Ifè. Uncle Special and Simple Photo reminisced fondly about the time they spent with Sprague nearly fifty years prior, examining with interest journal articles I shared in which they and their photographs appear. In the 1970s, black-and-white photography was in ascendancy and darkroom skills were uniquely valued. Ade de Love spent his formative years in Cotonou, Republic of Benin, a former French colony, where he apprenticed and trained from an early age as a photographer. Ade de Love is linked with innovation and photography in Ìlá Òràngún, from the first enlarger that he improvised using his motorbike as a power source to his involvement with the first color photography laboratory.[31] He attributes his ongoing interest in technology and advancements in his profession to the training and exposure he received in cosmopolitan Cotonou during his apprenticeship (figure 5.4).

These photographers were at the vanguard of weaving and retaining indigenous cosmologies, ways of seeing and being in the world, in a fast-changing contested sociopolitical landscape. Improvements in technology and lower equipment costs accelerated the expansion and diffusion of photography. Hajj Hammed reminisces that his initial training was on a Japanese Yashica G, a twin-lens reflex camera that he used from 1978 to 1990. By 1990 he had moved to a 135 mm Yashica, just as other affordable 35 mm cameras like the Zenit, manufactured in the Soviet Union, entered the market. Innovation was stimulated by access to technology but this was not the sole determinant driver. Uncle Special is still proud of his "invention" of mirror photography. This technique enabled him to seemingly merge a portrait within a reflective mirror without printing the photograph onto the mirror. Instead, using a secret that he says was imparted to him through a dream, the client's photograph becomes one with the mirror. Uncle Special has passed on his technique in strict secrecy to his apprentices, who have further adapted this special effect to great demand.

Simple Photo still practices photography and is proud to attend to the needs of his customers. The customer is king in the Nigerian setting, and when you enter any business, you are immediately greeted as "my customer," enunciating the future into being. As you walk past a shop, you are beckoned inside with the entreaty "Enter, my customer." This layered relationship is rendered especially poignant when you spend time with the elder photographers of this ancient city such as Simple Photo. The fact that the majority of his customers are elder denizens of Ìlá Òràngún is something that he regards as befitting their discernment. It reflects his professional stature, seasoned skills, expertise, and their shared history marked through a lifetime of photographs. This is a visual testimony of mutual revalidation in common with other elder photographers of Ìlá Òràngún. Simple Photo projects his relevance as a permanent fixture embedded within the fabric and pulse of Ìlá Òràngún, where camera work intrinsically links temporal and spatial ways of being and becoming in this world.

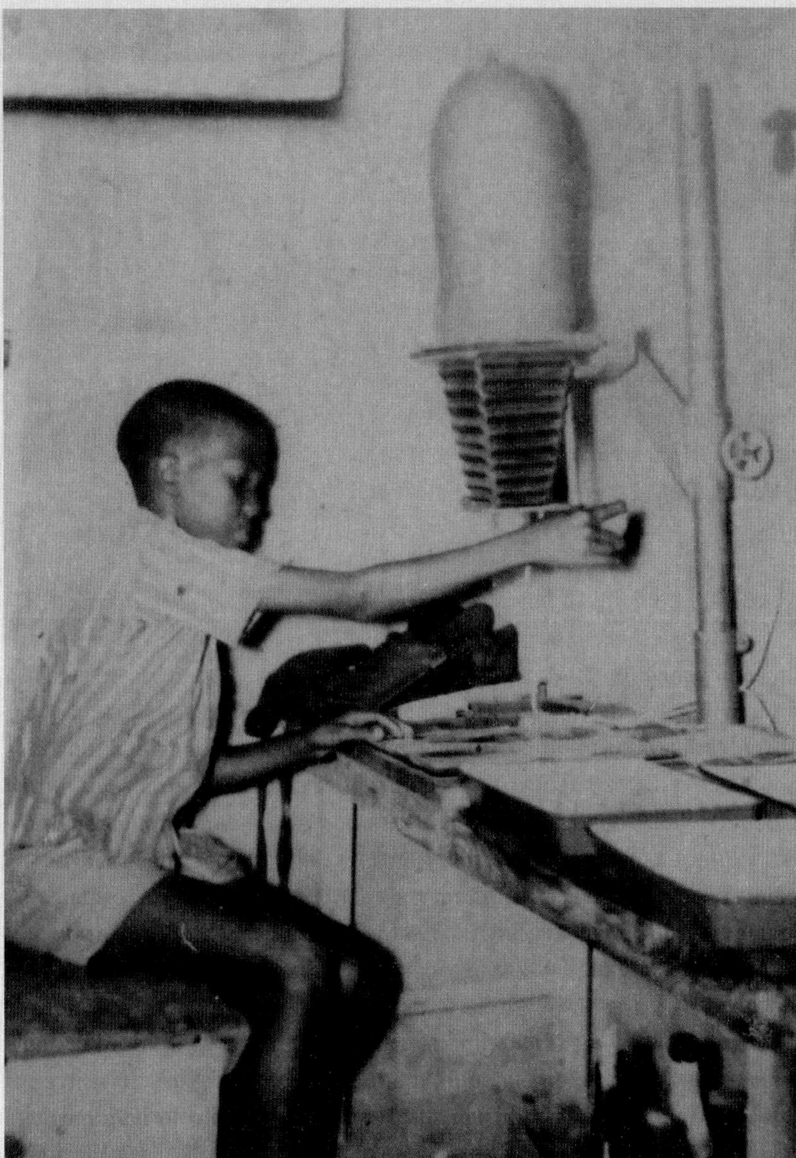

5.4 Ade de Love as a young apprentice in Cotonou, the capital of the Republic of Benin. The equipment was far more sophisticated than what Ade de Love found on his return to Ìlá Òràngún. Sprague names him as the innovator who built a homemade enlarger powered by his motorbike. Ade de Love is proud of his youthful exposure to what was then cutting-edge technology. Rephotographed by Naluwembe Binaisa, 2018.

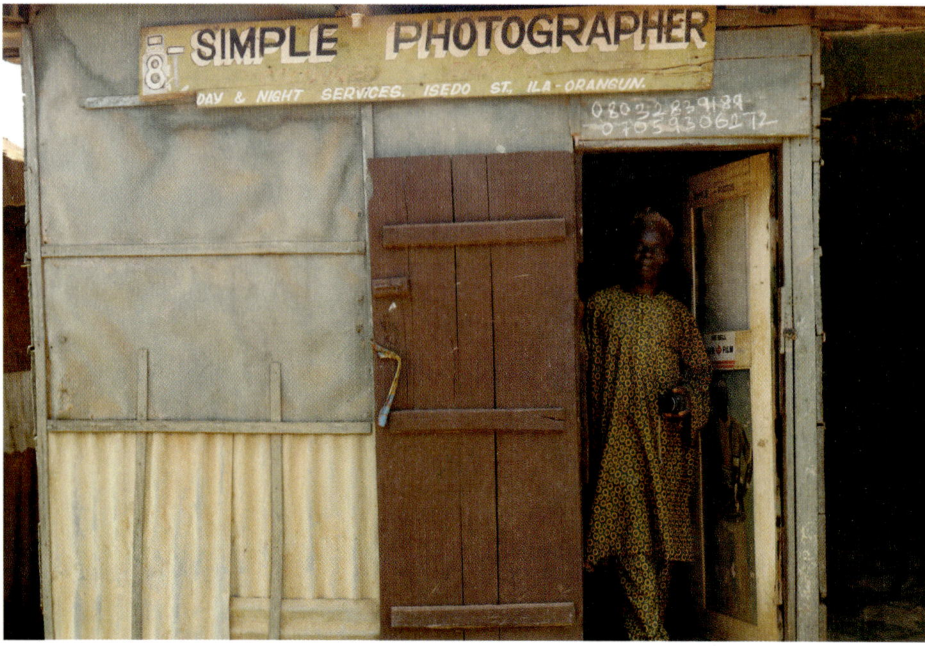

5.5 Simple Photo outside his studio. The vestibule is a time capsule lined with photographs, which span his career and life. Beyond the vestibule is the formal studio, now an empty room, its only adornment a simple backdrop of a potted palm frond painted on the wall. Photograph by Naluwembe Binaisa, May 2018.

In posing for me he is keenly aware that I will travel with his portrait to another clime and positions himself carefully, saying, "They will see that this is myself." I am struck by the thoughtful performance underlining his pose and words in a self-fashioning that might be lost in translation. He directs me carefully and checks my composition several times until he is semi-satisfied with my endeavors (figure 5.5). Simple Photo outside his studio, with signage that blends the traditional and contemporary accruements of his profession, including his mobile phone number, reflects continuities and change. The unique role that photography plays in the fabric of this community is exemplified in the representation of elder photographers in the formal institutions of governance. Uncle Special serves as an advisor based at the palace of the Orangun-Ila providing counsel for the development and betterment of the community. Similarly, Ade de Love meets regularly with a group of esteemed elders at the country seat or "palace" of Chief Adebisi Akande. "Photographers are very important in the community," Ade de love explained to me, because they are in close relation with the wide spectrum of society and are trusted as intrinsic to all life stage events in the community.

Mobilities are central to the trade of studio photographers as they follow community members' celebrations of key life moments. Their practice anchors affective mobilities and underscores the mutuality that embraces the photographer, the client, and the audience yet to come. This is reenacted many times, layering spatial and temporal vectors as these image-events move, interact, or are edited, digitized, or redigitized into new forms. These include timeless family portraits that bring siblings and parents together, despite being geographically apart. An appreciation of these layers and symbiotic ontologies gestures beyond the narrow economic lens through which Yoruba itinerant photographers are often understood. The demand for their services and insistence on formal portraiture, despite the ubiquity of the smartphone, goes beyond conspicuous consumption. Photographers attract a loyal clientele based on their technical skills and other transmutation attributes bestowed by satisfied customers. These include, as intimated to me by photographers and separately by interlocutors, the perceived success or good fortune that follows a particular portrait or ID photograph. An element of levity often accompanied these assertions, which were nevertheless repeated in a variety of ways as a compliment to the photographer's skills, accompanying a particular anecdote of success, or as an explanation for customer loyalty.

In the confines of Dr. Lukson's Star Photo Studio in Ilé-Ifè, I was able to view another example of the aesthetic and political arc within which the technics of photography are operationalized (figures 5.6a and 5.6b). Dr. Lukson was trained in Ibadan at a time close to its heyday as the capital of the western region and in direct competition with the grandeur of Lagos. As an indigene of Ilé-Ifè, Dr. Lukson ultimately returned in the mid-1970s to set up his studio there. It was a longtime fixture on the main thoroughfare of this ancient city. Unfortunately, by the time of writing, he had to close down these premises. Pride of place in his studio was the throne room chair with its plush red velvet and gold paint–covered wood trimmings (see figures I.17 and I.18 in the introduction to this volume). Dr. Lukson displayed with obvious pride a montage portrait of different clients who had their photograph taken in this chair. These ranged from one-year-old babies to middle-aged men and women. The bottom-right-hand corner of figure 5.6a illustrates the multiple functions of the photo studio, as one can just glimpse the edge of a wooden stool placed against a wall, which had the ubiquitous red curtain–mandated backdrop for official passport ID photographs.

The entanglement of photography with relations of power, aesthetics, and aspirations remains visible within the political landscape of postcolonial Ni-

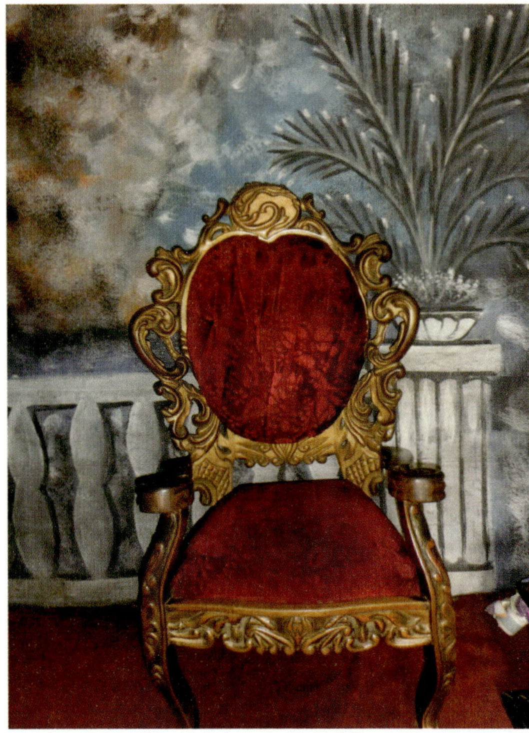

5.6a (right) Inside Dr. Lukson's Star Photo Studio, pride of place is given to the "throne chair" prop placed against a backdrop painted directly onto the wall, featuring atmospheric sky, formal balustrade, and palm frond. **5.6b (opposite)** An assemblage of sample photos created by Dr. Lukson hangs inside his studio. The clients who opt for the throne chair are diverse: in the top row center, an older middle-aged man poses in traditional attire; to his far right a toddler is propped up on the chair. In the middle row far left, a PhD graduate poses in their university ceremonial gown. In the bottom row middle left, twin boys drape their legs irreverently on the throne chair, while to the right a young married couple poses in front of a cityscape, projecting their aspirations into the future. Photographs by Naluwembe Binaisa, August 2017.

geria. Identity documents requiring ID photographs as a tool of governance were introduced to impose colonial authority and monitor geographical access to mobility, places, and spaces. To this day, Nigeria is a highly bureaucratized country, and as a consequence ID photographs are the mainstay of many popular small-scale photo studios. It is very common in a variety of everyday situations to be asked to produce four or even six ID photographs, such as when I had to register for a local clinic. This early aspect of photography as an instrument of surveillance remains today and casts a darker light on the multiple versions of citizenship that many Nigerians inhabit. The photographs, as Arjun Appadurai says, become like fingerprints or "face prints and their written backdrops are in fact foregrounds."[32]

The popular appeal of the photo studio as it spread deep into the countryside, where it thrived away from the metropole, leads us to consider its democratizing potential as clients and photographers actively participated in image making. The accessibility of the popular photo studio increased opportunities for self-fashioning, allowing clients to enter into local and transnational dis-

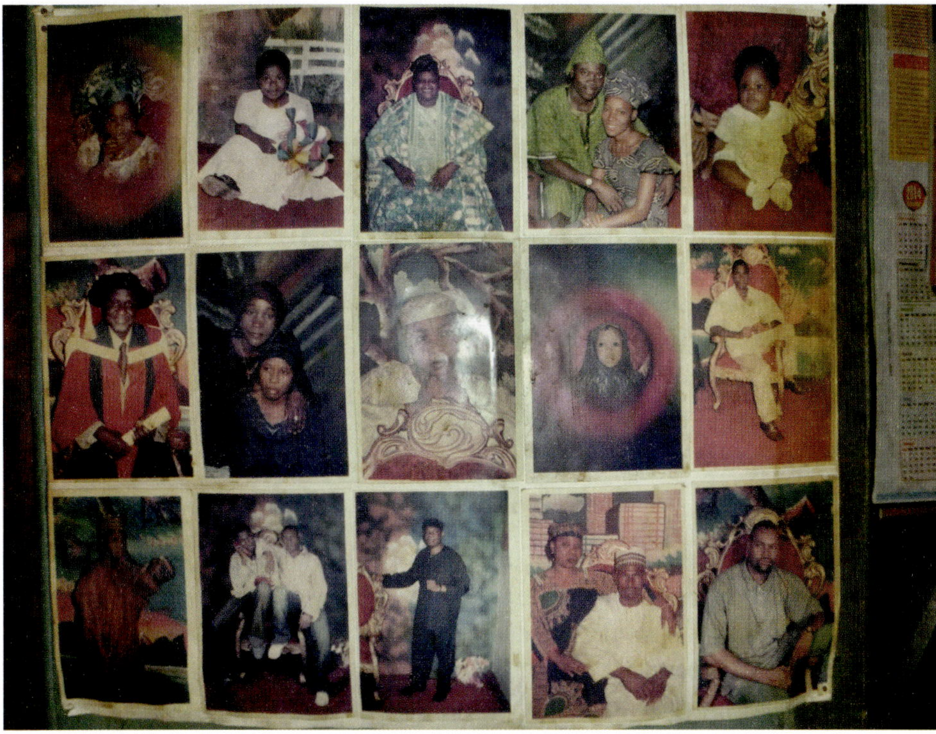

courses of modernity as well as maintain, adapt, and transform cultural forms of representation through this new medium. It is in this context that we can understand how the throne that was the preserve of kings and queens comes within the realm of political imagination for the ordinary woman, child, or man. The range of clientele captured in the throne chair montage validates an aspirational aesthetics of equality and nonimpaired citizenship, accessed through photography yet rooted through a traditional iconography of status.

In the rural city Ìlá Òràngún, I found a number of photographers whose studios depicted a painting of a palm frond directly on the wall similar to that in Dr. Lukson's Star Photo Studio. In different ways, these photographers explicitly and implicitly gesture toward the performance of aesthetics linked to enduring social norms while participating in global urban modernity through cityscape backdrops. The palm frond in Yoruba culture is symbolic of an agentic intermediary between the visible and invisible forces of the spiritual and physical world. In an exploration of what are termed Yoruba anti-aesthetics, cultural everyday objects and things (including palm fronds) are noted as imbued with *áále/áse*. David Dale quotes the renowned Nigerian art historian Rowland Abiodun, who defines áále as "áse-impregnated sculptural constructs" that have the ability to protect property.[33] Dale notes: "This is a useful definition because it suggests that in áále, áse—the generative 'power to make things happen' that lies at the heart of Yoruba cultural and social discourse—resides not only in the invisible interiors of things, but is also enacted through visual processes, in the creation and reception of surfaces."[34] Thus the power of indigenous aesthetics materialized in conjunction with the throne room chair sparks the transgressive power possibilities that everyday people seek to invoke. Here members of society in the Azoulayean schema who suffer from impaired citizenship aspire to climb above their social status in a country and community that is extremely hierarchical.[35]

Photography enters a sophisticated material culture realized by practitioners who are imbricated within the sociopolitical, religious, and moral economy of their society. Here their role transcends the category of mere photographer, artist, sculptor, or metal worker. Photographers "moving with technology" can be understood as preserving power, society, and cosmology by using the "new" master's tools. They subjugate this technology to indigenous beliefs and practices just as one would work iron, wood, or stone and open up "new" avenues of resistance and transformation. In many respects, the uptake and wide dissemination of photography in Nigeria frames a "new visual" aesthetics of value and social mobility, providing opportunities for alternative modes of identity and voice. In these quite distinct spaces—Ìlá Òràngún, Ilé-Ifè, and Lagos—as Tobias Wendl has noted elsewhere, photography is in essence "continuously shaped, reshaped and even transformed in order to fit into the local fabric of imaging and imagining."[36] Photography is always entwined with Yoruba forms of media and image traditions that predate colonialism. It is at this juncture that contemporary women sit tasked with the intimate work of reproducing the nation and as "care-keepers" of these fragile archives.

"Releasing" Photographs: Gender, Care, and Visibility

The reluctance to share photographs with a new stranger (myself) was the first insight into the many layers behind different practices that inflect and mobilize these image-events. A small vignette can serve to illustrate my many and diverse encounters in the field. It was the fourth meeting that I had with Mrs. Abimbola and we were talking as we often did about her family—her various challenges of living, working, and raising another generation of children in Ìlá Òràngún. The sun was shining high and we were seated outside her small provision shop that carried everything a small supermarket needs for local customers: cleaning products, tinned foods, rice, sugar, salt, a chest freezer stocked with various drinks, and the environmental-blight five hundred milliliter plastic sachets of "pure water" that young and old drink in the unrelenting heat. We sat on the bench she placed in the shade for those customers who wanted to stop by and rest, pass some words of greeting, evaluate how the day went, or just watch the foot and vehicle traffic passing along this main road into Ìlá Òràngún. It was a good place to meet interlocutors, yet I found reluctance to engage, particularly from those who were mothers or grandmothers. They directly queried my motivation, asking: "Why do you want to look at my photographs?" "What are you doing in our country?" "Why should I release my photographs to you?" "Will this put food on my children's table?" Others who joined these conversations were happy to show me their family albums in the privacy of their homes but did not consent to the rephotographing or sharing of their images.

One rare childhood photograph that was released into my care and which I was granted permission to reproduce came from the mother of one of my research assistants, Kehinde (figure 5.7). He was able to explain to his mother that I was from Uganda, an academic doctor from a London university conducting research on photography, and crucially that the photograph was only for research. Many of Kehinde's photographs are with his fellow twin, Taiwo. In Yoruba cosmology, names are very important; the names Kehinde and Taiwo are traditionally given to twins whether they are female or male to denote their age order.[37] Culturally Kehinde is considered the "elder" twin, although he is second-born and his name refers to the fact that he comes after Taiwo. Taiwo is considered the "junior" twin because although first-born, he was the one given the task to inspect what is awaiting their emergence from the womb. This photograph marks the twins' first birthday and is one of their mother's most treasured possessions. I was struck how when I tried to align these contemporary photographs with the ibeji traditions that Sprague highlights in his research, this was met with outright rejection by some of my interlocutors.[38] Instead, remembrance and practices of care were the main frame of reference stressed for these precious photographs, while at the same time the special regard for twins still persists.

Mothers in the Nigerian context (similar to what I found working with women in other parts of Africa) are often envisioned figuratively and practically as the custodians of the nation, through their multiple nurturing roles

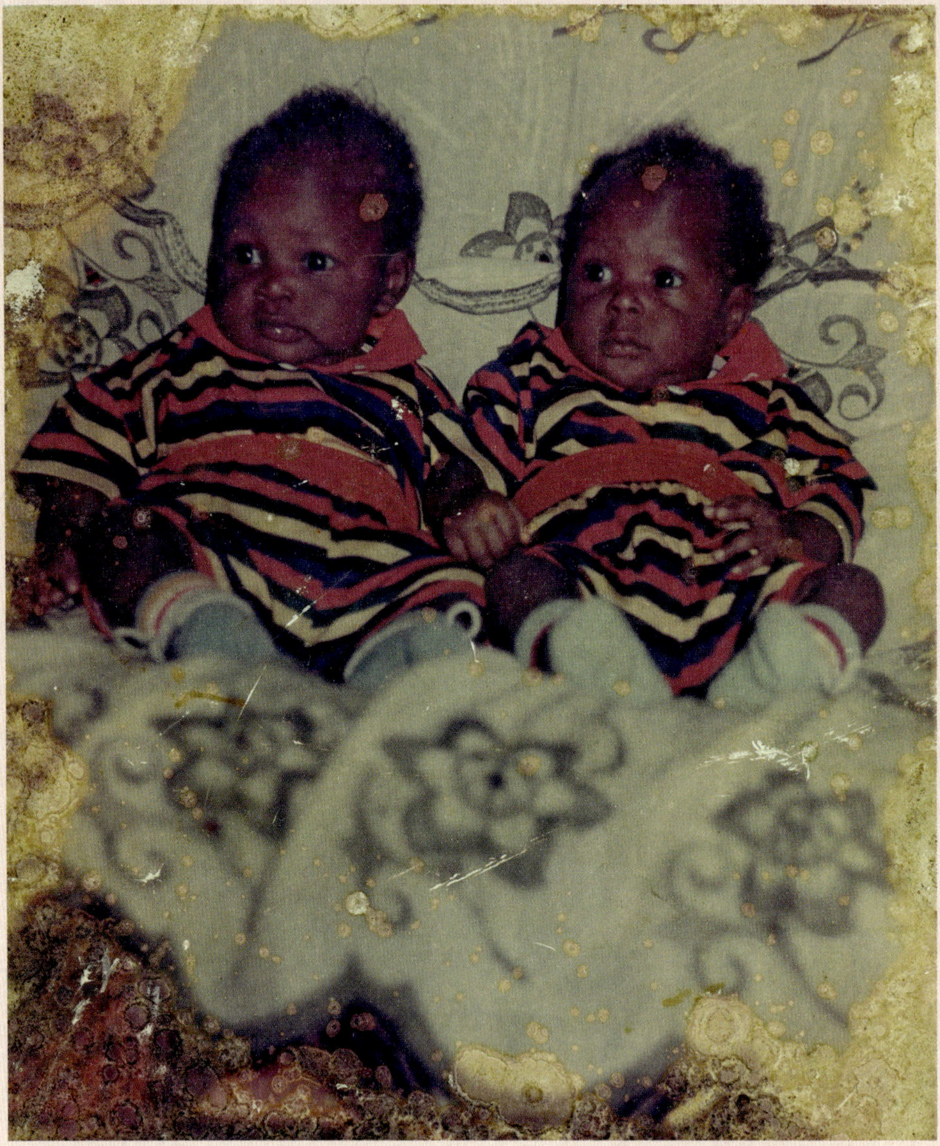

5.7 Kehinde and Taiwo, age one. Rephotographed by Naluwembe Binaisa, August 2018.

and social reproduction labor. The safeguarding of photographs of their children is a powerful enactment of guardianship for the nation and its futurity.[39] Many times, when I visited people in their homes, I was first shown the photographs on display around the room and then subsequently shown the private family album collection. Some of these photographs were more precious because of age, while others were considered particularly intimate as they featured elderly family relatives or a private family event such as funeral rites.

Mobility is part of the afterlives of photographs as they exit family albums, for example, when individual photographs are repatriated by grown-up children embarking on their own "family album journey" in cities far away. Employment, education, and evolving family commitments are key drivers of migration. This also stimulates much of the business that sustains studio photographers, who are often commissioned to reproduce or reconstitute family portraits. In these ways, photographs participate and enable the family work of mutual care and consideration, which keeps the family together. One elderly interlocutor showed me his most treasured possession, a beautiful portrait posed with his late wife in their youth, commissioned after her death. He chuckled and said, "Can I let you into a secret, we never posed for this photograph, the photographer put us together from two separate photos. I wanted us to be together in our youth."

The act of releasing photographs provocatively challenges one to think about the impetus behind the cycles of photography: commissioning, posing, the technics, photographer, the possession of photographs, and the known unknowns of future audiences. As Appadurai argues, the advent of the popular studio, the staging of ordinary people in front of a camera in relations of visibility, changes something crucial.[40] In these posed photographs, everyday citizens who are less visible or who suffer from impaired citizenship are brought into a shared visual regime with full citizens. This potentially gestures to future relations of visibility and equality. Mobility and migration are two common reasons raised for the dispersal of family albums that are intimately tied to the demands placed on photography to prophesize and enable social mobility. Practices of photography meld seemingly opposing needs to embrace movement, rootedness, the Strassler "as if" injunction, and the maintenance of indigenous cosmologies. For example, Simple Photo explains that it became custom to commission a portrait of an elderly relative, particularly if they had never had a photograph taken, as they approached their final years. Figures 5.8a and 5.8b show two examples of such elders carefully posed outside the studio in the "traditional formal" pose with its association of gravitas and social status.[41] They sit in natural light with the wall behind their backs,

5.8a & 5.8b
Two grandmothers in Ìlá Òràngún. Simple Photo archives, scanned images from black-and-white negatives. Original photographs taken around the 1960s to commemorate their lives. Re-photographed by Naluwembe Binaisa, October 2018.

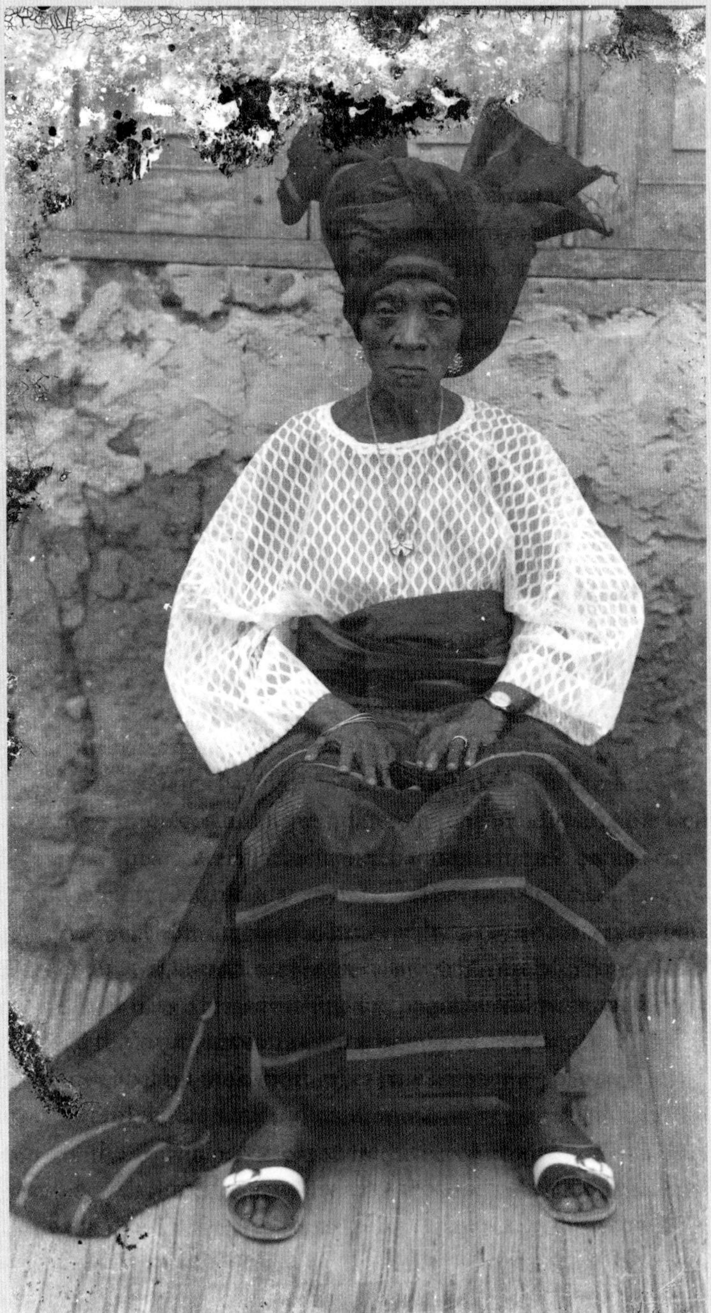

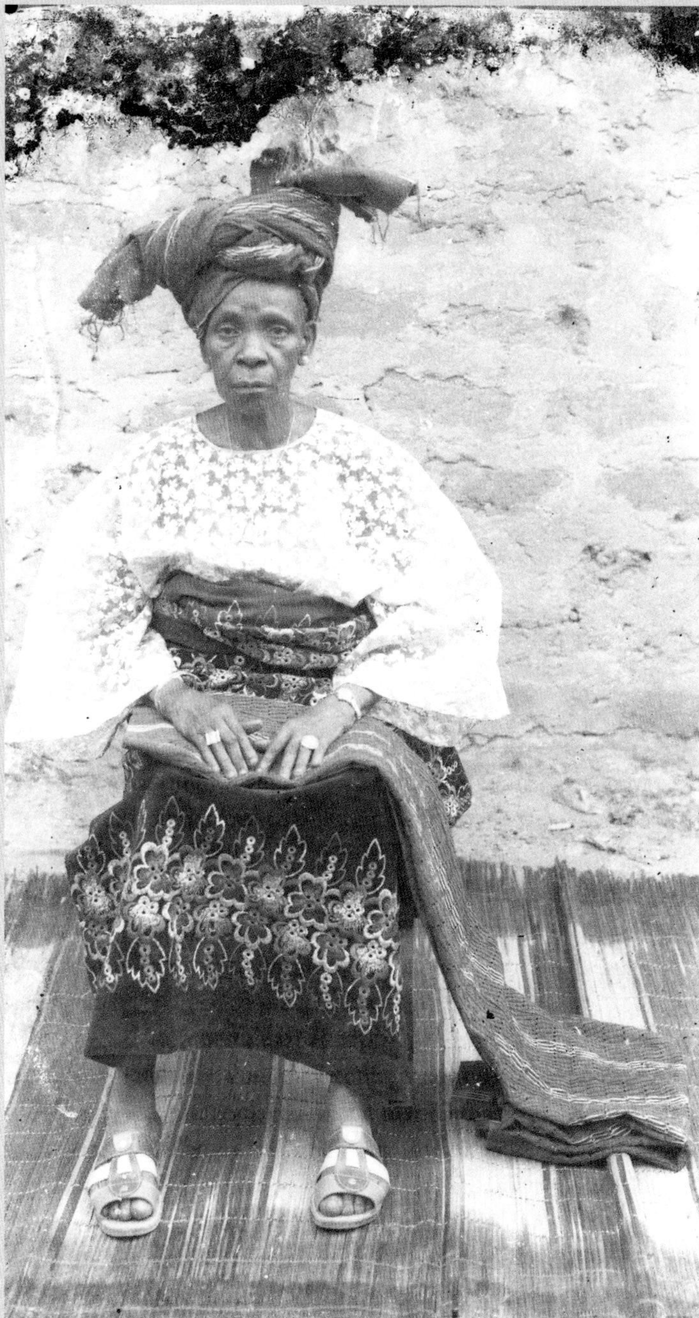

the traditional attire and mat adding to the poignancy and contingency that suffuses these images.

I showed these images in Lagos at the exhibition *The Photographs Are Always Speaking*, held in October 2018 as part of ongoing initiatives to share findings with different audiences in Nigeria. I was struck that of all the varied images in the exhibition, these drew by far the largest reaction. I had scanned the original 120 black-and-white negatives as positive unenhanced prints, displayed as a mounted strip of four images, showing their age and damage over the years. The most common refrain I heard was "I have a photograph just like this in my parents' album!" or "That is our culture!" In a gallery in Lagos far from the rural idyll of Ìlá Òràngún, visitors encountered their heritage and spoke about how life in Lagos sharply contrasted with life in the rural places where many claim indigeneity. Nostalgia was very evident in their longing to associate their personal family histories, values, and trajectories directly onto these portraits, peering closely to discern and connect with the vision of their ancestors.[42] There is an agentic power about these elders that transcends generations, space, and time, with contingency activated through these awed interactions in the exhibition space. Transposed onto these images were ideas interlocutors shared with me of the enduring tranquility, purity, and bastion of traditional values that the rural held in their imaginaries.

Women, men, and young people from the earliest period of photography in Nigeria sought engagement with and through this medium, not simply as a revolutionary call to embrace the colonizer's modernity but as a new aesthetic through which to project cultural traditions and embrace the disruptions and opportunities of the postcolonial promise. The power and honor placed on these grandmothers within a contemporary exhibition space highlights alternative constructions of social norms, often elided when read through a Western lens. There is a significant critique posed by many scholars who argue that gender as a concept has been applied in a problematic way when analyzing Africa's realities and its people. In the specific case of Nigeria and the Yoruba, scholars cite how in both language and culture one finds a lack of equivalence with Western norms.[43] Oyerónké Oyewùmí, one of the leading theorists of feminism in this context, notes the long-standing challenge to Western epistemologies from local discourses.[44] In particular, other scholars such as Mojúbàolú Olúfúnké Okome, in her work on political agency, stress that understandings of women's power within indigenous societal structures continue to be sorely misrepresented.[45]

In a photograph from the archives of the Ransome-Kuti family taken probably in the period preceding Nigeria's independence, we see in the center,

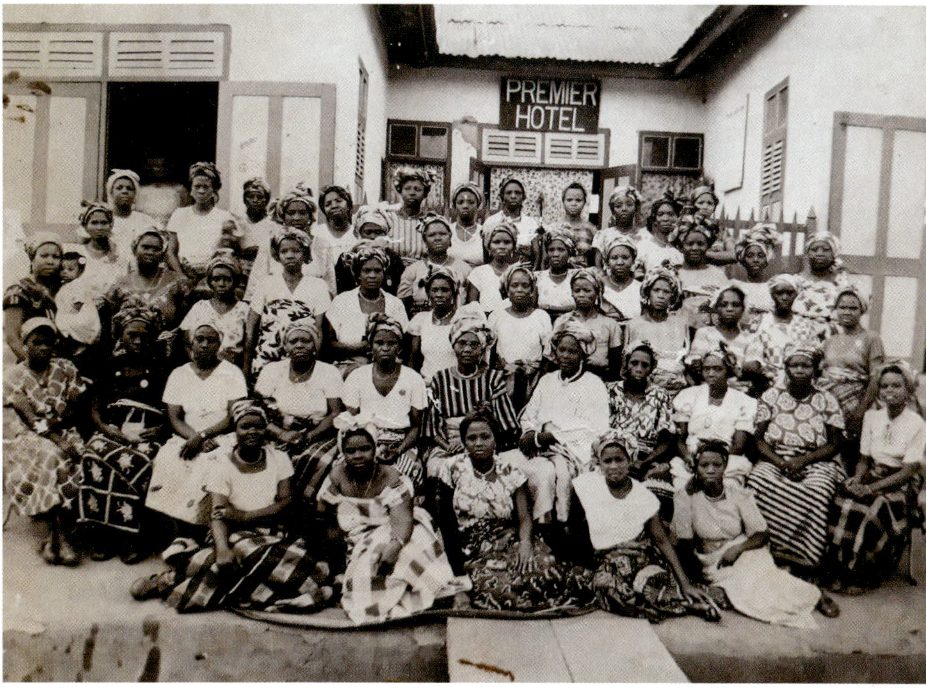

5.9 Mrs. Funmilayo Ransome-Kuti (*second row, sixth from left*) poses outside Premier Hotel, Ibadan, at that time the leading hotel in Nigeria's western region frequented by political elites and the colonial establishment. Original photograph circa 1960s. Rephotographed by Naluwembe Binaisa October 2018. © Special Collections, University of Ibadan.

second row from the front, in a vertical striped top, Mrs. Funmilayo Ransome-Kuti, the foremost organizer of the women's movement in Nigeria (figure 5.9).[46] She was an educator, politician, and activist and the only woman in the delegation who came to London to negotiate Nigeria's independence. Funmilayo Ransome-Kuti used photography very self-consciously as a campaign tool for political solidarity, as she forged a movement that placed women at the center of Nigeria's development. The wearing of what is termed *aso-ebi*, or "uniform," draws on traditional Yoruba culture when at important ceremonial events or life events, such as weddings or funerals, a family group or family compound and their friends wear different styles all made from the same fabric. This signals their unified relations of consanguinity and friendship.[47] In this photograph, the concept of aso-ebi is still performed, although the women's garments are made from different patterned cloth. This is because they dress in traditional Yoruba attire and adopt a seating composition that emphasizes their solidarity as a group. This strategy was adopted to ease differences in social status, reduce social distance (Mrs. Ransome-Kuti is also famously known as the first woman to drive a car in Lagos), and highlight their common cause to uplift women from across Nigeria beyond ethnic and class lines. It is interesting that the powerfully stylized and politically charged performance embedded in this image has disappeared from the public sphere. I also displayed this image in the exhibition *The Photographs Are Always Speaking* and was struck how visitors instantly recognized Mrs. Funmilayo Ransome-Kuti and commented in an astonished yet complimentary way on its revolutionary staging. They compared the unity of these women in the 1960s to contemporary Nigeria, where it is rare to view such an assemblage as social divisions based on class and wealth have worsened.

As Appadurai suggests, our attention to the foregrounded subject inevitably engages the discourse within which photography is located and brings into view underlying power relations.[48] These power relations include the moment of image making, that is, the photographer who poses the subjects, the client, and the intended audience who will view and consume the photographs. We should bear in mind that photographs are not static; neither are audiences static across space and time. Hence it is useful to think in terms of the social life of photographs,[49] particularly as these iconic Ransome-Kuti images that she used so effectively in her political campaigns are no longer visible in the public sphere. They are instead veiled within the family archive held at the University of Ibadan Special Collections, despite the ongoing issue of women's marginalization and exploitation. Their energy to provoke and lay down a marker remains pertinent to this present era. It suggests a future yet to be fully realized for women and the youth generation in their struggle against precarity and waithood.[50]

Youth, Precarity and Digital Imaginaries

During fieldwork, the elections (2018–19) were held for the governorship of Osun State and the office of the president of Nigeria. I asked many of my young interlocutors whether they would participate in the elections and met with varied answers. The majority cynically responded that elections did not lead to anything and that nothing changed except the possibility that one of the contenders would recruit youth as cheerleaders or poster boys to cover the posters of rival claimants. They spoke of minibuses, motorbikes, and food parcels, materials and objects that were emblazoned with contending candidates' photographs, as some of the incentives that election contenders dispersed in the community (figure 5.10). There are benefits as well as perils during election season. The political landscape in Nigeria is scarred by different periods of conflict at the national and the communal level. The years of military rule dashed the promise of independence that Mrs. Ransome-Kuti and so many had struggled to achieve. Instead, the cynicism underpinning the original independence constitution disintegrated into years of political and violent instability. The betrayal of the civil war, oil boom politics, structural adjustment policies, and years of military rule have dramatically changed the cultural, social, economic, and political fortunes of the country, to the detriment of today's youth.[51]

5.10 Portraits of competing politicians are emblazoned onto an entourage of brand-new cars to emphasize the contenders' stature, success, and wealth. Photograph by Naluwembe Binaisa, June 2018.

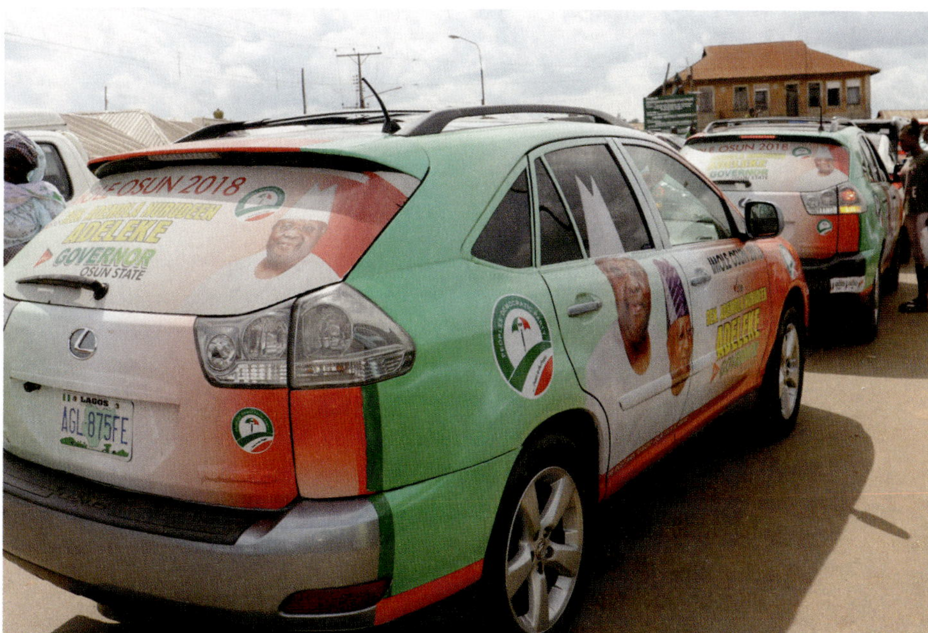

Conflict and insecurity, as indicated earlier, are on the rise across Nigeria. In rural Ìlá Òràngún, Ilé-Ifè, and neighboring ancient towns in South West Nigeria, the seemingly unchanging rhythms of life disguise the underbelly of conflict. This continues to sporadically affect communities during election seasons or in deadly communal violence that flares up from time to time between indigenes and non-indigenes. One example I was alerted to in Ilé-Ifè was the simmering unease that erupts periodically between the Modekeke and Ilé-Ifè peoples.[52] They are both ethnically Yoruba but the Modekeke are considered migrants, having first been invited nearly five hundred years ago to take refuge in Ilé-Ifè. Although these on/off clashes have declined in recent years, denizens remain sensitive and an element of self-curfew still permeates the town, with many opting for an early night despite a local student population. As I walk along the road with one of my interlocutors, I am struck by a poster extolling the virtues and benefits for indigenes who apply and obtain their Osun State ID cards (figure 5.11). It is my interlocutor who remarks on the pointed irony of the location of this billboard, placed on a road that is one of the demarcation boundaries between the two communities in Ilé-Ifè. This is a boundary devoid of any markings, invisible to the stranger yet highly visible to everyone else. Many youths are aware of these demarcation points because flare-ups are more likely to take place at these communal boundaries. However, this poster is deployed as an effort to revision citizenship by indigeneity and reference Osun State as the point of unity.

The poster's text reads:

Kaadi Omoluabi
Omoluabi ni wa!
Kaadi wa re
F'oruko sile l'oni
fun idagbasoke
ati ilosiwaju ise re

Good citizens card
We are good citizens!
Here is our card
Register today
for development/progress
and the advancement of your work

There is a striking contrast between the women in the group photograph taken in the 1960s with Mrs. Funmilayo Ransome-Kuti and the ones in this

2018 poster for the Osun State ID card. The two women in the poster are relegated to the space of domesticity as they are shown tending to their appearance, while the men are holding their Osun State ID cards ready for "development." This visually belies the renowned industriousness of women in Nigeria who suffer from generalized impaired citizenship that grows ever wider due to multiple long-standing disparities, many of them legal, between men and women.[53] In recent years, feminist political strategies to counter the underlying causes of these inequalities have gathered momentum, giving rise to the Womanifesto Charter led by a coalition of individual women and women's organization across Nigeria.[54]

The "reality" that the ID card captures is never static, although it implies purity and permanent access to "rights" for the indigene. The layering of roots

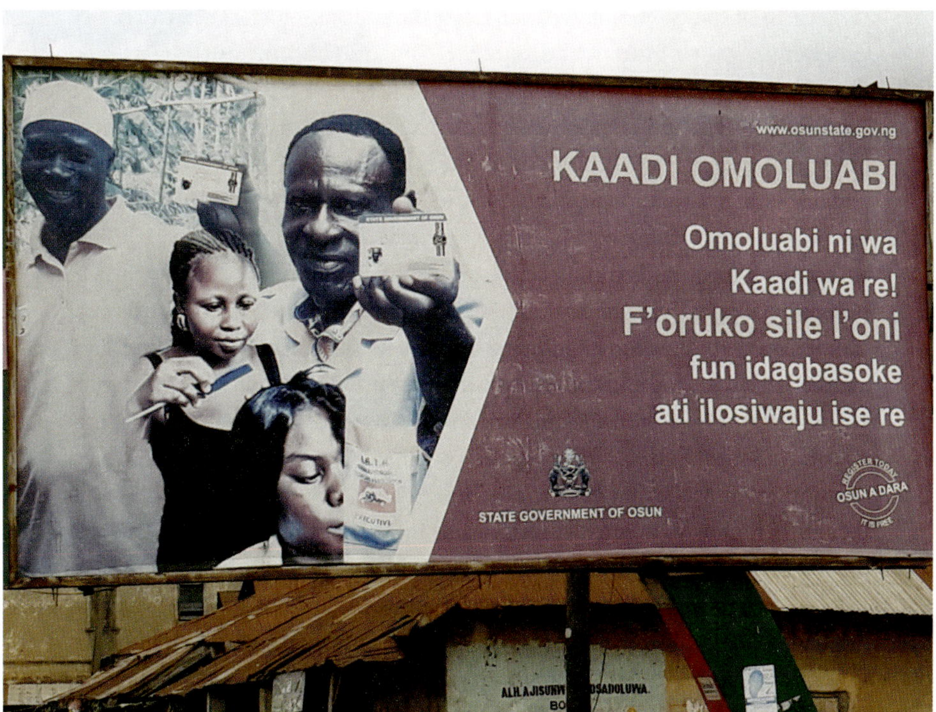

5.11 Official state government of Osun billboard in Ilé-Ifè, urging people to register for their Osun State indigene ID card. In Nigeria, rights at the state level as an indigene via patrilineal ancestry are recognized constitutionally. Photograph by Naluwembe Binaisa, April 2018.

and routes highlights the multiple meanings of identity, belonging, and regulation found within the landscape of Nigeria at the intersection of the private and bifurcated public sphere. The billboard aligns with colonial political imaginaries that relegate different groups into invented ethnic and gender silos, in order to solidify power through the politics of "divide and rule." It is such continuities that evidence what Peter Ekeh names as the civic public, one that is linked to amoral power structures of governance to include the military, police, and civil service and that has "no *moral* linkages with the private realm."[55] This billboard could be understood in Ekeh's theorization as an attempt to amalgamate the two publics through a collage of images that collapse the primordial within the civic public. The potential of improved family livelihoods and the intimacy of women's care work are juxtaposed as the prize offered by an ID card linked to the structures of what is ordinarily regarded as a violent, at best indifferent state. It is the occlusion of what Ekeh names as the violence and terror of the state that is at the crux of what I term "missing photographs."

The photographs I consider as "missing," a fluid, contested term, represent the scarcity of atrocity image-events in Nigeria's public sphere, despite a legacy of violence and conflict that predates independence. The Biafra war (also termed the Nigerian civil war), the ongoing Boko Haram insurgency, the kidnapping of schoolchildren, secessionist agitations in the East, and the so-called farmers and herdsmen conflict all illustrate endemic generalized violence and insecurity. This reveals the fragility at the core of a state–citizen compact as the nation-state struggles to deliver peace and stability for all its citizens. News censorship, an admittedly sensitive topic, is one answer for the scarcity of atrocity image-events in the mainstream press. However, this fails to capture the complexity of the situation because despite the frequent absence of an accompanying photograph, most conflict stories are covered in vivid detail with varying viewpoints reflecting different political stances. Photographs of the actual violence, conflict, and/or atrocities are not front and center in media coverage, particularly in the print media. Instead, what is often juxtaposed side by side with a conflict story is a separate news story told through a photograph of an event unrelated to conflict. This could be an event such as a dignitary opening a building, or a celebration, thus normalizing within a single visual field two politically disparate yet spatially conjoined image-events.

I was struck during fieldwork how sensitive the subject of Biafra was and how few image-events related to the conflict circulated in Nigeria's terrestrial public sphere. This contrasted sharply with the circulation of such image-events on social media platforms through international media organizations and the exhibition space.[56] In the majority of South West Nigeria, the war was rendered invisible despite the presence of some refugees who fled to the region and the presence of local and international photographers who covered the conflict. My first-level unpacking of these contradictions was to consider the role of political censorship and/or public indifference, which was proposed by some interlocutors. This was somewhat complicated through observing the reactions visitors had to other conflict images I displayed during the exhibition *The Photographs Are Always Speaking*.

In the exhibition, I included a group of photographs depicting the devastation and aftermath of communal violence in 2000 in Share, Kwara State, which borders Osun State. The visitors to the exhibition in part due to its location in Lagos represented a cross section of ethnicities from across Nigeria. I restricted the images to a small, far corner of the gallery where they nevertheless elicited a visceral reaction. Visitors often visibly recoiled, or even walked past with eyes averted. It was this forced encounter within the gallery space that helped deepen my understanding beyond the simplistic explanation that people from different ethnic groups lack empathy or interest in the suffering of people outside their ethnic group. After further discussions with visitors about averting eyes as an act of self-censorship, I drew the conclusion that the encounter with these image-events demonstrated a mutual stake in a primordial public sphere. Concern was expressed that freeing these images into more open circulation could foreground and fuel more blood-soaked narratives, thus negating the hope embedded in the portable photographs of formidable grandmothers invoking a brighter future for their migrating children far from home. These often unspoken yet enacted and embodied relations of care and healing reflected shared political imaginaries for a hoped-for better future, particularly for young people.

At the vanguard of political imaginaries and self-representation stand the youth of Nigeria. In some respects, their trajectories illustrate their consumption of a global youth culture that is easy to attribute to the coming of the smartphone and social media. However, much of what is evident today has antecedents in earlier photography. These visions of modernity not only relate to clothes, airplanes, technology, and consumerism; they also give us an insight into the changing social sphere.

The advent of the smartphone, digital technologies, and social media has led to a burst of entrepreneurial ventures by many youths in Nigeria. In a country of limited opportunities for a growing youth population, many of them experience "waithood." They sit within the liminality of poverty, underemployment, conflict, and insecurity. The digital platforms of social media are an access point where dreams can potentially flourish despite limited resources. One common saying is "The phone is my shop," as tailors, carpenters, shoemakers, photographers, musicians, and other independent traders photograph their merchandise and showcase their services and talent. Instagram, WhatsApp, and Facebook are as popular for artists as for community activists. In an image produced by H Boy, an Afro-pop artist, photographer, and graphics designer, he visualizes his aspirations and music to promote and align himself with a transnational visual music scene across a range of digital platforms (figure 5.12). H Boy says the right image is crucial because it can grab the attention of important social media influencers and further promote his music. To this end, he uses intersecting visual mediums (photography, selfies, video) and vernacular aesthetics of value and success such as "OMO G"—"Child of God" (*omo* means child in Yoruba, while "G" is the colloquial acronym for God). Together with digital manipulation, this calls to the prophetic and the "cool" an aesthetic that is grounded in the past and inserted into alternative futures.[57]

For many Nigerian youth, digital technologies are an intrinsic part of their everyday ecosystem of visual social mobility. Their embodied performativity elides the online/offline divide and through another modality reflects Hajj Hammed's assertion of "moving with technology." A visual allegiance to the aspiration of a global transnational youth culture could be viewed as a claim on the citizenry of photography. Contemporary youth mapped across the planet continually "borrow" and "sample" between and within their intersecting spaces. Their claim to visibility within global modernities is self-generated beyond the structures of governmentality. Nigerian youth, through cultural, social, and economic practices, engage innovation through shared praxis points with their transnational compatriots. More recently, frustration with waithood, inequality, and social justice has spilled across the streets as image-events flood social media, mobilizing a transnational politics of resistance against infrastructures of police brutality. This movement was part of a global-spanning #BlackLivesMatter, #BLM "call and response," during 2020 that intensified the #EndSARS protest, in Nigeria and across the diaspora.[58] Despite the brutal Lekki Bridge "massacre" that ended the demonstrations at their core in Lagos, a new generation mobilized across class, ethnicity, and international borders to claim new modalities of belonging, voice, and resistance. These fractured, decolonial political imaginaries live on as image-events, widely accessible and circulating through social media platforms.[59] They are powerful because they depict and archive the at times violent strug-

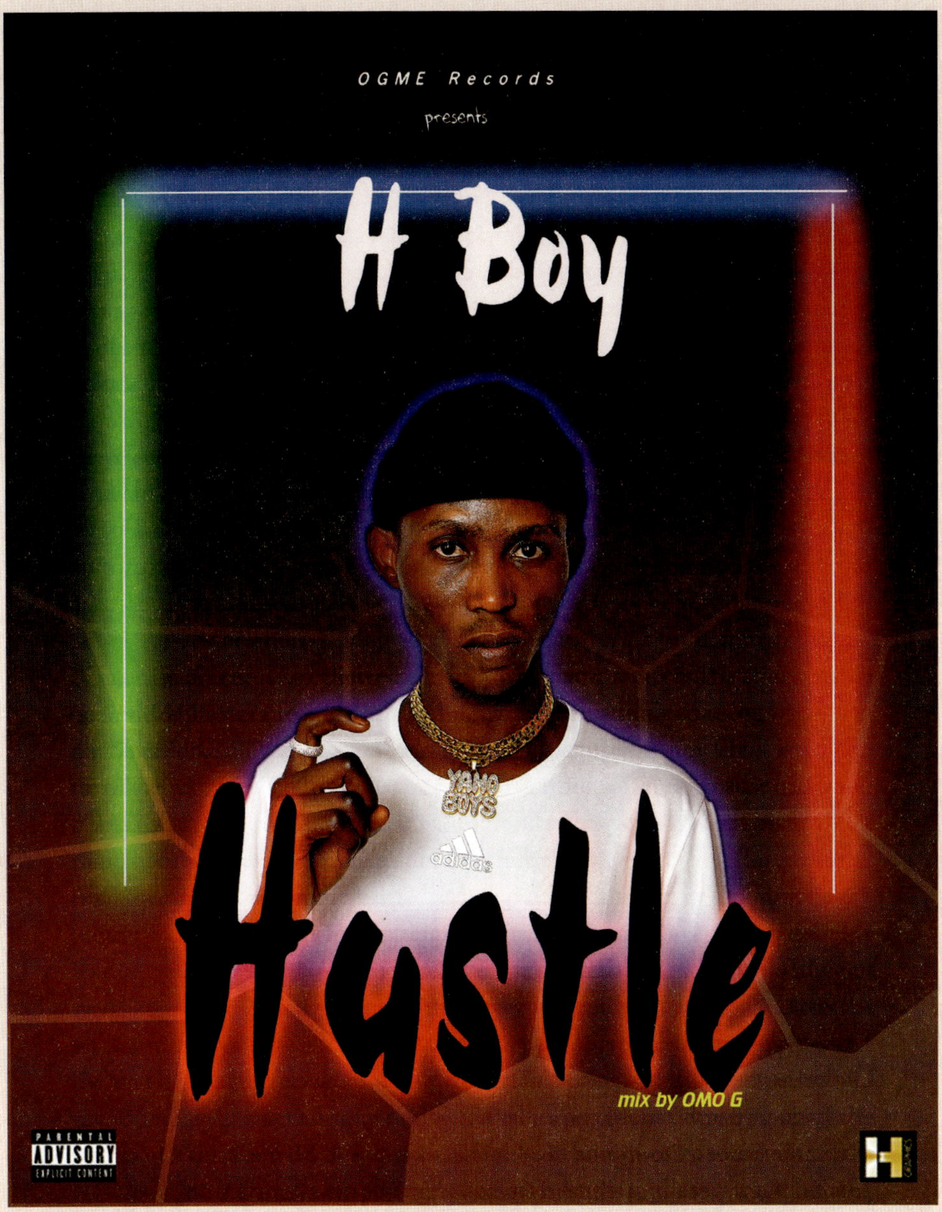

5.12 Digital image promoting the new single "Hustle" by H Boy, released on Instagram, WhatsApp, Facebook, and a range of digital streaming services. Photograph by © Wuraola Olanrewaju, January 2020.

gles beyond the studio from Lagos to London to Los Angeles, to materialize in very real ways a shared diasporic landscape.[60]

Conclusion

Photography has been pervasive in its spread and popularity in Nigeria from the earliest studio photographers to more recent self-anointed "photographers" who use smartphones as their tools of trade. In this chapter, I have sought to explore different affordances of demotic photography to trace transformation and modalities of belonging despite the echo and disruption of violence, conflict, and oppression. This chapter's point of departure is studio photographer Hajj Hammed's assertion that "we are the same" in his assessment of photography and disavowal of the prefix "Yoruba." I want to suggest that through the three main sections of this chapter—elder studio photographers, tradition, and transformation; gender, care, and visibility; and youth precarity and digital imaginaries—photography reflects popular practices of innovation. These draw on indigenous cosmologies to bring into view everyday political imaginaries where citizenship, as rights and responsibilities, is embodied at the local level. These are complex intersections and are not a direct challenge to the supra-level of nationhood. Rather, they are an inclusive sideways step that allows multiple modernities to coexist in conversation with each other through this medium.

The work of studio photographers in the rural ancient city of Ìlá Òràngún might seem far removed from the phrase "we are moving with technology," yet employing the active gerund *photographing*, as proposed by Christopher Pinney (introduction to this volume), enables us to trace these practices of active transformation and resistance. As we have explored in this chapter, there is a tension that intersects popular photography and political imaginaries for the many women and youth who occupy impaired citizenship. What comes to the fore is a discursive terrain where we understand demotic photographing as dynamic yet imbued with both nostalgia and innovation. Mobilities of belonging are reinscribed across the *longue durée* of generations photographing, despite the violence and trauma that pervades the country. This is rarely visualized in mainstream media but is rampant on social media. The reactions of urban dwellers who regard the countryside as the repository of an untainted purity that they shroud in nostalgia contrasts sharply with rural youth stuck within the limbo of waithood. In trying to think with Hajj Hammed's insistence on "sameness," I want to suggest that despite the specificities of Nigeria, we should revision Ìlá Òràngún as not peripheral but intrinsic to the center. This is because practices of photographing that emerge have resonance at home globally and are not restricted to Nigeria.

World systems photography as a concept challenges the territorializing logics that overemphasize the particularities of people "from elsewhere" encased in the "inferior" specificities of ethnicity, region, religion, and language that reinforce epistemic violence. It is vital to prioritize in our analysis indigenous knowledge frameworks and transform the continued ex-nomination of the global majority within the colonial logics of empire. In this chapter, I have explored photographing practices within particularities that nevertheless demand relevance within a broader citizenry of photography that "moves with technology." These are generative implications if one takes as a starting point the relations of "sameness" that Hajj Hammed and a host of other interlocutors propose in their rejection of the term *Yoruba photography*. The promise of world systems photography is that it potentially removes analysis from the cage and ghetto of "otherness" to recenter indigenous cosmologies as mainstream. It allows a reanalysis of photography within processes of globalization, resistance, and transformation through the lens of vernacular, demotic practices to potentially fulfill the promise of a citizenry of photography.[61] From the studios of elder photographers, through family albums and their care practices of hope, to youth co-option of the digital sphere, we find the resilience of Africa's cosmologies, ways of seeing and being in the world. It is from this center of photographing that political imaginaries bridge to the wider diaspora, giving voice to old/new forms of belonging.

Notes

My sincere thanks go to Obafemi Awolowo University, Ilé-Ifẹ̀, Osun State, which provided me with a Visiting Research Fellowship in the Fine Art Department. My thanks also to Osun State College of Education in Ìlá Òràngún and to my excellent resourceful research assistant Kehinde Wuraola Olanrewaju. I would like to thank the elder studio photographers Ade de Love, Hajj Hammad, Simple Photo, Uncle Special of Ìlá Òràngún, and Dr Lukson of Ilé-Ifẹ̀ for their time and patience. In Lagos, special thanks go to the Centre for Contemporary Arts and their late director Olabisi Silva. My time in Ìlá Òràngún would not have been possible without the generous hospitality of Chief Adebisi Akande and his family—a huge thank you for all your support. My final heartfelt thanks go to my son Kwame Owusu, to my family, friends, and the many people from all walks of life in Ila, Ife, Ibadan, Abeokutu, Osogbo,

Port Hartcourt, and Lagos, whose help, kindness, and love made my stay in Nigeria unforgettable. This work would not have been possible without you.

1 Sprague, "Yoruba Photography," 54.

2 See Okediji, *African Renaissance*, in which Moyo Okediji traces how art from Africa with a focus on the Yoruba has encapsulated resistance and renaissance within Africa and the diaspora through "old forms" and "new images."

3 Poole, *Vision, Race, and Modernity*, 7.

4 Chakrabarty, *Provincializing Europe*; Pinney, "Seven Theses," 1–2; Pinney, introduction to this volume.

5 Pinney, "Seven Theses," 2.

6 Pinney, "Locating Photography."

7 I draw on the generative scholarship of Gayatri Chakravorty Spivak, who posed the question in her seminal essay "Can the Subaltern Speak?," to highlight the epistemic violence of imperialism that constructs and animates the subaltern.

8 I am grateful to Mojúbàolú Olúfúnké Okome for this insight in a personal communication, February 2, 2021.

9 Hajj Hammed, interview with the author, August 12, 2017.

10 Azoulay, *Civil Contract*, 81.

11 Ekeh, "Colonialism and the Two Publics," 91–93.

12 Azoulay, *Civil Imagination*, 69–80; Azoulay, *Civil Contract*, 81–93.

13 Multisited ethnography is defined as moving "out from single sites and local situations of conventional ethnographic research designs to examine the circulation of cultural meaning, objects, and identities in diffuse time-space." Marcus, *Ethnography through Thick and Thin*, 96. South West Nigeria is a geopolitical zone consisting of Ekiti, Lagos, Ogun, Ondo, Osun, and Oyo States. My fieldwork was conducted primarily in Osun and Lagos States. I also consulted important archival resources in Oyo and Ondo States.

14 My use of the term *image-event/s* is doubly informed, following Ariella Azoulay's insistence on the photograph as encapsulating a dynamic discursive encounter that is more than an index, or a signifier of what is described through a caption, but also includes the camera, the photographer, and the gaze of an unsighted future audience, decentering sovereignty and at each intersecting temporal moment imbuing the photograph with context (*Civil Contract*, 263–66). I also draw on Karen Strassler's more explicit definition of "image-event" as "a political process set in motion when a specific image or set of images erupts onto and intervenes in a social field, becoming a focal point of discursive and affective engagement across diverse publics" (*Demanding Images*, 9–10).

15 Abiodun, *Yoruba Art and Language*.

16 Adebanwi, *Yoruba Elites*, 207–8.

17 Cf. Strassler, *Refracted Visions*, 77.

18 Azoulay, *Potential History*, 9.

19 Adebanwi, *Yoruba Elites*, 224–42.

20 Cf. Strassler, *Demanding Images*, 38. The billboard is mounted during the 2018 election campaign season for the presidency and federal governorships. The arresting composite group portrait blown up to monumental dimensions shows Chief Obafemi Awolowo, the "Father," etched through the gravitas of black and white, flanked in color by three contemporary leading political figures, the "sons" who all hail from Osun State. The first "son" to the right of Chief Awolowo is the late Chief James Ajibola Idowu Addegoke Ige (known as Chief Bola Ige), who served as former governor of Oyo State before it was split into Oyo State and Osun State, and who was appointed minister of justice and attorney general of Nigeria, before his murder in 2001. Following him are Chief Adebisi Akande, popularly referred to as Bisi Akande, an indigene of Ìlá Òràngún and former governor of Osun State. He is flanked by Ogbeni Rauf Aregbesola, who at the time was the outgoing governor of Osun State and who currently serves as minister in charge of the Federal Ministry of the Interior.

21 Ibiloye, "Rural Urban Migration in Kwara State 1970–1975," 98–99.

22 Lord Frederick Lugard was the first governor general of the united Nigeria between 1914 and 1919. He served as the last governor of the Southern Nigerian and Northern Nigerian Protectorates (1912–14) and was principally involved in their amalgamation. Akpan, "Nigerian Federalism."

23 Awolowo, *Path to Nigeria's Freedom*, 47–48.

24 Benjamin, "Little History of Photography" (1999), 510.

25 Azoulay, *Civil Contract*, 21.

26 Ferguson, *The Yorubas of Nigeria*, 17–19.

27 Benjamin, "Work of Art," 212–14

28 Lawal, "Àwòrán," 521–22; cf. Pinney, *"Photos of the Gods,"* 9.

29 Sprague, "Yoruba Photography," 56–58.

30 Cf. Buckley, "Self and Accessory."

31 Sprague, "How I See the Yoruba," 14.

32 Appadurai, "Colonial Backdrop," 5.

33 Abiodun, "Understanding Yoruba Art," 78.

34 Dale, "Symptoms and Strangeness," 26.

35 Azoulay, *Civil Contract*, 35–37.

36 Wendl, "Entangled Traditions," 79.

37 Leroy et al., "Yoruba Customs and Beliefs Pertaining to Twins," 134–36. See also Sprague's insightful discussion on Ere Ibeji and the transition from sculptor to 2D representations through photography ("Yoruba Photography," 56–57).

38 Sprague, "Yoruba Photography."

39 Campt, *Listening to Images*, 101.

40 Appadurai, "Colonial Backdrop," 5.

41 Sprague, "Yoruba Photography," 54.

42 Kalantzis, *Tradition in the Frame*, 213–14.

43 Oyewùmí, *Invention of Women*, 31–60.
44 Oyewùmí, *Invention of Women*, 1–27.
45 Okome, "African Women and Power."
46 Johnson-Odim and Mba, *For Women and the Nation*, 63–94.
47 See Nwafor, "Fabric of Friendship," 1: "In Yoruba, *aṣọ* means cloth while *ebì* means family. Translated literally, *aṣọ ebì* means family cloth. In recent times *aṣọ ebì* popularly refers to identical uniformed dresses worn by members of a particular family or groups of friends and well-wishers during important events such as weddings, parties, birthdays, house warmings, among others."
48 Appadurai, "Colonial Backdrop," 5.
49 Edwards, "Material Beings."
50 See Honwana, "'Waithood,'" for an important discussion of the concept of *waithood* applied to a global youth context.
51 Adebanwi and Obadare, "Introducing Nigeria at Fifty."
52 See Akanji, "Group Rights and Conflicts in Africa."
53 Igodo, "Nigeria's Missing Multipliers."
54 Womanifesto, "#Womanifesto: What Nigerian Women Want."
55 Ekeh, "Colonialism and the Two Publics," 92.
56 In 2019 Tate Britain held an important retrospective exhibition of the British photographer Don McCullin that included many of the important photographs he took during the Biafra war. The exhibition subsequently toured to Tate Liverpool in 2021 and has received wide international coverage and acclaim.
57 R. Thompson, "An Aesthetic of the Cool."
58 Obia, "#EndSARS, a Unique Twittersphere," and Ekoh and George, "Role of Digital Technology," both outline in detail the unique and fast-moving use that was made of social media platforms from the initial images and videos shared to mobilize audiences in Nigeria, the diaspora, and beyond. This acted as a conduit of information, channeling resources, and political strategizing despite the threat posed by the COVID-19 pandemic.
59 For an intergenerational discussion on decolonial imaginaries through the studio photography of Francophone West Africa, see Bajorek, *Unfixed*.
60 Binaisa, "Diasporic Landscape."
61 Pinney, "Locating Photography," 29.

6

Citizenship, Contingency, and Futurity

PHOTOGRAPHIC ETHNOGRAPHIES FROM NEPAL, INDIA, AND BANGLADESH

CHRISTOPHER PINNEY

This chapter eschews a national frame in favor of a regional focus. It may appear to open up a specifically South Asian world of aesthetic practices and forms. It is hoped that the texture of locality is vividly apparent, and yet the aim of this concluding chapter is to underline the medium-specific constraints within which locally nuanced photography appears. This chapter's account of practices that are "more than local but less than global" aspires to explore the space of the demotic that is reducible to neither culture nor technology.

The medium specificity of photography leaves its trace in many material manifestations, among which are photo studios, which often serve as museums for what were once avant-garde technologies and imaginaries. Photographic studios are repositories of entangled material histories.

Most proprietors will have a collection of their earliest cameras and a diverse variety of negatives, vintage prints, parts of enlargers and other defunct equipment, together with aging studio props. It is easy to be seduced by the apparent quaintness of these archaic fragments, but it is important to remember that they are all traces of what were once cutting-edge technologies, promising to lift the veil that hid the future in the ever-evolving practice of photography.

In Nepal, it is very common to encounter small tie racks on which are hooked several examples of a type of hat known as a *Dhaka topi*, so called because the batik-like pattern of the hat's material previously originated in Dhaka in what is now Bangladesh. New Golden Photo Service in the archaic city of Bhaktapur provides a good example. A tiny space situated on what was previously the main Kathmandu–Lhasa trade route that ran through the city (and now forms a meandering commercial artery), its street frontage is little more than a doorway wide and shows a glimpse of a small museum of cameras from the early days of the studio in the 1970s, above which is an extensive display of defunct early compact digital cameras that clients brought in for repair but then abandoned.

Past the proprietor Gajendra's work desk and a framed image of the Nepali Royal Family taken before the 2001 palace massacre, the cramped studio space opens up into a small room with an elaborate hand-painted luxury villa set in manicured gardens. On an adjacent wall is a faded photographically printed tropical beach scene in front of which stands a clutter of abandoned studio lights. Opposite this is a small rack from which hang three ties and two distinctly patterned Dhaka topis in contrasting colors, remnants of a compulsory sartorial regime that came to an end around 2005.

In a magisterial ethnography of Janakpur, in Nepal's Terai (the lowland region that borders India), Richard Burghart memorably contrasted temporal and atemporal sovereignty and identity. Burghart noted that in 1975 the district officer was instructed to issue identity cards to all Nepali citizens. In response, Maithili-speaking Hindu ascetics (and Burghart's implication is that not all of these were Nepali citizens) presented themselves to the district officer speaking Nepali and "with the *topi*, a cap which is identified particularly with the Nepali-speaking people of the hills, balanced upon their heads."[1]

This strategic impersonation is the starting point for Burghart's reflections on contrasting external forms of identity: "I was informed by . . . ascetics [who showed him their identity card photographs] that to wear the *topi* was to don the likeness, or *rup*, of the Nepalese people. The customary rup of the Hindu ascetic is that of the ruler of the internal kingdom of the body, speech and mind. The matted hair is his crown; his waterpot and begging bowl is his royal granary. His walking staff is likened to the staff of justice."[2]

Burghart provides an anthropological insight into the role that external apparel plays in the constitution of identity and conveys a sense of the paradoxical disjuncture between the tactical co-option of the Nepali topi and the profound semiology of the Hindu ascetic's attire. The journalist Amendra Pokharel, writing in 1986, provides a marvelous contrasting account, one that conveys the unexpectedly dramatic and transformative phenomenology of wearing the topi in the studio, vividly conjuring the sense of an unexpectedly profound identity that flowed from a dusty piece of headwear:

> Holding out a shabby Dhaka topi [. . .] the photographer asked the boy to put it on. He took the topi and peered inside only to find it dirty and frayed. Since the boy had reached the qualifying age for the Nepalese citizenship, he was in the studio to have his photo taken for the card. For that it was required [of] him to wear a Dhaka topi. He would have to wear it and bear it for [a] few seconds only, the boy thought, and never again, so the topi's condition didn't matter. He shook the topi in the air twice, patted against the palms to shake out the dust, then put it on. What he saw in the mirror stunned him. Suddenly the topi mattered, even a dirty, shabby and frayed one. His Nepali identity, buried in the recess of his subconscious mind, hit his consciousness in a flash. It reminded him who he was. His dispensation towards the piece of cloth now was completely different from the slipshod manner he handled it with in the beginning. He arranged the topi with a slight tilt on the left, covering half of the forehead on one side, and made a dent of a desirable shape at the top; the way he had seen kings, political figures, actors and commoners wearing it on television. After the photo, he took it off and placed it on the stand, folding [it] carefully, an act that spoke of the new meaning he just acquired of the topi.[3]

Pokharel's striking account directs our attention to the photo studio as a place of transformation and a place in which identities are precipitated rather than simply affirmed. Pokharel vividly animates a sense of the studio as a place of becoming and of photographing, as a verb, summoning new identities. It also powerfully echoes and makes concrete aspects of Ariella Azoulay's suggestion that there might be a "photographic citizenship" that the camera makes available in advance of conventional citizenship.[4]

A discussion with a textile workers' activist in Dhaka, Bangladesh, in 2018, however, suggests that the relationship between photographic representation and political representation can also operate in a sphere beyond the literal existence of photographic images. Subjunctive, imagined, or prophesized self-presentation through photography—a form of latent "photographability"—emerges as a form of entitlement parallel to those within more conventional citizenship claims.

This discussion in Dhaka was provoked by recollections of the Rana Plaza textile factory disaster and the work of the photographer and activist Taslima Akhter in reclaiming the visibility of the thousand-plus workers who died during the collapse in 2013. Akhter had undertaken a work of engaged visual anthropology, provoked by relatives' public display at the disaster site of photocopies of images of the missing.[5] With other activists, she met and interviewed the families of the missing and attempted to photographically document the lives of those who had died. This work echoed her broader project of making visible the faces and testimonies of textile workers.[6]

The discussion that I report here was part of a conversation with another activist, Nadvi, and focused on one group studio portrait, of Akhi Akhter and her friends, which featured prominently in a memorial quilt (*srmiti katha*) project inspired by Robin Bersan's New York Remember Triangle Fire Coalition. The quilts, made by relatives of the dead, were unveiled in front of the Rana Plaza site on the fifth anniversary of the disaster on April 20, 2018.

The particular image we discussed recorded a visit to a photo studio by eight female workers and friends who shared a hostel (figure 6.1). The occasion was Bangla New Year (Pohela Boishakh 1420), April 14, 2013, this being celebrated by the matching red and green colors worn by all the friends, these being the colors of the Bangladesh national flag. The studio backdrop shows a verdant foreground and a dramatic horizon punctuated by vertiginous blue mountains. Seven of the eight women would die in the building collapse.

I had asked the activist which of the images used in the quilt project he found the most powerful and he alighted immediately upon this one. His reasoning was that the collective nature of the portrait pointed to a double injustice: destruction through an act of what he saw as the corporate murder of so many, and the denial of the kind of individual visual representation that was every worker's right.

"Her relatives only had the group photo," the activist lamented. "There wasn't even a photo of her on her own."[7] The lament in part reflected the assumption that the lack of other ID photos that could have been used were symptoms of further disempowerment: she would not have had a bank account nor any voter ID. In other words, the absence of any individuated image indexed not only a life destroyed at a cruelly young age, but the absence

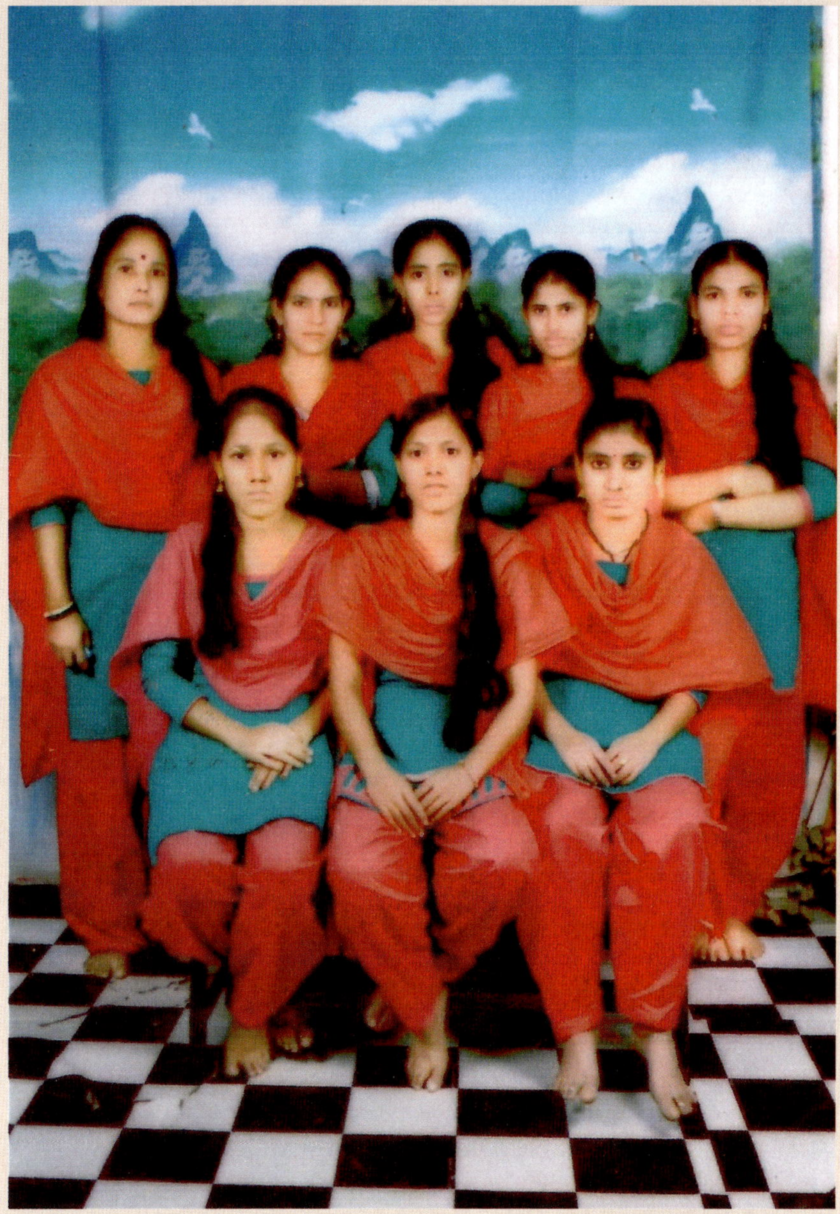

6.1 Group studio portrait of Ready Made Garment Workers. Akhi Akhter (*center of back row*) worked on the sixth floor of the Rana Plaza building at New Wave Style Ltd.'s factory. She and her friends were photographed in a local studio on Bangla New Year (Pohela Boishakh 1420), April 14, 2013. Akhi and six of the friends in this photograph died in the Rana Plaza collapse. A copy of the photograph was given by Akhi's family to the activist and photographer Taslima Akhter after the disaster. Courtesy of Taslima Akhter.

of representation also indexed itself: an absence of a visibility to which she was entitled tout court.

This memorable conversation left me reflecting on the other visual deficits and absences that are central to Bangladesh's history. The 1971 war of liberation (*mukti joddho*) is omnipresent in Bangladesh's civic space and endlessly memorialized through murals and architectural structures. However, the role of photographs in this key historical moment is ambivalent, to say the least. The national icon, a photograph taken by Nabil Uddin Ahmed showing a *birongona* covering her face with her hair, speaks to a kind of erasure made necessary by the unbearable nature of suffering.[8] In a parallel way, the great Indian photographer Raghu Rai's images of the war were lost for forty years, their oscillating presence serving as a metaphor for the striking absence of a photographic documentary record of the war in general.[9] While public space in Bangladesh is thoroughly saturated with Awami League iconography bearing the imprimatur of Sheikh Mujib (the nation's founding father) and his daughter Sheikh Hasina (the current prime minister) as an endless reminder of the traumatic coming into being of the nation, 1971 has only a partial photographic visibility. An image sent to a Dhaka studio for Photoshop revitalization, depicting two veterans of the war posing with their weapons against an incongruous studio backdrop, was among only a handful of images I encountered that marked this epochal struggle (figure 6.2). Images of monuments associated with the war (e.g., the Language Movement Martyrs' Memorial and the National Martyrs' Memorial at Savar) did occasionally appear as photoshopped studio backdrops, but these were not common.

Lifting the Veil That Hides the Future

Siegfried Kracauer opens his study of frivolity and catastrophe in nineteenth-century France with an arresting vignette of the Paris Salon of 1831. He describes how crowds gathered each day around Eugène Delacroix's *Liberty Leading the People*, a celebration of the July Revolution of 1830. The subject matter was dramatic (a "half-naked young woman" holding a musket and waving a tricolor, a "new Joan of Arc") and raised the question of whether she was "a terrestrial being or a supernatural apparition."[10] Kracauer surmises that the attraction of the picture may have reflected the possibility "that this picture was not just a graphic representation of the three glorious days of July, but that it also lifted a corner of the veil that hid the future."[11] Kracauer, whose work consistently demonstrates a concern with "'uncontemporaneous' sed-

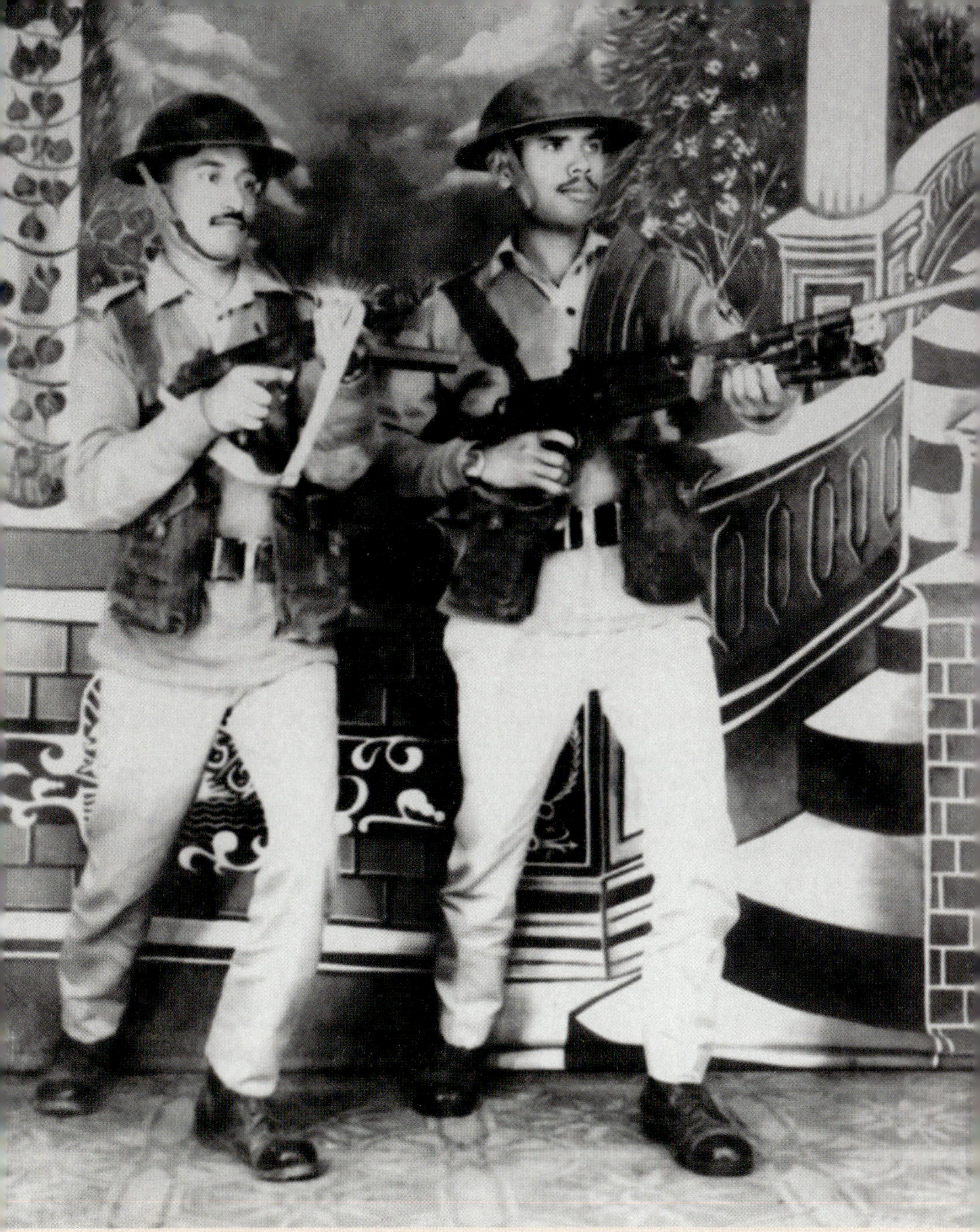

6.2 Reenacting the Liberation War of 1971. Studio photograph, probably mid-1970s, courtesy of Photo Movies and Stills, Newmarket, Dhaka.

imentation," here dramatizes a startling way of viewing images, suggesting a popular understanding and desire for pictures to point to what is yet to be rather than merely objectify what has already happened.[12]

For visual anthropologists, Pierre Bourdieu's *Un art moyen* (*Photography: A Middle-Brow Art*) has been a notable landmark in the study of vernacular photography and one that offers a very different perspective than Kracauer.[13] Its Durkheimian stress on what has already been achieved by the social also stands in strong contrast to Azoulay's emphasis on the "unpredictable" ends of photography and Karen Strassler's account of the subjunctive "as if" nature of photography in Java.[14]

Bourdieu was very concerned with the way in which photography acted as a mechanism of "integration," a "solemnization" *after the fact* that can be read as a "sociogram."[15] The family photographic album objectifies "social memory" and has, as he says in a memorable metaphor, "all the clarity of a faithfully visited gravestone."[16] This may well be an appropriate description of the nature of popular photography in France in the 1960s. It also, undeniably, describes some contemporary photographic practice in South Asia. For instance, one might read Gopalprasad's smartphone-generated "tree of life" as expressing a yearning for place and family (figure 6.3). Gopalprasad started the series of which this is a part in Qatar, where he worked as a security guard. He then opened a shop in Bhaktapur in the Kathmandu Valley on his return. His home and his shop were very badly damaged in the earthquake of 2015. In the tree template, a statue depicts the Buddha underneath Gaya's Bodhi Tree and is surrounded by key religious structures in Bhaktapur, including the Nyatapola Pagoda, the Bhairavnath Temple, and two smaller temples in the city's Durbar Square. These images of his hometown are interspersed with images of his wife and daughter. This demands to be read as a Bourdieuian "sociogram."

Strikingly, per Bourdieu, the "community" or "group" always preexists the photographic act whose destiny is to further integrate that group. The photograph is always a "reaffirm[ation]."[17] When he writes of acts that "must be photographed because it realizes the image that the group seeks to give of itself as a group," the camera serves only to make manifest a kind of visual echo of what the group has *already* achieved (not what in a future moment it *might* achieve).[18] As Bourdieu further states in a characteristically tautological manner, "The photograph itself is usually nothing but the group's image of its own integration."[19] There is no room here for Benjaminian, Azouleyan, or Strasslerian contingency, for the unexpected and subjunctive, and it is precisely these qualities that the ethnographic study of contemporary photography in South Asia reveals.[20]

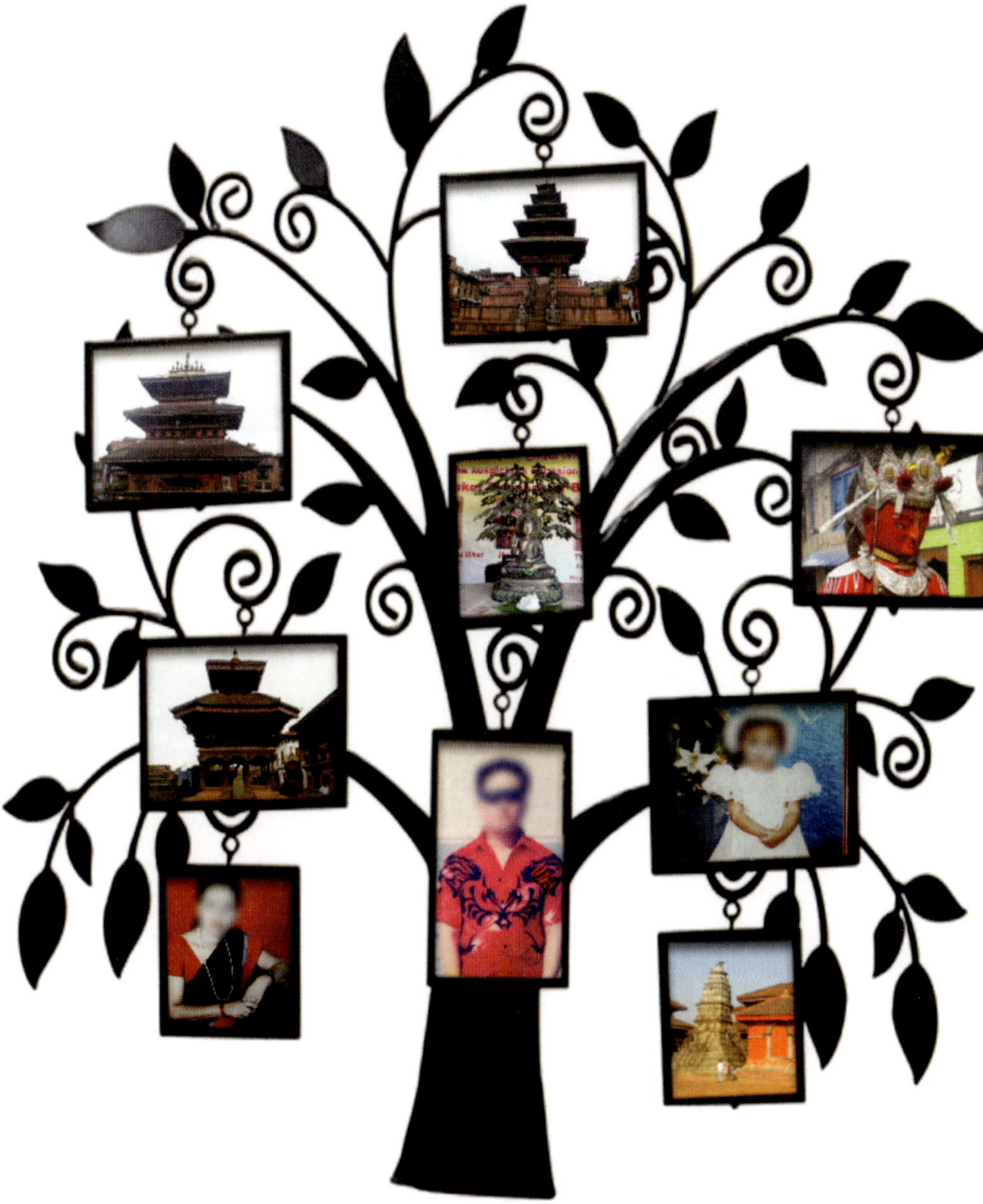

6.3 Mobile phone–generated montage bringing together ritually important Nepali structures, gods, and family members. Courtesy of Gopalprasad, Bhaktapur, 2018.

The future orientation of much popular photography was seen most strikingly at work at the popular tourist destination of Jaflong in northern Bangladesh. The river Piyain, which separates Bangladesh and the Indian state of Meghalaya, attracts numerous younger Bangladeshis, many of whom avail of the services of one of the dozens of photographers who use printers on floating barges to produce images for their clients. Tourists sit on rocks in the middle of the river and exchange WhatsApp details with Indian tourists who flock from the Meghalaya side. Photography is deeply entangled in this fantasy of border crossing and escape to a "beyond" (see introduction to this volume). The outward-looking direction of their gazes (from Bangladesh toward India and from India toward Bangladesh) seems to symbolize the manner in which photography not only consolidates locality and what is already familiar but also opens up new deterritorializing vistas (figure 6.4).

During the past three decades, photography has played a key role in Nepal in the bringing into being of "large-scale political subjects, or 'publics,' that are thinkable and practicable by means of mass-mediated communication."[21] Key here is the fact that photography did not merely record socialities that already existed (as in the Bourdieuan formulation) but that the camera helped precipitate emergent forms of citizenship in advance of conventional citizenship (as in Azoulay's formulation).

In each of the past three decades, a hugely significant photobook was published in Nepal that marks different stages in the emergence of new publics and counterpublics. The first of these three, Gopal Chitrakar's *People Power*, was self-published in 1992 and was crucial in establishing the domestic, Nepali presence of photojournalism. Prior to that, photographs as vehicles of political documentation and persuasion had been either exported or imported. Chitrakar himself worked as a photographer for *Gorkha Patra*; all images had to be submitted to the Press Secretariat, which decided which images could and couldn't be used. Photographs were reproduced through zinc blocks, which produced images of extremely poor quality (the caption would read: "King and Queen smiling while visiting X" and "all you could see were two black patches").[22] Gopal also wired images to Reuters in Hong Kong, which then only circulated externally in the foreign press, never reaching an internal Nepali audience (Indian and other foreign newspapers were regularly stopped at the Nepali border). In a reverse movement, foreign images (especially US, Russian, and Chinese) flooded Nepal with visual traces of global soft power. Gopal's own father-in-law, Ganeshman, worked for the US Citizenship and Immigration Services (USIS) in the US Embassy as a photographer. They produced *Swatantra Vishva* (Free world), a glossy color publication with arti-

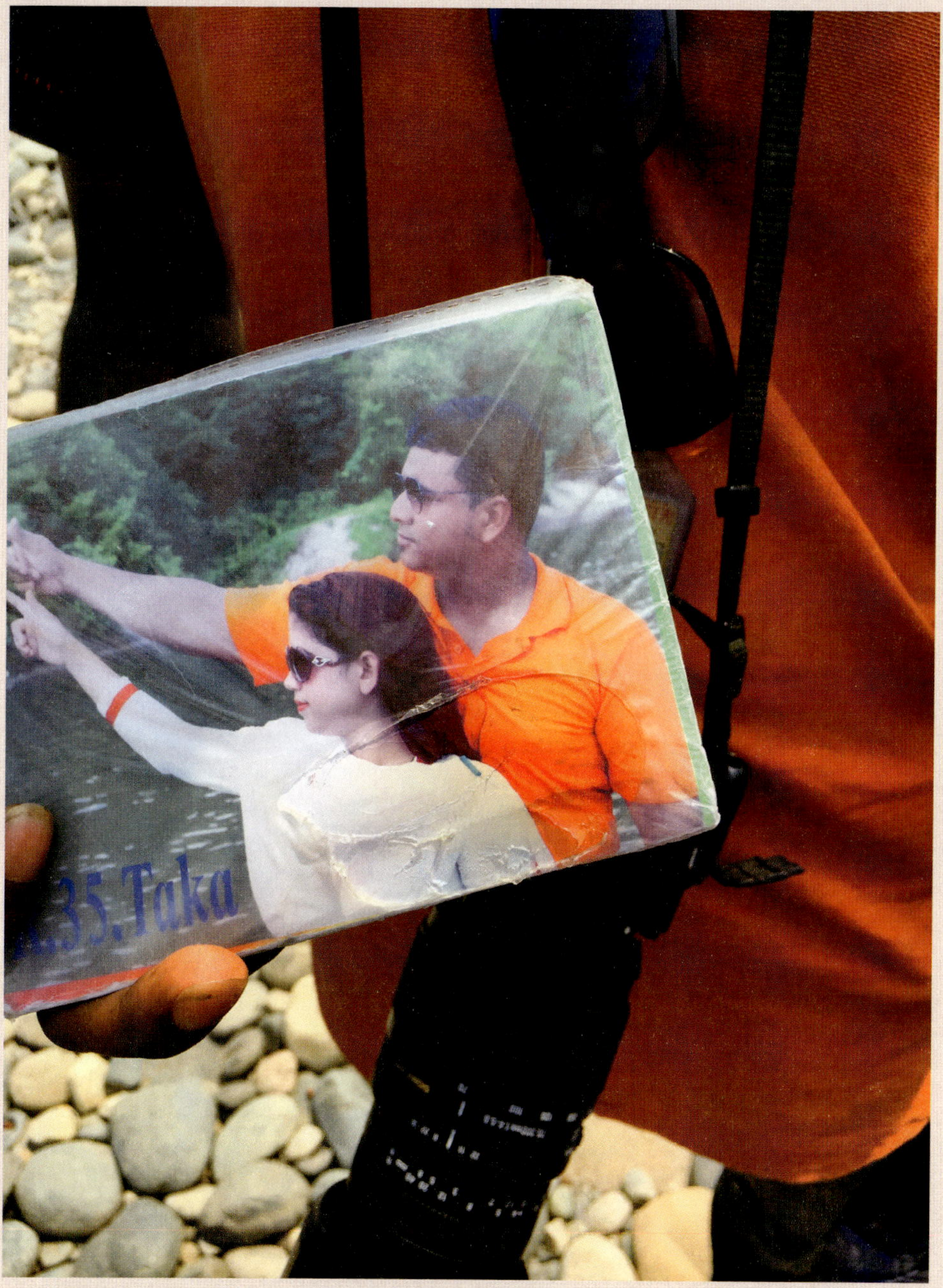

6.4 An itinerant photographer on the riverside at Jaflong (Bangladesh) with a sample image (costing Tk35) showing a Bangladeshi couple pointing across the river toward Meghalaya in India. Photograph by Christopher Pinney, April 2018.

cles on topics like democracy and multiparty systems. Many Nepalis still recall the superior printed quality of the publications in which they appeared, viewing them as formative influences in the formation of image worlds, although Gopal also recalled that Chinese and Russian glossy magazines were very cheap and mostly bought for their superior paper quality and used to make paper bags.

People Power, *A People War*, and the *People's War*

In Gopal Chitrakar's *People Power*, we can see the public learning to possess an image of itself. The book documents unfolding protests in the Kathmandu Valley in great detail, and the earlier images show protesters acting indifferently toward the camera. As the movement unfolds, we start to see crowds in the act of reflexively performing their collective image for the camera, a process brilliantly captured in Rosalind Morris's comments on the visibility of the crowd and "their ambition to access the media immediately. . . . This crowd, in order to achieve any objectivity—for the purposes of self-sustenance if not self-reproduction—must have an image of itself as such. The image, then, is the anticipatory origin of that force as well as its reproduction."[23] Later images from the struggle show sections of crowds acknowledging the camera and presenting a unity for its eye (figure 6.5).

It was during the Democracy Movement, specifically on April 9, 1990, following the lethal shooting of more than fifty demonstrators, that Min Bajracharya photographed a young woman named Durga Thapa rising from a large, predominantly male crowd with her hands raised in a victory salute after King Birendra had announced the end of Absolute Rule (figure 6.6).[24] This jubilant image would become known as *Dawn of Freedom* and become an icon of Nepali photojournalism, one that Bajracharya himself compares to Steve McCurry's *Afghan Girl*. The image is regularly reproduced in the press as the anniversary of that event is remembered and Durga Thapa's pose is regularly performed by demonstrators: Min recounts many instances where he subsequently photographed activists consciously acting out her iconic gestures.

The Democracy Movement of 1990, the subject of Chitrakar's work, was superseded by the People's War or Nepali Civil War. This period of insurgency lasted from 1996 until 2006 and would result in the assemblage and dissemination of two further major bodies of images. Issued as books and also promoted as exhibitions, these would have profound impacts on the political culture of the country.

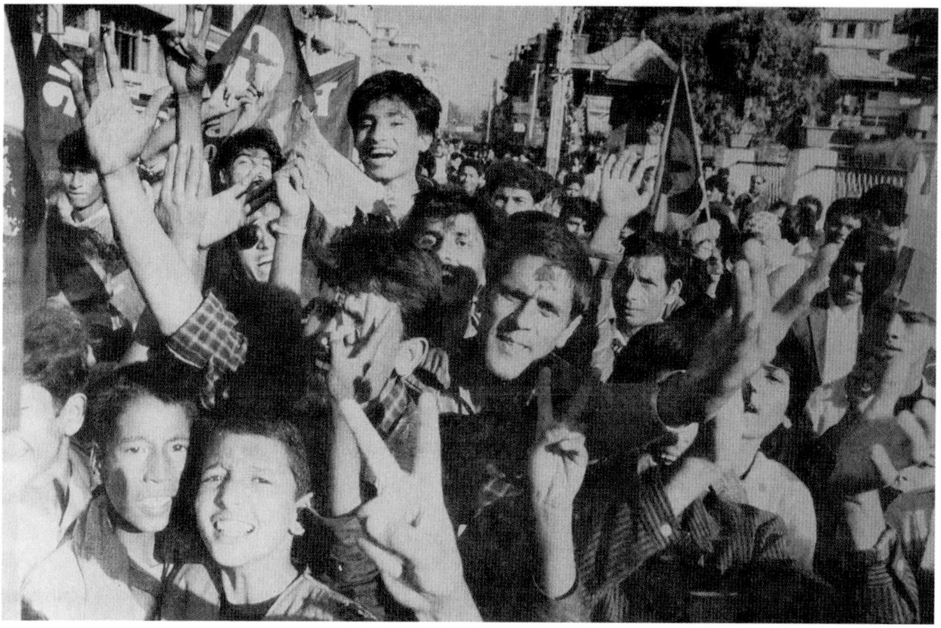

6.5 The crowd performing protest for the camera, Kathmandu, 1990. From Gopal Chitrakar, *People Power*.

The first of these was largely the work of Kunda Dixit, a leading journalist and editor of the *Nepal Times*. As the tenth anniversary of the start of the insurgency approached, he found himself in conversation with Shyam Tekwani, a Sri Lankan photojournalist who had covered the war in northern Sri Lanka, and Shahidul Alam, the Bangladeshi director of Drik Photoagency and the chief organizer of Dhaka's renowned biannual Chobi Mela photo festival.

Shyam Tekwani had been responsible for a celebrated image of a dead member of the ill-fated Indian Peace Keeping Force in Sri Lanka that was published as a front cover of the weekly journal *India Today* in November 1987. Dixit described it as "that iconic image . . . that changed the course of the war. . . . It was India's Vietnam. That one image was extremely powerful." This, together with a long acquaintance with Shahidul's activist practice, persuaded Dixit that the national political debate could be changed through the promotion of certain types of images. "There was tremendous brutality, human rights violations," and it was assumed that the war would continue for another ten years, Dixit recalls. He started with a special photo feature in the *Nepal Times* in January 2006, which then formed the basis for the book *A Peo-*

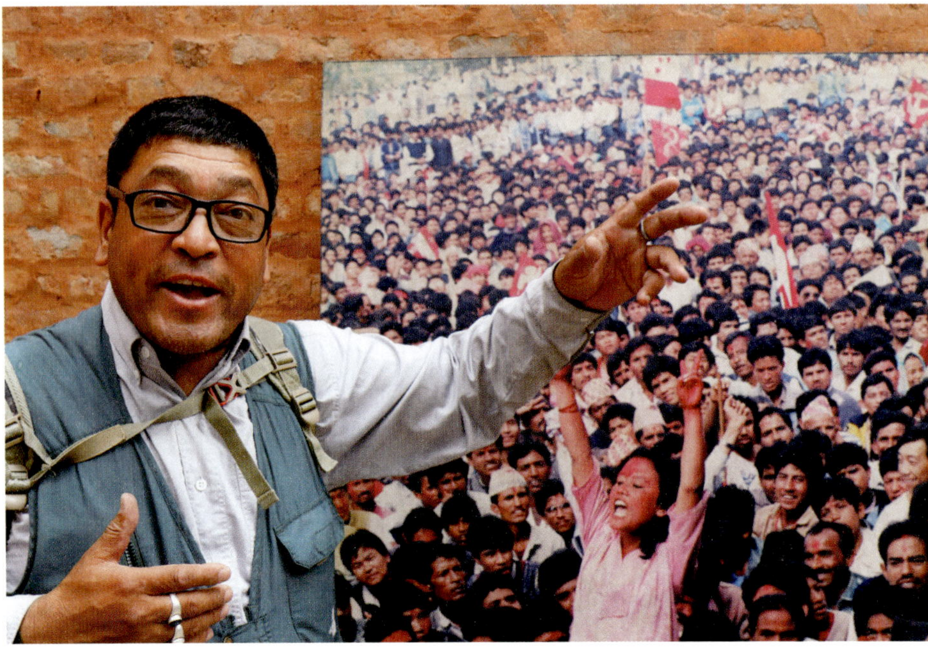

6.6 Min Ratna Bajracharya discussing his celebrated image known as *Dawn of Freedom*, taken on April 9, 1990. Photograph by Christopher Pinney, Patan, May 2019.

ple War: Images of the Nepal Conflict 1996–2006 in English with a parallel Nepali text (*Laraima Janata*).[25]

From the beginning, the intention was "to try and bring an end to the war by a photographic documentation of how the war had brutalized the people. And it was equally clear from the beginning that the emphasis was that it should focus on . . . civilians. Even if we had photographs of soldiers of combatants [we wanted to show how] their deaths affected civilians. We were not trying to take any sides in the conflict. But we wanted it to be an antiwar book."[26]

A key concern of the book was to focus on what Dixit calls "ordinary Nepalis," this being reflected in the title. "The Maoists had called [their struggle] the People's War just like Mao Tse Tung had . . . [and we used something similar but different because we wanted to show that] it was the people who were affected most by the war. . . . When we started working on the book, the big dilemma for us was do we choose the most shocking images because they showed you real violence or do we choose pictures that were . . . more subtle." As examples, he points to Narendra Shrestha's image of a grieving grandmother present

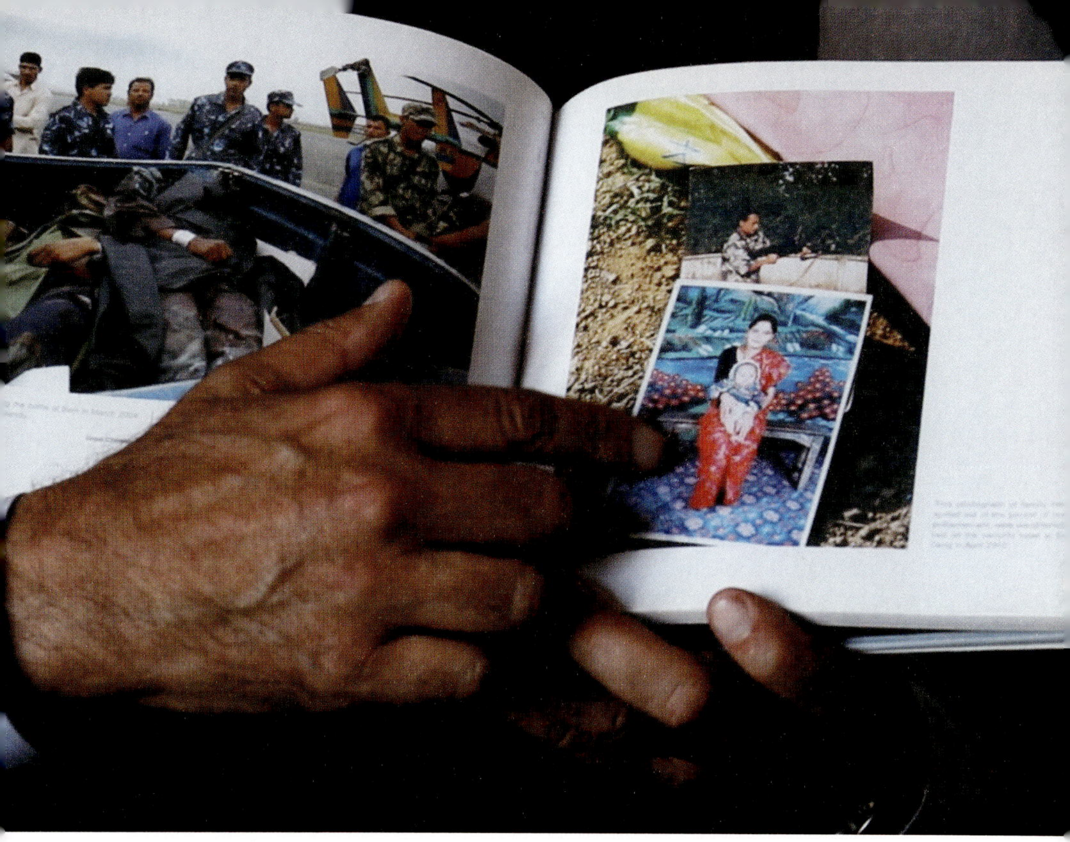

6.7 Kunda Dixit discussing an image in *A People War*. The caption to the image reads: "This photograph of family members had spilled out of the pocket of one of the 24 policemen who were slaughtered in a Maoist raid on the security base at Satbariya of Dang in April 2002." Video screenshot by Christopher Pinney, Kathmandu, December 2017.

at the mass cremation of fifty-six soldiers following a battle at Achham. Instead of sensational images of corpses or pyres, Shrestha captured the legacy of the violence. "Even when combatants were killed, we could see that it was civilians, those left behind, who were most affected," Dixit observed.[27]

Dixit says he is often asked what is the most shocking picture in the book. He thinks the most powerful and "emotionally wracking one" is one that he describes as "photographs of photographs," photographs that "spilled out of the pocket of a dead [policeman]" after a massacre at Dang in 2002. The photographer, who asked that a pseudonym be used in the book, was a helicopter pilot who was usually the first on the scene after a massacre. Dixit imagines that the top image shows the policeman and the one below shows his family (figure 6.7).[28]

A People War also became a traveling exhibition whose various continuing iterations have surely had as great an impact in Nepal as Edward Steichen's *Family of Man* had globally in its various circulating versions. Steichen's show, and its depoliticizing humanism, was of course the subject of a devastating and perfect critique by Roland Barthes. He saw its "myth of human 'community'" as involving a "failure of photography" that ought to be more analytical and more confrontational. Barthes also argues that *Family of Man*'s humanism also allowed the reappearance of God (for the "unity of [mankind's] gestures demonstrates his will") before contemptuously quoting André Chamson, one of the authors of the exhibition's introductory leaflet, to the effect that "this look over the human condition must somewhat resemble the benevolent gaze of God on our absurd and sublime ant-hill."[29] One can imagine the "photograph of a photograph" encouraging such sentiments.

Although "people" (rather than "the people") were foregrounded in the title of the project, it was only during the exhibitions that a "public" started to recognize an image of itself and mobilize reflexively. Dixit recalls a feeling of anxiety at the start of the process. In the second half of 2007, the exhibition commenced the first part of its tour—four districts, two east of Kathmandu, and then one south. "I was personally very apprehensive: many people had warned us you shouldn't be doing this—the war has just ended, the wounds are still fresh. You might restart some kind of a revenge thing. They might attack each other; you might be attacked."[30]

But from the first exhibition there was tremendous interest:

> We thought there'd be two thousand people and there'd be twenty thousand. There'd be a line of people who'd wait two or three hours to get in. So we thought we were onto something important. We had put some guest books outside the exhibition but there were not enough: people queued to write comments. They'd wait another hour to write in the guest books so we increased the number of guest books. Everyone was writing—fifth graders right up to grandfathers. It was clear when we read them—each evening we'd read what they'd written—it was clear that they were writing extremely personal things that some of them had not even divulged to their parents.[31]

Many of the responses are remarkable. A young college girl in Ilam wrote: "They killed my father, I know the murderer, he walks around openly and I have a deep sense of revenge, I wanted to kill him and then when I saw this exhibition and that there were so many others like me, my anger diminished." A comment from someone in Sukhet observed: "I was glad to see the photo exhibition because I suppose both the security forces and the rebels came to see them too."[32]

This sense of a shared spectatorship, and the quasi-religious nature of the exhibition space as itself the subject of new forms of photography, emerged as a key theme in Dixit's analysis:

> It would be like this: they'd waited maybe one or two hours to get in, the college kids would come in their uniform, they'd all be chattering and laughing and all that, they'd see the first two pictures and then complete silence. *It was like they were entering a temple or a church, the pictures brought them right down, they'd hug each other, hold each other's hands, whisper the captions to each other, there'd be former combatants, former guerrillas, soldiers in uniform—side-by-side*. They'd be taking pictures with their mobiles (we allowed that). What strikes me even today is that the silence was so loud."[33]

The Maoists would publish their own photo book response to *A People War* five years later, in 2011.[34] Titled *People's War in Pictures*, it was also accompanied by an exhibition that had local iterations and toured widely. These largely featured the work of the battlefront, and the subsequent official photographer to Prime Minister Prachanda, Dinesh Shrestha, whom I interviewed in September 2017 and who has generously shared his photographic archive.

Although Dinesh is clear that the party prioritized battlefield images for public dissemination, when he was asked to identify the most important images produced in the struggle, he pointed to images of the People's Liberation Army (PLA) in training, especially one taken at Rolpa depicting a commander (Pasang/Nanda Kishor Pun), who at the time of the interview was the deputy president of Nepal. This demonstrated to the public the seriousness of the Maoist preparations, Dinesh explained.[35]

Dinesh is coy about the relationship between Kunda Dixit's *A People War* and the Maoist response. He says he visited the earlier exhibition and found it (like the book) "a little negative." When pressed to specify why, he makes clear his objection not only to the anti-Maoist tone but also to Dixit's apparent desire to show through photographic evidence that the PLA recruited child soldiers: "they searched for those kind of photos and published those." Clearly troubled, Dinesh then also mentions *People War*'s commitment to showing that the "people" were punished: this was another dimension of the "negativity" of Dixit's project.

Then, discussing horrific images of a Nepali Army ambush of Maoists in Makwanpur, Dinesh points to an image of a dead comrade and says, "*This* is the people" (figure 6.8). Here one might recall the point at which Barthes, fed up with "gnomic" obfuscations where truism no longer has any value except in the realm of a purely 'poetic' language," exasperatedly asks, "Why not ask the parents of Emmett Till, the young [African American] assassinated by the Whites what *they* think of *The Great Family of Man*?"[36]

But sixty years after it was written, and in this conflicted Himalayan context, Barthes's critique of humanism is difficult to attach fully to *A People War*. There is much that does seem to apply to it (as indeed Dixit, a perceptive and generous self-critic, would readily acknowledge). When I asked Dixit about the Maoist photo book, for instance, he said (to my surprise) that he wished he'd been able to include images from the Maoists in his book and exhibition.

People's War in Pictures (the Maoist project), for its part, might be accused of an equal determination to produce a magical unity out of pluralism, not least through the transformational structures of the People's Liberation Army. It trades in thoughts from the Great Chairman rather than *Family of Man*'s Old Testament, but both serve, in Barthes's words, to "define an eternal wisdom, a class of assertions which escape History." Its "earth mother" shares much in

6.8 Dinesh Shrestha, a former battlefront photographer, pointing to one of his own photographs of a revolutionary martyr of the Nepalese Civil War. Video screenshot by Christopher Pinney, Kathmandu, 2017.

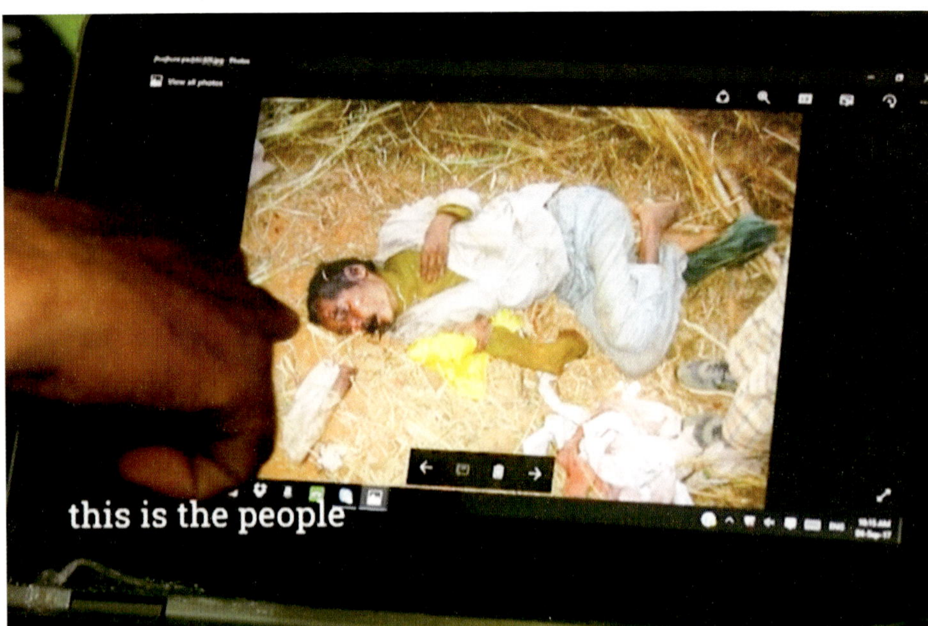

common with Edward Steichen's essentializations (Barthes derisively quotes: "The Earth is a Mother who never dies").[37] However, the PLA one comes armed with an MI6.

One of the most striking pages toward the end of *People's War in Pictures* pairs two images of life and death. The caption reads: "Proclamation programme of the 5th Division of the People's Liberation Army held at Manimare Chaur of Jinawang, Rolpa on 29 November 2005. Division Commander Com[rade] Kim Bahadur Thapa 'Sunil' is seen at the centre-row among guests. Com[rade] Sunil and BN VC Com[rade] Nirman were martyred half an hour through the programme in an aerial attack by the Royal Nepalese Army. Dead body of Com[rade] Sunil (right)."[38]

This may recall for some the famous image by Alexander Gardner of the assassin Lewis Payne awaiting execution. It is reproduced by Barthes in *Camera Lucida* with the memorable caption "He is dead and he is going to die."[39] The *People's War in Pictures* pairing seems to point to the same impossible double temporality of photography in which the "there then" and "here now" collide and often disalign. But it also brings to mind Barthes's comments toward the end of his critique of the *Family of Man* of what he calls "the eternal lyricism of birth" (and of "death").[40]

People's War in Pictures, not surprisingly, celebrates martyrdom. At the back of the book, there are several pages recording the faces of comrades who "were disappeared" by the state during the "great People's War," and the preamble records the deaths of various senior martyrs "as one after another unparalleled records of supreme sacrifice were set in the drive to inaugurate a new epoch."[41] "Must we really celebrate [birth or death's] essence once more and thus risk forgetting that there is still so much we can do to fight it?" Barthes asks at the end of his essay. "It is this very young, far too young power that we must exalt, and not the sterile identity of 'natural' death."[42]

Dixit would want to replace "natural" with "revolutionary." His argument is that we should not exalt revolutionary deaths and martyrdoms that occur under the ahistorical cloud of dialectical materialism and the utopian belief in a "new epoch." Barthes's critique of Steichen's humanism remains powerfully perceptive and its resonance with some aspects of the *People War* project is unavoidable. But it seems also to critically illuminate aspects of this new insurgent family of man: the Nepali Maoist photographic construction of the "people."

The camera's role in bringing "the people" into being in these three photographic projects bears restating. In the first project, Gopal Chitrakar's *People Power*, the crowd becomes increasingly reflexively aware, gradually developing an image of itself, affirming Rosalind Morris's suggestion that "the image . . . is the anticipatory origin of that force as well as its reproduction." In the second project, Kunda Dixit's *A People War,* although the public is announced in the title as the victims of war, it only emerged after the event through an audience responding, by means of a "loud collective silence," to exhibited images, to the performative dimension of visiting a photographic exhibition. In the third and final project, the Maoist rejoinder, a ghostly martyred rebel population is required to summon the "people" of whom they are the shadowy vanguard. Martyrdom proves to be immensely generative, and anticipatory, of the "people." In all three instances, photography's function is quite unlike the "solemnization" and "reaffirmation" of what already exists that Bourdieu describes. Photography is revealed through these closely connected projects as a practice lifting the "veil," to recall Kracauer, "that hid[es] the future."[43]

Thresholds of Visibility in the Photograph

The portrait of a young man called Hira is featured on the cover of *Camera Indica* in a *mise en abyme*, a kind of visual black hole, through which the image fell backward to an impossible moment of past capture.[44] I had known him when I first conducted field research in the early 1980s in central India, and shortly after, he was killed by a train. The image I encountered of Hira in 2019 in the breakaway Dalit settlement near the village railway station, where his brothers now live, seemed to move in the opposite direction, falling forward into a future in which he served as a guide. Gokul, the son of Hira's brother Naggulal, thrashed with the presence of Hira at least twice a year (during each of the "nine nights of the goddess") and served as a conduit for an eager audience of Hira's advice on relationships, and medical and employment anxieties. The memorial photograph of Hira directly animated the thrashing, Hira's *pret* (soul) passing from the surface of the photographic image into Gokul's body (figure 6.9).

These two iterations of Hira's photographs (the *Camera Indica* incarnation and his current animated presence) dramatize two different modes of photography, one solemnizing the past as in the Bourdieuian formula, and the other prophetic and future-oriented and filled with unknowability, something close to what Azoulay describes as the recognition that "not only were the photographed people there [at the moment of exposure], but . . . they are still present at the time I'm watching them."[45]

The future-oriented nature of memorial portraits is also apparent in their endlessly changing form. These images are not "conserved" as repositories

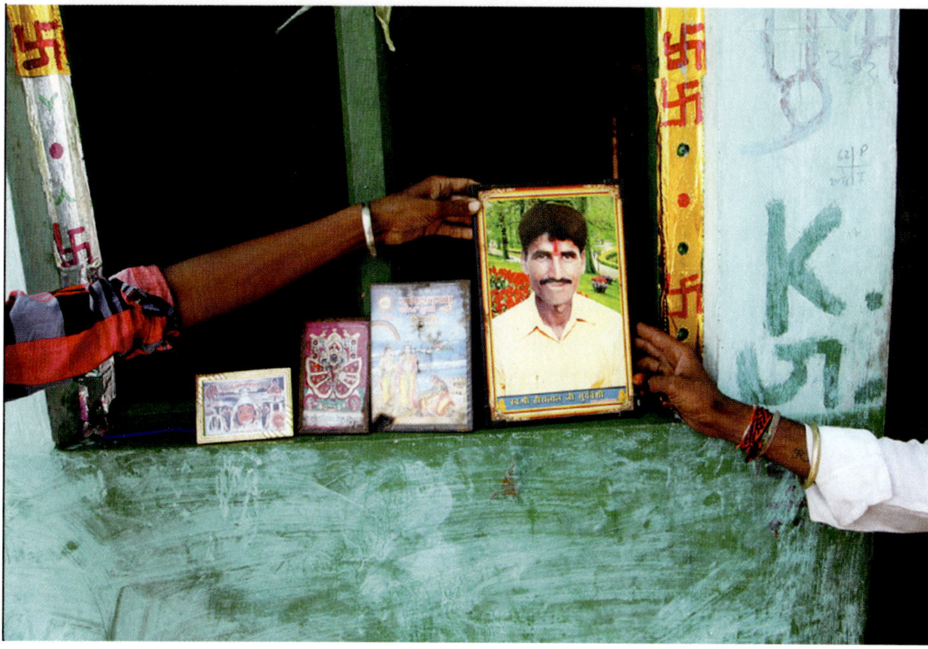

6.9 Gokul's and Narji's outstretched arms hold a memorial photograph of Hira, in Bhatisuda, Madhya Pradesh, India, 2016. Photograph by Christopher Pinney.

of indexical effect but rather serve as generative templates for continual upgrading. Sitting for several hours in any Nagda photo studio will inevitably lead to encounters with mostly rural customers arriving with old memorial portraits with requests that they be "made new." This usually involves rephotographing the old image, further saturating its colors and photoshopping it against new, usually garish, backdrops. Through time, photographic renewal leads the image further and further away from its primal indexical trace and fortifies it for the future.

Narratives that underline the camera's inability to capture the sacred are common, and this threshold of visibility threads its way through village discussions that concern themselves with the ethics and complexities of photographic consent. Among these narratives were ones I heard from members of the religious community of Jains relating to photography at pilgrimage sites. One concerned a visit, in early 2019, by a mixed group of high caste villagers (Ram Maharaj, a Brahman; Radhashyam Nai, of the barber caste; and Bapu, a Mukati) to Mohankheda, a Jain complex about two hours' distance away in

Dhar district. When they arrived, they were told by the *chowkidar* (watchman) not to take photographs, advice that they disregarded. They all took photos on their smartphones and could see what they had illicitly taken. Then they went to do their puja (ritual/prayers) and, so the story goes, planned to post their photos on WhatsApp. At this point, they realized that all their photos had disappeared.

The same location appears as the destination of a similar story told by a younger village Jain. He had gone to Mohankheda during the Jain festival of *paryushan* and had stayed there for eight days. There is a large banyan tree at the entrance to the site; that young pilgrim took between eight and ten selfies in front of it. He then entered the temple for prayer, which involved him depositing his phone in a secure locker. Upon exiting, he discovered that the photographs were no longer visible. They had not disappeared completely but had become completely black: they were somehow still present but tabooed.[46]

It is clear that these narratives limn the shape of an ontological ethics of photography, revealing in the end that what is not allowed cannot be permanently photographed. There is an echo of this in some aspects of Muslim practice in which an evanescence of the image seems to be privileged. We should be clear that although the Hadith contains a famous association between "images" and "dogs," there is nothing in the Quran that prohibits image use, and many Muslims are enthusiastic commissioners and consumers of photography.[47] Research in Bangladesh documented a range of engagements with photography, from wedding albums to portraiture to devotional images of local holy men. Often, as in the case of Gas Pir ("Tree Saint") of Srimongol, near Sylhet, local traditions are montaged into the central traditions of Islam through the use of photoshopped backdrops of Mecca and Medina. When I was collecting printed copies of Gas Pir's photographs from the Oparupa Photo Studio, a client grabbed one of the images and kissed it, demonstrating how actual Muslim practices often have little difficulty in venerating images (figure 6.10).

In Bangladesh, although it is very common for studios to destroy their negative archives on the grounds that they could be "misused" (and further inquiry reveals this to be a concern specifically about how images of female customers might be abused), there are plenty of studios that are skilled in depicting their female subjects through highly glamorous aesthetics. A prime example of this was Rixon Digital Studio in the semirural location of Banaripara, about one hour from Barisal in southern Bangladesh. One of the smallest studios I encountered in South Asia, it deployed scenic backdrops that had been gifted by a much larger studio in Barisal to glamorous effect (figure 6.11).

6.10 Gas Pir. Print made from a file kept by Oparupa Photo Studio, Srimongol, Bangladesh, 2019.

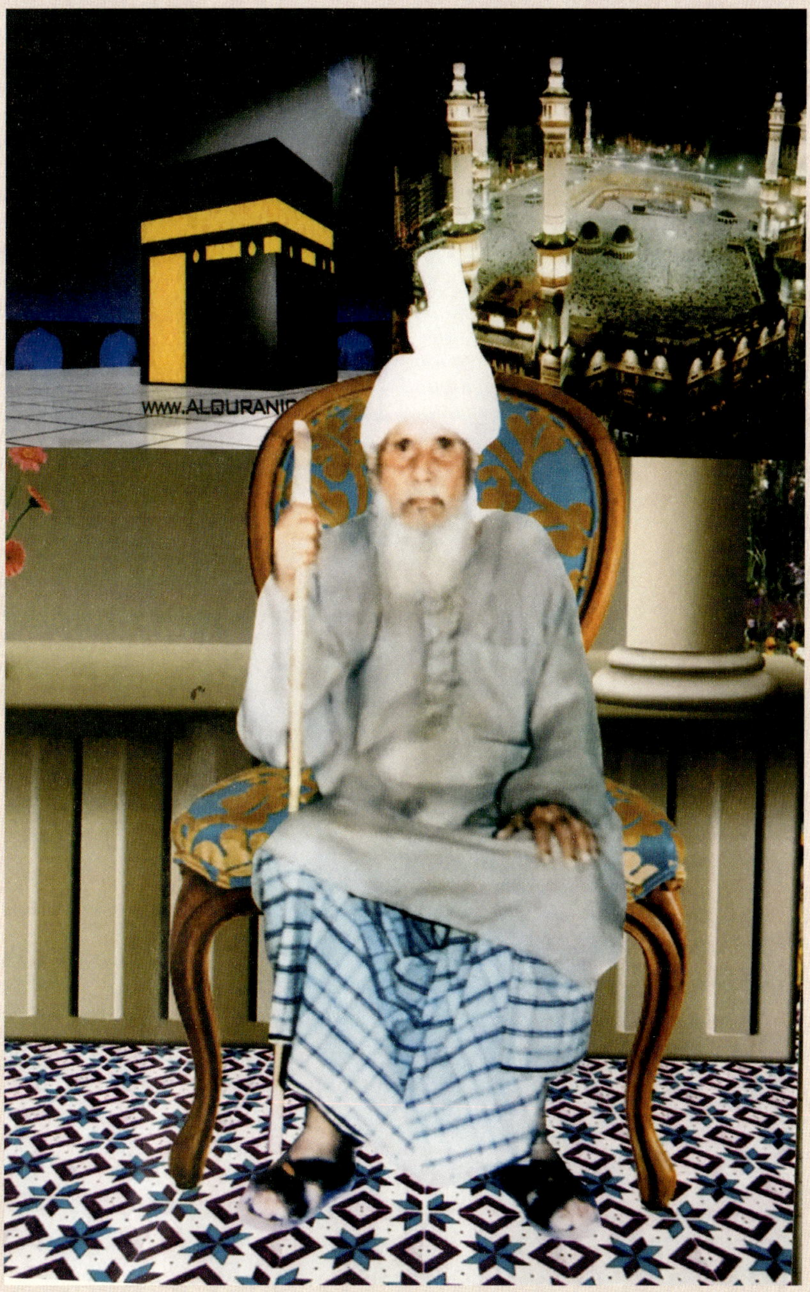

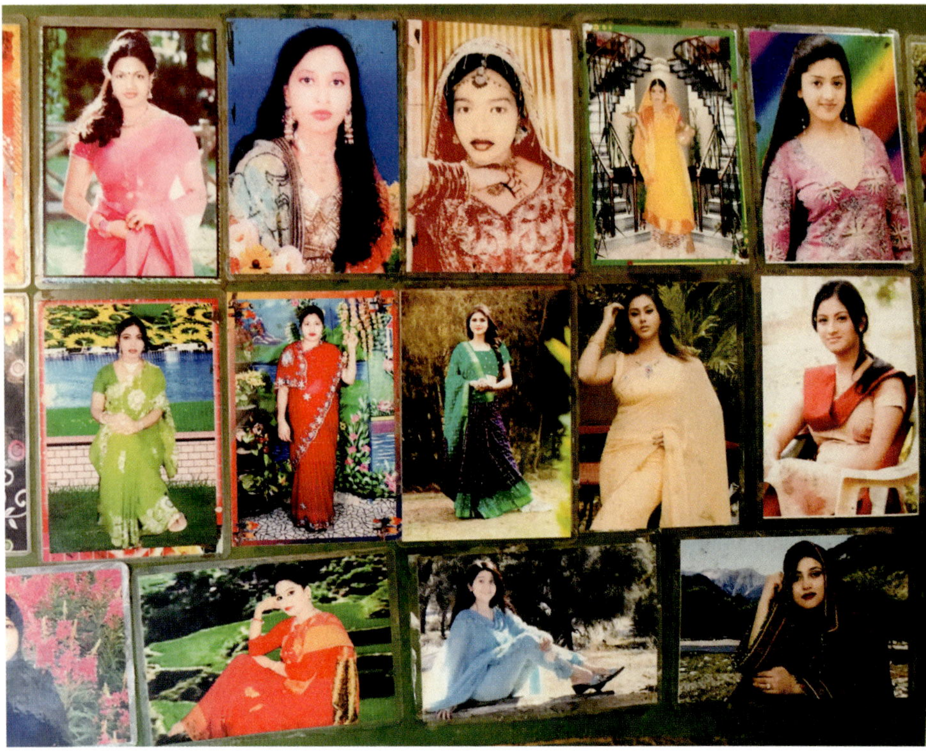

6.11 Display inside the tiny studio space of Rixon Digital Studio, in the semirural area of Banaripara, southern Bangladesh. Rixon makes extensive use of digital backdrops supplied by a Barisal studio. Photograph by Christopher Pinney, 2019.

It is also worth noting that of the only two female photographers encountered during the whole of the field research, one ran a studio in Kathmandu (Rita of Chakra Studio) and the other was a Muslim woman, Israt Jahan Sonya of "nthFotoz" (*sic*) in Barisal in Bangladesh.

Because there are always many exceptions, it is difficult to align generalizations about image use with different religious identities. Nevertheless, many Muslims (interlocutors in Madhya Pradesh, Lucknow, and Bangladesh) exhibit a striking ambivalence toward the photograph as a stabilized object.[48] In Madhya Pradesh, one is often struck by an extreme enthusiasm for cell phone photography in Muslim domestic settings that are otherwise devoid of visible imagery. Across South Asia, there is a notable contrast in the importance that Hindus and Muslims invest in images of ancestors. For Hindus, the production of images of ancestors for worship (notionally for seven generations) is practically obligatory (figure 6.12), whereas among Muslims, this practice is very unusual, though certainly not unknown.[49]

Nineteenth-century commentators on photography often called it a "mirror with a memory," that is, a technology that rescued fleeting images from the ravages of time, and this prompts the idea that Muslim practice celebrates the absence of a memory, or at any rate the absence of any permanent materialization of the photographic image. In Lucknow, two key Shia shrines, the Bada Imambara and Chhota Imambara, feature numerous huge, prominent mirrors between the alcoves housing *tazias* and other sacred regalia.[50] Watching (a mix of Shia and Sunni) visitors, I was struck by the dominant use of video on visitors' cell phones as if they were consciously rejecting the ossifying "memory" potential of photography. This echoes the conclusion of Timothy Cooper's research in Lahore, which emphasizes greater acceptance of evanescent and fleeting images (which he also establishes as a key theme in texts by Iqbal).[51]

6.12 Images of the (Hindu) proprietor's parents garlanded in Khanna Photo Studio, Aminabad, Lucknow, 2019. Photograph by Christopher Pinney.

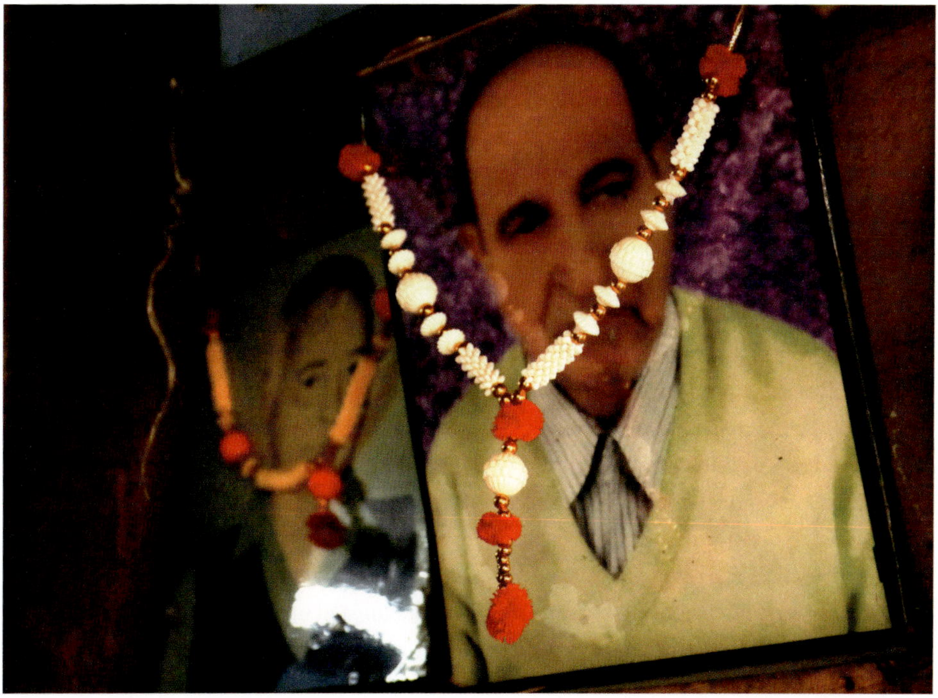

In an Aminabad (Lucknow) studio, I requested permission to rephotograph old framed images that lined the walls. "No problem," the (Hindu) proprietor responded, so I started, but then he urgently requested me to halt: "Not the Muslim women! You can copy the Nepali girl at the end." Given that Aminabad is a largely Muslim area where chaste dress for females is the norm, this was not surprising, and it recalled the nonvisibility of females in Darogah Abbas Ali's *Rajas and Talaqdars of Oudh*. In that publication of 1880, all female landowners were represented by a medallion with the inscription *pardanashin* ("under the rule of parda").[52]

My research over eighteen months during 2018–2019 suggests that very few South Asian Muslims keep any permanent visual trace of ancestors for devotional purposes. Perhaps alongside the dominant theory of photography's temporality as "memory" (in the sense of stable image), we need another conceptualization of equally important photographic practices, a kind of *camera lucida* or *camera obscura* in the original sense (an imaging device without a memory) that acknowledges the image but stresses active remembering in the absence of a settled or static image.[53]

This frontier between sense experience and what is finally deposited in the image is further explored in rural Madhya Pradesh narratives. One story of oscillating visibility recalls an event in which a twenty-foot-long snake, in reality a *sagas* or *jujhar* (the unsettled soul of a warrior who had been beheaded in battle) taking the identity of the Nag Maharaj, or King Cobra, makes itself known to the group and complains that they were having so much fun that they had forgotten to give offerings (of *agabatti* [incense sticks] and *dhup* [sacred smoke]). The group took photos of the snake, but in the developed images it appeared only as a black void.

The snake was visible to sense experience but not via photography, a relationship partly inverted in another story, told by the same villagers, in which the spirit world makes itself fully apparent only through photography. Because the photographs around which the story revolves are dated on their verso by the studio that printed them, it is possible to say with certainty that the events described took place in September 1977.[54]

The occasion was Tejas Dasmi (Tejas's tenth lunar day), a festival celebrating the pastoral deity Tejaji, who through the allied figure of Nag Maharaj (King Cobra) provides protection from snakebites. The festival centers on a Tejaji *autla* (shrine) in the center of the village from where participants make a procession around the village, bringing out colored umbrellas on long poles decorated with cobra designs that are then installed above the shrine (figure 6.13). In 1977, at least, the festival also involved a *matki phod*, a human tower

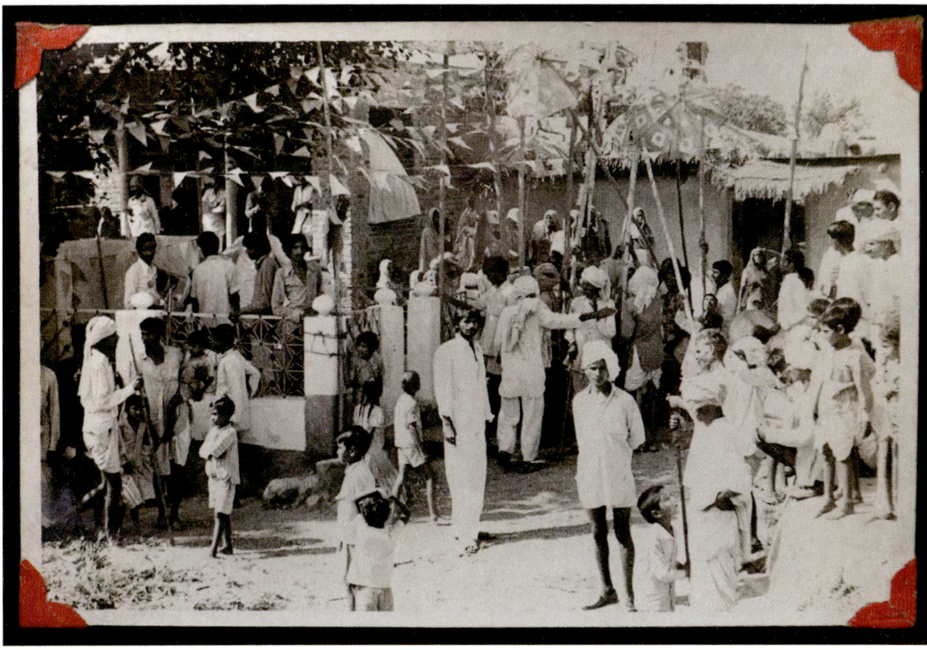

6.13 Tejas Dasmi in Bhatisuda village. Photographed by Krishna Studio, Nagda, September 1977. Courtesy of Manoharlal Bharatiya.

associated with mythology concerning Krishna in his guise as the *makhan chor* (butter thief).[55]

Photographs carefully preserved in a village album by a leading Jain document villagers congregating around the shrine after the procession that circumambulates the village. Later images in the series show the matki phod, a human tower, being constructed by thirty or perhaps forty people in three tiers. It was while this living pyramid struggled to take form that the participants became aware of a mysterious presence, a zone of energy of the kind that someone fifteen to twenty feet high might exert. Everyone was aware of something helping them as they clambered upward, and the same force came to their rescue when the tower collapsed onto hard stony ground, for they were all magically cushioned as they fell. One of the photographs from the middle of the series connects vividly with the evocative narrative given by Pukhraj and Manoharlal. They are identifiable in the center of the image and convey a sense of being in the experiential midst of puzzlement and excitement—the sense that something unusual was happening triggered by the perception that there was a fifteen- to twenty-foot-high being helping them push the tower higher and higher (figure 6.14).

The final image in the series delivers the denouement, placing the tower at the center of the image and showing some of the many small colored flags suspended from the shrine (figure 6.15). Parallel to the tower on the left side of the image, a towering, mottled, snakelike stripe sears the image. For the participants in the matki phod, and the many excited spectators whose presence the image also documents, the photograph clarified what they had experienced: the King Cobra whom the festival remembers had been the presence assisting in its own effervescent celebration.

6.14 Tejas Dasmi, 1977. Manoharlal and Pukhraj can be seen in the center of the image, the matki phod on the left. Courtesy of Manoharlal Bharatiya.

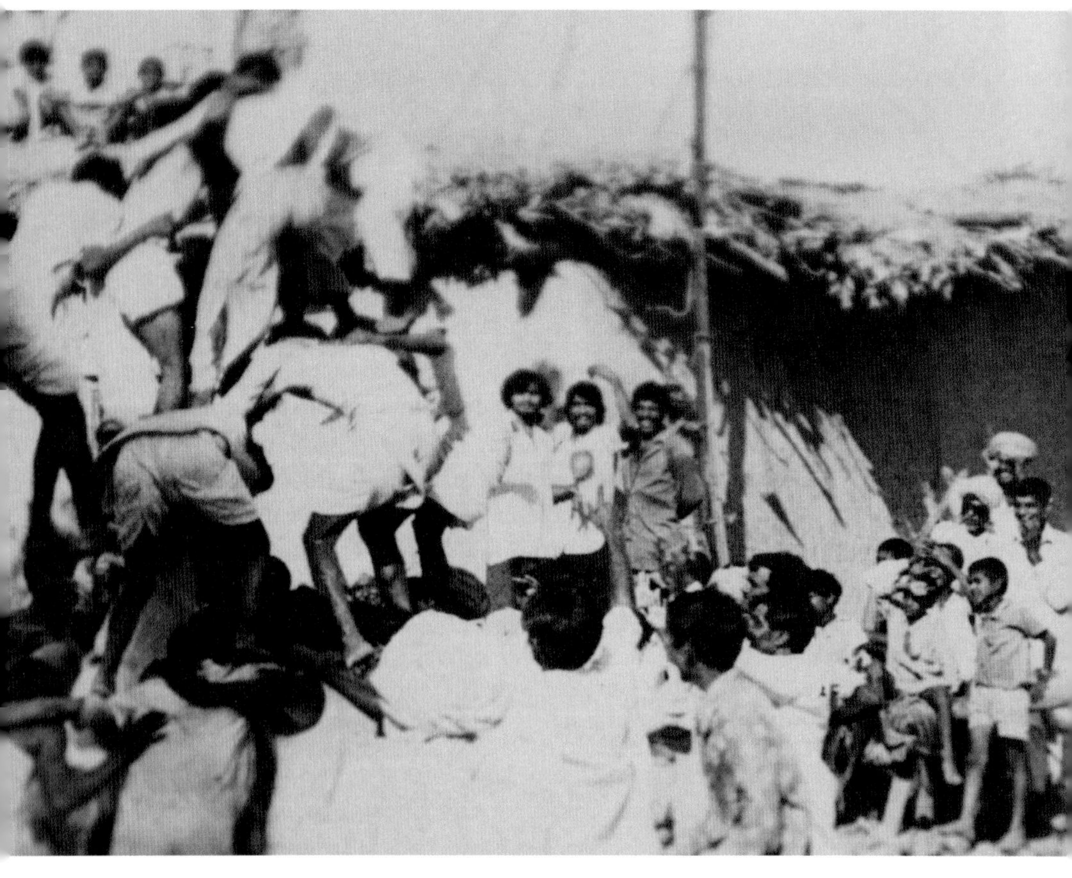

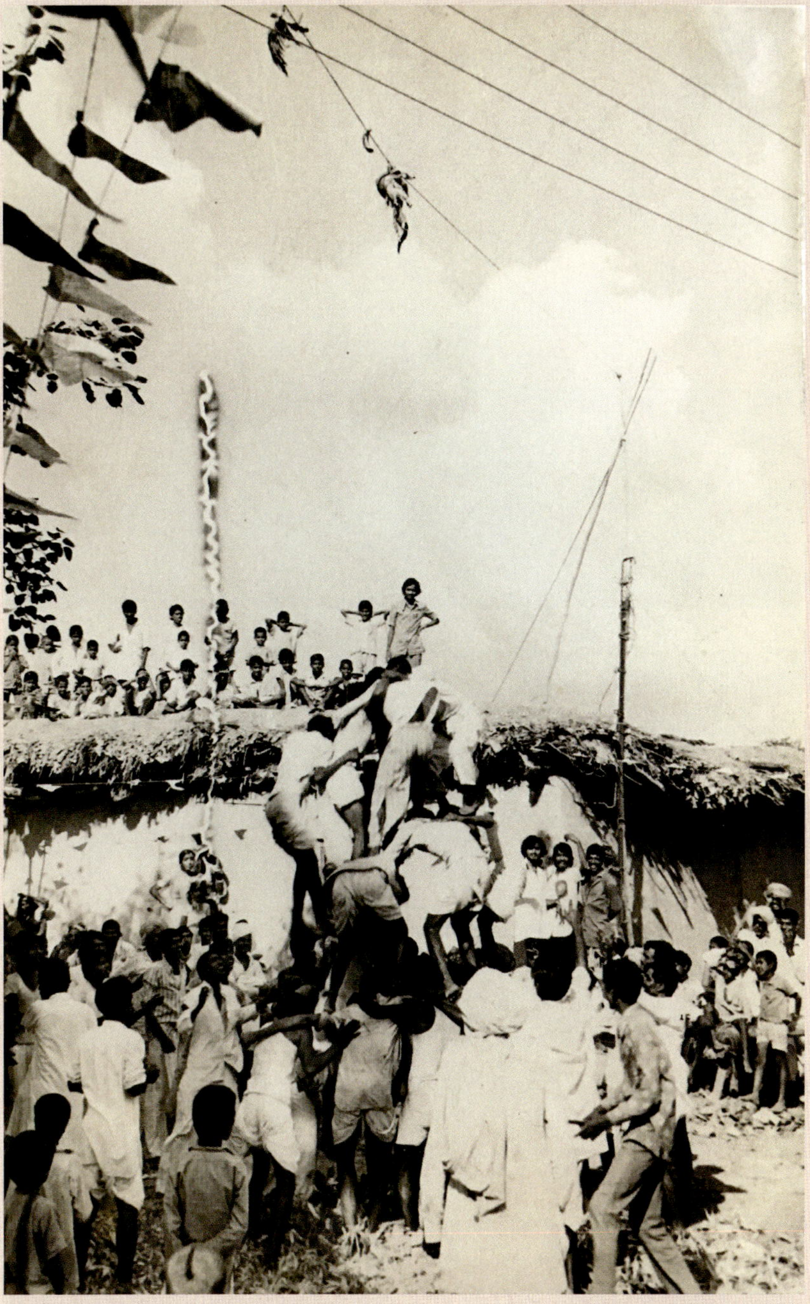

6.15 The Tejas Dasmi matki phod, with the Naga Maharaj visible on the left of the photograph. Courtesy of Manoharlal Bharatiya.

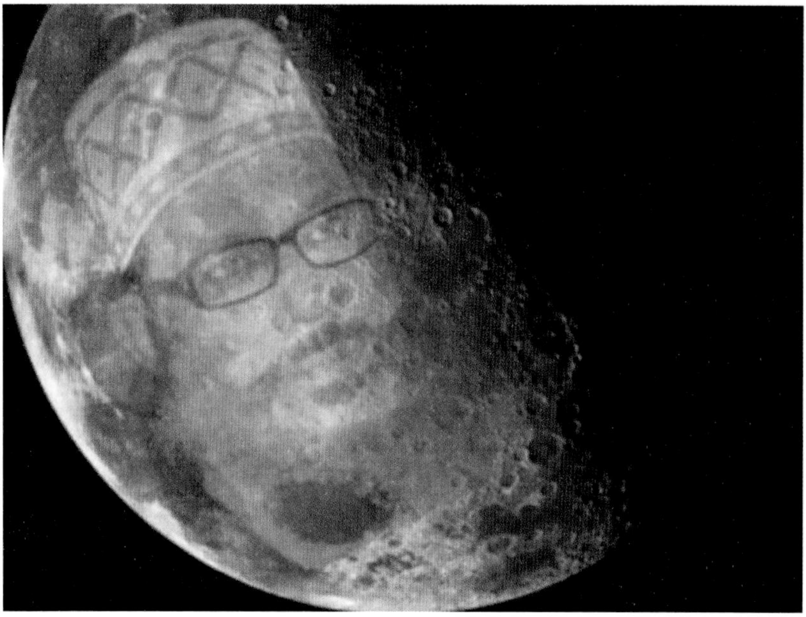

6.16 Facebook-disseminated image of the *razakar* Delwar Hossain Sayedee appearing in the moon in 2013.

Professional photographers in the nearby town are highly skeptical of the rural ontology of photography, which prizes it as a medium in which the world of sagas and jujhar becomes visible. Suresh Punjabi of Suhag Studio observed that when developing 120 film, the negative can easily get scratched, producing confusing noise on the surface of the image. Deep scratches in the emulsion can also start to "melt" at high temperatures, and for this reason many photographers would add a little ice (if they could obtain it) to the developer. Split negatives often produced a mottled pattern on the final printed image.

A similar reaction of both belief and skepticism marked responses to the circulation of an image of the face of the *razakar* ("collaborator") Delwar Hossain Sayedee appearing in the moon in Bangladesh in 2013 (figure 6.16). He had been sentenced to death for war crimes in the liberation struggle of 1971. The image was circulated by the radical group Jamaat-Shibir through Facebook with an accompanying text declaring that the appearance was an omen and a sign from God. Local mosques, conscious of their followers who lacked internet access, also broadcast announcements by loudspeaker.[56] Whenever I showed this image in local presentations in Bangladesh on my research (e.g., to the students' Visual Anthropology Club of Dhaka University), it occasioned ribald laughter.

Contingency and Its Minimization

Contingency may have been an intrinsic part of every photographic event according to Walter Benjamin, but Indian photographers often take trouble to eliminate or at least minimize its presence. One example was prominently placed in a rural Jain home in Madhya Pradesh and depicted family members in the Shantinath temple in the nearby town of Nagda (figure 6.17). This had been designed and largely funded by Babulal, one of the family members who

6.17 Shri Shantinath Jinalay. Laminated photograph taken inside the Shantinath Jain temple in Nagda, January 2005. Courtesy of Pukhraj Bohara.

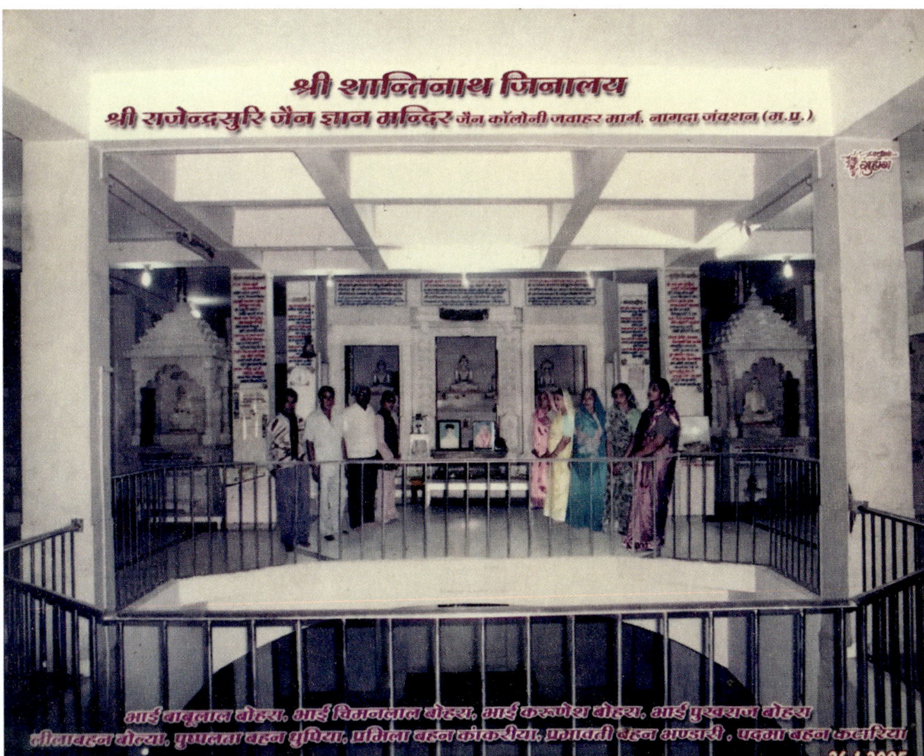

appears in the image. The taking of the photograph was a regular event every few years, organized by Chattersinghji, the husband of one of the sisters.

The image enacts a gendered symmetry, with laminated photographs of the deceased parents, Hookmichand and Ratanbai, placed at the center of the image beneath the statue of the *tirthankara* Shantinath; four brothers stand on the left and five sisters are on the right arranged by birth order. Gender and time are thus structured spatially under the divine gaze of Shantilal in this geometricized sociogram.

This image conforms to the iconography of a genre known as *manoratha* ("minds vehicle"), a very particular form of image making that depicts Pushti Margi devotees symmetrically flanking the Nathdvara deity Shrinathji.[57] Formal expressions of devotees' desire to receive *darshan* (to see and be seen) and offer *seva* (service, but in this context, puja), the images declare the virtue of a foundational symmetry that attempts to suppress contingency. Commissioned by devotees originally as paintings, then as paintings with photographic elements and subsequently as photographic events, the images depict the worshipper(s) in proximity to the deity. The increasing use of photography amplified the contingent mishaps that the symmetrical template was designed to minimize.

Photography, Contingency, and Ritual: Back to Nepal

Dakshinkali lies in a small valley to the south of Kathmandu, about one hour up a circuitous and ruined road that leads into the hills. It is the location of a major temple to the goddess Kali, and on Tuesdays and Saturdays it attracts large crowds, many of whom sacrifice cockerels and have their photographs taken by one of many studios in the bamboo shacks that line the road that descends toward the shrine.

The studios, twenty in total, are all very recent (the oldest, Ram Studio, having been established only in 2013). They are all dependent on an equally recent (and puzzling) interdiction: the prohibition of photography inside the temple precincts. Dakshinkali is located in a grove in a small valley, and its ancient Kali *murti* (idol) is open to the elements and visible from the forecourt of the shrine. Devotees wait in this area and frequently photograph each other on their mobile phones in front of the general backdrop of the temple.

However, photography is forbidden in the visually similar area ten or fifteen feet nearer the actual murti. A flex banner hung above the perimeter of the shrine declares the prohibition in Nepali and English, together with images of cameras crossed through with red lines. This very specific interdiction, which nevertheless operates within a regime of general laxity, provides the ostensible alibi for the enthusiastic photographic studio activity that surrounds the shrine.

Clients tend to be regular visitors to Dakshinkali; they are familiar with the topography and ritual architecture and know in advance that it makes sense to be photographed on their way down to the shrine and to collect the framed image on their way back to the bus stand. Although referred to as "studios," most of the photographic establishments photograph their clients in the street since they lack the space to do this inside. The first one, which one encounters as one alights from the bus, is Mahakali Photo Studio, run by two phlegmatic Tamang brothers who also sell chickens (presented in two iron cages at the front of the studio) for sacrificial purposes.

There is a plenitude of studios but a remarkable singularity of practice. Clients are almost always posed with females on the left side of males (inscribing a gender hierarchy common throughout South Asia) and are most commonly given a plastic bowl to hold, which will be substituted via Photoshop with an elaborate and opulent display of floral and fruit offerings of the kind that are for sale at the stalls adjacent to the studios. Photographing clients with a camera is the speedy part of the process, after which the image is composed on computers housed in the main part of the shacks.

The prohibition of photography (for reasons unknown) provoked Ram, the proprietor of the first studio, to import Photoshop templates from Manakamana, the famous goddess shrine on the Kathmandu–Pokhara Highway. These are now in the possession of all the studios and depict goats, doves, garlands, and cable cars, among other motifs, alongside the English text "Sweet Memory of Manakamana" and in Nepali "Manakamana Darshan," with the date according to the Vikram Samvat (VS) calendar (figures 6.18 and 6.19).[58]

The boldest twentieth-century theorization of photography, by Walter Benjamin, has pitted photography against the cultic. But for Benjamin, this was a prescriptive and programmatic exercise in what photography "ought" to do if it was able to pursue what was "closely related to the camera."[59] Benjamin's approach was hardly ethnographic, and he often has cause to lament the divergence between the effects photography should have and the uses to which it was actually put.

Siegfried Kracauer's method, by contrast, engaged popular uses of the camera. As Philippe Despoix has noted, he "approache[d] photography primarily as a vector of mass culture."[60] Kracauer's more anthropological concerns encouraged close attention to the circulation and reading of images. It is in this

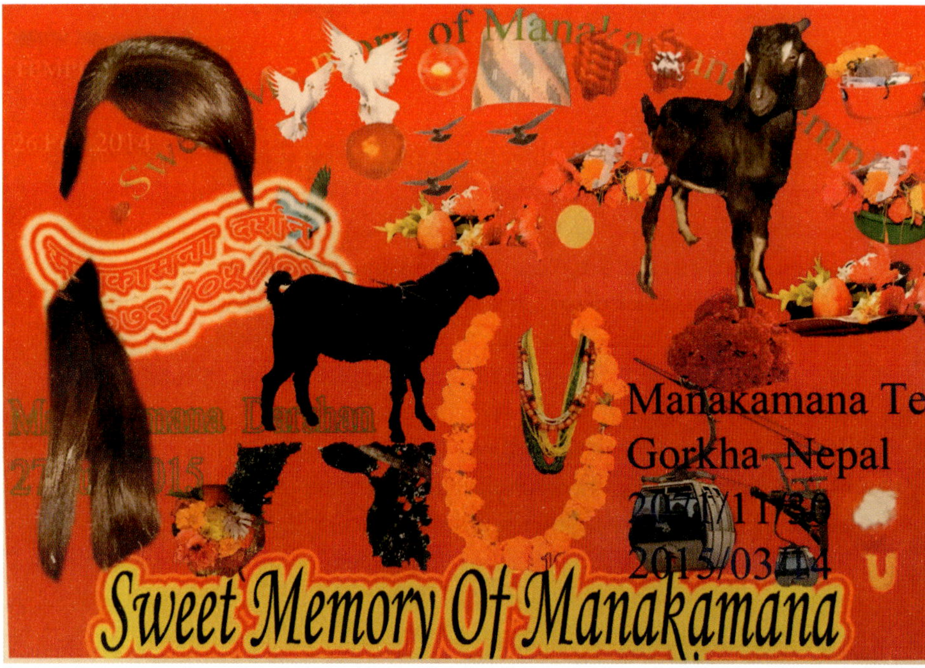

6.18 Photoshop template in use at Dakshinkali, Nepal. As is apparent from the image, all the elements have been imported from studios in the pilgrimage destination of Manakamana.

context that Kracauer focused on the manner in which "the definitive fixing of an *ephemeral* moment" became one of "the sharpest indicators of the crisis in the modern relation to transcendence and to eternal time that religion promised."[61] Dakshinkali photographic practices seek to recuperate eternal time through the minimization of contingency.

If modern Dakshinkali is viewed as a machine for the suppression of contingency, we can hypothesize the following: *pujaris* (priests) collaborated with the earliest photo studios to prohibit the direct photography of the Dakshinkali murti. This prohibition could be framed alongside similar interdictions elsewhere in Nepal (most markedly with respect to the Kumari in Kathmandu's Darbar Square, but in a broader South Asian context alongside restrictive systems of visibility such as those established in the Shrinathji *haveli* in Nathdvara, and Jain stipulations (e.g., at Ranakpur) allowing the photography of the general temple milieu but actively prohibiting the pho-

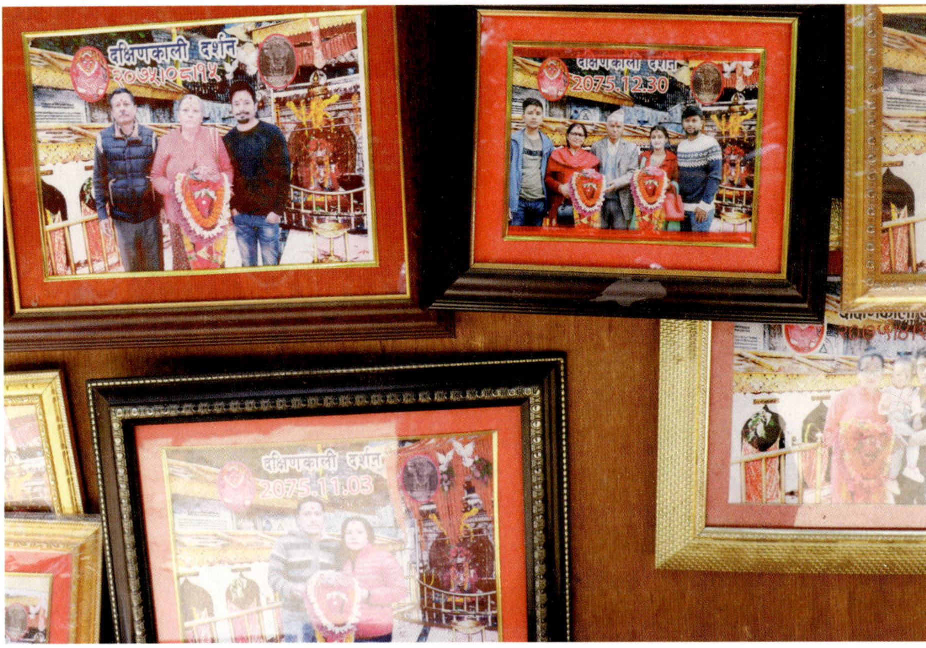

6.19 Photoshopped pilgrimage souvenirs awaiting collection from a studio at Dakshinkali, 2018. The shrine murti can be seen both in the medallion to the left of the Devanagari text (*Dakshinkali Darshan*) and on the right-hand side of the background image. Photograph by Christopher Pinney.

tography of "idols" (i.e., murti). In Nepal, the tolerance of "environmental" photography of general temple settings and the interdiction of idol photography may also be related to (well-founded) anxieties about the role of photography in facilitating the theft of idols and the manufacture of identical copies.

The minimization of photographic contingency apparent in Nathdvara manorathas and the move from the Dakshinkali shrine to the highly mediated photoshopped space of the studio recalls a central argument in Maurice Bloch's classic essay "Symbols, Song, Dance and Features of Articulation," which we might think of as an anthropological reinvention of some of the key concerns of Benjamin's "Work of Art" essay. What Benjamin termed the "cultic" becomes for Bloch "traditional authority," a political force that he contrasts with "everyday speech acts." Elsewhere in his oeuvre, Bloch associates these two kinds of power with cyclical time and linear time. In "Symbols, Song, Dance," he maps the opposition between "everyday speech acts" and "formalized speech acts." The former are characterized by a complete vocabulary, the absence of stylistic rules, and numerous choices concerning presentation. The latter involve exclusions, limitations, and fixity. This language of traditional authority is, Bloch notes, an "*impoverished* language," one in which "many of the options at all levels of language are abandoned so that choice of form, or style, of words and of syntax is less than in ordinary language."[62]

Impoverishment may be one way of grasping the normative approach to photographing the Nepalese royal family as advocated by its chief recorder, Mangal Mohan Shrestha. The former royal photographer, whom I met on the occasion of the publication of his autobiography, perfectly formulated the paradoxes that attend photography's revolutionary *and* auratic potential. He conjured a matrix in which camera angles and "communist" or "Congress" sympathies operated. These were "top" and "low" angles, the former providing the vantage point from which the "mass" (the people) could be conjured, the latter being the perspective from which one could imagine the great leader.[63]

By contrast, royalty demands to be pictured "just as it is" (*jastako testai*). Here Mangal recognizes the hieratic and frontal aesthetic that characterizes his many images of various royals. But he also clearly marks out the ideologically inviolable naturalization of power effected through this visual mode of address and Mangal's theorization of it. Jastako testai is a camera angle that points to a kind of ultimate *studium*, a what-it-is-ness, that squeezes out political alternatives and proposes the dominance of the sovereign as inevitable (figure 6.20).

Most of the Nepalese royal family was massacred by Crown Prince Dipendra in the Narayanhity Palace on June 1, 2001. Dipendra was king for three days, until his death while in a coma, and he was succeeded by Gyanendra, who reigned until the abolition of the monarchy in 2008 by the Constituent Assembly. Gyanendra remains in Kathmandu, and there are frequent calls for his return to office from diehard royalists and others disappointed by the corruption at the heart of Nepali politics.

That royalty remains a focusing point for the accumulation of aura through photography is vividly apparent in the numerous images that Mangal and his son produce of Gyanendra dispensing *tikka* (a ritual mark) on the festival of Dashain. Commoners arrive in great numbers (Mangal estimates between 1,500 and 2,000) to receive this ritually efficacious benediction but also to be photographed receiving it. Most of them order 12 × 8 enlargements from a wall display outside Mangal's downtown studio that are then framed and hung in customers' living spaces.

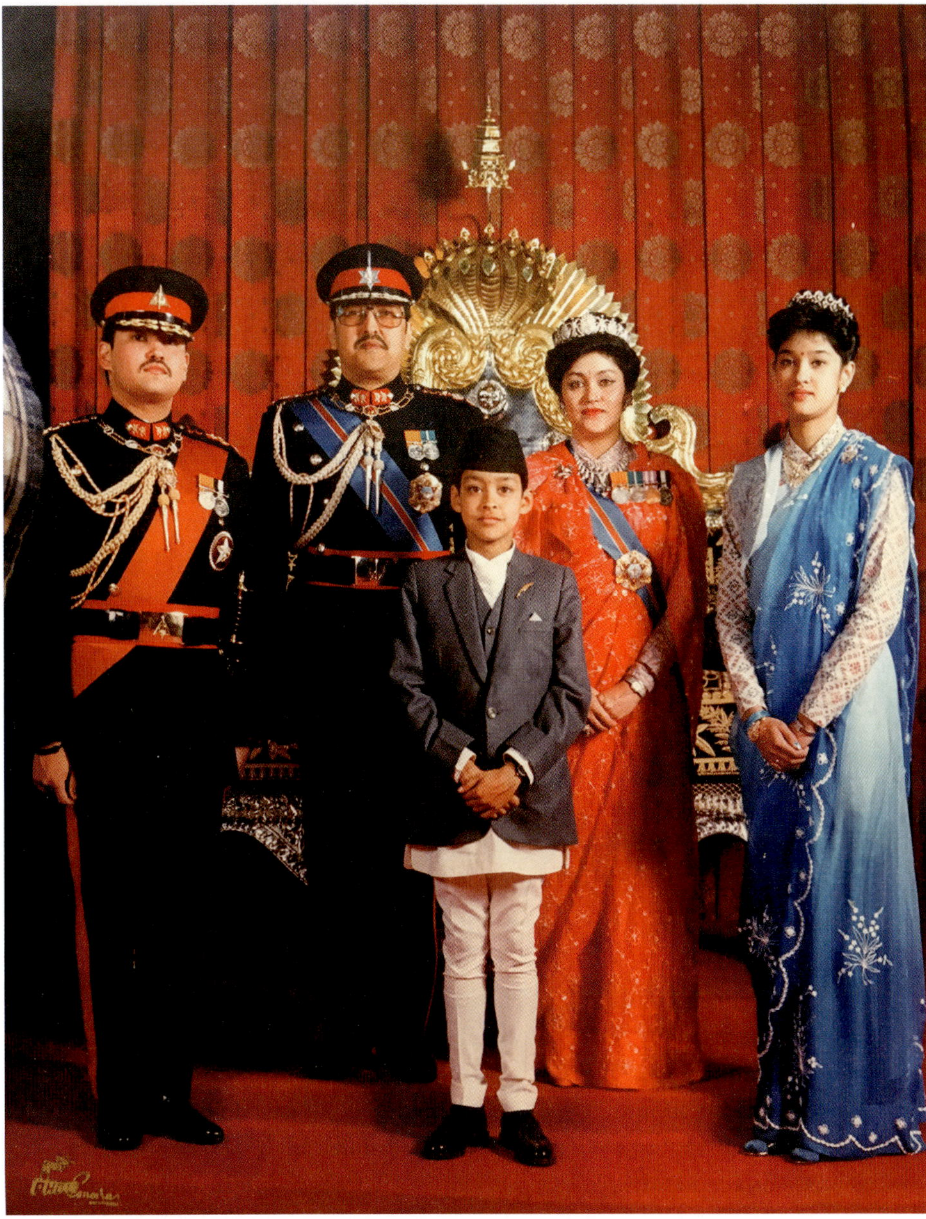

6.20 A widely distributed print of the Nepali royal family (*from left*): Prince Dipendra, King Birendra, Prince Nirajan, Queen Aishwarya, Princess Shruti. This is a perfect example of what Mangal Mohan Shrestha termed "the royal angle."

However, the sovereign's power is always vulnerable to photographic dethroning, as Azoulay has shown (see introduction to this volume).[64] Min Ratna Bajracharya, the renowned Nepali photojournalist whose image of Durga Thapur protesting (*Dawn of Freedom*) we encountered earlier in this chapter, is also renowned for another image (a copy of which I have so far been unable to source; the hunt continues). Shortly after Gyanendra had resumed the throne after the 2001 massacre, he had to address Parliament in the Singha Darbar, and Bajracharya was assigned to cover it. He photographed Gyanendra as he exited from his car and exchanged namastes with then Congress prime minister Sher Bahadur Deuba. Bajracharya says he was shooting rapidly ("click, click, click, click . . .") and found that he had two frames in which the prime minister had dropped his hands while those of the king remained folded together in a formal namaste greeting. Contingency had delivered a highly subversive image, one that demonstrated that "the photograph escapes the authority of anyone who might claim to be its author, refuting anyone's claim to sovereignty."[65] Min relates how he received an angry and threatening call after the image was published in *Himal*; the Press Secretariat demanded, "Min, this is not good! You think the king is inferior?"

Bajracharya credits the image with a transformation in public opinion, hastening the move toward democracy: "It changed public attitudes—the public saw it and said Oh! Our prime minister [the metonym of democracy] is so dynamic!" That Bajracharya's image alerts us to an ever-present (even when suppressed) feature of photography points to its inevitably contingent nature. Many years earlier, in 1990, Gopal Chitrakar (whose *People Power* we encountered earlier) had taken an image at a political meeting that subsequently became known as *The Three Faces of Congress* for the manner in which contingency delivered what would soon be seen as an iconic image (figure 6.21). The meeting involved the three leading political stars of the democracy movement—Ganesh Man Singh, K. P. Bhattarai, and G. P. Koirala. Gopal Chitrakar captured a moment in which they appeared as though they were a three-headed hydra, each facing in a different direction, and in this manner contingency delivered an image that for many seemed to crystallize the divergent thinking of the movement's leaders. Clearly the power of the image rested upon a sentiment that was already at large, but it amplified these and accentuated them, creating and distilling in the image a conclusion that was in advance of existing ideology.

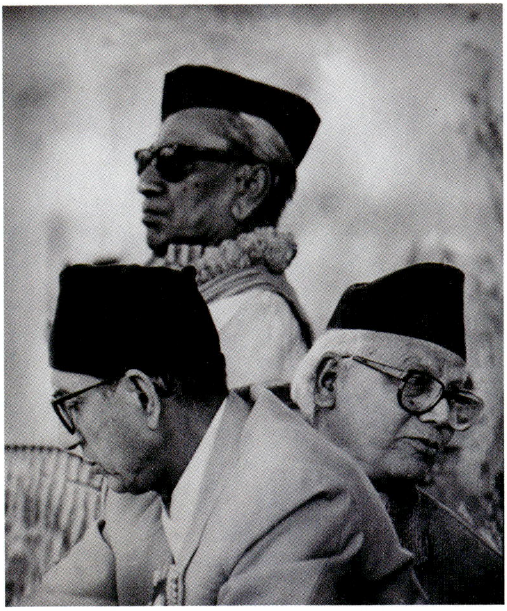

6.21 Gopal Chitrakar, *The Three Faces of Congress* (Ganesh Man Singh, K. P. Bhattarai, and G. P. Koirala), 1990. Courtesy of Gopal Chitrakar.

The Third Eye of Democracy and the Messianic Imagination

When I first met Min Ratna Bajracharya, he gave me a copy of that week's *Nepali Times* (editor: Kunda Dixit). The front-page lead, marking World Press Freedom Day, was titled "Long Shadows" and featured a large image by Bajracharya showing a DSLR held above coils of barbed wire framed by the shadows of a row of riot police.

Allegorical, and worthy of a stock library, the image offered a secular photojournalistic icon of an argument that Bajracharya also made in a quite different register. Bajracharya has also argued that photojournalism should be seen as the third eye of the god Shiva. In Hindu mythology, this is a third eye that opens in his forehead and sends out a beam of fire, igniting and energizing its targets at great distances.[66] I first encountered this idea in the subtitle of a 2006 book by Prakash A. Raj illustrated with many of Bajracharya's color photographs of protests and riots. This book, *The Dancing Democracy: The Power of the Third Eye*, fails to shed any light on the rationale for the subtitle, but he clarified this during an interview in Kathmandu in 2019.[67] In conversation with him, it became clear that his usage is largely metaphorical and is formulated as an idea—which he propagates in lectures and talks to Mass Communication students and others—about the need to conceptualize the photograph one hopes to make rather than merely rely on state-of-the-art equipment in order to take it. As he puts it, he urges students to "believe in their body's lens and eye, the power of the third eye." A "big lens and big camera are just tools. . . . Make sense first, then use the lens." At this point in the conversation, I asked about the Saivite connotations, observing that Shiva's third eye emits a "beam of fire" (*ag ki dristhi*). Bajracharya enthusiastically elaborated on this, suggesting that the political potential of photography turned it into a beam of fire. He recalled an image by a photographer friend, Shaligram, that depicted a girl on a wall forlornly viewing an assembly in a school from which poverty excluded her. The picture was published and "that power, that fire" resulted in a public mobilization that got her a place in the school. The "fire" of the third eye was thus for Bajracharya a metaphor for public pressure, the demand for what Azoulay terms a new "civil political space," an actionable space ripe for fiery transformation in which "photographers, photographed subjects and spectators share a recognition that what they are viewing is intolerable."[68]

A different kind of anxiety marks the understanding that technology is also gradually liberating the public from the studio. In the part of central India with which I'm familiar, it is not simply that cell phone cameras are occupying the space previously taken by studios (for example, by producing images of friends at Diwali, or capturing the moment when you first wear new clothes). Rather, the cell phone camera can be seen to be enfranchising a whole new worldview. When allied to digital platforms such as WhatsApp and divisive issues such as "cow protection," the camera can act as a tool for the denial of citizenship to those who thought they had already acquired it.[69] Photography, confounding Azoulay's initial optimism, is showing itself capable of reducing the size and shape of "civil political space" through its alliance with a messianic politics that imagines sinister futures.

In rural central India, there is what might be termed "Hindu citizen journalism," which is more benign but no less messianic. It is capable of imagining *literally* what for Min Bajracharya is only metaphorical. In 2011 Kishor Sharma was walking down the main street in Bhatisuda village, his phone in hand, when he looked up at some fellow villagers who were placing a brass *kalash* on top of a newly built Shiva temple. As they were doing this, Kishor realized that Shiva was sending down a beam of light from his third eye to perform Prana Prathishtha (an idol consecrating ceremony) to energize the temple. Kishor had seen this happen several times before, but thanks to his phone camera, this time he was able to capture the process as it happened (figure 6.22). He then had a 12 × 8 print of this made at a local photo studio; this was laminated and formed part of his puja ensemble.

Mobile photos are implicated in other interruptions of the sacred into the everyday, such as the appearance of five-headed snakes. Rural puja rooms give space to photoshopped images showing miraculous cobras, images that are sold by local photo studios (figure 6.23).[70] They might be seen as the digital version of the Tejas Dasmi/Nag Maharaj image discussed earlier. However, whereas the Nag Maharaj image (figure 6.15) arose from contingencies in the dark room, its digital successors are a more deliberate invention.

Villagers are invested in the photography of these occurrences because they provide evidence for, and validation of, their subjugated worldview. It promises to extend a citizenship to messianic paradigms that dominant Nehruvian critical rationality disavowed.[71] In rural lifeworlds, wondrous events have, un-

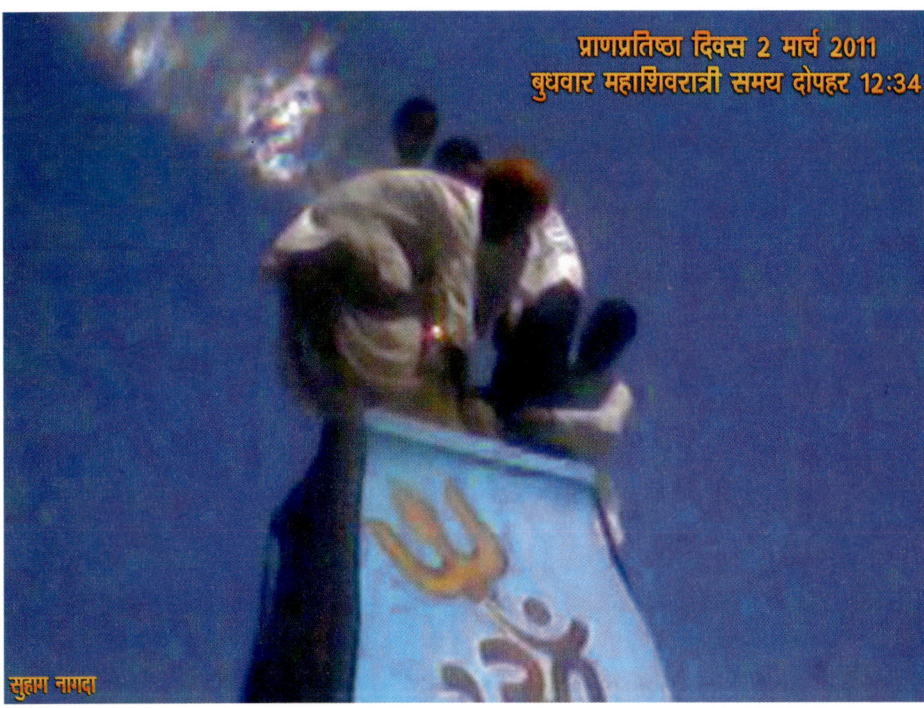

6.22 The third eye of Shiva in action. Cell phone photograph by Kishor Sharma, pranpratishtha divas 2 march 2011/budhvar mahashivratri samay dopahar 12:24. Laminated print by Suhag Studio. Courtesy of Suhag Studio.

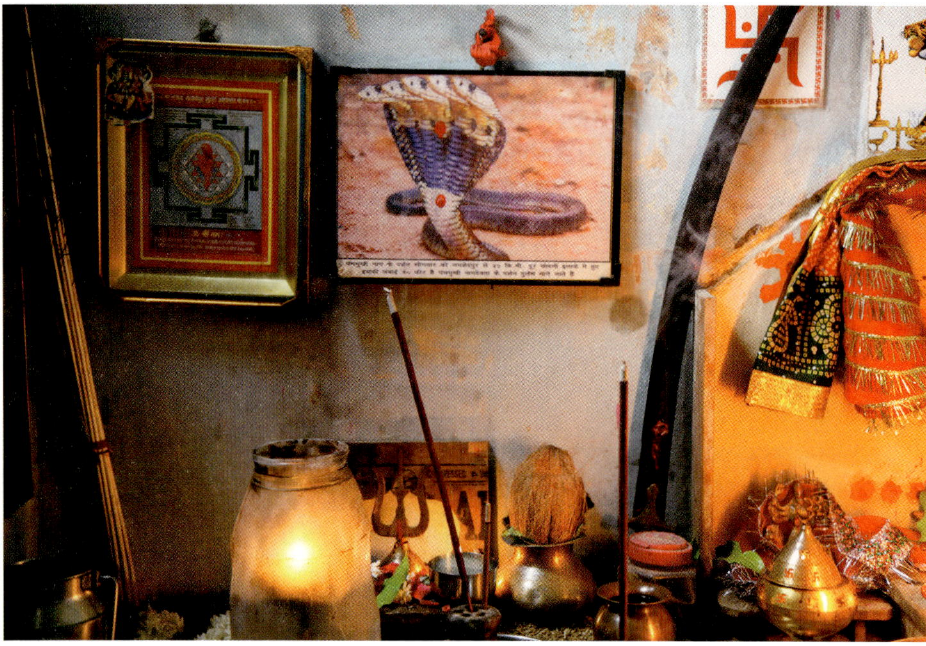

6.23 Puja room in rural Madhya Pradesh with laminated print showing a Panchmukhi Nag (Five-Faced Cobra), July 2014. Photograph by Christopher Pinney.

til now, largely gone unrecorded, remaining unvalidated. A five-headed snake might be seen fleetingly, but it was never photographable; it could never be placed inside the walls of the studio. Now, that studio is always in your pocket. This studio without walls poses an increasing threat to the livelihoods of small-town photographers, but it poses a bigger challenge to what we might think are the kinds of phenomena capable of being made visible, and also to the political potential of photography. It promises to lift the veil on a new kind of messianic future.

Notes

The research in this chapter was fundamentally dependent on the assistance in Nepal of Usha Titikshu, and in Bangladesh of Nadvi Abdullah and Habib Ahsan.

1 Burghart, *History of Janakpurdham*, 410.

2 Burghart, *History of Janakpurdham*, 410.

3 Pokharel, "Dented Pride."

4 Azoulay, *Civil Contract*, 23–26.

5 See Olin, *Touching Photographs*, for the parallel case of images displayed at Ground Zero in New York following 9/11.

6 Akhter, *Lives Not Numbers*. See also the Bengali and English documentation at "Outcries of a Thousand Souls," Bangladesh Garment Sromik Samhati, accessed November 17, 2022, http://www.athousandcries.org.

7 Nadvi Abdullah, interview with the author, Dhaka, Bangladesh, May 6, 2018. Her relatives had used the group photo as part of a "missing" poster.

8 Mookherjee, *Spectral Wound*, xv–xvi. The birongona had been raped during the 1971 war and was subsequently valorized by the state as a "war heroine."

9 Rai, *Bangladesh*.

10 Kracauer, *Orpheus in Paris*, 3.

11 Kracauer, *Orpheus in Paris*, 3–4.

12 Koch, *Siegfried Kracauer*, 120.

13 While the argument is made elsewhere (Pinney, introduction to this volume) that "demotic" better characterizes the "more than local, less than global" position of a distributed popular photographic practice, in the case of Bourdieu, his theorization is precisely that of "vernacularization," a local oppositional distillation from dominant class practices.

14 Azoulay, *Civil Contract*, 96; Strassler, *Refracted Visions*, 108.

15 Bourdieu, *Photography*, 27, 23.

16 Bourdieu, *Photography*, 30–31.

17 Bourdieu, *Photography*, 29.

18 Bourdieu, *Photography*, 24.

19 Bourdieu, *Photography*, 26.

20 On the subjunctive, see Pinney, "Bruises and Blushes," 27–33.

21 Cody, "Publics and Politics," 38.

22 Gopal Chitrakar, interview with the author, Kathmandu, October 6, 2017.

23 Morris, "Theses on the New Öffentlichkeit," 108, quoted in Gürsel, "Visualizing Publics," S139.

24 On the shooting, see *The Guardian*, "From the Archive."

25 Dixit's project has received surprisingly little academic attention. Exceptions include Allan, "Documenting War," esp. 160ff.

26 Kunda Dixit, interview with the author, Maya Yala Kendra, Patan, September 1, 2017

27 Kunda Dixit, interview with the author, Maya Yala Kendra, Patan, September 1, 2017.

28 Kunda Dixit, interview with the author, Maya Yala Kendra, Patan, September 1, 2017.

29 Barthes, *Mythologies*, 100.

30 Kunda Dixit, interview with the author, Patan, December 3. 2017.

31 Kunda Dixit, interview with the author, Patan, December 3, 2017.
32 Dixit, *Never Again*, 186.
33 Kunda Dixit, interview with the author, Patan, December 3, 2017
34 One of its main functions seems to have been to serve as a prestation to visiting delegations from communist regimes.
35 Dinesh Shrestha, interview with the author, Kathmandu, September 2, 2017.
36 Barthes, *Mythologies*, 101.
37 Barthes, *Mythologies*, 101.
38 Shrestha, *People's War*, 118.
39 Barthes, *Camera Lucida*, 95–96.
40 Barthes, *Mythologies*, 101.
41 Shrestha, *People's War*, 131, n.p.
42 Barthes, *Mythologies*, 102.
43 Kracauer, *Orpheus in Paris*, 3.
44 Pinney, *Camera Indica*.
45 Azoulay, *Civil Contract*, 16.
46 This is a very common visual trope in India that I have heard on many other occasions and features in a number of popular Hindu movies, such as *Aa Dekhen Zara* (2009).
47 Per the Hadith, neither images nor dogs should be kept domestically. See Bhatti and Pinney, "Optic-Clash," on the overlap between Hindu and Muslim practices.
48 For an introduction to diverse Muslim attitudes to images, see Saeed, *Muslim Devotional Art in India*, 1–3. One is tempted to say (following Marriott's claim for a Hindu "ethno-sociology") that there is a pronounced Muslim privileging of "fluidarities" over "solidarities" (Marriott, "On 'Constructing an Indian Ethnosociology'").
49 As part of his research in Pakistan, Danial Shah (personal communication, February 15, 2021) documented the display of commemorative portraits by the Hazara minority in Baluchistan.
50 Their utility is partly explained by the online Shiavault ("Islamic Etiquettes"):

> 10 Manners of using the mirror: According to the reliable tradition related to Imam Ja'far-e-Sadiq (a.s.), the Holy Prophet (s.a.w.a.) had said that heaven is definitely rewarded to that young fellow who looks in the mirror and thanks God for the beauty given to him.
>
> According to another tradition, the Holy Prophet (s.a.w.a.) kept on looking in the mirror while combing his hair and beard. He also ordered his wives and other companions to beautify themselves as God liked that a muslim should, before meeting another person, make himself acceptable to the other's eyes.
>
> According to a tradition related to Hazrat Ali (a.s.), one should recite the following prayer while looking into the mirror:

"All praise is worthy of that Allah who has created me and made my creation the best. He has made my face as it was the best possible to make. He has beautified me with such things, had these been found in others, they would have been considered as faults and then He has blessed me with Islam."

51 Cooper, "3D *Ziyarat*"; Cooper, "Cinema *Itself*."
52 See Pinney, *Coming of Photography*, 39–40.
53 The camera lucida and camera obscura both allowed the evanescent projection of an image through a lens but lacked any means of recording that image permanently.
54 The images were only disclosed to me in 2019, more than thirty years after I started visiting the village it depicts, thus demonstrating the value of long-term fieldwork.
55 The several occasions on which I have witnessed this festival since 1983 did not involve a matki phod.
56 Staff Correspondent, "Lie Worked Well."
57 Nardi, *Portraits of Devotion*, 24; Pinney, *"Photos of the Gods,"* 80–104.
58 The cable cars feature in *Manakamana*, a 2014 documentary by Pacho Velaz and Stephanie Spray.
59 Benjamin, "Little History of Photography" (2008), 279.
60 Despoix, "Kracauer as a Thinker," 11.
61 Despoix, "Kracauer as a Thinker," 8.
62 Bloch, "Symbols, Song, Dance," 25.
63 Mangal Mohan Shrestha, interview with the author, Kathmandu, June 8, 2019. See also Shrestha, *Mero Jivan-Chitra (Atmakathma)*.
64 Azoulay, *Civil Contract*, 110–13.
65 Azoulay, *Civil Contract*, 112.
66 See Pinney, *"Photos of the Gods,"* 30, for an 1880s lithographic example depicting this.
67 Min Ratna Bajracharya, interview with the author, Kathmandu, June 24, 2019.
68 Azoulay, *Civil Contract*, 12, 18.
69 Pinney, "Digital Cows."
70 See Pinney, "For an Ethnosociology of Photography and Sculpture."
71 See Nandy, *Time Warps*, 6.

Bibliography

Abiodun, Rowland. "Understanding Yoruba Art and Aesthetics: The Concept of Ase." *African Arts* 27, no. 3 (1994): 68–78, 102–3.

Abiodun, Rowland. *Yoruba Art and Language: Seeking the African in African Art*. Cambridge: Cambridge University Press, 2014.

Adebanwi, Wale. *Yoruba Elites and Ethnic Politics in Nigeria: Obafemi Awolowo and Corporate Agency*. Cambridge: Cambridge University Press, 2014.

Adebanwi, Wale, and Ebenezer Obadare. "Introducing Nigeria at Fifty: The Nation in Narration." *Journal of Contemporary African Studies* 28, no. 4 (2010): 379–405.

Aguilar, Ilich Buitrago, and Roy Moncada. "'Árboles de la vida' cumplen cuatro años." *La Prensa*, June 14, 2017.

Akanji, Olajide. "Group Rights and Conflicts in Africa: A Critical Reflection on Ife-Modakeke, Nigeria." *International Journal on Minority and Group Rights* 16, no. 1 (2009): 31–51.

Akhter, Taslima. *Lives Not Numbers*. Dhaka: Samhati Prokashon, 2017.

Akpan, N. U. "Nigerian Federalism: Accidental Foundations by Lugard." *Journal of the Historical Society of Nigeria* 9, no. 2 (1978): 1–20.

Amnesty International. "Nicaragua: Silence at Any Cost. State Tactics to Deepen the Repression in Nicaragua." February 15, 2021. https://www.amnesty.org/en/documents/amr43/3398/2021/en/.

Anderson, Benedict. *Imagined Communities*. Rev. ed. London: Verso, 2006.

Appadurai, Arjun. "The Colonial Backdrop." *Afterimage* 24, no. 5 (March/April 1997): 4–7.

Appadurai, Arjun. "Disjuncture and Difference in the Global Cultural Economy." *Public Culture* 2, no. 2 (April 1990): 1–24.

Arunasalam, Kannan, dir. *Paper*, 2011.

Austin, J. L. *How to Do Things with Words*. 2nd ed. Cambridge, MA: Harvard University Press, 1985.

Awolowo, Obafemi. *Path to Nigeria's Freedom*. London: Faber and Faber, 1947.

Azoulay, Ariella. *The Civil Contract of Photography*. New York: Zone Books, 2008.

Azoulay, Ariella. *Civil Imagination: A Political Ontology of Photography*. Translated by Louise Bethlehem. London: Verso, 2012.

Azoulay, Ariella Aïsha. *Potential History: Unlearning Imperialism*. New York: Verso, 2019.

Baer, Ulrich. *Spectral Evidence: The Photography of Trauma*. Cambridge, MA: MIT Press, 2002.

Bajorek, Jennifer. *Unfixed: Photography and Decolonial Imagination in West Africa.* Durham, NC: Duke University Press, 2020.

Barthes, Roland. *Camera Lucida: Reflections on Photography*. Translated by Richard Howard. New York: Wang and Hill, 1981.

Barthes, Roland. *Mythologies.* Translated by Annette Lavers. New York: Hill and Wang. 1972.

Batchen, Geoffrey. *Burning with Desire: The Conception of Photography*. Cambridge, MA: MIT Press, 1997.

Batchen, Geoffrey. "Vernacular Photographies." *History of Photography* 24, no. 3 (2000): 262–71.

Batchen, Geoffrey, Mick Gidley, Nancy K. Miller, and Jay Prosser, eds. *Picturing Atrocity: Photography in Crisis*. London: Reaktion, 2012.

Baudrillard, Jean. "Simulacra and Simulations." In *Jean Baudrillard: Selected Writings*, edited by Mark Poster, 166–84. Cambridge: Polity, 1988.

Bendiksen, Jonas. *The Book of Veles*. London: GOST, 2021.

Benjamin, Walter. "Little History of Photography." In *Walter Benjamin: Selected Writings*, vol. 2, part 2, *1931–1934*, edited by Michael W. Jennings, Howard Eiland, and Gary Smith, 507–30. Translated by Edmund Jephcott and Kinglsey Shorter. Cambridge, MA: Belknap Press of Harvard University Press, 1999.

Benjamin, Walter. "Little History of Photography." In *The Work of Art in the Age of Its Technological Reproducibility and Other Writings on Media,* edited by Michael W. Jennings, Brigid Doherty, and Thomas Y. Levin, 274–98. Translated by Edmund Jephcott and Kinglsey Shorter. Cambridge, MA: Belknap Press, 2008.

Benjamin, Walter. "The Work of Art in the Age of Mechanical Reproduction." In *Illuminations*, edited by Hannah Arendt, 211–44. Translated by Harry Zohn from the 1935 essay. New York: Schocken Books, 1969.

Berger, John. *Ways of Seeing*. London: Penguin, 2008.

Bhabha, Homi K. *The Location of Culture*. London: Routledge, 1994.

Bhatti, Shaila, and Christopher Pinney. "Optic-Clash: Modes of Visuality in India." In *A Companion to the Anthropology of India*, edited by Isabelle Clark-Decès, 225–40. Oxford: Blackwell, 2011.

Biesta, Gert. "A New Logic of Emancipation: The Methodology of Jacques Rancière." *Educational Theory* 60 (2010): 39–59.

Binaisa, Naluwembe. "Diasporic Landscape: Theoretical Reflections on African Migrants' Everyday Practices of 'Home' and 'Belonging'." *Journal of Intercultural Studies* 34, no. 5 (2013): 553–68.

Bloch, Maurice. "Symbols, Song, Dance and Features of Articulation: Is Religion an Extreme Form of Traditional Authority?" In *Ritual, History and Power: Selected Papers in Anthropology*, 19–45. LSE Monographs on Social Anthropology. London: Athlone, 1989.

Bourdieu, Pierre. *Outline of a Theory of Practice*. Translated by Richard Nice. Cambridge: Cambridge University Press, 1977.

Bourdieu, Pierre. *Photography: A Middle-Brow Art*. Translated by Shaun Whiteside. Cambridge: Polity, 1990.

Broomberg, Adam, and Oliver Chanarin. *Mr. Mkhize's Portrait and Other Stories from the New South Africa*. London: Trolley, 2004.

Brown, Elspeth H., and Thy Phu. "Introduction." In *Feeling Photography*, edited by Elspeth H. Brown and Thy Phu, 1–25. Durham, NC: Duke University Press, 2014.

Brun, Catherine. "Birds of Freedom." *Critical Asian Studies* 40, no. 3 (2008): 399–422.

Buchsbaum, Jonathan. *Cinema and the Sandinistas: Filmmaking in Revolutionary Nicaragua*. Austin: University of Texas Press, 2003.

Buckley, Liam. "Self and Accessory in Gambian Studio Photography." *Visual Anthropology Review* 16, no. 2 (2000): 71–91.

Burghart, Richard. *The History of Janakpurdham: A Study of Asceticism and the Hindu Polity*, edited by Martin Gaenzle. Kathmandu: Social Science Baha/Himal Books, 2016.

Buthpitiya, Vindhya. "Absence in Technicolour: Protesting Enforced Disappearances in Northern Sri Lanka." *Journal of the Royal Anthropological Institute* 28, no. S1 (April 2022): 118–34. https://doi.org/10.1111/1467-9655.13758.

Buthpitiya, Vindhya. "Naveena Camera." *Dastavezi | The Audio-Visual South Asia* 4 (October 2022). https://doi.org/10.11588/dasta.2022.1.19131.

Butler, Judith. *Frames of War: When Is Life Grievable?* London: Verso, 2010.

Butler, Judith. "Photography, War, Outrage." PMLA (*Publications of the Modern Language Association of America*) 120, no. 3 (2005): 822–27.

Campt, Tina, M. *Listening to Images*. Durham, NC: Duke University Press, 2017.

Candea, Matei. "*Derrida en Corse*? Hospitality as Scale-Free Abstraction." *Journal of the Royal Anthropological Institute* 18, no. 1 (2012): 34–48.

Candea, Matei, and Giovanni da Col. "The Return to Hospitality." *Journal of the Royal Anthropological Institute* 18, no. 1 (2012): 1–19.

Cardenal, Ernesto. *La revolución perdida*. Memorias 3. 2nd ed. Managua: Anamá Ediciones Centroamericanas, 2004.

Cardenal, Ernesto. "Revolución es cultura y cultura es revolución." In *La revolución es un libro y un hombre libre: Los afiches políticos de Nicaragua Libre 1979–1990 y del Movimiento de Solidaridad Internacional*, edited by Erick Aguirre, 64–78. Managua: INHCA-UCA, 2009.

Caswell, Michelle. *Archiving the Unspeakable: Silence, Memory, and the Photographic Record in Cambodia*. Madison: University of Wisconsin Press, 2014.

Chakrabarty, Dipesh. *Provincializing Europe: Postcolonial Thought and Historical Differences*. Princeton, NJ: Princeton University Press, 2000.

Chheng, Niem. "Second Man Charged under Country's Lese Majeste Law." *Phnom Penh Post*. Accessed September 9, 2019. https://www.phnompenhpost.com/national/second-man-charged-under-countrys-lese-majeste-law.

Chheng, Niem, and Leonie Kijewski. "Woman Who Threw Shoe at CPP Sign in Video Sought." *Phnom Penh Post*. Accessed September 10, 2019. https://www.phnompenhpost.com/national/woman-who-threw-shoe-cpp-sign-video-sought.

Chheng, Niem, and Andrew Nachenson. "Lese Majeste Law Now in Effect." *Phnom Penh Post*. Accessed September 12, 2019. https://www.phnompenhpost.com/national-politics/lese-majeste-law-now-effect.

Chitrakar, Gopal. *People Power*. Kathmandu: n.p., 1992.

Cody, Francis. "Publics and Politics." *Annual Review of Anthropology* 41 (2011): 37–52.

Cole, Jennifer. "The Work of Memory in Madagascar." *American Ethnologist* 25, no. 4 (1998): 610–33.

Cooper, Timothy P. A. "Cinema *Itself*: Cinephobia, Filmic Anxieties, and Ontologies of the Moving Image in Pakistan." *Visual Anthropology Review* 31, no. 3 (2018): 253–67.

Cooper, Timothy P. A. "3D *Ziyarat*: Lenticularity and Technologies of the Moving Images in Material and Visual Piety." *Material Religion* 17, no. 3 (2021): 291–316.

Courtright, Paul B. "The Iconographies of Sati." In *Sati, the Blessing and the Curse: The Burning of Wives in India*, edited by John Stratton Hawley, 27–48. New York: Oxford University Press, 1994.

Craven, David. *Art and Revolution in Latin America, 1910–1990*. New Haven, CT: Yale University Press, 2002.

Cusicanqui, Silvia Rivera. *Ch'ixinakax utxiwa: On Practices and Discourses of Decolonization*. Cambridge: Polity, 2020.

Dale, David T. "Symptoms and Strangeness in Yoruba Anti-Aesthetics." *African Arts* 92 (Winter 2005): 24–31.

Das, Veena, and Deborah Poole. *Anthropology in the Margins of the State*. Santa Fe, NM: School of American Research Press, 2004.

de Mel, Neloufer. *Militarizing Sri Lanka: Popular Culture, Memory and Narrative in the Armed Conflict*. London: SAGE, 2007.

Derrida, Jacques. *Limited Inc*. Translated by Samuel Weber. Evanston, IL: Northwestern University Press, 1988.

Despoix, Philippe. "Kracauer as a Thinker of the Photographic Medium." Translated by Conor Joyce. In *The Past's Threshold: Essays on Photography*, by Siegfried Kracauer, edited by Philippe Despoix and Maria Zinfert, 7–24. Zurich: Diaphenes, 2014.

Didi-Huberman, Georges. *Désirer désobéir: Ce qui nous soulève 1*. Paris: Éditions de Minuit, 2019.

Didi-Huberman, Georges. *Images in Spite of All: Four Photographs from Auschwitz*. Chicago: University of Chicago Press, 2008.

Didi-Huberman, Georges. *Uprisings*. Paris: Jeu de Paume, 2016.

Dijck, José van. *Mediated Memories in the Digital Age*. Stanford, CA: Stanford University Press, 2007.

Dixit, Kunda, ed. *Never Again: Testimonies from the Nepal Conflict*. Kathmandu: Nepalaya, 2009.

Dixit, Kunda. *A People War: Images of the Nepal Conflict 1996–2006*. Kathmandu: Nepalaya, 2006.

Droumpouki, Anna-Maria. *Mnimeia tis lithis: Ihni tou B' pagosmiou polemou stin Ellada kai stin Evropi*. Athens: Polis, 2014.

Edwards, Elizabeth. "Material Beings: Objecthood and Ethnographic Photographs." *Visual Studies* 17, no. 1 (2002): 67–75.

Edwards, Elizabeth. "Performing Science: Still Photography and the Torres Strait Expedition." In *Cambridge and the Torres Strait: Centenary Essays on the 1898 Anthropological Expedition*, edited by A. Herle and S. Rouse, 106–35. Cambridge: Cambridge University Press, 1998.

Edwards, Elizabeth. "Photographs and the Sound of History." *Visual Anthropology Review* 21, nos. 1–2 (2005): 27–46.

Edwards, Elizabeth. *Raw Histories: Photographs, Anthropology and Museums*. Oxford: Berg, 2001.

Eiss, Paul. *In the Name of El Pueblo: Place, Community, and the Politics of History in Yucatán*. Durham, NC: Duke University Press, 2010.

Ekeh, Peter P. "Colonialism and the Two Publics in Africa: A Theoretical Statement." *Comparative Studies in Society and History* 17, no. 1 (1975): 91–112.

Ekoh, Prince Chiagozie, and Elizabeth Onyedikachi George. "The Role of Digital Technology in the EndSARS Protest in Nigeria during COVID-19 Pandemic." *Journal of Human Rights and Social Work* 6, no. 2 (2021): 161–62.

Eng, David. L. "Colonial Object Relations." *Social Text* 34, no. 1 (2016): 1–19.

Engage Sri Lanka. *Corrupted Journalism: Channel 4 and Sri Lanka*. London: Engage Sri Lanka, 2013.

Enwezor, Okwui. *Snap Judgments: New Positions in Contemporary African Photography*. New York: International Center of Photography; Göttingen: Steidl, 2006.

Fanon, Frantz. *Black Skin, White Masks*. Translated by Charles Lam Markmann. 1952. Reprint, London: Pluto, 1986.

Fasan, Rotimi. "'Wetin dey happen?': Wazobia, Popular Arts, and Nationhood." *Journal of African Cultural Studies* 27, no. 1 (2015): 7–19.

Ferguson, John. *The Yorubas of Nigeria*. Bletchley, UK: Open University, 1970.

Ferme, Marianne. *The Underneath of Things: Violence, History and the Everyday in Sierra Leone*. Berkeley: University of California Press, 2001.

Fiofori, Tam. "J. A. Green: Pioneer and Legend." In *African Photographer J. A. Green: Reimagining the Indigenous and the Colonial*, edited by Martha G. Anderson and Lisa Aronson, 335–54. Bloomington: Indiana University Press, 2017.

Fisher, Mark. "What Is Hauntology?" *Film Quarterly* 66, no. 1 (Fall 2012): 16–24.

Flusser, Vilém. *Towards a Philosophy of Photography*. 1983. Reprint, London: Reaktion, 2000.

Foucault, Michel. *Discipline and Punish: The Birth of the Prison*. New York: Vintage, 2012.

Frazer, James George. *The Golden Bough: A Study in Comparative Religion*. New York: Macmillan, 1894.

Gadihoke, Sabeena. *India in Focus: Camera Chronicles of Homai Vyarawalla*. Ahmedabad: Parzor Foundation in association with Mapin, 2006.

Gago, Véronica. "Introduction: The Silvia Rivera Cusicanqui Principle," In *Ch'ixinakax utxiwa: On Practices and Discourses of Decolonization*, by Silvia Rivera Cusicanqui, vii–xxxiii. Cambridge: Polity, 2020.

Gell, Alfred. *Art and Agency: An Anthropological Theory*. Oxford: Oxford University Press, 1998.

Gensburger, Sarah. "Visiting History, Witnessing Memory: A Study of a Holocaust Exhibition in Paris in 2012." Translated by Katharine Throssell. *Memory Studies* 12, no. 6 (2017): 1–26.

GIEI (Grupo Interdisciplinario de Expertos Independentes). "Report on the Violent Events That Took Place in Nicaragua between April 18th and May 30th." December 21, 2018. https://gieinicaragua.org/en/#section00.

Gómez Cruz, Edgar, and Eric T. Meyer. "Creation and Control in the Photographic Process: iPhones and the Emerging Fifth Moment of Photography." *Photographies* 5, no. 2 (2012): 203–21.

González C., Alejandra. "Así se vive la caída de un 'árbol de la vida' en Managua." *La Prensa*, May 20, 2018.

Gourgouris, Stathis. *Dream Nation: Enlightenment, Colonization and the Institution of Modern Greece*. Stanford, CA: Stanford University Press, 1996.

Graeber, David. "Radical Alterity Is Just Another Way of Saying 'Reality.'" *HAU: Journal of Ethnographic Theory* 5, no. 2 (2015): 1–41.

Gruzinski, Serge. *Images at War: Mexico from Columbus to Blade Runner (1492–2019)*. Translated by Heather MacLean. Durham, NC: Duke University Press, 2001.

Guardian. "From the Archive: April 9, 1990: Nepal King Bows to Protests." April 9, 2015.

Gürsel, Zeynep. "Visualizing Publics: Digital Crowd Shots and the 2015 Unity Rally in Paris." *Current Anthropology* 58, Supplement 15 (2017): S135–S148.

Hariman, Robert, and John Lucaites. *No Caption Needed: Iconic Photographs, Public Culture, and Liberal Democracy*. Chicago: University of Chicago Press, 2007.

Harrison, Frances. *Still Counting the Dead: Survivors of Sri Lanka's Hidden War*. London: Portobello Books, 2012.

Haviland, Charles. "Sri Lanka Government Publishes War Death Toll Statistics." BBC News, February 24, 2012. https://www.bbc.co.uk/news/world-asia-17156686.

Hawley, John Stratton, ed. *Sati, the Blessing and the Curse: The Burning of Wives in India*. New York: Oxford University Press, 1994.

Herzfeld, Michael. "The Absent Presence: Discourses of Crypto-Colonialism." *South Atlantic Quarterly* 101, no. 4 (2002): 899–926.

Herzfeld, Michael. *Anthropology through the Looking-Glass: Critical Ethnography in the Margins of Europe*. Cambridge: Cambridge University Press, 1987.

Herzfeld, Michael. "'As in Your Own House': Hospitality, Ethnography, and the

Stereotype of Mediterranean Society." In *Honor and Shame and the Unity of the Mediterranean*, edited by David D. Gilmore, 75–89. Washington, DC: American Anthropological Association, 1987.

Herzfeld, Michael. *Cultural Intimacy: Social Poetics in the Nation-State*. 1997. Reprint, London: Routledge, 2005.

Herzfeld, Michael. *Subversive Archaism: Troubling Traditionalists and the Politics of National Heritage*. Durham, NC: Duke University Press, 2021.

High, Holly. "Melancholia and Anthropology." *American Ethnologist* 38, no. 2 (2011): 217–33.

Hinton, Alexander. "A Head for an Eye: Revenge in the Cambodian Genocide." *American Ethnologist* 25, no. 3 (1998): 352–77.

Hirsch, Eric, and Charles Stewart. "Introduction: Ethnographies of Historicity." *History and Anthropology* 16, no. 3 (2005): 261–74.

Hirsch, Marianne. "The Generation of Postmemory." In *On Writing with Photography*, edited by Karen Beckman and Liliane Weissberg, 202–26. Minneapolis: University of Minnesota Press, 2013.

Hirsch, Marianne, and Leo Spitzer. *School Photos in Liquid Times: Reframing Difference*. Seattle: University of Washington Press, 2020.

Hirschkind, Charles, Maria José A. de Abreu, and Carlo Caduff. "New Media, New Publics? An Introduction to Supplement 15." *Current Anthropology* 58, Supplement 15 (2017): 3–12.

Hirschon, Renée. *Heirs of the Greek Catastrophe: The Social Life of Asia Minor Refugees in Piraeus*. 1989. Reprint, New York: Berghahn Books, 1998.

Honwana, Alicinda. "'Waithood': Youth Transitions and Social Change." In *Development and Equity: An Interdisciplinary Exploration by Ten Scholars from Africa, Asia and Latin America*, edited by Dick Foeken, Ton Dietz, Leo de Haan, and Linda Johnson, 28–40. Amsterdam: Brill, 2014.

Huard, Adrienne, and Gabrielle Moser. "Editorial Introduction: Reparation and Visual Culture." *Journal of Visual Culture* 21 no. 1 (2022): 3–16.

Human Rights Watch. "Sri Lanka: Protect Civilians in 'Final' Attack." April 20, 2009. https://www.hrw.org/news/2009/04/20/sri-lanka-protect-civilians-final-attack.

Human Rights Watch. "Sri Lanka: Repeated Shelling of Hospitals Evidence of War Crimes." May 8, 2009. https://www.hrw.org/news/2009/05/08/sri-lanka-repeated-shelling-hospitals-evidence-war-crimes#Hospital.

Ibiloye, E. O. "Rural Urban Migration in Kwara State 1970–1985." *Canadian Social Science* 6, no. 4 (2010): 97–108.

Ichijo, Atsuko. "Sovereignty and Nationalism in the Twenty-First Century: The Scottish Case." *Ethnopolitics* 8, no. 2 (2009): 155–72.

Igodo, Chynthia. "Nigeria's Missing Multipliers: Women, Vision 2020 and Nigeria's Legal Blindspot." *The Republic* 4, no. 2 (2020). https://republic.com.ng/april-may-2020/nigerias-missing-multipliers-women-vision-2020/.

Inden, Ronald B. "Orientalist Constructions of India." *Modern Asian Studies* 20, no. 3 (1986): 401–46.

Inglis, Tom. "Empowerment and Emancipation." *Adult Education Quarterly* 48, no. 1 (1997): 3–17.

International Crimes Evidence Project (ICEP). "Island of Impunity? Investigation into International Crimes in the Final Stages of the Sri Lankan Civil War," 2014. https://piac.asn.au/2014/02/12/island-of-impunity/.

International Truth and Justice Project Sri Lanka. "Death Toll in Sri Lanka's 2009 War." International Truth and Justice Project Sri Lanka, 2021.

International Truth and Justice Project Sri Lanka. "War on Civilians Exhibition." International Truth and Justice Project Sri Lanka, London, 2019. https://itjpsl.com/reports/war-on-civilians-exhibition.

Jain, Kajri. *Gods in the Bazaar: The Economies of Indian Calendar Art*. Durham, NC: Duke University Press, 2007.

Jameson, Fredric. *The Political Unconscious: Narrative as a Socially Symbolic Act*. London: Methuen, 1981.

Jay, Martin. *Downcast Eyes: The Denigration of Vision in Twentieth-Century French Thought*. Berkeley: University of California Press, 1994.

Jeganathan, Pradeep. "Eelam.com: Place, Nation, and Imagi-Nation in Cyberspace." *Public Culture* 10, no. 3 (1998): 515–28.

Jeganathan, Pradeep. "On the Anticipation of Violence: Modernity and Identity in Southern Sri Lanka." In *Anthropology, Development, and Modernities: Exploring Discourses, Counter-tendencies, and Violence*, edited by Norman Long and Alberto Arce, 111–25. London: Routledge, 2000.

Johnson-Odim, Cheryl, and Nina E. Mba. *For Women and the Nation: Funmilayo-Ransome Kuti of Nigeria*. Urbana: University of Illinois Press, 1997.

Josephides, Lisette. "Being Held Accountable: Why Attributing Responsibility Matters." *Journal of the Royal Anthropological Institute* 28, no. S1 (2022): 34–49.

Journeyman Pictures. *Truth Tigers—Sri Lanka*. ABC Australia, 2002.

Kalantzis, Konstantinos. "'Fak Germani': Materialities of Nationhood and Transgression in the Greek Crisis." *Comparative Studies in Society and History* 57, no. 4 (2015): 1037–69.

Kalantzis, Konstantinos. "Picturing the Imaginable: Fantasy, Photography, and Displacement in the Highland Cretan 'Village.'" *Journal of Modern Greek Studies* 38, no. 1 (2020): 59–84.

Kalantzis, Konstantinos. "Proxy Brigands and Tourists: Visualizing the Greek-German Front in the Debt Crisis." *Visual Anthropology Review* 32, no. 1 (2016): 24–37.

Kalantzis, Konstantinos. *The Sfakian Screen: Looking and Living in the White Mountains of Crete*. London: University College London, 2018. Exhibition catalog.

Kalantzis, Konstantinos. *Tradition in the Frame: Photography, Power, and Imagination in Sfakia, Crete*. Bloomington: Indiana University Press, 2019.

Karinkurayil, Mohamed Shafeeq. "Reading Aspiration in Kerala's Migrant Photography." *South Asia: Journal of South Asian Studies* 43, no. 4 (2020): 598–612.

Keane, Webb. "On Semiotic Ideology." *Signs and Society* 6, no. 1 (2018): 64–87.

Keane, Webb. "Semiotics and the Social Analysis of Material Things." *Language and Communication* 23, nos. 3–4 (2003): 409–25.

Kennedy, Liam, and Caitlin Patrick, eds. *The Violence of the Image: Photography and International Conflict*. London: I. B. Tauris, 2014.

Kittler, Friedrich. *Optical Media: Berlin Lectures 1999*. Cambridge: Polity, 2010.

Klein, Melanie. "Love, Guilt, and Reparation." In *Love, Hate, and Reparation*, by Melanie Klein and Joan Riviere, 55–119. New York: W. W. Norton, 1964.

Kleinman, Arthur, and Joan Kleinman. "The Appeal of Experience; The Dismay of Images: Cultural Appropriations of Suffering in Our Times." *Daedalus* 125, no. 1 (1996): 1–23.

Knight, Daniel M. "Cultural Proximity: Crisis, Time and Social Memory in Central Greece." *History and Anthropology* 23, no. 3 (2012): 349–74.

Koch, Gertrud. *Siegfried Kracauer: An Introduction*. Translated by Jeremy Gaines. Princeton, NJ: Princeton University Press, 2000.

Kofoworola, Ziky. *Yorùbá Names, Cosmology, Worldviews and Dramatic Exploration*. Lagos: International Institute of Theatre in conjunction with DorcAmos Tops Publishers, 2015.

Kracauer, Siegfried. *Orpheus in Paris: Offenbach and the Paris of His Time*. Translated by Gwenda David and Eric Mosbacher. New York: Knopf, 1938.

Kratz, Corinne A. *The Ones That Are Wanted: Communication and the Politics of Representation in a Photographic Exhibition*. Berkeley: University of California Press, 2002.

Kunzle, David. *The Murals of Revolutionary Nicaragua, 1979–1992*. Berkeley: University of California Press, 1995.

Latour, Bruno. *Pandora's Hope: Essays on the Reality of Science Studies*. Cambridge, MA: Harvard University Press, 1999.

Latour, Bruno. *We Have Never Been Modern*. Translated by Catherine Porter. Cambridge, MA: Harvard University Press, 1993.

Latour, Bruno. "What Is Iconoclash? Or Is There a World beyond the Image Wars?" In *Iconoclash: Beyond the Image Wars in Science, Religion and the Arts*, edited by Bruno Latour et al., 16–40. Cambridge, MA: MIT Press, 2002.

Lawal, Babatunde. "Àwòrán: Representing the Self and Its Metaphysical Other in Yoruba Art." *Art Bulletin* 83, no. 3 (2002): 498–526.

Lefebvre, Henri. *The Production of Space*. Oxford: Blackwell, 1991.

Leroy, Fernand, Taiwo Olaleye-Oruene, Gesina Koeppen-Schomerus, and Elizabeth Bryan. "Yoruba Customs and Beliefs Pertaining to Twins." *Twin Research* 5, no. 2 (2002): 132–36.

Levin, Laura. "The Performative Force of Photography." *Photography and Culture* 2, no. 3 (2009): 327–36.

Lewis, Mark, and Laura Mulvey, dirs. *Disgraced Monuments*. London: Channel 4 Television, 1994.

Li, Zhensheng. *Red-Color News Soldier: A Chinese Photographer's Odyssey through the Cultural Revolution*. London: Phaidon, 2003.

Lies Agreed Upon. Ministry of Defence, Sri Lanka, 2011.

"Lie Worked Well." *Daily Star*. March 4, 2013. https://www.thedailystar.net/news-detail-271242.
Linfield, Susie. *The Cruel Radiance: Photography and Political Violence*. Chicago: University of Chicago Press, 2010.
Linfield, Susie. "Syria's Torture Photos: Witness to Atrocity." *New York Review of Books*, February 9, 2019. https://www.nybooks.com/daily/2019/02/09/syrias-torture-photos-witness-to-atrocity.
Longoni, Ana. "Photographs and Silhouettes: Visual Politics in the Human Rights Movement of Argentina." *Afterall* 25 (Autumn 2010): 5–17.
Lubkemann, Stephen C. *Culture in Chaos: An Anthropology of the Social Condition in War*. Chicago: University of Chicago Press, 1997.
Ly, Boret. "Devastated Vision(s): The Khmer Rouge Scopic Regime in Cambodia." *Art Journal* 62, no. 1 (2003): 66–81.
Ly, Boret. *Traces of Trauma: Cambodian Visual Culture and National Identity in the Aftermath of Genocide*. Honolulu: University of Hawai'i Press, 2020.
Macrae, Callum, dir. *No Fire Zone: In the Killing Fields of Sri Lanka*. CinePhil, 2013. https://nofirezone.org/.
Macrae, Callum, dir. *Sri Lanka's Killing Fields*. Channel 4, 2011. https://www.channel4.com/programmes/sri-lankas-killing-fields.
Macrae, Callum, dir. *Sri Lanka's Killing Fields: War Crimes Unpunished*. Channel 4, 2012. https://www.channel4.com/programmes/sri-lankas-killing-fields.
Malinowski, Bronisław. *Argonauts of the Western Pacific: An Account of Native Enterprise and Adventure in the Archipelagoes of Melanesian New Guinea*. New York: Dutton, 1922.
Mani, Lata. "Contentious Traditions: The Debate on Sati in Colonial India." In *Recasting Women: Essays in Colonial History*, edited by K. Sangari and S. Vaid, 88–126. New Delhi: Kali for Women, 1988.
Marcus, George E. *Ethnography through Thick and Thin*. Princeton, NJ: Princeton University Press, 1998.
Marriott. McKim. "On 'Constructing an Indian Ethnosociology.'" *Contributions to Indian Sociology* 25, no. 2 (1991): 295–308.
Mattenklott, Gert. *Karl Blossfeldt: The Alphabet of Plants*. Munich: Schirmer Art Books, 2007.
Maunaguru, Siddharthan. "Brides as Bridges? Movements, Actors, Documents and Anticipation in Constructing Tamilness." In *Pathways of Dissent: Tamil Nationalism in Sri Lanka*, edited by R. Cheran, 55–80. New Delhi: SAGE, 2009.
Maunaguru, Siddharthan. *Marrying for a Future: Transnational Sri Lankan Tamil Marriages in the Shadow of War*. Seattle: University of Washington Press, 2019.
Mazzarella, William. "Internet X-Ray: E-Governance, Transparency, and the Politics of Immediation in India." *Public Culture* 18, no. 3 (2006): 473–505.
Mbembe, Achille. *Necropolitics*. Durham, NC: Duke University Press, 2019.
McDowell, Sara. "Symbolic Warfare in the Ethnocratic State: Conceptualizing Memorialization and Territoriality in Sri Lanka." *Terrorism and Political Violence* 24, no. 1 (2012): 22–37.

Mech, Dara. "Man Held after Calling Government 'Authoritarian' on Facebook." *Phnom Penh Post*. Accessed September 9, 2019. https://www.phnompenhpost.com/national/man-held-after-calling-government-authoritarian-facebook.

Mehta, Harish C. *Cambodia Silenced: The Press under Six Regimes*. Bangkok: White Lotus, 1997.

Meiselas, Susan. *Nicaragua, June 1978–July 1979*. New York: Pantheon Books, 1981.

Michaud, Philippe-Alain. *Aby Warburg and the Image in Motion*. Translated by Sophie Hawks. New York: Zone Books, 2007.

Mirzoeff, Nicholas. *How to See the World*. London: Pelican Books, 2015.

Möller, Frank. "Photography after Empire: Citizen-Photographers or Snappers on Autopilot?" *New Political Science* 32, no. 4 (2010): 501–13.

Montague, Joel. *Picture Postcards of Cambodia, 1900–1950*. Bangkok: White Lotus, 2010.

Mookherjee, Nayanika. "The Aesthetics of Nations: Anthropological and Historical Approaches: The Aesthetics of Nations." *Journal of the Royal Anthropological Institute* 17 (May 2011): S1–20.

Mookherjee, Nayanika. "Introduction: On Irreconciliation." *Journal of the Royal Anthropological Institute* 28, no. S1 (2022): 11–33.

Mookherjee, Nayanika. "The Raped Woman as a Horrific Sublime and the Bangladesh War of 1971." *Journal of Material Culture* 20, no. 4 (2015): 379–95.

Mookherjee, Nayanika. *The Spectral Wound: Sexual Violence, Public Memories, and the Bangladesh War of 1971*. Durham, NC: Duke University Press. 2015.

Morris, Rosalind. "Theses on the New Öffentlichkeit." *Grey Room* 51 (2013): 94–111.

Moser, Gabrielle. "When Photographs Fail, When Monuments Fall: Photography and Reparations in Canada." *Photography and Culture* 15 no. 1 (2022): 1–17.

Mroué, Rabih. "The Pixelated Revolution." Translated by Zial Nawfal, with an introduction by Carol Martin. *TDR: The Drama Review* 56, no. 3 (2012): 18–35.

Nandy, Ashis. "Sati: A Nineteenth-Century Tale of Women, Violence and Protest." In *At the Edge of Psychology*, 1–31. Delhi: Oxford University Press, 1980.

Nandy, Ashis. *Time Warps: Silent and Evasive Pasts in India's Politics and Religion*. London: Hurst, 2002.

Nardi, Isabella. *Portraits of Devotion: Popular "Manorath" Paintings from Nathdvara in the Collection of Anil Relia*. Ahmedabad: Mapin, 2019.

Natali, Christiana. "Building Cemeteries, Constructing Identities: Funerary Practices and Nationalist Discourse among the Tamil Tigers of Sri Lanka." *Contemporary South Asia* 16, no. 3 (2012): 22–37.

Navarrete, Oscar. "Mi déjà vu." Fundación Violeta Barrios de Chamorro, Managua, 2019. Accessed October 1, 2020. http://memoria-multimedia.violeta-chamorro.org.ni/mi-deja-vu-2/.

Nordstrom, Carolyn. *A Different Kind of War Story*. Philadelphia: University of Pennsylvania Press, 1997.

Norén-Nilsson, Astrid. *Cambodia's Second Kingdom: Nation, Imagination, and Democracy*. Ithaca, NY: Cornell University Press, 2018.

Nwafor, Okechukwu C. "The Fabric of Friendship: *Aṣọ Ebì* and the Moral Economy of Amity in Nigeria." *African Studies* 72, no. 1 (2013): 1–18.

Obia, Vincent A. "#EndSARS, a Unique Twittersphere and Social Media Regulation in Nigeria." *LSE Blogs*, November 11, 2020. https://blogs.lse.ac.uk/medialse/2020/11/11/endsars-a-unique-twittersphere-and-social-media-regulation-in-nigeria/.

Okediji, Moyo. *African Renaissance: Old Forms, New Images in Yoruba Art*. Boulder: University Press of Colorado, 2002.

Okome, Mojubaolu. "African Women and Power: Labor, Gender and Feminism in the Age of Globalization." *SAGE Race Relations Abstracts* 30, no. 2 (2005): 3–26.

Olin, Margaret. *Touching Photographs*. Chicago: University of Chicago Press, 2012.

Olin, Margaret. "Touching Photographs: Roland Barthes's 'Mistaken' Identification." *Representations* 80, no. 1 (2002): 99–118.

Osaghae, Eghosa E. *Crippled Giant: Nigeria since Independence*. Bloomington: Indiana University Press, 1998.

Oyewùmí, Oyerónké. *The Invention of Women: Making an African Sense of Western Gender Discourse*. Minneapolis: University of Minnesota Press, 1998.

Pagden, Anthony. *European Encounters with the New World: From Renaissance to Romanticism*. New Haven, CT: Yale University Press, 1993.

Papagaroufali, Eleni. *Ipia diplomatia: Diethnikes adelfopoiiseis kai eirinistikes praktikes sti sighroni Ellada*. Athens: Alexandreia, 2013.

Papataxiarchis, Evthymios. "O adianoitos ratsismos: I politikopiisi tis filoxenias tin epohi tis krisis." *Singkhrona Themata* 127 (2014): 46–62.

Peirce, Charles Sanders. *Philosophical Writings of Peirce*. New York: Dover, 1955.

Perera, Sasanka. *Violence and the Burden of Memory: Remembrance and Erasure in Sinhala Consciousness*. New Delhi: Orient Black Swan, 2016.

Perera, Sasanka. *Warzone Tourism in Sri Lanka: Tales from Darker Places in Paradise*. New Delhi: Orient Black Swan, 2016.

Phelan, Peggy. "Atrocity and Action: The Performative Force of the Abu Ghraib Photographs." In *Picturing Atrocity: Photography in Crisis*, edited by Geoffrey Batchen, Mick Gidley, Nancy K. Miller, and Jay Prosser, 51–61. London: Reaktion, 2012.

Phu, Thy, and Elspeth H. Brown. "The Cultural Politics of Aspiration: Family Photography's Mixed Feelings." *Journal of Visual Culture* 17, no. 2 (2015): 152–65.

Pinney, Christopher. "Accidental Ramdevji." In *India's Popular Culture: Iconic Images and Fluid Spaces*, edited by Jyotindra Jain, 32–45. Mumbai: Marg, 2007.

Pinney, Christopher. "Bruises and Blushes: Photography 'beyond' Anthropology." In *Documentary across Disciplines*, edited by Erika Balsom and Hila Peleg, 20–38. Berlin: Haus der Kulturen der Welt; Cambridge, MA: MIT Press, 2016.

Pinney, Christopher. *Camera Indica: The Social Life of Indian Photographs*. London: Reaktion, 1997.

Pinney, Christopher. "Civil Contract of Photography in India." *Comparative Studies of South Asia, Africa and the Middle East* 35, no. 1 (May 2015): 21–34.

Pinney, Christopher. *The Coming of Photography in India*. London: British Library, 2008.

Pinney, Christopher. "Digital Cows: Flesh and Code." In *PhotoObjects: On the Mate-*

riality of Photographs and Photo Archives in the Humanities and Sciences, edited by Julia Barnighausen, Costanza Caraffa, Stefanie Klamm, Franka Schneider, and Petra Wodtke, 199–210. Berlin: Max-Planck-Gesellschaft zur Förderung der Wissenschaften, 2019.

Pinney, Christopher. "For an Ethnosociology of Photography and Sculpture in India." In *Photography and Sculpture: The Art Object in Reproduction*, edited by Sarah Hamill and Megan R. Luke, 222–34. Los Angeles: Getty Research Institute, 2017.

Pinney, Christopher. "Introduction: 'How the Other Half . . .'" In *Photography's Other Histories*, edited by Christopher Pinney and Nicolas Petersen, 1–14. Durham, NC: Duke University Press, 2003.

Pinney, Christopher. "Locating Photography." In *A Companion to Photography*, edited by Stephen Bull, 29–47. Hoboken, NJ: Wiley-Blackwell, 2020.

Pinney, Christopher. "The Parallel Histories of Anthropology and Photography." In *Anthropology and Photography, 1860–1920*, edited by Elizabeth Edwards, 74–95. New Haven, CT: Yale University Press, 1992.

Pinney, Christopher. *Photography and Anthropology*. London: Reaktion, 2011.

Pinney, Christopher. *"Photos of the Gods": The Printed Image and Political Struggle in India*. London: Reaktion, 2004.

Pinney, Christopher. "Seven Theses on Photography." *Thesis Eleven* 113, no. 1 (2012): 141–56.

Pokharel, Amendra. "Dented Pride: The Story of Daura Suruwal and Dhaka Topi." *ECS Nepal*, no. 70 (July 2010). http://ecs.com.np/features/dented-pride-the-story-of-daura-suruwal-and-dhaka-topi.

Pollock, Sheldon. *The Language of the Gods in the World of Men: Sanskrit, Culture, and Power in Premodern India*. Delhi: Permanent Black, 2006.

Poole, Deborah. *Vision, Race, and Modernity: A Visual Economy of the Andean Image World*. Princeton, NJ: Princeton University Press, 1997.

Punjabi, Suresh, and Christopher Pinney. *Artisan Camera: Studio Photography in Central India*. Chennai: Tara Books, 2013.

Rai, Raghu. *Bangladesh: The Price of Freedom*. Delhi: Niyogi Books, 2013.

Raj, Prakash A. *The Dancing Democracy: The Power of the Third Eye*. New Delhi: Rupa, 2006.

Rakopoulos, Theodoros. "Solidarity: The Egalitarian Tensions of a Bridge-Concept." *Social Anthropology* 24 no. 2 (2016): 142–51.

Rancière, Jacques. *The Politics of Aesthetics*. Translated by Gabriel Rockhill. London: Continuum, 2009.

Rejai, Mostafa, and Cynthia H. Enloe. "Nation-States and State-Nations." *International Studies Quarterly* 13 (1969): 140–18.

Richardot, Sarah. "Cinema Reborn: A Profile of Cambodian Films." Asia-Europe Foundation, February 13, 2013. https://culture360.asef.org/magazine/cinema-reborn-profile-cambodian-films.

Riding, Alan. "National Mutiny in Nicaragua." *New York Times Magazine*. July 30, 1978.

Roberts, Allen, and Mary Nooter Roberts. *A Saint in the City: Sufi Arts of Urban Senegal*. Los Angeles: UCLA Fowler Museum, 1993.

Roberts, Michael. "Saivite Symbols, Sacrifice, and Tamil Tiger Rites." *Social Analysis: The International Journal of Social and Cultural Practice* 49, no. 1 (2005): 67–93.

Roberts, Michael. "Tamil Tiger 'Martyrs': Regenerating Divine Potency." *Studies of Conflict and Terrorism* 28, no. 6 (2005): 493–514.

Rocha, José Luis. *Autoconvocados y conectados: Los universitarios en la revuelta de abril en Nicaragua*. Managua: IHNCA-UCA, 2019.

Roitman, Janet. *Anti-Crisis*. Durham, NC: Duke University Press, 2014.

Rosaldo, Renato. "Introduction: Grief and a Headhunter's Rage." In *Culture and Truth: The Remaking of Social Analysis*, 1–21. Boston: Beacon, 1993.

Rubenstein, Daniel, and Katrina Sluis. "The Digital Image in Photographic Culture: Algorithmic Photography and the Crisis of Representation." In *The Photographic Image in Digital Culture*, 2nd ed., edited by Martin Lister, 22–40. London: Routledge, 2013.

Ruthless: LTTE's Final Crimes against Humanity. Ministry of Defence, Sri Lanka, 2012.

Saeed, Yousuf. *Muslim Devotional Art in India*. New Delhi: Routledge, 2012.

Sanmugeswaran, Pathmanesan, Krishantha Fredricks, and Justin W. Henry. "Reclaiming Ravana in Sri Lanka: Ravana's Sinhala Buddhist Apotheosis and Tamil Responses." *South Asia: Journal of South Asian Studies* 42, no. 4 (2019): 796–812.

Sant Cassia, Paul. *Bodies of Evidence: Burial, Memory, and the Recovery of Missing Persons in Cyprus*. New York: Berghahn Books, 2005.

Schalk, Peter. "Resistance and Martyrdom in the Process of State Formation of Tamililam." In *Martyrdom and Political Resistance*, edited by Joyce J. M. Pettigrew, 61–82. Amsterdam: VU University Press, 1997.

Schalk, Peter. "The Revival of Martyr Cults among Ilavar." *Temenos* 33 (1997): 151–90.

Scott, James. *Seeing like a State: How Certain Schemes to Improve the Human Condition Have Failed*. New Haven, CT: Yale University Press, 1998.

Seangly, Phak "Billboard Cutter Held." *Phnom Penh Post*. Accessed September 9, 2019. https://www.phnompenhpost.com/national/billboard-cutter-held.

Selejan, Ileana L. "Vandalism as Symbolic Reparation Imaginaries of Protest in Nicaragua." *The Cambridge Journal of Anthropology* 39, no. 2 (2021): 19–38.

Seppanen, Janne. "Unruly Representations: Materiality, Indexicality and Agency of the Photographic Trace." *Photographies* 10, no. 1 (2017): 113–28.

Seremetakis, C. Nadia. *The Last Word: Women, Death, and Divination in Inner Mani*. Chicago: University of Chicago Press, 1991.

Shiavault. "Tahzeeb-ul-islam (Islamic Etiquettes): Etiquette of Wearing Jewellery, Applying Surma, Looking in the Mirror and Applying Hair-Dye for Men and Women." Shiavault. Accessed November 14, 2022. http://www.shiavault.com/books/tahzeeb-ul-islam-islamic-ettiquettes/chapters/2-etiquette-of-wearing-jewellery-applying-surma-looking-in-the-mirror-and-applying-hair-dye-for-men-and-women.

Shrestha, Dinesh. *Tasbirama Janyuddha 1/People's War in Pictures 1*. Kathmandu: Unified Communist Party of Nepal, 2011.

Shrestha, Mangal Mohan. *Mero Jivan-Chitra (Atmakathma)*. Kathmandu: Shrimati Maiya Shrestha, 2019.

Shryock, Andrew. "Breaking Hospitality Apart: Bad Hosts, Bad Guests, and the Problem of Sovereignty." *Journal of the Royal Anthropological Institute* 18, no. 1 (2012): 20–33.

Siegel, James T. *Fetish, Recognition, Revolution*. Princeton, NJ: Princeton University Press, 1997.

Sliwinski, Sharon. *Human Rights in Camera*. Chicago: University of Chicago Press, 2011.

Sliwinski, Sharon, and Shawn Michelle Smith, eds. *Photography and the Optical Unconscious*. Durham, NC: Duke University Press, 2017.

Smith, Matthew, and Taimoor Sobhan. "Capturing Their Genocide on Their Cellphones." *New York Times*. August 27, 2018. https://www.nytimes.com/2018/08/27/opinion/capturing-their-genocide-on-their-cellphones.html.

Sontag, Susan. *On Photography*. London: Penguin Books, 1977.

Sontag, Susan. *Regarding the Pain of Others*. New York: Farrar, Straus and Giroux, 2003.

Spivak, Gayatri Chakravorty. "Can the Subaltern Speak?" In *Marxism and the Interpretation of Culture*, edited by Cary Nelson and Lawrence Grossberg, 271–313. Basingstoke: Macmillan Education, 1988.

Sprague, Stephen F. "How I See the Yoruba See Themselves." *Studies in Visual Communication* 5, no. 1 (1978): 9–28.

Sprague, Stephen F. "Yoruba Photography: How the Yoruba See Themselves." *African Arts* 12, no. 1 (1978): 52–59, 107.

Spray, Stephanie, and Pacho Velez, dirs. *Manakamana*. Cinema Guild, 2013.

Spyer, Patricia, and Mary Margaret Steedly. "Introduction: Images That Move." In *Images That Move*, edited by Patricia Spyer and Mary Margaret Steedly, 3–40. Santa Fe, NM: School for Advanced Research Press, 2013.

Sri Lanka Campaign for Peace and Justice. "Event: 'Tamils of Lanka: A Timeless Heritage,' 18–19 May 2019, London." https://www.srilankacampaign.org/event-tamils-of-lanka-a-timeless-heritage-18-19-may-2019-london/.

Staff Correspondent, "Lie Worked Well." *Daily Star* (Dhaka), March 4, 2013. https://www.thedailystar.net/news-detail-271242.

Stewart, Charles. *Dreaming and Historical Consciousness in Island Greece*. Cambridge, MA: Harvard University Press, 2012.

Steyerl, Hito. *Duty Free Art: Art in the Age of Planetary Civil War*. New York: Verso, 2019.

Steyerl, Hito. "In Defense of the Poor Image." *e-flux journal* 10 (November 2009). https://www.e-flux.com/journal/10/61362/in-defense-of-the-poor-image/.

Stimson, Blake. *The Pivot of the World: Photography and Its Nation*. Cambridge, MA: MIT Press, 2006.

Stokke, Kristian. "Building the Tamil Eelam State: Emerging State Institutions and Forms of Governance in LTTE-Controlled Areas in Sri Lanka." *Third World Quarterly* 27, no. 6 (2006): 1021–40.

Strassler, Karen. *Demanding Images: Democracy, Mediation, and the Image-Event in Indonesia*. Durham, NC: Duke University Press, 2020.

Strassler, Karen. *Refracted Visions: Popular Photography and National Modernity in Java*. Durham, NC: Duke University Press, 2010.

Stuart, Allan. "Documenting War, Visualising Peace: Towards Peace Photography." In *Expanding Peace Journalism: Comparative and Critical Approaches*, edited by Ibrahim Seaga Shaw, Jake Lynch, and Robert A. Hackett, 147–67. Sydney: Sydney University Press, 2011.

Sutton, David E. *Memories Cast in Stone: The Relevance of the Past in Everyday Life*. Oxford: Berg, 1998.

Tagg, John. *The Burden of Representation: Essays on Photographies and Histories*. London: Palgrave Macmillan, 1988.

Tagg, John. "The Currency of the Photograph." In *Thinking Photography*, edited by Victor Burgin, 110–42. London: Macmillan, 1982.

Tambiah, Stanley J. *Buddhism Betrayed: Religion, Politics, and Violence in Sri Lanka*. Chicago: University of Chicago Press, 1992.

Tambiah, Stanley J. *Sri Lanka: Ethnic Fratricide and the Dismantling of Democracy*. Chicago: University of Chicago Press, 1986.

TamilNet. "LTTE Announces Unilateral Ceasefire." TamilNet, April 26, 2009. https://www.tamilnet.com/art.html?catid=13&artid=29178.

TamilNet. "Source Files from One of Digital Cameras Witnessing 2009 Genocide Released to Public Domain." TamilNet, July 3, 2018. https://www.tamilnet.com/art.html?catid=13&artid=39117.

Taylor, Diana. *The Archive and the Repertoire: Performing Cultural Memory in the Americas*. Durham, NC: Duke University Press, 2003.

Thiranagama, Sharika. *In My Mother's House: Civil War in Sri Lanka*. 2011. Reprint, New Delhi: Zubaan, 2013.

Thompson, Krista. *Shine: The Visual Economy of Light in African Diasporic Aesthetic Practice*. Durham, NC: Duke University Press, 2015.

Thompson, Robert Farris. "An Aesthetic of the Cool." *African Arts* 7, no. 1 (1973): 41–91.

Thompson, Robert Farris. *African Art in Motion: Icon and Art*. Berkeley: University of California Press. 1974.

Tyner, James. "Dead Labor, Landscapes, and Mass Graves: Administrative Violence during the Cambodian Genocide." *Geoforum* 52 (March 2014): 70–77.

Tyner, James. *The Nature of Revolution: Art and Politics under the Khmer Rouge*. Athens: University of Georgia Press, 2019.

Tyner, James, Sokvisal Kimsroy, and Savina Sirik. "Landscape Photography, Geographic Education, and Nation-Building in Democratic Kampuchea, 1975–1979." *Geographical Review* 105, no. 4 (2015): 566–80.

UNHCR. "Number of Displaced Nicaraguans in Costa Rica Doubles in Less Than a Year." March 25, 2022. https://www.unhcr.org/uk/news/briefing

/2022/3/623d894c4/number-displaced-nicaraguans-costa-rica-doubles-year.html.
Valéry, Paul. "The Centenary of Photography." In *Classic Essays on Photography*, edited by Alan Trachtenberg, 191–98. New Haven, CT: Leete's Island Books, 1980.
Varoufakis, Yannis. "Being Greek and an Economist while Greece Is Burning! An Intimate Account of a Peculiar Tragedy." *Journal of Modern Greek Studies* 32, no. 1 (2014): 1–23.
Varzi, Roxanne. *Warring Souls: Youth, Media, and Martyrdom in Post-Revolution Iran*. Durham, NC: Duke University Press, 2006.
Venugopal, Rajesh. *Nationalism, Development and Ethnic Conflict in Sri Lanka*. Cambridge: Cambridge University Press, 2018.
Virilio, Paul. *Open Sky*. London: Verso, 2008.
Vokes, Richard, and Darren Newbury. "Photography and African Futures." *Visual Studies* 33, no. 1 (2018): 1–10.
Vuth, Lyno. "Cambodian Photographers Document War and Violence: Vandy Rattana, Khvay Samnang and Sovan Philong." *Trans Asia Photography Review* 3, no. 1 (Fall 2012).
Wall, Jeff. "Photography and Liquid Intelligence." In *Jeff Wall: Selected Essays and Interviews*, edited by Peter Galassi, 109–10. New York: Museum of Modern Art, 2007.
Wani. "Por qué Wani? Dia mata Wani? Why Wani? Ampadawak Wani?" *Wani* 1 (1984): 3–7.
Warner, Michael. "Publics and Counterpublics." *Public Culture* 14, no. 1 (2002): 49–90.
Weaver, Matthew, and Gethin Chamberlain. "Sri Lanka Declares End to War with Tamil Tigers." *Guardian*. May 19, 2009. https://www.theguardian.com/world/2009/may/18/tamil-tigers-killed-sri-lanka.
Wendl, Tobias. "Entangled Traditions: Photography and the History of Media in Southern Ghana." *RES: Anthropology and Aesthetics* 39 (Spring 2001): 78–101.
Wendl, Tobias. "Ghana: Portraits and Scenery." In *Revue Noire Collection of African and Indian Ocean Photography*, 142–55. Paris: Revue Noire, 1998.
Whitaker, Mark P. "Some Reflections on Popular Anthropology, Nationalism, and the Internet." *Anthropological Quarterly* 77, no. 3 (2004): 469–98.
Witharana, Dileepa. "Ravana's Sri Lanka: Redefining the Sinhala Nation?" *South Asia: Journal of South Asian Studies* 42, no. 4 (2019): 781–95.
Womanifesto. "Womanifesto: What Nigerian Women Want." WARDC, 2022. Accessed November 2022. https://wardcnigeria.org/womanifesto-what-nigerian-women-want/.
Wood, Alex. *Thomas Young, Natural Philosopher, 1773–1829*. Cambridge: Cambridge University Press, 1954.
Wright, Chris. "Material and Memory: Photography in the Western Solomon Islands." *Journal of Material Culture* 9, no. 1 (2004): 73–85.
Young, Sokphea. "Citizens of Photography: Visual Activism, Social Media and

Rhetoric of Collective Action in Cambodia." *South East Asia Research* 29, no. 1 (2021): 53–71.

Young, Sokphea. "Internet, Facebook, Competing Political Narratives, and Political Control in Cambodia." *Media Asia* 48, no. 1 (2021): 67–76.

Young, Sokphea. *Strategies of Authoritarian Survival and Dissensus in Southeast Asia: Weak Men versus Strongmen*. Singapore: Palgrave Macmillan, 2021.

Youngblood, Gene. *Expanded Cinema*. Introduction by R. Buckminster Fuller. London: Studio Vista, 1970.

Zelizer, Barbie. *About to Die: How News Images Move the Public*. New York: Oxford University Press, 2010.

Zelizer, Barbie. "Atrocity, the 'As If' and Impending Death from the Khmer Rouge." In *Picturing Atrocity*, edited by G. Batchen, M. Gidley, N. K. Miller, and J. Prosser, 155–66. London: Reaktion, 2012.

Zuberi, Muhammad Nabil. "The Man on the Moon: A Semiotic Analysis of Scopic Regimes in Bangladesh." In *Global Digital Cultures: Perspectives from South Asia*, edited by Aswin Punathambekar and Sriram Mohan, 261–79. Ann Arbor: University of Michigan Press, 2019.

Zuboff, Shoshana. *The Age of Surveillance Capitalism: The Fight for a Human Future at the New Frontier of Power*. London: Profile Books, 2019.

Contributors

NALUWEMBE BINAISA is an interdisciplinary scholar and creative practitioner researching mobilities, belonging, and identities within Africa and her diaspora. She has conducted research for leading institutions, including the University of Oxford, University College London, and the Max Planck Institute for the Study of Religious and Ethnic Diversity. She is a 2021 recipient of a Writing Our Legacy/Shifting the Gaze bursary for her project *Sacred Trees Sacred Landscapes*.

VINDHYA BUTHPITIYA is an anthropologist by training, and has more than a decade of research and policy experience in the international development sector in Sri Lanka. She is lecturer in social anthropology at the University of St Andrews.

KONSTANTINOS KALANTZIS is an assistant professor of anthropology at the University of Thessaly. He is the author of *Tradition in the Frame: Photography, Power, and Imagination in Sfakia, Crete* (2019) and the director of the ethnographic films *Dowsing the Past* (2014) and *The Impossible Narration* (2021). He has published extensively on the intersections of visual culture and the political imagination in Greece.

CHRISTOPHER PINNEY is a professor of anthropology and visual culture at University College London and has published a number of books on the visual culture of India. He was a coeditor of *Photography's Other Histories* (Duke University Press, 2003).

ILEANA L. SELEJAN is a lecturer in art history, culture and society at the University of Edinburgh. She was previously a research fellow with the Decolonising Arts Institute at the University of the Arts London, a research associate in the Department of Anthropology at University College London, and the Linda Wyatt Gruber '66 Curatorial Fellow in Photography at the Davis Museum at Wellesley College.

SOKPHEA YOUNG obtained his PhD from the University of Melbourne, Australia, and is currently an honorary research fellow at University College London. He is the author of *Strategies of Authoritarian Survival and Dissensus in Southeast Asia: Weak Men versus Strongmen* (2021).

Index